To all my customers who'\

To Liz, for understanding when I work late, and to Cameron, for jumping into my arms when I don't.

—Dave Greely

To my friend Leon Schiffman, and my uncle Alan Sawyer, who have supported me vigorously as I chase my dreams.

—Ben Sawyer

Acknowledgments

For Ben and Dave, *Creating Stores on the Web* was a landmark of sorts. After building a solid career as a computer book author, Ben dragged Dave away from his cushy job as a sportswriter and together they formed Digitalmill, which, among other things, writes technology-related books. This is the first. It would never have happened without a lot of help. This is where we get to thank the people who did the helping:

Corbin Collins, our outstanding editor at Peachpit. Corbin had reason on many occasions to pull out either his hair or ours. Instead he sent us e-mail that quoted Wavy Gravy. He also kept us on track when we started to drift. Corbin's involvement made this book far better than it would've been otherwise.

Peachpit Publisher Nancy Aldrich-Ruenzel, who believed in our idea and let us run with it.

Mimi Heft, for her gorgeous design, and Maureen Forys, for her excellent implementation of that design.

Everyone else at Peachpit who will help make this book a success.

David Rogelberg and Sherry Rogelberg of StudioB, our book agency, who helped us prepare and present this project to Peachpit and served as a source of feedback throughout its development.

Alan Sawyer, a professor of marketing at the University of Florida and Ben's uncle, who provided valuable information for Chapter 4.

Peter Carlisle, our attorney (and friend), who not only helped get Digitalmill off the ground but also wrote Chapter 21.

Marc Harrison from Jupiter Communications, who provided some important statistics for the book.

Sarah De Marchi of TRUSTe, for allowing us to use some of TRUSTe's documentation.

Joann Meyer of Digitalmill, who puts up with Ben and Dave every day and hasn't jumped out a window. Yet.

Adam Mattessich, who housed the Digitalmill crew in New York during their trip to Fall Internet World.

Barbara Holt, for straightening us out.

Ben and Dave would also like to thank Joe Cataudella for giving this book a voice of experience.

Additionally, Joe would like to thank the following:

David Bango, whose suggestions concerning Tronix have helped tremendously. David was also a great help with my part of the writing.

Dominick Bruno, my nephew and a Tronix's co-founder.

His family and all of Tronix's customers, who continue to make the store a success to this day.

Table of Contents

PART I

Introduction

Before you learn how to build an online store, it is important to know why you should do so. Part I answers those questions and also shows you how Tronix and some other online retailers have survived and thrived. You'll also learn about why people shop online and why they don't, how many are doing so know, and how many are expected to do so in the future. You'll also have a chance to study some proven online store business models.

Part I Table of Contents

CHAPTER ONE

Frequently Asked Questions

Let's cut to the chase. If you're like most people, you have questions, and it's likely that some of them are answered right here.

What kind of person does it take to run an online store?

An aggressive one! Running an online store takes the same kind of personal traits necessary to run any business. You have to be committed, a bit of a risk taker, willing to work long and late hours, and driven to succeed. Being a little crazy doesn't hurt either. Online stores are a new frontier.

You also have to be organized and able to deal with setbacks without flipping out. You have be committed to providing better customer service than your competitors. And if you ever want to grow past a one- or two-person operation, you need to have vision and a clearly defined plan.

It also takes someone who is willing to learn and change. Internet commerce is a growing field that will mature over the next few years. Be prepared to grow with it.

How much will it cost to get my store up and running?

There are so many variables, it's tough to put an exact figure on it. Will you hire a lawyer and an accountant or will you try to deal with incorporation and tax issues on your own? Do you plan to work out of an office or your home? Will you have any employees? Do you plan to start with a large inventory of products or will you order as demand warrants? Can you build your own Web site or will you hire someone to do it for you? All of these factors will determine how much money you spend to get your store launched.

Tronix's entire initial investment was about $12,000. Of course, we didn't have much of a cushion for inventory, but in our case we only stocked what had already been ordered.

What equipment and software do I need?

A computer!

Okay, there's a bit more than that. You'll need to download the top two Web browsers: Netscape Communicator (or Navigator) and Microsoft Internet Explorer. You'll have to choose e-mail and newsgroup reading software, a File Transfer Protocol program to upload files to your site, a visual design and HTML code editor, image editing software, a point of sale program, shipping and tracking software (available from the various shipping companies), America Online, CompuServe, a scanner, and possibly a digital camera.

To find out what your options are, check out Chapter 6: Launching Your Online Store.

You'll also need a good deal of equipment for shipping purposes. Packing materials, boxes, a shipping table on which to pack boxes, a scale to keep shipping charges accurate, etc. For more about shipping-related needs, see Chapter 17: Everything About Shipping.

Can I run my store out of my house or apartment or should I find an office?

That largely depends on the volume of business you're doing and, of course, the size of your home. If you're just getting started, don't have an overwhelming inventory, and don't have the money yet to spend on an office, working out of your home may be your best—or only—option.

Also, if you have an empty basement or garage in which you have absolute privacy and which is capable of being wired for phones and a cable modem, using this space to limit your overhead might be a good idea. However, as your business grows, you'll probably need an office for a number of reasons.

One is the separation of work and the rest of your life. No matter how hard you try, you'll never be able to escape work if it's just a few steps away. Although starting any small business requires a strong commitment of both time and effort, you need to be able to get away from it or you'll eventually grow tired of your so-called life and bag the whole thing. And no matter how many times you tell your kids to stay away while you're working, eventually one of them will skin his or her knee and coming running for your help. Or they'll just decide they're bored and want to play.

Additionally, as your business grows you just won't have the space to run your store out of your home. You also have to be aware of local zoning laws.

So, to answer your two-part question, yes and yes.

How many employees do I need? Can I do it myself?

That's the beauty of running an online store. You *can* do it yourself. Tronix started that way and is still a one-person operation (with a friend occasionally helping out). Sure you'll need some help getting started—a lawyer, an accountant, and someone to design your site if you decide you can afford it or realize you don't have the ability to do it yourself.

Other than that, you can go it alone and add employees as growth warrants. You'll work long and hard, but that's a given for any small business owner. And no matter how big your business gets, you'll never need to hire someone to staff the cash register and lock up on Saturday night.

How much money can I make running an online store?

That depends on what you sell, how organized you are, how well you publicize your store, etc. Much like a traditional store, your future is in your hands. Some people start a small community restaurant and they're happy to remain at that level. And some become McDonald's.

The opportunity to make money on the Web is expected to grow dramatically as the public becomes more aware of its advantages and less concerned about placing credit card orders. Commerce on the Web is expected to grow from $2.6 billion in 1996 to more than $220 billion in 2001, according to a report by International Data Corporation (www.idc.com). The report, the highlights of which are available on IDC's Web site, also said the number of devices accessing the Web will grow from 32 million in 1996 to more than 300 million by the end of 2001.

The opportunity to make a lot of money is there and is only expected to increase.

What are some advantages and disadvantages of running an online store?

There are plenty of both. First the bad news:

When you run an online store, you're at the mercy of your Internet Service Provider. If the ISP goes down, you go down. It is also easy for competitors to get started and is, therefore, a very competitive field. Since e-commerce is still relatively new, your pool of customers can be small, and you have to really reach out to those potential customers. Since you don't have a storefront on Main Street, people aren't going to just walk by, poke their heads in, and buy something. If you don't make yourself known to potential customers, they may never find you. And if you treat one of those customers poorly, word can spread very rapidly on Usenet.

You can also fall prey to stores that have the ability to stock larger inventory, provide better customer service, and do more extensive marketing, but that is also true of traditional stores. You either need some technical ability or the money to pay someone who does. There are security and fraud issues, and running an online store can be extremely time-consuming.

Now the good news:

Your startup costs are potentially much lower than those of a traditional store owner. Operating on the Web allows you to have an immediate international sales presence from wherever you decide to set up shop. Speaking of which, you can set up shop anywhere in the world provided you have good Internet access. There is no need to relocate.

You can also create a personalized shopping experience. Depending on your budget, there are a number of high-end software products that help guide shoppers to the items they want. You have the option of providing electronically distributed goods for immediate fulfillment. Small operations with slim inventories can more effectively compete with larger companies. As long as your ISP doesn't go down, you can be open 24 hours a day, 365 days a year without hiring anyone.

If that isn't enough, there's a book of more reasons to follow.

How much content do I need to generate?

You can either generate your own product descriptions or rely on the manufacturers' literature, assuming you don't make the products you sell. The content for pages dealing with company policy, common questions, what's new, shipping, etc. will be provided and updated by your company. News and reviews of products can be culled from other sources.

You'll also have to type in prices and product descriptions, even if they've been provided for you. Although you'll have to generate a large percentage of your site's content, it won't account for the majority of your total workload.

Are there any special laws and regulations covering online stores?

In short, yes. In medium, get a lawyer. In a long-winded answer, there are a plethora of laws that govern both the online and retail universe that will affect your business.

A lot of Internet law has yet to be developed—cases either haven't come up or are still pending. As a store owner, you need to stay on top of the news and have a lawyer who can keep you apprised of the shifting legal winds. Some good online legal sources are FindLaw (www.findlaw.com), the Cyberspace Law Center (www.cybersquirrel.com/clc/), The Cyber Law Encyclopedia (http://gahtan.com/techlaw/home.htm) by Alan M. Gahtan, CyberSpace Law (www.ll.georgetown.edu/lr/rs/cyber.html) by the Georgetown University Law School, and the Web Law FAQ (www.patents.com/weblaw.sht).

Many of the legal issues are the same as those dealt with by traditional stores: advertising regulations, export laws, customs, guidelines for shipping perishables, etc. Interstate commerce as it pertains to the Web is another unresolved issue.

The only legal advice we're qualified to give is this: consult an expert. You should never assume you are sure about anything. If you have even an inkling that you might be misinterpreting or overlooking a law, talk to your lawyer. There's nothing like a temporary shutdown and a fine to kill your cash flow.

How do I find a good lawyer?

There are plenty of lawyers out there. Some people would say there are too many. It's important to find a good business lawyer who is sensitive to your needs as a new business owner, if you're just starting out. You should be able to find a good lawyer without dragging your business down with legal expenses.

If you don't know a lawyer, ask around. Someone you know will almost surely be able to point you in the right direction. If not, ask the owners of similar-sized businesses to recommend a lawyer.

What products sell best on the Web? What should I sell?

Most of the best-selling products are small items like books, CDs, video games, software, and so on. Don't limit your options to these. What you decide to sell is up to you. Something to think about is a computer-related product since the majority of people shopping online are computer owners. Tronix has been successful in selling computer games because the people who buy them are likely to be online.

You should also sell something you are enthusiastic and knowledgeable about. If you think roughing it is not having a cable modem for your Internet connection, don't sell hiking gear. And if you think punk is the only music worth listening to, don't sell violins.

Of course you may be just taking your traditional store online, in which case you'll know which of your products sell best. Now we know what you're going to ask next.

Once I've started selling things, how do I get the products to the customers?

You have a number of shipping options you can make available to your customers. Depending on how quickly your customers want their products, and how much they want to pay in shipping charges, you can ship using everything from standard first class mail to FedEx First Overnight.

Shipping isn't as complicated a process as setting up your shipping accounts and figuring out which company or companies best suits your variety of needs. You'll probably patch together a quilt of shipping coverage that meets all the needs and demands of your customers. To learn more about this, ship yourself to Chapter 17.

Can I make my store almost totally virtual?

Your marketing and sales are virtual. It's possible to run a completely virtual store in which you never see a product and never pack a box by using fulfillment companies. Expect to see an increase in these large warehouses, which store your inventory for you. Web merchants pay a storage fee and when orders come in, they simply tell the warehouse what to send and where to send it. Passing along the risk of holding inventory is the difference between being very virtual and totally virtual.

Is there anything I can sell and send directly to my customers over the Web?

The Web isn't just a place to sell goods, it can also be an excellent distribution medium for items, provided they are electronically transferable (please e-mail us if someone has figured out how to download milk and eggs).

While most stores sell goods that have to be shipped to users, there are number of stores that don't. For example, music stores eventually will transfer your new CD to you electronically. Many software stores are already turning to ESD (Electronic Software Distribution) instead of shipping the product to the user on disk or CD. The software is downloaded directly over the Internet. Electronic distribution is not limited to music or software. Expedia (expedia.msn.com), Microsoft's airline tickets and travel services "store," sells airline tickets that are nothing more than a password to be given at the gate. This same type of password sale will eventually be used for all sorts of things like car rentals, hotel rooms, movie tickets, concert tickets and more. Eventually these items could even be transferred to so-called *smart cards,* which you just slide through a scanner as you walk through the terminal gate or into your favorite theater.

Three keys to electronically distributed sales are security, bandwidth, and record keeping. Security is needed to protect items like distributed music and software from being easily replicated by end-users. Also, since the product itself is stored on a server, no one wants to have a virtual break-in where a hacker can copy all the wares and distribute them for free. Bandwidth is crucial because end-users need fast access like that provided by a T-1 or cable modem to receive a full-length CD, movie or video game.

Finally, record keeping is critical because it's harder to count how many copies have been properly sold through electronic distribution. That is why companies have created sophisticated and secure systems that will tell companies how many downloads of a top software package have been properly handled by a particular merchant.

The technology is still catching up, but it won't be long before a number of major products will be bought and distributed directly over the Web.

Should I consider combining my traditional store with an online store?

Yes. Well, maybe. Let it be said that not everyone has to be on the Web. A store that's doing well might not do any better if taken to the Web. And a struggling store won't necessarily be saved by the Web. Sometimes building a site can even be a mess, sucking out money you have and creating headaches you don't want.

However, existing traditional stores have a number of compelling reasons to get online and compete for sales. The most obvious reasons to get online are to expand sales and avoid losing sales to competitors who are online. However, why take the "scared stiff" approach? Existing stores should be compelled to go online by the inherent advantages they have over cyber-only competitors.

An existing store already has a lot of the infrastructure set up for such an operation. It will already have stock, distribution relationships, shipping accounts, product knowledge, a name, and a customer base. The trick is transferring your store's ambiance, reputation, and operational style so it shines through on the Web. Let your traditional customers know you're on the Web by posting your URL in your store and on all of your mailings, stationary, business cards, etc.

Maine mail order and retail behemoth L.L. Bean (www.llbean.com) is a great example. The company thrives on its reputation for excellent customer service, product knowledge, and outdoors expertise. When L.L. Bean launched its carefully created Web site, this was apparent. L.L. Bean didn't immediately accept orders on its site, explaining that it would wait until its customers' transactions would be guaranteed to be safe. L.L. Bean also warned that color representation of items shown on the Web was not an exact match to reality. These were classic reinforcements of L.L. Bean's customer service reputation.

L.L. Bean also launched with an extensive database of park and camping site information. Not only was this interesting content to offer as a draw to the site, but it also reinforced L.L. Bean's image as an expert in camping and outdoor activities.

As L.L. Bean shows, traditional retailers can benefit from having a Web presence. However, you don't have to rush and stumble. Instead, create a true cyberspace equivalent to your existing store.

What are some of the most successful online stores?

The most successful online stores have been pioneers that launched interesting new ways to shop online but didn't forget that online stores, like traditional stores, have to be focused, provide outstanding customer service, and create an interesting shopping experience.

However, *successful* is a relative term. Some operations that are considered successful haven't actually turned a profit. These stores are considered successful because they are projected to earn a profit once a critical mass of accustomed online shoppers is available.

Then there are stores like Tronix Multimedia—smaller operations that are run profitably on shoestring budgets by aggressive proprietors who have combined a good store choice with a readily available market and built a loyal clientele. Though most of these stores will never reach millions of dollars in sales, they don't have to in order to be profitable and provide excellent returns for their owners.

Some traditional retailers have also done well building a Web presence. Although not every store has successfully managed to add online sales to its repertoire, some stores and catalogs like L.L. Bean.com, Insight.com, and Walmart.com have taken early leads.

What are online auctions?

Most online auctions deal with computer-related items while some have gone into other areas of merchandise. Online auctions are a newer phenomenon than online stores, but there are an increasing number of players. The big difference between stores and auctions, besides the way you procure goods, is the entertainment value involved in auction sites. Online auctions are also able to generate large profit margins by purchasing excess goods at well below retail price, starting the bidding at less than that, and riding a bidding process that drives the final price well past what the auctioneer paid but still well below the retail price. Everyone goes home happy.

Onsale, Inc. (www.onsale.com) is the early leader in the online auction battle. Onsale requires participants to bid upward in $25 increments to help guarantee lucrative profit margins. First Auction (www.firstauction.com), which is affiliated with the Internet Shopping Network (www.internet.net) and launched in mid-June 1997, could be another serious contender.

What's the difference between simply selling products on the Web and running an online store?

It's the same as the difference between building a lemonade stand in front of your house and opening a store that happens to sell lemonade.

The online equivalent of a lemonade stand would be to simply go online and inform people that you have a particular item that you'd like to sell, and anyone who is interested can contact you via e-mail, regular mail, or phone.

Building an online store is much more involved. You'll probably be selling a variety of related products through a virtual inventory. You'll have to make your store known to potential customers and work to get them and keep them. In short, selling something online takes no time, little effort and will likely provide minimal income. Opening an online store requires long hours of work, tireless effort and will hopefully provide you with a living. Selling online is a hobby. Running an online store is your job.

Isn't online retailing really competitive? Will I be able to succeed?

Online selling is extremely competitive; so is selling cars, insurance, or anything else. As an online store owner, you must find out exactly who your competition is. Make sure you can answer the following questions.

- How many online companies are selling similar products?
- What are their prices and shipping options?
- How fast are they getting their products to their customers?
- What is the word of mouth on Usenet newsgroups about your competition?
- How slick/functional are their Web sites?
- Where does your competition advertise (e.g., links, major magazines)?

Will you be able to succeed? What kind of question is that? Of course you will be able to succeed. That doesn't mean you will.

A little luck never hurts, but success, as Boston Celtics coach Rick Pitino says, is a choice. Cliché alert: You'll get out of it what you put into it.

Can't I just open my store and let the orders roll in?

That would be nice wouldn't it? Unfortunately you can no more do that than you could open a store on a rural road, never advertise, and stay in business for more than a couple of months. In other words, NO!

There are a number of things you should do to increase your visibility—so many in fact that we have an entire section devoted to promoting your store. Chapter 10 will show you how to find customers through Usenet, online forums and referrals. Chapter 11 discusses promoting your store on the Internet: submitting to search engines, where to get your store listed, how to do link exchanges, how to set up leads and bounty programs, and more. Chapter 12 is The Store Owner's Guide To Advertising and will show you how to advertise on a shoestring budget. Chapter 13 focuses on international sales. These chapters will not only show you what to do but what not to do.

What's Spam? Is it a good thing?

Spam is unsolicited e-mail sent out in bulk without any regard to the recipients' interest in the subject. This type of spam, unlike that tasty, canned meat of the same name, is not good. If you decide to use spam as a way to promote your store, be prepared to incur the wrath of a large number of people. You will probably lose more customers than you gain. If you happen to annoy a hacker, you might end up with a trashed Web site. There are plenty of ways to promote your store without spam.

I don't know much about computers, much less HTML code. What should I learn before I open a store?

If you're the management type, you might just outsource the entire project, set the goals, pay the experts to build you a killer store, and watch the cash roll in. If you're in the real world, you'll want to learn some fundamentals and dig in a little so that you can keep your costs low and stay on top of the ever-changing Internet. The best management comes from being able to do the work but choosing, for other compelling reasons, not to. That way no one will pull a fast one on you and you can step in when something goes wrong.

You should be familiar with how to use a computer and pick up some Internet experience. After you know your way around, you'll want to learn some HTML and how to use a basic editor. You don't need to be an expert but some basics will help. To gain this knowledge, you can start with this book. You should also look into some other books and check out some of the major online resources and guides listed throughout this book. There is a lot of learning to do, but there are some very good aides available—especially the ones listed in this book.

For those of you more versed in the Web, we recommend that you get intimately familiar with a top-rate e-mail package. As you'll learn later, your ability to command an e-mail program is paramount. Brush up on the ability to quickly edit Web pages and learn the ins and outs of uploading and downloading from your site. I will be critical to know how to make minor edits and changes throughout the life of your store. You might also want to learn how to operate a scanner and/or digital camera and subsequently fix up the imagery in a good paint program.

For those of you who are computer experts but not well-versed in the retailing trade, stop thinking you're ready to go. Running a store on the Web is a lot more than just hacking out some cool HTML code and uploading JPEGs. You need to provide top-notch customer service, make correct orders, maintain stock, deal with the local UPS driver, and collect and maintain all the taxes and money. This stuff is enough to make even the most knowledgeable Java programmer curl into the fetal position. We're here to help.

Should I just hire someone to develop my site or do it myself?

That depends on your knowledge, your willingness to learn, and your cash flow. If you don't know HTML, don't care to know HTML, and have enough money, you can have someone do the work for you. If you're an established retailer like L.L. Bean or Eddie Bauer looking to build a Web presence, of course you'll want to hire someone to do the work. But if you're a small startup, learning HTML will allow you to do your own site maintenance while keeping your costs low.

Designing your own site is also a creative, if grueling, process. It can be satisfying to put together your own site from scratch, much like creating a piece of art. Anyone can buy a painting and hang it in the living room. Few people can create that painting themselves.

Are there any "Shop In A Box" products on the market?

Yes. An example is Viaweb Store, which is a combination of an authoring tool and a hosting service. You can build your store on their browser and Viaweb serves your finished site. Pricing is reasonable at $100 per month for a store selling up to 20 items and $300 per month for up to 1,000 items. You don't have to know any HTML; you just enter the information you want to provide such as names prices and descriptions. You can update your site as often as you want and all you need for software is an ordinary browser: Netscape Navigator or Microsoft Internet Explorer.

However, these products cost money, and if you want to keep your costs down, you're better off creating your own Web site.

What are Open Market and Microsoft Merchant Server?

These are kits for Internet storefronts that help solve some issues such as creating a shopping environment, order and user tracking, demographic information, and secure payments. But they still leave a lot of work for you to do and are almost certainly out of your price range as a start-up business owner. However, some Web hosts set up servers which run Open Market or Merchant Server and allow you to set up a store on that server while paying a licensing fee. Eventually commerce-based servers should become easier to use and less expensive and can be useful for a large volume store.

What are online malls and how do they work?

Thankfully they aren't where online Valley girls hang out to you know, like, *chat*.

Actually, the idea behind online malls is similar to that of traditional shopping malls. A developer will launch a site on the Web that offers entrances and integrated shopping experiences across a multitude of product lines and vendors. Everyone is under the same roof; that roof could be the same URL or a similar looking interface with different vendors.

Behind the scenes many of the stores run on the same server, taking advantage of a unified shopping infrastructure including credit card checking, digital cash acceptance, personalization tools, etc. The mall operator charges vendors a rental fee for space on the system or takes a percentage of every transaction. As a small operator, launching a store as part of an online mall allows you to reside on a server that has been specifically created online selling. The mall operator may also offer other services such as promotions help and design assistance. The downside is that you might not have as much control over your site.

The biggest existing mall areas are on the specialized online services like America Online and CompuServe. However, several groups—including IBM—have experimented with Web-based malls. There is still a question about how well the mall concept will translate to the Web. Since any site is as close as any other site on the Web, how important it is to have a store located on the cyberspace equivalent of the local mega-mall?

Instead, what may arise are closer affiliations and seamless linking and purchasing ability between vendors selling complementary goods. It won't exactly be a mall, but the concept of pulling a variety of stores together for a unified online shopping experience could be powerful.

I hear there is a risk involved in accepting credit card orders. Should I accept them?

Purchasing goods over the Internet using a credit card is becoming a more secure process, although it is not yet perfect. As the industry moves closer to a secure transaction standard, credit card purchases will continue to become less worrisome.

Whether or not you accept credit cards is up to you. Most Web stores, including Tronix, accept them. The risk is for the shoppers and, as long as they understand no transaction is guaranteed to be secure, they'll likely decide whether or not they want to send their credit card number off into cyberspace.

In a purely business sense, the more payment options your store offers, the better your sales will be. In the end, it's tough to run a successful cyberstore without accepting credit cards.

What other kinds of security risks do I have to worry about?

The biggest risk is fraudulent credit card usage and the proper handling of customer's personal e-mail information. You also need to make sure your provider is secure enough to block break-ins. To learn more about eliminating these risks, see Chapter 16: How to Spot and Catch Online Thieves.

What are SET, SSL, e-cash, and TRUSTe?

If you're going to run an online store, it's best to know what technologies you're dealing with.

SET (Secure Electronic Transaction) is an open industry standard detailing the use of payment cards over open networks like the Internet. SET uses digital certificates to authenticate parties involved in a transaction. Introduced by Visa and MasterCard, with assistance from technology partners IBM, Terisa Systems, GTE, VeriSign, RSA, Netscape, Microsoft and SAIC, the SET specification was completed in May 1997. The SET consortium is working on creating a SET software compliance process; a structure to manage and issue the SET digital certificates to the payment brands; validation of vendor software against the 1.0 spec and the deployment into the global market; roll-out of programs through financial institutions, merchants, and cardholders.

SSL (Secure Sockets Layer) was introduced in Netscape 2.0 as a technology to protect credit card numbers. Users are often advised if they are using an older browser without built-in SSL to phone in their order.

E-cash systems such as Digicash and NetCash allow the customer to deposit cash into an account and then use that cash to purchase items off the Internet. E-cash is untraceable, which improves privacy. You can only lose as much cash as is in your electronic wallet as opposed to someone stealing your credit card number and maxing it out. However, e-cash is uninsured. If your hard drive crashes or your e-bank goes under, there is no way to retrieve the lost cash.

IBM is also launching a payment server called eTill, that will allow Web merchants to accept a variety of forms of payment.

TRUSTe is a coalition that has been formed to limit the amount of junk e-mail you get. If a store has a TRUSTe tag, that store agrees not to release any of its customers' information to other businesses or to mailing list companies.

I've heard a lot about VeriSign. Who are they?

VeriSign, Inc. (www.verisign.com) provides digital authentication services and products for electronic commerce and other forms of secure communications. Digital IDs are crucial to establishing confidence in the security of electronic transactions. A Digital ID binds a person's or company's identity to a digital key which can be used to conduct secure communications or transactions. The Digital ID is intended to give the parties involved in a transaction confidence in its origin and can then be attached to electronic transactions and communications as the critical authentication component.

VeriSign was selected by Visa in July 1997 to operate an Internet-based authentication service for electronic commerce solutions based on SET. VeriSign will operate the Digital ID service for Visa which, in turn, will make it available for Visa member financial institutions wanting to roll out secure electronic commerce services.

Don't confuse VeriSign with VeriFone, the company that was recently purchased by Hewlett-Packard and which manufactures and provides services for credit card transaction equipment.

Are there any good references to help online store proprietors?

Some of the best information will come from simply checking out other established Web sites. There are also a number of good books out there, including *Getting Hits: The Definitive Guide to Promoting Your Website* by Don Sellers (published by Peachpit Press) and *How to Grow Your Business on The Internet* by Vince Emery (published by Coriolis Group Books).

There are also some Usenet spots such as alt.business.misc, comp.internet.net-happenings, and alt.internet.commerce where online merchants can share ideas. To search for more Usenet spots, try searching with DejaNews (www.dejanews.com).

Of course, we're partial to *Creating Stores On the Web*, but you probably figured that.

All right, I'm going to start an online store. Where do I start?

That's easy. Read this book.

CHAPTER TWO

The Story of Tronix

Since launching Tronix (www.tronixweb.com) in late 1993, Joe Cataudella, a long-time video game devotee, has seen the World Wide Web change dramatically as the technology has allowed for more interesting graphics and more secure transactions. A swarm of new businesses hoping to ride the Internet to increased market share has come and gone. During that time Tronix, Cataudella's own company, has gone from a struggling start-up selling five or six games a day to an established online presence handling 30 or 40 orders a day that is on the brink of expansion.

Through it all, Cataudella's philosophy of honest customer service, a user-friendly Web site, and the ability to fulfill orders while maintaining a relatively small inventory has kept Tronix near the front of the pack of online video game retailers. As with most start-ups, Tronix has had to be innovative and flexible while learning from early mistakes. For anyone hoping to dive into online retailing, Tronix is an example of success that shows what is possible with a little sweat, a lot of creativity, and the willingness to change with the ever-shifting Internet.

This chapter focuses on what Tronix has done to become a solid, profitable business. You can apply most of the lessons here to your own philosophies as you move toward the reality of running an online store.

A Beginning in Retail

Cataudella's retailing roots were laid in New York City as a jack-of-all-trades at Leigh Computers.

"I've been a game player all my life," Cataudella says. "That inspired me to get involved in the business. I started with an Apple computer and took the game playing route rather than programming. I had studied graphic design before it was done on computers, and that aspect of games intrigued me. When I first got a computer, I did a few freelance projects. I did graphic development for a game that, because of a lack of planning, eventually fell through."

Shortly after graduating from high school, Cataudella went to work at a computer center in New York. The company folded about a year later, but when Leigh Goldstein, a co-worker, opened Leigh Computers, Cataudella joined him. As the only initial employee, Cataudella worked as a manager and a salesperson, learning all aspects of retailing along the way.

"I did a bit of everything and became pretty successful at it," he remembers. "But I didn't always want to do things Leigh's way. I had a lot of suggestions—in fact, I set him up with his first Nintendo account before it was a big name. If he was still in existence he could be a Nintendo dealer and a lot of other things, but he was afraid to take any risks."

Cataudella was more of a risk-taker. Although his customer service ideas weren't perfectly tailored to retail, they helped him gain the trust and admiration of the store's customers. Rather than push product out the door, Cataudella offered his honest opinions. If a product wasn't good for a customer, he said so.

"At some of the big retail outlets, the salespeople will tell the customer everything's great," he said. "The idea of retail is to get rid of inventory. Telling a customer that a product isn't great doesn't fit in with retail. I was always honest. I didn't feel right about telling a customer a certain product was great if I hadn't looked at it or if I didn't believe it myself."

Cataudella's approach helped build a loyal customer base.

"People believed my advice and kept coming back, but Leigh didn't really agree with the way I was doing things," Cataudella said. "He didn't think it was helping business if I wasn't pushing stuff out the door. Customers became friends. They'd come in and we'd have conversations and it was a real family atmosphere. It was someplace people wanted to shop."

But Goldstein eventually lost his enthusiasm for the business and, after nine years, Leigh Computers folded in 1993.

The Birth of Tronix

With Leigh Computers out of business, Cataudella went the entrepreneurial route with his nephew serving as the primary investor. A few months after Leigh Computers folded, Cataudella began the arduous task of starting his own business—an online video game store.

"My nephew and I had talked about starting our own business," Cataudella says. "We never thought it would happen but we had to follow that dream."

Starting a small business requires more than just dreams of fame and fortune. Simply getting Tronix off the ground was Cataudella's biggest challenge. While his nephew took care of the financial end of the start-up, Cataudella did the legwork, scouting out office space in New York City and setting up merchant accounts with credit card companies.

"Looking for office space in New York wasn't easy and that's probably the case everywhere," Cataudella said. "I looked at a lot of spaces that weren't great. That was probably the most frustrating part. My nephew was the investor and he already had a lawyer, so that gave us a head start. He took care of all the paperwork with the lawyer."

Even more difficult than finding a suitable space, which Cataudella eventually settled into on Seventh Avenue, was convincing the credit card companies to give him the merchant accounts necessary to allow credit card orders. Credit card companies are hesitant to deal with strictly mail-order businesses. Cataudella had to convince the companies that he would be doing some retail sales as well. A lot of former customers from Leigh Computers made the trip to Cataudella's office, but his business quickly became primarily mail order.

Another hurdle—one faced by all but the most fortunate start-ups—was money. Tronix was launched in late 1993 with an investment of about $12,000.

"At the beginning it was hard to see how much money you needed," Cataudella remembers. "We weren't thinking about profits, we were just thinking about paying the rent and surviving. I paid the rent and security deposit and all the start-up costs, which didn't leave much money for inventory. We had a very, very small inventory and started out basically doing special orders. Not everybody will be able to work with such small inventory but we're within walking distance from our distributors. That was a big advantage."

By the summer of 1994, things were starting to fall into place for Tronix. But success didn't come without some early struggles.

Learning on the Fly

When Tronix was launched, customers didn't exactly flock to the Web site and spend hundreds of dollars. Not only was Tronix new, the idea of shopping on the Web was also in the embryonic stage. For about the first five months of existence, Tronix filled five or six orders a day as Cataudella learned some important lessons about mail-order sales and operating on the Web.

"We used to have periods when the orders would really come in," he says. "We just barely survived in the summer and then the holidays would come and we'd make enough money to get caught up. It was a survival thing. Little by little, I stumbled on things that made us more efficient. Even now we're picking things up to help us get orders out faster. Anything to save a minute."

Cataudella said one of his early mistakes was making himself too vulnerable in accepting credit card orders. "I had a few charge-backs at the beginning," he remembers.

Cataudella also says he wasted a lot of time addressing envelopes and packing boxes. But as the number of orders grew, Tronix became more efficient out of necessity. Envelopes are now self-addressed ahead of time and boxes are pre-padded during down times.

"I have a lot better process now," Cataudella said. "I'm obsessed with everything being perfect, as any business owner would be. We've had to become a lot more efficient as the number of orders have grown."

Keys to Success

As Cataudella continued to learn, Tronix's chances of surviving grew. By 1995, Cataudella was confident Tronix would survive and thrive. He credits his commitment to honest customer service, his ability to stay ahead of the competition in terms of his Web site, and his belief and interest in what he's selling as keys to Tronix's success.

Honest Customer Service

"Customer service is the reason we've been successful," Cataudella said. "At Leigh's, I learned a lot about customer service—how to treat people and how not to treat people. Now with a lot of orders coming through e-mail it's a bit different because there isn't that face-to-face contact, but you still have an opportunity to make shopping at your site an enjoyable experience. If your site is easy to use, and you get the products to your customers on time, people will want to come back. If they have to spend a lot of time navigating your site, or it takes forever to load, or you promise two-day delivery and it takes a week, you're going to lose customers, and before long you'll be out of business."

For Cataudella, honesty is the best policy. As a store operator, the obvious goal is to sell things to people who want or need them. But, Cataudella insists, that doesn't mean pushing inferior products on unsuspecting customers.

"You can avoid selling bad products by not stocking many of them," he says. "That way you never have to tell somebody something's fantastic if it's not, and you won't be stuck with lousy products. It also keeps your inventory from getting too big."

In the world of online sales, speed is of the essence. The Web provides immediate gratification and, in the case of Tronix, a young clientele which wants its orders immediately.

"Everyone wants it yesterday," Cataudella said. "When we get something in, it's like bees to honey. A lot of people call because their local store hasn't gotten a particular game yet. They want new releases as soon as they're available."

And if an online store can't provide a compelling reason to shop there rather than walking down to the corner, what's the point?

"You have to provide a reason for them to shop online," Cataudella said. "If you can get them an item faster than anyone else or if you can give them a good price, they'll shop online."

A Clean Web Site

In the beginning, there were limited options for Web site construction, but Cataudella spent a lot of time monitoring the competition.

"I had many sleepless nights," he said. "I'd see a site that was better than mine and it would drive me crazy. The competition was the most overwhelming thing. You see something and immediately have to counteract it. For the first two years I spent about 30 minutes a day just checking Web sites. Now I'm comfortable checking them once a week."

And the more he saw, the more he realized he was near the front of the pack.

"For the most part I was able to beat people to the punch and make them react to what I was doing," Cataudella said. "The more time I spent in front, the more I realized that's the way it was going to be. I always seemed to be a step ahead of them in terms of balancing my Web site and being innovative."

Cataudella says he was the first video game merchant to include reviews on his site. He wrote the reviews and stuck to his credo of honesty. Great games got great reviews. Mediocre games got mediocre reviews. "Not everyone reads the reviews, so you can be honest and it's not going to cost you a lot of sales. In the long run it's better to lose one sale because of a fair review. If you write how great a product is and people buy it and find out it's not so hot, you might lose them as a customer. That could end up costing you dozens of sales in the long run."

As the technology to create snazzy Web sites grew, Cataudella admits to getting carried away with the possibilities. As soon as a particular graphical item became available, up it went.

"I felt like I had to use everything that was available, but I soon realized that wasn't the case," he said. "A clean Web site without all the whip cream works best. It makes things faster because you don't have to wait for the animation to load. A lot of other sites have scrolling marquees, but I don't think they're worth it. Eventually you fall back to the basics. The way the Tronix Web site is laid out you can tell we didn't mess around."

The Tronix site has evolved and continues to do so. Rather than enticing customers with fancy graphics, the site is simple, easy to read, easy to navigate and quick to load. The customers are there to shop, not to "ooh" and "ahh" over the graphics.

The home page is primarily black with a navigation bar down the left side. The Tronix logo runs vertically down the left half of the screen. Centered near the top of the screen is the company's motto—"No-Nonsense Mail Order For The Serious Gamer"—followed by the address, phone number and fax number. The inclusion of the contact information in such a prominent spot seems like an obvious choice until you consider the number of sites which seem intent on burying it.

The only other graphics are for a couple of current games and, near the bottom of the page, the logos of accepted credit cards.

The lettering on the navigation panel is an easy-to-read white and links to price lists are divided by companies such as Nintendo and Saturn. The price lists include brief descriptions of each game and newer releases are highlighted by an aqua-colored bar. You can also jump to Specials, What's New (a calendar of new and upcoming releases), Read Me (Frequently Asked Questions), Shipping Info (rules and sample rates), Reviews (categorized by Playstation, Saturn and Nintendo), Email Tronix, and Order (in aqua).

The navigation panel remains black throughout the site, while the primary color of some pages is gray rather than black. The site is consistent and clearly spells out the terms of sale. The Specials page informs customers that all sales are final, and the Shipping page also includes Tronix's policies. The Reviews page not only has capsule reviews of some games, it also includes a few lengthy game FAQs submitted by customers. Tronix's secure online order form offers full explanations and warnings.

A Love for Games

For all his customer service experience and sound Web site philosophy, Cataudella says Tronix wouldn't be as successful as it is if he didn't love what he was doing. He shares his customers' enthusiasm for video games, which makes it easy to put the necessary extra thought and effort into his business.

"It's essential that you have an interest in what you're selling," he says. "If you don't care about it, eventually the competition is going to beat you into the ground. You see people who are purely in it to make a buck and have no idea about what they're selling. Of course you want to make money, but you see a lot of store owners just checking the top 10 lists and selling those products. They usually fail because there is no connection with the customer."

If you sell what you know—and what you love—you'll have a better chance of making it through the tough times. Besides making your job more fun, it's just good business. If your customers can sense your enthusiasm for and knowledge of your product, they'll keep coming back. If they think you're just trying to turn a buck with no regard to their happiness, they'll go elsewhere. Let your passion set you apart.

Cataudella also has the benefit of retail experience, further easing his transition to the entrepreneurial life. He launched Tronix already knowing how to operate a credit card machine and other business hardware. His nine years at Leigh Computer also helped shape his customer service philosophy.

"If you have some retail experience, that's just another advantage," Cataudella said. "The best combination is to have some retail experience as well as a genuine enthusiasm for what you're selling. You see a lot of people trying to start online businesses who might be fanatical about (their products) but have no idea about the business end."

Why Many Companies Fail

While Tronix has survived, many of its competitors have come and gone. Many of the reasons for failure aren't unique to operating on the Web.

"Extensive inventory of the wrong items has led to a lot of failed companies," Cataudella said. "And you see companies trying to make extra money on shipping charges or not getting shipments to customers on time. Those things will kill you."

Choosing the right products to stock just requires a little research. In Tronix's case, a visit to the annual Electronic Entertainment Expo (E3) helps Cataudella find the hottest new products. Almost every industry will have similar trade shows.

Some online store owners think the Internet will do all the work for them. Although the Internet provides some advantages over traditional mail order or retailing, you have to work to reap those benefits. Otherwise it's like taking steroids and sitting on the couch with a bag of chips, a six pack and a remote control.

"Some people think they can just put up a Web site and ride the Internet to success, which is a mistake," Cataudella said. "A lot of them aren't even aware of the newsgroups, which are the best places to spread the word about your store."

Others jump into a supposedly hot market only to find it is already saturated or they deliver poor customer service. With an immediate medium such as the Internet, word spreads in a few days. If you don't treat your customers right, there won't be any left.

Becoming a Workaholic Out of Necessity

Cataudella says he enjoys his social life too much to be a workaholic. But running an online store requires a commitment, if not a workaholic schedule.

Cataudella's typical day includes 10 or 11 hours of Tronix-related work, although only about seven of those hours are spent at his Seventh Avenue office. He spends at least an hour a day upgrading the Tronix Web site. "We're constantly making changes even if they're only minor changes," Cataudella said. "If I see a word spelled wrong, I change it immediately."

In the morning, Cataudella spends about two hours going through his e-mail and separating the orders from the inquiries. He processes the orders immediately and deals with the inquiries at night at home. The rest of the day is primarily dedicated to ordering stock, packing boxes and getting them shipped. Cataudella also spends some time answering phones, the avenue through which about 25 percent of orders are placed.

"We used to get about 90 percent of our orders through e-mail," Cataudella said. "Most of the people who call are long-time customers who want to know about a certain game. The phone calls slow me down, but I grin and bear it."

He also spends about six hours on the Internet on weekends and the Christmas rush often means a full Saturday in the office. The heaviest Web upgrading is done at night when Cataudella gets home. It's something he wishes he had more time for.

"I'd like to spend more time on the creative end of things, like upgrading the Web site and writing reviews," he said. "Packing boxes can get old. I'm in the process of hiring another person who will be there to process orders and pack boxes so I can do more creative work. When I first opened I did a lot of reviews and really liked that. It lured a lot of customers. Now I don't need it as much and I don't have the time."

The most obvious measure of success is financial. When Cataudella launched Tronix, he hoped to make a living and he has. He has also enjoyed more subtle rewards than a growing bank account.

"When a customer comes back and says he's never dealt with a better business, that keeps you going," Cataudella says. "When you get written up in a magazine and the article says how great your store is, that makes you feel good. And when you keep seeing your name on the newsgroups and it's always in a positive light, you know you're doing things the right way. And of course there's no boss. You're in control."

Looking Ahead

Although the online retailing business has changed dramatically since Tronix's 1993 launch, the metamorphosis isn't complete.

Cataudella says Tronix needs to be flexible enough to grow with the Web.

"The whole industry has changed," he said. "Secure transactions, rather than just e-mailing credit card numbers back and forth, have given it a more professional atmosphere and helped online retailing become more established. The Web itself has come a long way with Java and some other languages. At the beginning, the most you could do was a simple list."

Cataudella agrees with the forecasts of massive growth in online retailing. He also admits he never saw it coming back in the early days of Tronix.

"We live in such a busy society, people don't have time to run to stores," he said. "I know I don't. The Internet can take care of a lot of things and allow people to use their free time for something more enjoyable than shopping. The growth has taken me completely by surprise. At the beginning I thought the Web might be a phase that wouldn't last. Then I never thought there would be a method for secure credit card transactions. That was a big step."

Now it's just a matter of the public becoming aware of the possibilities of online shopping.

"I see the whole thing getting more professional and more well-done as people see what works and what doesn't," Cataudella says. "The next generation version of the shopping cart will be more automated. The way credit cards are taken and approved will run more smoothly."

And Tronix, which hopped on the Web wave early, hopes to keep growing along with the rest of the industry. Cataudella may add a rental end of the business or expand to non-game computer products. More money could be spent on advertising.

"We have a lot of potential for growth," Cataudella said. "We can't really handle any more orders without growing. There are a few routes we can go, but I'm still playing it by ear."

CHAPTER THREE

Lessons From Other Online Retailers

Although Tronix has certainly been successful, it is just one of thousands of online stores that continue to be profitable as electronic commerce flourishes. This chapter focuses on a few successful stores that cover the spectrum from small to enormous.

On the gigantic end of the spectrum, we have L.L. Bean, which has expanded its sales potential and highlighted its corporate image through a marvelous Web site. We'll take a close look at its site because there is plenty to learn here. We'll also visit Reel, which is as much a resource for film buffs as it is a video rental cyberstore.

There is also Amazon.com, which claims to be "Earth's Biggest Bookstore" with more than 2.5 million titles. Amazon.com has a number of features than can be scaled down to fit the needs of a small cyberstore owner. We'll also check out Sub Pop Online, an independent record label that went from bankruptcy's door to booming on the coattail's of Nirvana's record sales. Finally there are The Cassette House and Billy's Florida Stone Crab Claws, which are small and somewhat different from one another, but still successful operations.

As an online merchant, you can learn something from all of these businesses, no matter how big or small. Hopefully the information here will spark some ideas for your own store. We encourage you to visit the various Web sites to learn even more.

L.L. Bean
www.llbean.com

L.L. Bean, based in Freeport, Maine but known worldwide for its boots, casual clothes, and outdoor gear, has built an empire on quality products and near-legendary customer service. L.L. Bean's Golden Rule, spelled out simply by founder Leon Leonwood Bean, is "Sell good merchandise at a reasonable profit, treat your customers like human beings, and they will always come back for more." If Bean were alive today, he might add, "Keep your Web site functional, fun, and organized." L.L. Bean's online presence is all of that and more thanks to a partnership with Strategic Interactive Group of Boston and IBM's Internet Division and Integrated Systems Solutions Corporation.

When L.L. Bean first went online a couple of years ago, it didn't even offer the option to cybershop. The company didn't think electronic transactions were secure enough to ask its customers to take a risk. Besides being a smart public relations move, this underscored L.L. Bean's commitment to its customers. Now you can not only shop at llbean.com, you can use the Park Search to get information on state and national parks, forests, and wildlife refuges. The site also has information on L.L. Bean's Outdoor Discovery Program and perfectly conveys the spirit and feel of L.L. Bean.

Options

L.L. Bean runs its internal links across the bottom of the page to allow for maximum horizontal screen usage on the top 90 percent of each page. There are six buttons: Home, Search, Shop L.L. Bean, Let Us Help You, Explore The Outdoors, and About L.L. Bean. Each leads to a number of easily navigated subcategories.

Home page

L.L. Bean's home page features a set of rotating outdoors photos—three kids running through a field, a family in a canoe, friends sitting on a rocky coastline—and the L.L. Bean logo as the primary art. You can link to the Online Product Guide

FIGURE 3.1
L.L. Bean's home page.

and the Catalog Quickshop and get information on FedEx delivery. (The L.L. Bean factory includes its own self-contained FedEx shipping unit.) There is an immediate link to a featured product, an order form for free catalogs, What's New, and the Park Search (more on that later).

Search

There's nothing surprising here. If you have a good idea of what you're looking for, it's a quick way to find it, order it, and get outside. Type in a concept or keyword, hit search, and you'll be presented with a number of product links. For example, a search for **mountain biking** returns links to Mountain Pile Vest, Bean's Approach Mountain Bike, Gore-Tex Mountain Treads, and more.

Catalog page

Chose one of the options and you'll be sent to a catalog page of the item. Depending on the item, the catalog page includes a standard photo of the item, a photo of the product in use or being worn by a model, price, catalog number, and a short description of the item. There is also a warning that international customers must order by phone. As this book went to press, L.L. Bean said it was still not confident enough in secure transactions to allow international online shopping.

Ordering

If you decide to order, a form asks you to enter the style, size, color, quantity, etc. depending on the item order. You can also sign up as an online shopper, which allows you to simply sign in on return visits and eliminates the need to repeatedly enter all of this information.

Shop L.L. Bean

Choosing Shop L.L. Bean takes you through a number of shopping-related options. All are easily navigated and fully explained.

FIGURE 3.2
One of L.L. Bean's many catalog pages.

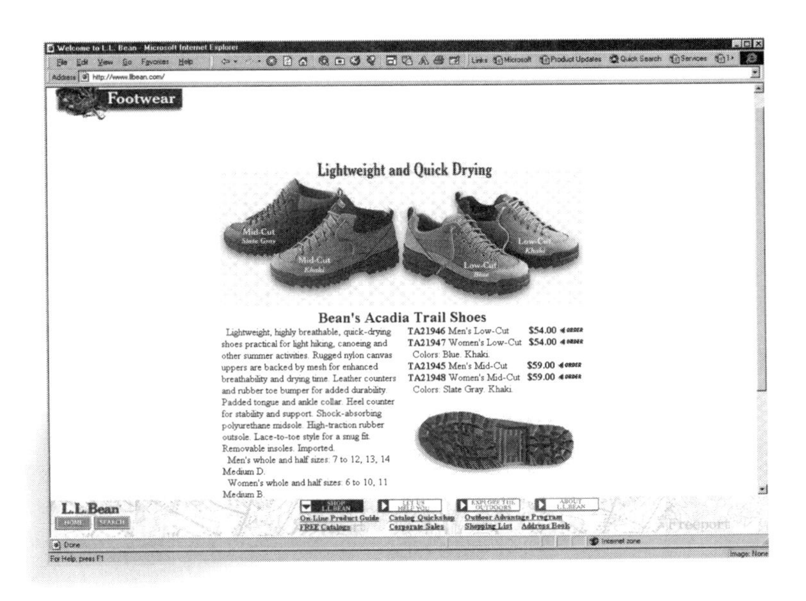

The Catalog Quickshop is for shoppers who have found an item in their mail order catalog and simply want to order through the Web site rather than making a phone call.

The Address Book is for people who have signed up to be online shoppers. It allows you to keep track of people to whom you might like to ship items. This can be particularly useful when a customer suddenly realizes Christmas is a few days away and she still hasn't picked anything up for Aunt Edna in Topeka. Go to the Address Book, order a pair of hip waders, and off they go.

If you'd rather sit in bed with a cup of hot chocolate flipping through one of L.L. Bean's catalogs than surf the Web site, you can click on Free Catalogs and get just that.

Shopping List takes you to a list of items you've already ordered on your current spree.

The Online Product Guide takes you through L.L. Bean's massive inventory. The major categories are Clothing, Home & Camp, Sporting Goods, and Gift Certificate. Each has a number of sub-groups. For example, you can go from Home & Camp to Indoor Furnishings, which provides a list of specific items. While the Search option is good for shopping when a customer has an idea of what he wants, the Online Product Guide allows a customer to start with a broader range of desires.

Let Us Help You

This is an informational category. The first subgroup is Customer Service, which spells out L.L. Bean's philosophy and the aforementioned Golden Rule. The Customer Service option also includes information on gift registry, a FAQ, and an assurance of privacy and a secure shopping environment.

TIP ▸ ***It's a good idea to include your customer philosophy on your Web site, not just for the benefit of your customers, but for yourself. If you put your customer service philosophy into words for your Web site, you'll be forced to think about it and be more likely to stick to it.***

How Are We Doing is another great idea for cyberstores of all sizes. It's a simple, seven-question survey that only takes a minute or so to answer and can provide valuable feedback on what is working and what isn't. With this option, customers might also be less likely to send e-mail about your site, therefore decreasing the time you need to spend reading and responding to complaints and compliments. The key is to keep it brief, as L.L. Bean has. Remember, people shop online to *save* time, not to waste it filling out 30-question surveys (unless they're *really* mad).

Explore The Outdoors

Here's where the L.L. Bean Web site gets fun and moves from being just a functional cyberstore to one of the best on the Web. Explore The Outdoors isn't directly about selling boots. It's about providing information, building a sense of community and reinforcing L.L. Bean's Web site as a great place to visit. Which, in an indirect way, is about selling boots.

The first option is the L.L. Bean Outdoor Discovery Program. The program includes schools for Fly Fishing, Paddling Cycling, Shooting, and Outdoor Skills. You can find information and classes offered for each school and registration and contact information.

Selecting Outdoor Sports includes informational tidbits on fitness, cycling, camping and day hiking, fly fishing, winter camping, cross country skiing, snowshoeing, hiking, a guide to the outdoors, and a link back to the Outdoor Discovery Programs. Choosing a category leads the user to more detailed bits of information.

But the most interesting spot on the L.L. Bean site is the Park Search, a database of 766 state parks, 171 national parks, 590 national wildlife refuges, 156 national forests, and 99 Bureau of Land Management lands. L.L. Bean licensed the database from Deep River Publishing in Portland, Maine. Each park page includes photos, a brief description of the park, activities available, and contact information.

The Park Search further solidifies L.L. Bean's image as an outdoors expert and provides a service that many customers find useful. If you have an area of expertise, providing an informational page such as L.L. Bean's Park Search is a nice bonus. Obviously, something as extensive as the Park Search is beyond the grasp of a small store. Scale this kind of area to fit your ability.

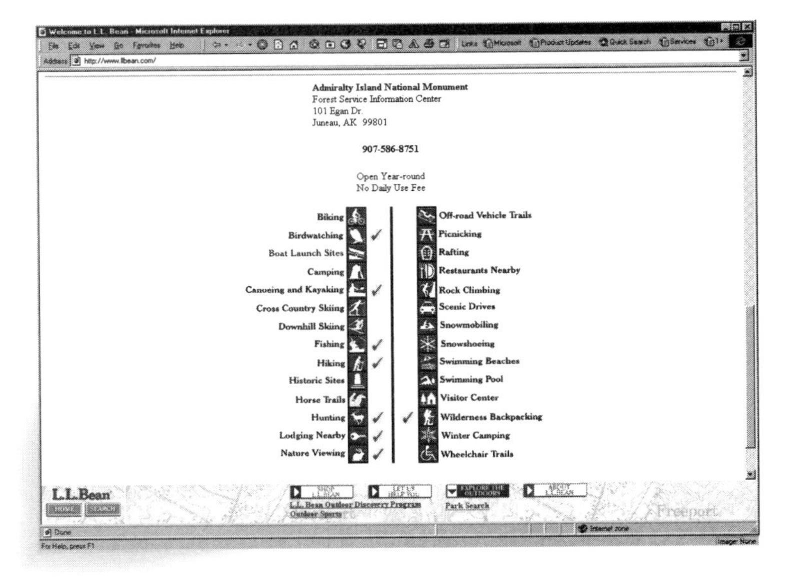

FIGURE 3.3
L.L. Bean's Park Search attracts potential customers to the site.

About L.L. Bean

About L.L. Bean takes you to a number of informational spots on the site. What's New has information on how to shop, FedEx shipping, a product plug, news on the new L.L. Kids store, free catalog ordering and e-mailing.

The Company Behind The Catalog includes the story of company founder Leon Leonwood Bean, Bean's Golden Rule, a collection of favorite catalog covers from 1927 to 1975, a spot on Made In Maine craftsmanship, and information on Bean's conservation efforts, creating and testing products, and suggested corporate gifts.

One of the best

Obviously L.L. Bean has immense resources that are unavailable to most companies. That doesn't mean you can't learn a few lessons from the mail order/retail giant. L.L. Bean has created an attractive, easily navigated site that not only provides users an opportunity to shop, but also to learn more about the company. It's nearly impossible not to walk away from this site without a positive feeling about L.L. Bean.

Follow L.L. Bean's example by making your site easy to navigate. Provide as much information about your goods as time and space allow.

While L.L. Bean paid for the information included in the Park Search, you can create similar features by using your expertise and the available resources without spending money. If you're selling sporting goods, your customers might be interested in a page that provides the sports news of the day or week. You can also link to related sites, but keep in mind that's taking customers away from your site. And if you rent or sell videos, why not include reviews and notes about the films? Which brings us to Reel.

Reel

www.reel.com

Reel claims to be "The Planet's Biggest Movie Store," and with 80,000 movies for sale and 35,000 for rent, it's hard to dispute that claim. Reel is a new San Francisco-based company that grew from the Empire Video Superstores, founded in Vermont in 1985. Empire founder Stuart Skorman sold his chain of stores in 1994 and moved to California with a group of video store veterans and movie experts. Reel has a partnership with Internet Movie Database of England. The site was built by Lynch Industries.

Other than its massive selection, Reel is interesting to study for two reasons: it offers rentals and is an incredible resource for movie fans even if you never rent a movie through the site. It would've been easier and cheaper for Reel to just slap up a list of available movies for people to order. Instead it has also become a comprehensive movie guide and a must-see site for film buffs.

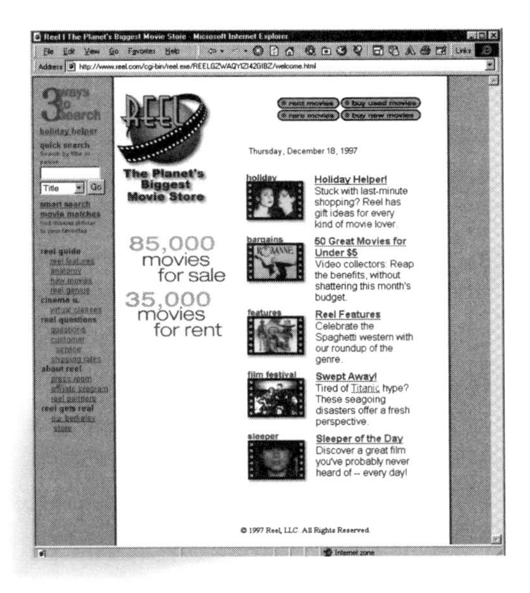

FIGURE 3.4
Reel's home page.

Search

There's a great scene in the movie *Clerks* that goes something like this. A guy walks into a video store and asks the clerk if he has "that movie with that guy who was in that movie that came out last year." Reel won't be able to help you if that's all you have for information, but if you have the name of "that guy" you'll be headed in the right direction.

Reel has a Quick Search by actor, director, and title. The Smart Search adds price range, format, genre, time period and rating (no X-rated movies).

Movie Match

Pick a favorite movie and Movie Match will return a list of other movies you might like. An entry of *Pulp Fiction* returns *Reservoir Dogs*, *True Romance*, and a few other ultra-violent, darkly humorous films.

Reel Guide

The Reel Guide includes New To Video, Cinema U., and Reel Festival. New To Video is a list of new releases categorized under Art-House Movies and Mainstream Movies and includes honest, one paragraph reviews. Cinema U. is a place for movie fans to meet and register for inexpensive film-related classes. Reel Festival spotlights the movies of a specific genre, in this case "Twisted Romances" (i.e. *9 ½ Weeks*).

But the most useful and interesting parts of Reel Guide are Anatomy and Reel Genius.

Anatomy

Anatomy rates a movie in a number of categories such as character development, drama depth, humor, action, violence, suspense, cinematography, etc. The ratings are based on audience responses. If you're in the mood for a particular type of movie and have a few titles in mind, you can check them out before you rent. For example, if you want a light-hearted movie, Anatomy

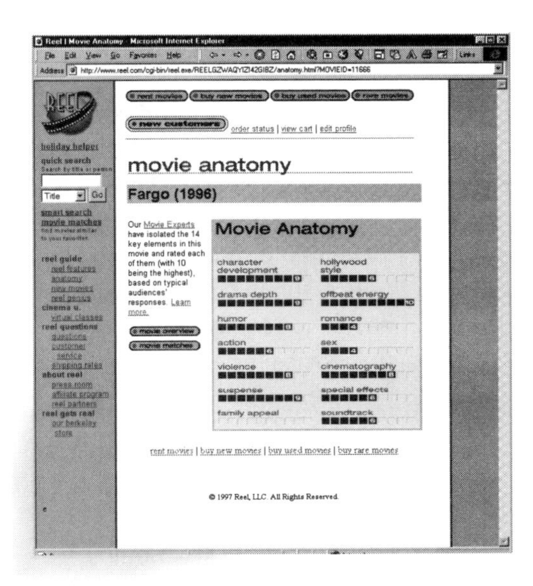

Figure 3.5
The Reel Anatomy of *Fargo*.

will tell you tonight's not the night to rent *Seven*, which rates highly in suspense and violence while drawing a bottom-of-the-barrel score in humor.

It's even fun to check some of your favorite movies and see how they rate. "What do you mean *Ernest Goes To Jail* has lousy character development?! It's brilliant!"

Reel Genius

Reel Genius is real addictive. After registering (it's free), you get a list of four or five movies, which you either rate on a scale of 1-10 or indicate that you haven't seen the movie. Then you can choose to rate more movies or get a list of movies Reel Genius thinks you should see. The more movies you rate, the larger and more exact the list of recommendations will be.

We rated 75 movies, stopping every 25 to check our list of recommendations. At each interval, our top choice was *The Usual Suspects*, proving Reel Genius is real genius. *The Usual Suspects* is indeed one of our favorites.

The Reel Genius filtering technology was developed by Entertainment Decisions.

Providing a Reel service

Reel hopes people who visit its site will rent movies. If a static percentage of Reel visitors eventually become renters, it's in Reel's best interest to increase the number of visitors. Plenty of people might use Reel's features to find movies then drive down to the video store and rent there. But after four or five trips result in no available copies of *Fargo*, someone might just decide to rent from Reel. And since the customer gets to keep the movies for a week, they might as well rent four or five.

It's obvious the people who started Reel are movie fans dedicated to helping other movie fans find something worthwhile. Not surprisingly, the credo of the Empire Video Superstores was that it was better to send a customer home empty-handed than with something she wouldn't like. Reel is an example of how providing information and good customer service can lead to a successful online business.

Amazon.com

www.amazon.com

"Earth's Biggest Bookstore" (Barnes & Noble would disagree with that assessment) offers more than 2.5 million titles and, it claims on its home page, up to 40 percent savings. Amazon.com and Barnes & Noble have been embroiled in a heated battle that would make Coke and Pepsi proud. Whether or not Amazon.com is indeed "bigger" than Barnes & Noble is irrelevant here. Instead, we'll look at what Amazon.com has done to achieve its success and what you can learn from it.

Instead of focusing on the snappy (and expensive) look of Amazon.com's site, we'll stick to some features that you might be able to approximate on your site.

Oprah Book Club

Talk show host Oprah Winfrey has a flock of loyal fans that follows her advice when it comes to reading, so Amazon.com's landing of

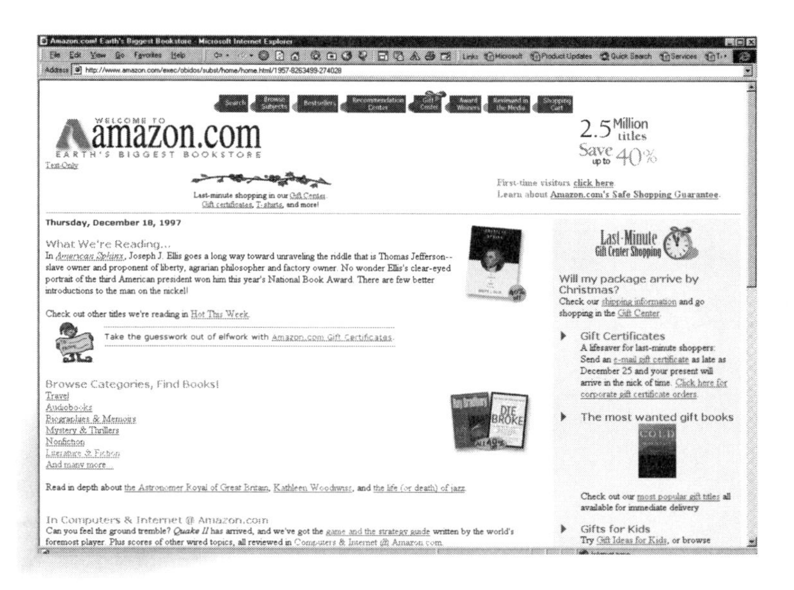

FIGURE 3.6
Amazon.com's home page.

the Oprah Book Club was a coup. It is unlikely you'll have the money needed to attach a celebrity's name to your store, but you can approximate the effect, albeit on a smaller scale.

While Amazon.com doesn't need to explain who Oprah Winfrey is in order for her name to sell books, you might want to find an expert in your field to recommend something each month. For example, if you're selling computer software, maybe you can convince a friend who is a software expert to regularly recommend products. You should clarify this person's expertise—simply offering "Ed's Hot Software Of The Month" doesn't do any good unless your customers know who Ed is and why he is recommending software. A short bio with Ed's background will give your customers confidence in his recommendations. Eventually, repeat customers will know Ed and, assuming he gives good advice, consider his advice. This brings up an obvious point. Don't ask for Ed's help simply because he's your pal, ask for his help because he's an expert. Eventually "Ed's Hot Software"—like the Oprah Book Club—could become a solid brand for your store.

It's also good to have someone other than yourself recommending products. It gives your store a more diverse feel and Ed just might build his own loyal following. Since he's on your site, Ed's fans are your fans. If Ed's really good, he may even come up with some products to pitch that you would've missed.

In Computers & Internet @ Amazon.com

This is a review of a recently released computer book that Amazon.com feels is good enough to be featured. Anyone accessing Amazon.com or any other online store will have at least some interest in computers, since that's how they got to the site in the first place. Think about what you're selling and consider whether or not there are any computer-related products that you can include on your site.

TIP ▸ ***If you sell bicycles and related products, there might be a good CD-ROM on bike maintenance and repair. If you sell luggage and other travel-related products, you might want to include Delorme's excellent mapping and trip planing CD-ROMs. Doing this could lead to some easy sales and makes your site more diverse and user-friendly.***

What We're Reading and Other Spotlights

Are they really reading this? Who knows. This is just a way to spotlight a product on the home page. In Amazon.com's case, there is a quick summary and a link to a book. You probably don't want to use something like this to push a lousy product out the door. If you sell music CDs and the What We're Listening To category this month is that old classic "Girl You Know It's True" by Milli Vanilli, your customers are probably going to think "What you're listening to stinks." If we visited a music store that recommended Milli Vanilli, we'd never shop there again.

Amazon.com has a number of spotlights on its home page, including Read All About It (books on timely topics) and Books of the Day (new arrivals). If you have different categories of products, this is a good idea. Sticking with the music store example, you could have a different spotlight on a CD from a number of different genres. Highlighting new products is smart.

More To Explore

This section includes links to customer reviews, author interviews, Want To Play? (a chance to voice opinions on questions such as "What's your favorite book-to-film adaptation?"), and Win Prizes (drawings and contests). A section like this takes a bit of extra time and money. The customer reviews, however, only take a couple of minutes to edit.

There are a couple of issues to consider with customer reviews. They will not always be very well written and you will have to spend some time editing them for spelling, grammar, and content. They also might not be positive. Anyone taking the time to write a review is probably going to feel strongly one way or the other about the product. A spectacular review might mean a few more sales. A lousy review might mean a few less. By all means, if you are going to include customer reviews, don't just post the good ones. Word will get out that you're eliminating the negative reviews and you'll look dishonest.

If you feel confident that most of your products will get good reviews, you should include a customer reviews section. The additional sales from good reviews will outnumber the lost sales from bad reviews.

In the age of e-mail, interviews don't take much time. If there are people in your industry worth interviewing, you can do one a month through e-mail without spending much time. Plan ahead. You don't want to be scrambling for an interview at the last minute.

Resources For

Amazon.com provides resources for publishers, authors, and associates. Authors are allowed to fill out a questionnaire that Amazon.com will make available to its customers. Publishers are made aware of partnering opportunities. The associates program, which Amazon.com pioneered and Barnes & Noble has since imitated, offers incentives for companies providing sales referrals to Amazon.com.

Search

Do you plan on including a search option on your site? Amazon.com, due to its immensity, has to help customers around the site with a number of different searches. There is a basic search in which you enter a keyword or keywords and a number of book titles are returned. Click on the title to link to the book's informational page.

Narrow your search by author and/or title. Options for an author search include the exact name or just the start of the last name. This is a particularly helpful option. If you're looking for more books by the author of *On The Road* but aren't sure how to spell Kerouac, just type in the first three letters of the last name and you'll find him. The title search is similar.

Browse

You can also browse through 22 categories including Arts & Music, Biographies & Memoirs, Business & Investing, Computers, Literature & Fiction, and Travel. Clicking on a category gives you What We're Reading, Our Customers Recommend, Amazon.com Recommends, and Amazon.com Delivers (a chance to sign up for e-mailed reviews) for the selected category.

You can also browse by Best Sellers, Award Winners, New In Paperback, Reviewed In The Media, Essential Bookshelf, American, Genre Fiction, and more.

The Best Seller browse delivers lists of hardcover, paperback, fiction, non-fiction, the Amazon Hot 100 (top-selling books among Amazon.com shoppers). You can also read profiles of top authors and check out books available for pre-order at Hot Books.

Award Winners provides a list of book awards. Pick one and you get a page describing the origin of the award, books eligible to win the award and a list of winners. From the list of winners you can link to the book's page and, of course, order it.

Reviewed In The Media provides reviews of recent releases from 23 sources such as *Business Week*, the *New Yorker*, and the *New York Times Book Review*.

Recommendation Center

Amazon.com's Recommendation Center is another area available more to larger operations because of the cost of the software required. It's interesting to note because it can be an important resource for customers.

The Instant Recommendations are based on what you have already bought. The Book Matcher asks for you to provide what you like in a book and it will return recommendations based on this information. The Mood Matcher offers books for different occasions (retirement, high school graduation, 30th birthday, etc.). If You Like This Author asks you to pick a genre and a favorite author and it will give you a number of other authors you might enjoy.

The Customer Buzz, while informative, will raise the eyebrows of cynics. There are two categories to learn about—books that customers are raving about, and books that customers are divided over. What about the books that customers universally hate?

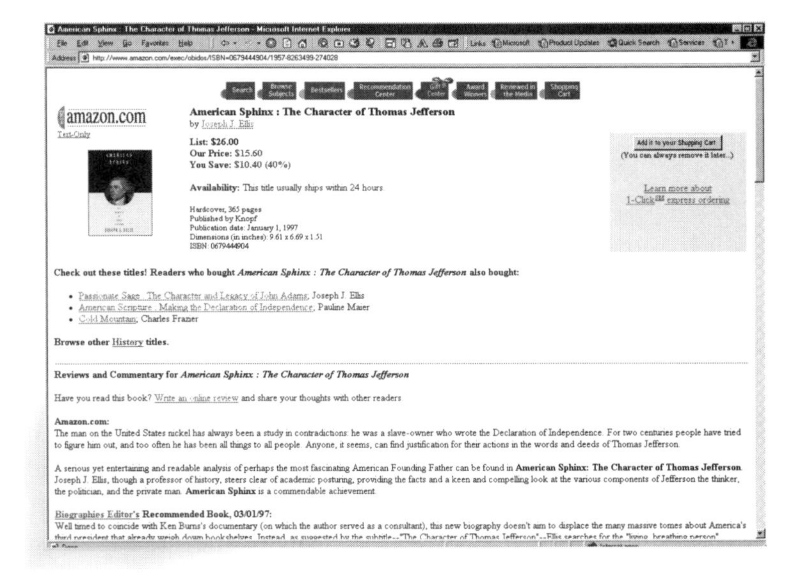

FIGURE 3.7
One of Amazon.com's book pages.

About Amazon.com

This section provides all the information you'll need about the site. There's a spot for new visitors, which is easy to do and should be a part of all online stores. This area makes it easier for customers to navigate even the most intricate sites. It's also another good place to explain how people can order from your store.

Amazon.com also has a FAQ, a spot about ordering out-of-print books, and information on audio books and videos, credit card and payment options, shipping, tracking your package, pricing and availability, and its returns policy.

Reading Groups

Amazon.com hosts reading groups to foster a community atmosphere and even provides possible questions for specific groups to help spark debate and conversation. Consider the benefits of an onsite chat forum for your customers.

Ordering

Unless an Amazon.com customer is ordering gifts, chances are she'll order one of any particular book. With this in mind, Amazon.com offers 1-Click Express Ordering. If you know you want one book and nothing else, instead of adding it to your shopping cart, registered shoppers can simply click the "Buy One Copy And Ship It" button.

Blanket Your Niche

Amazon.com doesn't sell much—just books. It's the variety of that one item that makes Amazon.com so enormous and comprehensive. You can offer a similarly wide variety of one specific product, such as baseball bats. There certainly aren't as many different kinds of baseball bats as there are book titles, but if you sell every bat available on the market, your smaller operation is just as comprehensive within its own niche. Amazon.com has simply selected a very large niche and blanketed it. Amazon.com would have failed long ago had it tried to be a comprehensive bookseller, but only carried a handful of authors. If you only offer one or two different baseball bats, your future will be similarly limited.

Sub Pop Online

www.subpop.com

Fans of alternative rock, especially the grunge explosion of the early 90s, know Sub Pop as the early label of grunge icons like Nirvana, Soundgarden, Mudhoney, and Green River. The independent Seattle label wasn't rolling in money until Nirvana's *Nevermind*, which wasn't even released on Sub Pop, changed the face of popular music. Pearl Jam singer Eddie Vedder wore a Sub Pop "Loser" T-shirt during a Saturday Night Live performance. As the world began lusting after all things flannel and Seattle, Nirvana's earlier Sub Pop release *Bleach* suddenly became a big seller. Sub Pop lives.

Sub Pop Online not only sells Sub Pop records and merchandise, it sells Sub Pop as a last bastion of indie cool as major labels continue to sign grunge mimics like Bush and Silverchair.

Home page

Sub Pop's home page includes links to the Megamart, Summer Hits!, Original Grunge, and New School. The home page not only gives you quick directions to where you want to shop, it establishes Sub Pop's image—sarcastically funny, cool, and fun. It would run counter to the independent grunge/punk ethos to appear interested in making mountains of cash, so Sub Pop intentionally sticks to its grungy roots.

The link to the Megamart tells the customer it's "the only place you can order all of the music (such as an exclusive Sebadoh single and the new Supersuckers LP) and the cultural accessories that make you a giant among your peers and a darn good person in our book." Sub Pop sounds like it's kidding, but there are plenty of kids out there wearing Sub Pop T-shirts because, well, it makes them a giant among their peers. Mentioning ultra-cool, lesser-known bands like Sebadoh and the Supersuckers keeps with Sub Pop's image.

FIGURE 3.8
Sub Pop Online's home page.

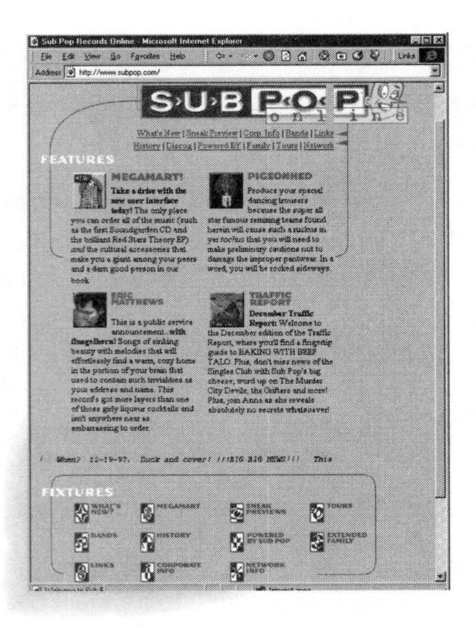

Summer Hits! is a snappy way to spotlight sales while Original Grunge includes classic Sub Pop releases like Nirvana's *Bleach*, Soundgarden's *Screaming Life*, and Mudhoney's *Touch Me I'm Sick*. Any kid who stumbles into the Sub Pop site will at least have heard of Soundgarden and Nirvana. Maybe even Mudhoney. New School spotlights some of Sub Pop's newer acts like Pigeonhed and Plexi.

Searching Sub Pop

You can buy music and merchandise at Sub Pop Online. Click on Music and you choose from a list of artists. Each artist page includes a band photo, a list of records, prices and an order button. For more information on a particular record, click on the title and you'll link to a record page where you can look at the cover art, see a list of songs and notes on the record, and access sound samples.

You can also buy merchandise, such as one of those ubiquitous early-90s "Loser" T-shirts. You can access photos of the merchandise by clicking on a rather lengthy list. Of course, beautiful models posed on the beach wearing Sub Pop gear would look pretty silly. Instead, an employee is shown lounging around in a hat or holding a T-shirt in front of her face.

Traffic Report

The Traffic Report is Sub Pop Online's news area. A news area, if you have the time, is nice to have. Even if someone isn't planning to buy something for a while, a good newsletter will keep them checking out the site.

Sub Pop's Traffic Site includes information on label bands, links to discographies, and the Megamart and the 45 Korner, which is dedicated to current 45s. In September 1997, Sub Pop didn't have any 45s coming out, but that didn't mean the 45 Korner was empty. Instead, readers were treated to a collection of Spam haikus by owner and CEO Jonathan Poneman. Yes, Spam haikus—haikus dedicated to that pink, canned, sorta-meat Spam. It's stuff like this that makes Sub Pop cool. If a major label tried something like this, it would look fake.

Fixtures

A collection of items listed under "Fixtures" at the bottom of the page includes What's New (recent and upcoming releases), Corporate Info (contact information), Sneak Previews (sound clips from future releases), Network Info (FAQ, ordering instructions, tour schedules, release schedules, etc.), Powered By Sub Pop, and History. History and Powered By Sub Pop are the two items most worth checking out.

Powered By Sub Pop

Powered By Sub Pop is a link trading partnership. Download the Powered By Sub Pop logo and put it on your site with a link to Sub Pop's site. In return you get a link from Sub Pop's site to your site as well as a Sub Pop catalog, a Powered By Sub Pop Sticker, and some other goodies. The top five sites each month get a Sub Pop Online T-shirt.

The link program is useful in this case if you think Sub Pop customers might find something interesting at your site. Getting a link from Sub Pop to your classical music site wouldn't make much sense.

History

You need a history to have a history section. Sub Pop certainly has that and it's all on display in this section. There are old press releases and publicity photos here that would fit in at the Rock 'n' Roll Hall of Fame. You'll also find background on the label and the Seattle music scene and columns written for the local music newspaper *The Rocket* by Sub Pop co-founder Bruce Pavitt.

TIP ▸ ***Your company might not have a history, but it has something that can make it seem more personal. It might be a page dedicated to your employees and their interests. It might be a story about the early days of your business if you've been around a while. Anything to let the customers know that your store is really run by nice people and isn't just a money-making blip on a computer screen will make them feel better about shopping there.***

It's Sub Pop's World and We're Just Visiting It

Sub Pop Online feels like Sub Pop should. It is, for lack of a better word, grungy. It's not corporate slick even if the intention of the site is to help the company make money. It is exactly the way a modern rock fan would hope it would be.

Someone unfamiliar with grunge, Sub Pop, and youth culture might not get Sub Pop Online. Who cares? They're not going to be there anyway. When designing your site, make sure your customers will identify with its feel. An investment bank with Sub Pop's design would likely be out of business in a hurry. And a record label hawking old Green River records on a slick site like L.L. Bean's would similarly alienate its customers.

Billy's Florida Stone Crab Claws

www.crabs.com

Billy's Florida Stone Crab Claws started as a restaurant and store. A few years ago, Bill Hershey began shipping crab claws overnight. This site is an extension of that and resides on the Miami City Web mall.

Billy's is a simple site that specializes in one thing—crab claws. You can order by fax, phone, or online. For every order of 10 pounds or more, you get a free key lime pie. Billy's is a good site to check out if you're a small retail and mail order business that is looking to expand a bit. Click around the site with the crab claw icons.

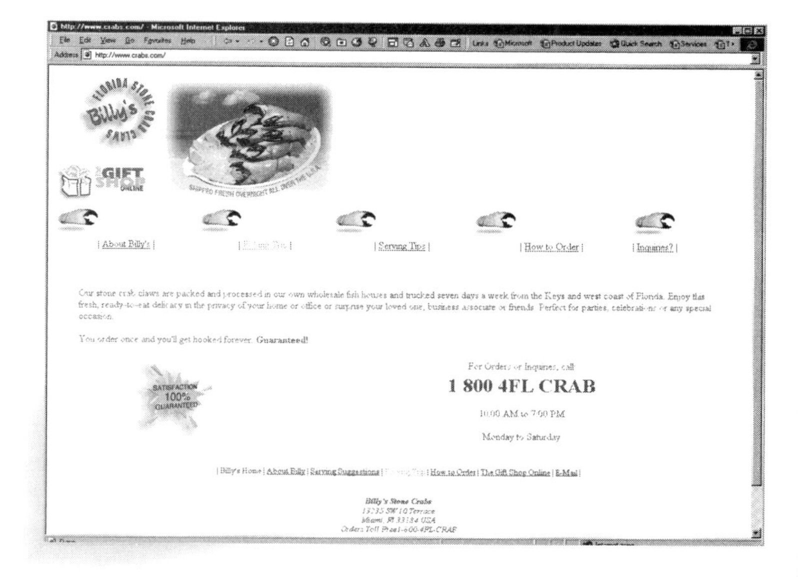

FIGURE 3.9
Billy's home page.

Fishing Trip

Do you want to know how your crab claws went from being appendages on crustaceans off the coast of Florida to dinner? The Fishing Trip, complete with photos, takes you through the entire process. This a fun spot or customers and could work for any store selling stuff like maple syrup, lobsters, or any hand-made goods.

Serving Tips

Does your customer know the best way to use your product? Probably not as well as you do. A spot like this helps emphasize your expertise and strengthen customer confidence. Any site shipping food that should be prepared in a certain way needs something like this.

Crab claws? Best served chilled with a side order of mustard sauce, drawn melted butter, or fresh lemon. If you drink wine, a chilled Sauvignon blanc or Chardonnay is nice.

The Cassette House

www.tape.com

The Cassette House is a basic, no-frills operation run from Tennessee by Art Munson. Munson has an impressive background in music as a guitarist, engineer, writer, and producer. He has worked with artists as diverse as surf music legends Dick Dale and the Deltones, John Lennon, the Righteous Brothers, David Sanborn, and Barbra Streisand, among others. He has also been involved in commercials, film, and television shows.

Munson originally began selling cassettes to clients from his Los Angeles recording studio in 1981. He eventually started a mail order catalog but has been strictly on the Web since April of 1995. The Cassette House's gross annual sales have doubled each year since and now top $1 million. Munson's success shows what you can do without all the bells and whistles of larger, better-funded sites. Munson designed his own site.

"It's not necessary to spend a lot of money on your site," Munson says.

The Cassette House sells recordable media such as blank cassettes, DATs (well-suited for recording live music), and CDs. The Cassette House offers low prices (as all cyberstores should) and builds customer loyalty through these prices and a commitment to the growing and very dedicated group of people who trade tapes of live performances. Fans of the Grateful Dead have always swapped concert tapes. Younger acts such as Phish, Blues Traveler, and Pearl Jam, which place an emphasis on their live shows, now allowing taping of their concerts and the taper community has begun to take advantage of the Web to find other tapers.

FIGURE 3.10
The Cassette House's home page.

A Simple, Successful Site

Hit The Cassette House home page and you'll get a good idea of what's to come. You are greeted by a white background and a "Welcome To Cassette House—DAT Tape, Blank Cassettes, Blank CDs and Recording Supplies" message. You are told you can order 24 hours a day, seven days a week and are provided with toll free phone and fax numbers as well as the Web, e-mail, and snail mail addresses. If this doesn't seem like a big deal, surf the Web for an afternoon and see how many sites force you to hunt for that information.

From the home page you can hop to price lists for specials, cassettes and cassette supplies, DAT, blank CDs, etc. From the price lists, you can order what you want. Nothing special except the prices.

You can also link to The DAT Web and DAT Ring, Free Info, Testimonials, Musician and Songwriter Resources, Independent Recording Artists, and Short Stories and Articles. These are the parts of the Cassette House that are most worth checking out if you're launching an online store.

The DAT Web and DAT Ring

This is an excellent resource for anyone interested in using DAT, especially for taping live music. While this seems like a narrow interest group, it is one whose members are very passionate about their hobby.

The DAT Web and DAT Ring is divided into four different sections. The first is an extensive informational spot with tips for using DAT.

There is a link to a list of bands that allow taping at their shows. It used to be that only a very small number of bands, most notably the Grateful Dead, allowed fans to tape their shows. The majority of big-time bands are still anti-taping because they are worried someone will use the recordings to make money and they'll get none of it. But many bands that have particularly dedicated fans have begun to allow taping, knowing their fans will trade the recordings rather than buy them from a professional bootlegger.

There are also links to tapetrading.com and tapetracker.com, a pair of Web sites for people who trade concert recordings of their favorite musicians.

Catering to the trader community is a natural for someone with a musical background. It's also good business. One thing every tape trader needs is blank tapes. Lots of them. If someone plans to buy hundreds of blank tapes each year, they'll certainly want to find the best deal possible. Providing resources for tapers only helps The Cassette House's business grow as more musicians allow taping. Catering to the taper community has helped "a lot," Munson said.

Free Info, Testimonials, and Musician and Songwriter Resources

Free Info is just that. More tips on taping live music and CDs.

Testimonials are e-mails from satisfied customers. Munson was wise to include a message from a customer who received defective tapes and quickly received a hassle-free credit. This lets the customer know that when mistakes happen they will be quickly rectified.

The resources page is a set of links that could be useful for musicians and songwriters.

An Attainable Goal

Most people starting a one-person online store will never be Amazon.com, but they might be Art Munson. Munson, his wife Robin, and one other person are The Cassette House. Munson has taken his personal interest in music and computers and turned it into a successful online business. Munson has kept his site streamlined and has done the work himself.

"You should be computer literate, do as much as you can yourself, and learn the technology or your chances of being successful will be much less," Munson says.

In Case You Want More

We could fill an entire book with online stores. As electronic commerce grows at a staggering rate, new stores open every day. Some will succeed (yours, we hope) and others will fail. Here are a few more successful stores that you might want to check out.

- **ONSALE.COM** is a leading example of an online site specializing in auctions. Fans swear by it as the place to find the best deals on the Web.

- **Cbooks.com** is a computer bookstore that shows how narrow "in-stock" strategy can be a successful business model.

- **CDNow** (www.cdnow.com) has an enormous selection for the music fan with better things to do than wander around a record store. It's the Amazon.com of Web music stores.

- **Buydirect.com** is ClNet's software store. You can buy software and receive it electronically without having to wait for a CD to arrive in the mail.

- **Viewpoint Datalabs** offers stock art at viewpoint.com, corbis.com, and photodisc.com.

Even if a store doesn't sell what you do or has a far larger (or smaller) budget, you can always learn more by checking it out. When you think you know everything there is to know about operating a successful online store is when you should go back to the drawing board and see if you really know half of it. The more you absorb, the better.

Online retailing continues to grow and evolve. To find out where it might be headed and why, move on to Chapter 4.

CHAPTER FOUR

Understanding the Online Store Market Opportunity

This chapter has a simple goal. We want you to understand the specifics of why online shopping is such a big growth market and, more importantly, learn something about the traits of online shoppers. To do that you first must understand the basic breakdown of the Web. That includes knowing who is accessing the Web and exactly how they are doing it, understanding what people do when they're online, and how they approach shopping. Finally, we'll look at the future of online shopping and how this all fits together.

The reason for the expected success of online shopping is twofold. First, there are easily identifiable reasons for people to shop online. This creates direct demand for Web-based stores; it is not just a pure demand for the goods, but also a demand for the way in which they are bought and sold. Also, there are a number of compelling reasons for merchants to move much of their business online. Not only can merchants take part in the Web's growth, but they can also streamline customer interaction and other operations to extract extra profits from the same sales.

Thus you must understand as much about the customer universe. That requires a look at key hardware growth, current Web demographics, and the psychology of shoppers in general.

Starting With the Fundamentals

Before one looks closely at the specifics of online shopping, an examination of the nature of computer owners, Internet connections, and usage of the World Wide Web is necessary. Before anyone can order something from your Web store, they must fulfill a number of prerequisites. They must own a computer, connect it to the Internet, and begin using the Web. These are the critical building blocks for understanding the online shopping market.

From Computers to Devices

When people think of surfing the Web they almost always envision the use of a standard personal computer, an image that has been etched into our minds since the first IBM PCs and Apple Macintoshes shipped more than ten years ago. However, in today's technological world there are a number of new computer-like devices that also offer connections to the Web. At the gut level, they are very capable computers. But on the outside, they will be very different devices such as screen phones, Web TVs, and even video game consoles.

The notion of what is or isn't a computer will change over time. Even today there are cellular phones and handheld PCs that are capable of providing Web access. This is why most market researchers count more than the number of personal computers in use, but also consider an array of Web-capable devices.

Despite the rise of alternative devices, common personal computers will remain the dominant form of Web access for some time. PC sales are booming on a worldwide level, not just in the United States, Japan and major European countries, but also in places such as China, Brazil, Singapore, India, and Korea. According to market research firm Dataquest, nearly 71 million PCs were sold worldwide in 1996 (the last year for which complete figures are available). Sales are growing at an annual clip of more than 20 percent, meaning that close to 85 million PCs shipped worldwide in 1997.

When it comes to Web TVs, the figures vary widely. Dataquest released a report that downplayed other studies that show positive signs for Web TVs. Dataquest's study found that 93 percent of households in 1997 were *not* planning to purchase an Internet set-top box or Internet-enabled TV (Dataquest press release). Meanwhile, Jupiter Communications predicts that the TV-based access devices, as they fall in price, will reach nearly 13 million in U.S. households by 2002. Incidentally, Jupiter also said that Web-enabled Screen Phones, a cousin of the TV device, will probably hit more than 2.5 million installed units by the same time. One research group has even gone so far as to predict that there will be 50 million TVs with Internet capabilities by 2005 and that Internet TVs will account for half of the total number of non-computer Web capable devices.

Also shedding additional light on the Web TV market is Alexander & Associates, which found in a 1996 study that nearly 30 million homes were aware of the Internet TV box-type devices and even more so after a multimillion-dollar ad campaign by Philips Magnavox and Sony during Christmas 1996.

Alexander & Associates further found that 12.6 million people said they would either definitely or probably purchase such a device, which seems to support Jupiter's findings. In a release explaining the apparent contradictory findings of Dataquest—that only seven percent of households were likely buyers of Web TV devices—Alexander & Associates Director Bob Alexander said that Dataquest's figure was probably accurate, and that the initial interest was actually very strong for a newly introduced consumer electronics device.

Summarizing Key Computer Hardware Figures

71 million PCs were sold worldwide in 1996. Growth is averaging more than 20 percent yearly. —*Dataquest*

13 million TV-based Internet access devices will be in U.S. households by 2002. —*IDC*

5.5 million handheld PCs, like Newton or Windows CE, sold in 1997. —*IDC*

210 million computers and other devices will be linked to the Internet by the end of 2000. —*Jupiter Communications*

Overall, Web TVs appear destined to become an interesting platform that should grow as the devices mature and, most likely, combine with their video game console cousins. As more TVs and set-top cable boxes ship with built-in capabilities, the market may even piggyback on the overall television sales and cable installation market.

Another potent group of devices that will surf the web are handheld PCs like Newton or Windows CE. Research firm IDC predicts total shipments will hit 5.5 million units in 1997, with 3.6 million of those sales coming in the form of PDAs such as the Newton or the Sharp Zauras. No matter how you look at it, the PDA market is growing rapidly.

A new category in the handheld market is the so-called *smartphone*. These devices, such as the Nokia 9000, combine voice phones with small screens and keyboards, enabling them to offer some common handheld functionality to access Web-based information. Research firm IDC distributed a press release saying that it expects shipments to reach 8.8 million units by 2001.

So between just PCs, Web TVs, and hand-held devices, there will be plenty of new computer capable hardware sold over the next few years. Almost all of it will be attached to the Web.

Jupiter Communications predicts that the number of devices accessing the Web will grow to more than 210 million by the end of 2000, with more than 160 million users. This includes many different devices, not just computer workstations or servers, and not just items people use at home or at work. Eventually, all sorts of devices—copiers, fax machines, ATMs, pagers, and even Coke machines—could be connected in some form to the Internet, enabling a rich, worldwide e-commerce system.

This is important because it indicates that many Web surfers, and therefore shoppers, will access the Internet through more than just common home computers. Stores that can appeal to buyers, whether they are on a Web TV, home computer, or even a portable phone, will have an advantage.

Software

A critical aspect of Web-connected devices is the underlying access software. As many Web developers know, the software that is used to get access to the Internet greatly dictates the capabilities of its users. While Microsoft and Netscape try to be relatively compatible, both implement things the other doesn't. Thus, all eyes are on browser platforms from Netscape and Microsoft so that developers (and storeowners) can better discern what their sites should support.

The browser battle was originally won by Netscape, which crushed a room full of hopefuls to gain close to an 80 percent market share. One late hopeful, however, has come back to push the race into overdrive and knock back Netscape's browser. Microsoft's Internet Explorer has gained a significant share, especially among home users, against Netscape's Navigator. In fact, recent estimates from Jupiter indicate that in the consumer market, Netscape's share of the market will drop to less than 40 percent in 1998, although Netscape's recent announcement that it will give away its browser may halt or reverse Microsoft's momentum.

TIP ▸ ***Watch the browser upgrades carefully as features added to newer versions of the browser platforms have the potential to greatly transform the Web and Web based commerce. Upcoming browser technology like XML (eXtensible Markup Language) and electronic wallets will usher in an even more mature technology framework upon which to build Web stores.***

Web-User Demographics: From Hardware and Software to Users

The underlying hardware and connections turn traditional store customers into Web customers. Once someone acquires the necessary hardware to go online, they join a fast growing populace that makes up the strong demographic mix that is quite attractive to Web merchants on the Web. Several companies do demographic research of online users. One major group is Georgia Tech's Graphics, Visualization, & Usability Center (GVU) and its WWW User Surveys.

Web-user demographics are exceedingly important to developers creating content, Webcasts or, in general, trying to build audiences for their Web sites. When the need for market research about Web-user demographics began in 1994-95, several studies raised eyebrows because of their methodology. Researching Web-user demographics isn't an exact science. By far, the most cited and well received studies are those conducted by researchers at the Georgia Institute of Technology and the University of Michigan Business School.

This self-selected Internet use and demographic survey (as opposed to a random phone poll) brings together a wealth of information about the current demographic state of the Web. The latest survey compiled thousands of statistics, including information about gender, political affiliation and registration, usage numbers, geographic location, access speeds, and more.

General Demographics

Web users tend to be white/Caucasian, male, slightly older, much wealthier, and more educated than the general public. According to the latest GVU study, 40 percent are married.

The average Internet user is approximately 36 years old. Market researcher FIND/SVP, which used a random-digit dialing poll, reported in its 1997 American Internet User Survey that the average age as 36.5 years old while the GVU survey reported that its respondents had an average age of 35.7.

Additionally, the average age has been steadily increasing as the Internet expands. Since its fourth survey, the GVU study has seen a steady rise in average age. GVU also reports that European respondents are generally younger (30.19 years old) than U.S. respondents, and there is a skew toward a younger demographics in Europe. This is because younger users tend to be early adopters of technology and gain access from college and other institutions.

TIP ▸ ***Targeting young demographics may be useful for some stores. Jupiter Communications tracks the emerging children's Web market. According to Jupiter, as of 1996 about 4 million children between the ages of 2 and 17 were accessing online content. That market is expected to grow to more than 20 million by 2002 and reach almost $2 billion in revenue for developers according to a Jupiter press release. America Online is the leader in this market, but Web-based content and other specialized content, such as Disney's Daily Blast, is expected to be big as well.***

In terms of the gender reports, there appears to be a 60/40 split between men and women on the Internet. The FIND/SVP study pegged it at 60/40 and the GVU percentage of female respondents to its survey was 38.5 percent. Female Internet use has been steadily rising over the last two years. However, European respondents continue to be overwhelmingly male.

In terms of ethnicity, the GVU study reported that 88 percent of its respondents classified themselves as white/Caucasian.

Education Attainment

Education attainment has been steady in most of the GVU studies. In the latest survey, 46.96 percent had completed college or had advanced degree. This is down from the previous survey and seems to represent the broadening of the Internet's user base. Respondents from Europe have consistently had higher levels of educational attainment than U.S. respondents. This is because Europeans users of the Internet are disproportionately skewed toward upper-income households with college degrees due to the higher costs of computers and Internet in Europe.

Household Income

GVU pegs the average U.S. household income of Web users at $53,000. European respondents reported a lower average household income ($48,500). One finding was particularly interesting: people who classified themselves as expert Internet users were, as a group, earning much more than other Internet users. This seems to be supported by the fact that many longtime Web users are highly educated technical people in high-paying jobs.

Based on these major statistics, Table 4.1 compares the major demographics to general U.S. population statistics.

TABLE 4.1 COMPARING U.S POPULATION WITH MAJOR WEB STATISTICS

CATEGORY	GENERAL U.S. DEMOGRAPHICS		RELEVANT INTERNET POPULATION STATISTIC	
Average Age	All	34.6	All	36.5
	Male	33.5	Male	36
	Female	35.8	Female	35
Gender	Male	49.0%	Male	60%
	Female	51.0%	Female	40%
Average Household Income		$42,300		$53,000
Education	College Grads	23.6%	College Grads	46%
Race	White/Caucasian	73%	White/Caucasian	88%
% Married		40%		40%

Occupation

The primary occupations of Internet users tend to be computer-related or education-related. This is logical given the computer bent of the Internet, and that many academic institutions offer free access to the Net and have been connected to it for quite some time. The GVU survey reported "Professional" was emerging in third place.

However, the computer-related category is dwindling quickly. There is much statistical research and empirical evidence that supports the fact that, while the Net is the domain of millions of computer-related workers, that number has peaked while people in other occupations stampede online. Occupation type tends to be divided noticeably between younger users who are involved in education and computers and older users who tend to work in other fields.

Special Web Statistics

There are also a number of statistics specific to the Web and its users that are worth studying.

Community Membership

How people relate to communities of interests is an important factor in Net use. The GVU survey reports that 45 percent of U.S. respondents feel more connected to people with similar hobbies. Female respondents also had strong connections to their families and with people in similar life situations. Men were more likely than women to feel connected by hobbies and professions.

TIP ▸ ***Many people who pursue communities of interest on the Internet also tend to create Web pages. The GVU summary supports this by reporting that 46 percent of all respondents have created a Web page. The percentage of respondents that creates Web pages of course increases with computer experience, from 19 percent among novices to 78 percent of experts. These numbers are significant when you consider that many merchants target Web pages with affiliate programs.***

Years on the Internet

The number of years that a user has spent on the Internet is a significant demographic to understand. GVU breaks usage into three categories: Novice, Intermediate, and Expert users. In its latest study, roughly 72 percent of people were categorized as experts, having been on the Internet for 4–6 years. Note that the GVU summary may have a slightly disproportionate number of users who are long time users. Respondents from the U.S. are more likely to have started on the Internet within the past year, while respondents from Europe are more likely to have been on for 1–3 years.

According to GVU and others, female users are still flocking to the Internet. GVU says that 42 percent of women currently online have gone online in the past year, compared to 32 percent for males.

Overall, the strong growth of the Internet should continue to see many first year users for some time. At the same time, it is already apparent that the population of experienced Internet users is growing.

Access, World Breakdown, and Language

Where people log on and in what parts of the world they live is another important factor. The GVU study showed the majority of respondents (65 percent) report accessing the Web from home, although this appears to be largely a U.S. phenomenon. Only 28 percent of users in Europe reported having their primary access from home. In Europe and internationally, the lack of home-based use is clearly tied to high phone costs—people try to log on from their company's computers or from universities.

European growth of the Internet is slower than in the United States. The telecommunications infrastructure being what it is in Europe, coupled with a lower household rate of quality PCs, means that overall usage, while experiencing significant growth, is still lagging. IDG recently developed a Web index to "measure the intensity" of the development of Internet activity in Western Europe. The most recent index indicates that Web usage in Western Europe will go from around 10.9 million users in 1997 to around 27.5 million by 2000—significant, but not overwhelming. Another study, which pegged Germany as the leading online country in Europe (a result of the presence of the online service T-Online, with more than 1.4 million users), expects the combined home and business population of Internet users to climb to more than 35 million by 2000.

However, the number of personal computers connected to the Internet jumped 71 percent over the past year to 82 million and is expected to more than triple to 268 million by 2001. According to one of the most bullish and comprehensive studies yet on Net usage, the percentage of PCs worldwide with Net access is expected to grow from 30 percent today to more than 50 percent four years from now. Much of the growth comes from big businesses connecting their employees to the Net.

IDG recently reported on the number of households with PCs connected to the Internet as of 1997 for major countries, as shown in Table 4.2. The numbers show that even in the United States, there is still a lot of room for growth.

TABLE 4.2 PERCENTAGE OF TOTAL HOUSEHOLDS WITH PCS CONNECTED TO THE INTERNET (EARLY 1997).

Country	*Percentage*
Japan	18.0%
United States	16.0%
Hong Kong	12.0%
Germany	11.7%
Taiwan*	10.3%
United Kingdom	9.5%
Australia	8.9%
Singapore	7.0%
France	6.5%
South Korea*	6.3%
Italy	5.8%

* IN THESE COUNTRIES, THE SAMPLE WAS ONLY AMONG MAJOR URBAN AREAS.

Even with a growing international presence, English is the primary language of users. Among GVU's European respondents, 43.92 percent reported English as their primary language. Beyond English, European languages that were high were German (12.17 percent) and Dutch (10.53 percent)—all other languages were less than 5 percent.

Most Important Issues Facing the Internet

GVU asked its users what the biggest issues on the Net were. The top three were privacy, censorship, and navigation. Among women, privacy was the most important issue. For men censorship is most important, with privacy a close second. This is important for storeowners because they are at the center of the privacy issue. Censorship is less of an issue unless you run Web boards and chat rooms.

Poor navigation through information and choices can actually hurt the sales ability of a site. As shown by this information, users are quite concerned about the ability to quickly find the information they seek. The navigation issue is also important because people are primarily turning to online shopping because of the easy access it offers to product information.

Are People Shopping Online?

People are definitely shopping online. Although the number is increasing rapidly, a recent IDC study showed it still had plenty of room for growth. In that study it was said that one out of three Web surfers engages in online shopping. Home-based shoppers spend an average of more than $50 per month while business shoppers (many of whom order computers and other equipment) are said to spend more than $500 per month.

According to GVU findings, 85 percent of Web users access it daily, with the largest category of respondents accessing the Web 1–4 times per day.

Female users access the Internet slightly less frequently than males and users between the ages of 19 and 50 use it more frequently than other age groups. IDC reports that cybershopping sessions are vigorous, with customers visiting an average of eight storefronts per session.

People are warming up to purchasing online. The GVU survey reported that two-thirds of its respondents had ordered products or services using the Web. Men are much more likely to have done so than women (73 percent vs. 60 percent).

One thing that is apparent is that as people are feeling increasing confident about online use of credit cards and, if they find satisfying stores, will quickly become Web shoppers. An IDC e-commerce study in 1996 reported that that 19.3 percent of its survey respondents use credit cards to conduct transactions over the Internet with 63.8 percent of respondents planning to buy products online with credit cards in the near future.

Understanding the Nature of Online Shoppers

It is important for online merchants to understand why people shop on the Internet. To better understand this, we turned to a range of academic based research that attempts to explain what is so attractive about online shopping.

In one paper titled "Interactive Home Shopping: Consumer, Retailer, and Manufacturer Incentives to Participate in Electronic Marketplaces," the authors explain that the biggest factors are:

- **Vast Selection:** Consumers like the access to a large number of choices, making it more likely they will find the item they want.
- **Screening:** Consumers are drawn to the ability to easily and quickly sort through choices.
- **Reliability:** The ability for stores to overcome the users' interest in physically seeing a product in order to make a buying decision is critical to online shopping's success.
- **Product Comparisons:** The true strength of online shopping is in the customer's ability to quickly compare similar products for the optimal choice (e.g. best quality, price, shipping terms, etc.).

What the paper argues is that people are most attracted to online shopping because it much easier to view the entire universe of available choices, whittle them down to the crucial choices, and obtain the information to make a final choice.

Critical to this observation is basic knowledge of how consumers shop in general. Researchers note that shopping is a process of searching, comparing, and gathering information. However, what researchers also know is that when someone shops, he can't consider the entire universe of available choices due to time constraints.

Instead, consumers tend to only examine a subset of all the possible choices. Researchers say this is because the time consumers save by not searching for and then comparing every available choice is worth more than the risk of overlooking the overall best choice. With this in mind, it becomes obvious that computers and online stores can greatly aid the shopping process. It is much easier for online stores to offer huge inventories. Using search engines and databases to screen those choices is easy. Finally, by offering extensive product information, Web stores can help people make the best choice after they have compiled a list of leading choices. The result is that people should feel better about the choices they make as a result of shopping online.

Another important aspect is that many consumers rely on their own memory when trying to recall alternative product choices—an imperfect process at best. By shopping online, consumers have their alternatives readily available on a computer screen. Again, this results in higher satisfaction and more efficient shopping.

Understanding the Detriments

While users are turning to the Web for efficiency in the shopping process, consumers will sometimes find traditional stores better than online stores. It is important to understand when and why.

The primary detriment to online shopping described by researchers in "Interactive Home Shopping: Consumer, Retailer, and Manufacturer Incentives to Participate in Electronic Marketplaces" are those buying decisions in which experiential information is truly needed. Experiential information comes from the ability of the consumer to smell, taste, feel, or see something. Therefore, selling items like house paint or fragrances on the Internet may be a more difficult process.

Experiential information is also a factor when a high level of in-store assistance is useful. As the paper points out, Home Depot is one store that doesn't translate as well to the Web as a store like Barnes & Noble, due to the highly specialized, in-person assistance you can receive at a real-world Home Depot.

Interestingly, brand experience can lessen the need for experiential analysis. Once a consumer is satisfied that a product is to her liking, she may subsequently shop online for that product because of the expectation that the brand quality and characteristics will be equal to the original purchase. This eliminates the need for repeated evaluation. For example, the first time someone buys a particular perfume, it will likely be done at a traditional store where it can be smelled. However, subsequent reorders may be done over the Web. There is also the brand of the store to consider. Clearly people buy from L.L. Bean without seeing all the merchandise in person because they expect a certain level of quality from LL Bean merchandise.

Another detriment to online shopping discussed by researchers is the application of delivery and consumers' interest in delivery. Many products do not lend themselves to delivery. Again, Home Depot is an example of a store that sells products (such as fencing or other large items) that are more easily bought in person. Additionally, some people simply don't like home delivery. They either fear the delivery people or are concerned about lost or stolen packages. Finally, in most cases the need for shipping eliminates the possibility of same-day procurement of the product. While Electronic Software Delivery (ESD) promises to bring impulse immediacy to the Web for items such as software and music, many products can only be transferred through physical means. That means waiting for at least a day.

In the End, Information Is the Key

Researchers boil the psychology of online shopping down to the supply of information. Once consumers have created a final set of selections after studying the available universe of choices, the thing they crave is extensive information in making the final choice. In addition, a plethora of information can help eliminate the need for experiential evaluation of the merchandise. For example, Web stores such as Amazon.com that offer customer reviews, provide information that can actually exceed the experience of flipping through the book.

Consumers are turning to Internet shopping because they can more rapidly assemble the best information needed to make a purchasing decision. That stems directly from one of the Web's best attributes, delivery of information, and one of the best aspects of computers, rapid processing of comparative features. This combination helps make online shopping a compelling, if not superior, choice alternative to traditional shopping.

Relating the Consumer Psychological Profile to Available Statistics

Do statistics back up consumer psychology studies? Apparently so. The most recent GVU study shows that three of the top four reasons people cited for personal Web shopping were directly related to the consumer psychological profile. The reasons the GVU respondents cited for shopping online were convenience (65 percent), availability of vendor information (60 percent), the lack of pressure from salespeople (55 percent), and saving time (53 percent).

As a side note, the GVU survey states that personalized services are, for most people, not a primary reason to shop online. Researchers wrote that this "could be a result of unfamiliarity with personalized shopping services."

What Does All This Mean?

We have established three critical components of online shopping. First, there is a growing base of devices that can connect to the Web and enable people to join and interact on the Web. That base of hardware and software is growing at a rate of more than 20 percent annually and, in terms of browsers, it is splitting between market leaders Netscape and Microsoft. Second, a healthy universe of Web users offers more desirable characteristics than the general U.S. or world population. Third, there is strong evidence that online shopping has inherent advantages that will attract shoppers to the Web even if prices are no less than those offered by traditional stores. These three factors are brewing a market that, according to Jupiter Communications, will grow from $706 million in 1996 to more than $35 billion in 2002.

What's a Web merchant to Do?

How can you, as a Web merchant, take advantage of this knowledge? First you must realize how you can use these factors to your advantage. Here are some recommendations:

- **BUILD A CUSTOMER BASE AND KEEP IT WITH VALUE-ADDED SERVICES.** Stores that are able to withstand losses as they spend to grab market share will have an advantage. Audience growth is critically expensive in the start-up phase. Since advertising doesn't guarantee a sale, top sites will use cash cushions to wait out costly advertising campaigns and search engine links as audiences grow to a profitable level. This notion is a based on a common Web business model in which sites deem it important to grab the audience first and keep them by offering superior content and user interaction.

- **DON'T ASSUME THAT STORES WIN ON PRICE.** Los Angeles Times technology editor Jonathan Weber summed it up best when he wrote, "Viewing the Web not as a cost-cutting tool but as a way to add unique new service helps explain a lot of what's happening—or not happening—in the online commerce arena these days." What Weber meant was that cutting costs and offering lower prices won't be at the heart of e-commerce success. Instead he, like many consumer behaviorists, argues the bond a store develops with its customers and via its inventory scope and information, will be the key. Price is a factor in a purchase decision, but its importance is often overstated in relation to the Internet. Instead, stores like Amazon.com, Virtual Vineyards, and L.L. Bean have designed online sites and business ethics that aren't focused as much on price as they are many other parts of the store equation.

- **Inventory scope is important.** Consumers feel an important aspect of the Web is that it helps them analyze many choices and quickly examine nearly complete selections of the products they want to buy. Stores that offer a subset of a product type may lose out to stores that push inventory availability to the maximum. The best way to maximize inventory availability is to have partnerships streamlined to manufacturers and distributors. This way you can offer a larger selection of items that aren't necessarily in stock. Incidentally, it is situations like these that infer that middlemen and distributors will not just fade away, as many predict.

- **Focus on category killer markets.** In order to focus informational offerings and inventory, many stores simply try to solve one specific subject area of shopping while avoiding others. The reason is that users respond to the depth of a site's expertise and information, not the breadth.

- **If possible, avoid items that require high experiential exposure.** If not, overwhelm the customer with information. Experiential buying will never be overtaken by mail order or Web-based stores because some things are just better shopped for in person. If you plan to compete in an area that has a high experiential need, you will need to increase the information available in order to offset the desire of the consumer to shop traditionally.

Numbers Can't Make Your Idea Work

Don't assume that the numbers and market survey presented here validate any Web store plan. Thousands of online stores are launched each month around the globe and all of them are chasing customers. Good numbers will never offset a bad idea. What they can do is help you understand which elements of your fantastic idea should be emphasized. Market research is never a stand-in, it's always about understanding. Now that you have an understanding of what's happening in the Web store market space, you have to go out and make that knowledge work.

Further Reading

Several studies, research companies and papers will help you learn more about what we've written about here, and with new numbers and analysis in the future as the Web shopping market matures.

Academic Papers and Studies

- **"Interactive Home Shopping:** Consumer, Retailer, and Manufacturer Incentives to Participate in Electronic Marketplaces" by Joseph Alba, John Lynch, Barton Weitz, Chris Janiszewski, Richard Lutz, Alan Sawyer and Stacy Wood. *Journal of Marketing,* July 1997. This paper takes apart the online shopping process, and dissects exactly how its benefits consumers and how consumers specifically gain benefits from online shopping that are critical to its success. Excellent reading.

- **The 8th GVU WWW Survey** by The GVU WWW Survey Team (www.gvu.gatech.edu/user_surveys/). The 8th version of this well respected self-selected Web survey is now out. The survey is constantly being reissued, and the writings and data sets for it and all the past surveys.

Research Companies

Several major research companies are actively producing studies, and numbers , of interest to online store owners. They're all worth checking. Many times abstracts, press releases and excerpts from their reports can be found on their Web sites.

- **Jupiter Communications** (www.jup.com). Jupiter produces a number of key studies, and produces a newsletter and conference about online shopping.

- **IDC** (www.idc.com). The research division of publishing giant IDG (*PC World, Macworld* magazines) conducts research to determine the size and characteristics of the e-commerce markets as well as the total worldwide installed base of computers and other technology systems.

- **Forrester Research** (www.forrester.com). Forrester has done a number of reports on e-commerce, and has several reports on growth overall, as well as rankings of e-commerce capability by country.

- **Dataquest** (www.dataquest.com). Like IDC, a large research group focused on tracking the size and characteristics of the worldwide e-commerce market as well as the total worldwide installed base of computers and other technology systems.

CHAPTER FIVE

Web Store Business Models

Despite the fact that the Web is still in its infancy, people often take for granted some of the truly unique opportunities it offers. Before attempting to operate a store on the Web, having a solid understanding of the Web and its uniqueness is essential to structuring a successful store business model.

This chapter first discusses the unique advantages of the Web before tackling specific business models for cyberstores.

One-to-One Relationships

One aspect of the Internet that makes it such a strong medium for business is that it offers the opportunity for people to directly interact with one another. Without the Internet, it is difficult for a company to give close, personal service to a large number of customers. Successful companies and retailers previously shied away from the idea of personal treatment and one-on-one marketing. The companies that dominated business in the 1950s, 1960s, and 1970s, were giants that created a common-denominator product line and treated everyone equally to create incredible efficiency both in manufacturing and sales. Some of these companies were McDonald's, Radio Shack, Wal-Mart, and, later, The Gap.

Computers and the Internet provide the power and efficiency to create extremely targeted, even personal relationships with customers. That helps smaller operations to compete against major stores. Knowing your customers' sizes, favorite shipping method, or other personal information allows you to provide better customer service.

Narrow Interest Aggregation

Although one advantage offered by the Web is the ability for large entities to "get small" and interact with customers on an individual basis, another aspect to consider is how normally narrow interests can become major markets. The Web's reach aggregates scattered groups into a single market.

For example, if one of every 25,000 people is a collector of antique bottles, would it be wise to open an antique bottle store in New York City? Considering that the New York metro area has a population of about 20 million people, there would only be 800 avid potential customers (excluding tourists) in the New York City area.

However, with the population of the Internet expected to be 100 million by the year 2000, a similar store on the Web would have a potential customer base of 4,000. These are not actual numbers, but rather are examples that prove a point. A quick search of the Net found more than 400 pages or sites related to bottle collecting, including Reggie's Antique Bottle Shelves (http://www.ipass.net/~rlynch/bottles/mylist.html), where bottle collector Reggie Lynch sells antique bottles (Figure 5.1).

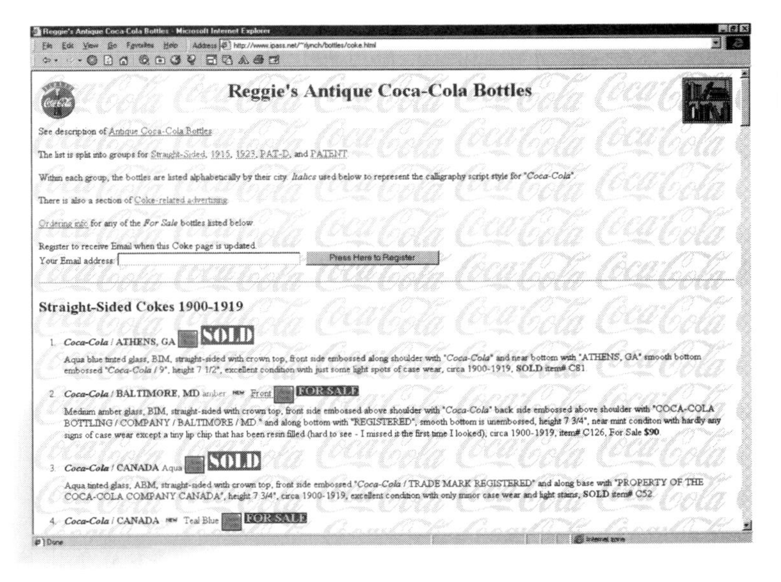

FIGURE 5.1
Reggie's Antique Bottle Shelves. Where else but on the Net could such a narrow interest store thrive?

The ability of the Internet to help communities of interest—especially narrow ones—exist in a significant enough form to foster commerce is at least as important as its ability to support personalized customer service. Many smaller markets are served not by enormous corporations such as Wal-Mart and L.L. Bean, but rather by individuals and small companies that, in many cases, serve the passions of both customers and merchants.

Low Cost of Entry

The barrier to launching a Web store is extremely low when compared to opening up a significant traditional retail store or mail order operation. Although major Web stores with significant site infrastructure, staffing, and content can cost millions to launch, these costs are not necessary for, or a guarantee of, success. Successful sites like Tronix can be built and run for less money than almost any other type of store. Larger sites can also be interesting. Disney has poured millions into its site, which quickly began to generate sales equal to that of four traditional Disney Stores. Disney executives expect the Web store to grow significantly. At the low end, opening a store on the Web can cost as little as $10,000 to $20,000. Not only does this make the Web an enticing place to open a store, it also means that new competition may arrive at any time.

Leveraging Technology

Technology can create immense changes in the way any entity operates. The Web makes it easy to utilize and present new technology to customers in a way that is easy to use. A Web page may look very simple on the surface—click here, answer this question, fill out that. But behind that interface could be software that automatically routes orders to manufacturing plants around the world, remembers a customer's previous presence, or checks the authenticity of a customer's credit card. This automation makes Web selling very productive. Examine the leverage that even a small store can gain by moving onto the Web—a constant, worldwide presence. Before the Web, that was almost impossible to have without a huge staff, a call centers, and extensive infrastructure. Today it's an afterthought.

The Sea Is Changing

The Internet represents a new way of doing business. One-to-one relationships, narrow interest aggregation, the low-barrier to entry, and technology's leverage are the major reasons behind the Web that are behind the growth of online stores and shopping. At every opportunity, storeowners should:

- **Build systems** that create one-to-one relationships with customers.
- **Look for narrow interest communities** that can be aggregate and to which their store can appeal.

- **Use the cost advantage** of the Web to compete against real-world counterparts.
- **Utilize computer technology** to become more productive while keeping things simple for users.

These are the pillar advantages of the Internet that allow storeowners to utilize various business models to create a compelling shopping site.

Choosing a Model

Deciding on a Web business model is paramount to a store's success. Opening a Web store is more than just slapping together a nice Web site and offering products for sale. A storeowner must decide how her store will make money. As you will see, there is more than one way to operate a store on the Web.

The rest of this chapter will identify, explain, and discuss all of the pure online store models. Many stores will actually use a combination of these pure models. Although the Web is still very young and online stores are younger still, the Internet is filled with an amazing array of stores, some of which are discussed in Chapter 3. From online auction houses like OnSale.com to import specialists like Tronix to sales lead stores like Microsoft's Carpoint, there are a number of successful examples from which to learn.

Traditional Online Store

We should first define a traditional online store. If there is in fact such a thing, a traditional online store offers hard goods for sale. Customers browse for items that are presented on a Web site in catalog fashion and can order directly through the site or via telephone, fax or mail. Most products are kept in stock and orders are sent out as soon as they are assembled and ready for shipping.

Auction House

The online auction model has been very well executed. With computers running the show and processing bids, online auctions provide a great model that is rooted in the real world. Online auctions combine the excitement of bidding with the opportunity to get a great price in real-time. Onsale.com (Figure 5.2) uses this model to sell surplus office and computer equipment. Other sites use it to sell used computer equipment.

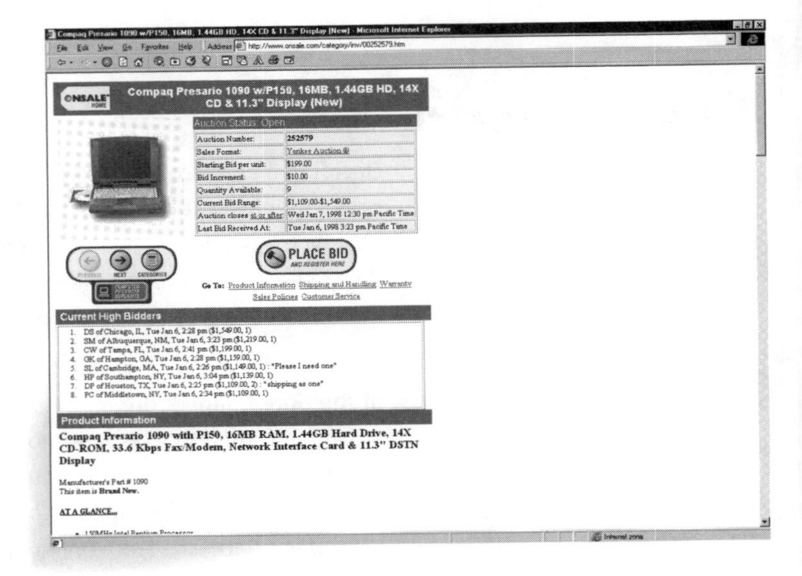

FIGURE 5.2
Onsale.com uses an auction model to attract buyers of office equipment and other high-end merchandise.

Broker/Virtual Store

A broker is someone who arranges and consummates a sale often without owning the item in question. Brokers may even sell items before they are in stock. It is a model that works well for online stores that want to be as virtual as possible.

The virtual store model is based on limiting stock and infrastructure costs that are generally associated with traditional stores or mail order companies. It also relies on receiving an order before actually procuring the resulting product from a supplier. The other goal is to automate as much of the sales process at the site level as possible. Costs are kept low by limiting the amount of store-to-customer contact during the ordering process.

The key to this model's success is minimizing the time needed to fill an order. To accomplish this, a store must be close to its suppliers in order to receive products as quickly as possible. It also needs to turn those items around immediately while providing a high level of customer service. The customer service element is crucial in the instance that the time required to deliver an item is longer than expected.

Associate Store

The associate store model draws strength from combining a real-world store with a virtual store. Many catalog outfits such as J. Crew, Eddie Bauer, and L.L. Bean operate retail stores as extensions to their mail order businesses. Web stores can consider similar opportunities. The goal of this model is two-fold. The model allows the storeowner to extend a link to the physical world to make the store more visible. The existence of a traditional store can make a virtual store appear more stable while attracting customers. Also, a successful Web store brand can be an asset to leverage into the retail world. For example, if Amazon.com continues to grow, it could decide to open physical Amazon bookstores. This would create a synergistic relationship between the virtual and real-world stores.

Of course associate stores will primarily be those that existed in traditional form prior to the growth of the Web which add an Internet presence to take advantage of its retailing potential. Either way the associate model is arrived at allows a store to increase overall sales by combining traditional and Web-based retailing.

Electronic Distribution Store

The electronic distribution model is a new breed. Why ship a product through the mail when it can be immediately transported over the Internet? The major advantage of this model is the ability to rapidly distribute products. There is no faster way to deliver a product than directly over the same phone, cable, or T-1 line that received the order. Of course, electronic distribution is limited to certain electronically transferable products such as software and music. When someone creates a way to electronically distribute such hard items as furniture, clothes, or sporting goods, it won't be limited to one part of one chapter in one book.

The success of the electronic distribution model also depends on the increase of faster distribution options and the security of electronic delivery. For more on electronic software delivery, see Chapter 16.

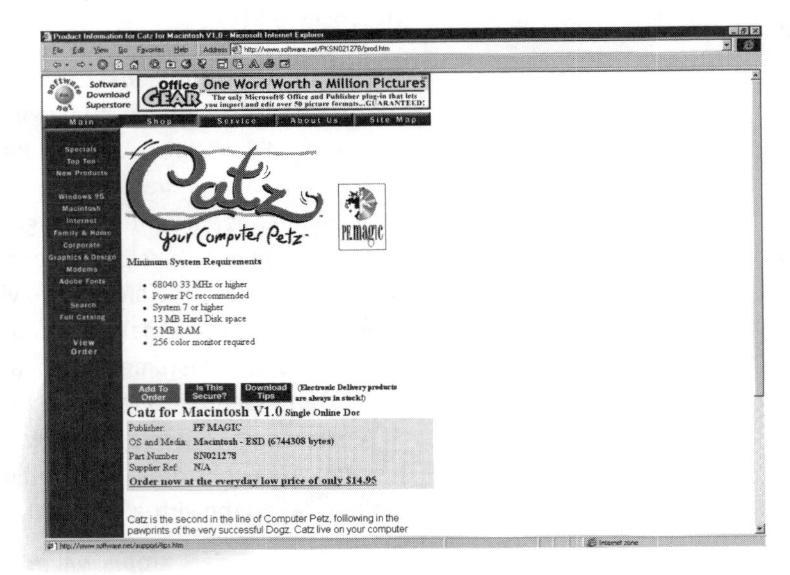

FIGURE 5.3
Software.net utilizes electronic software delivery to sell directly to users over the Internet.

In-Stock Advantage

The in-stock advantage model attempts to compete against broker stores by shortening the time between the placing of an order and the receiving of the product by the customer. This model works very well against stores that work with little or no inventory and compete on price. If an in-stock store can keep its prices close to those of a broker store, it can win sales on the ability to deliver the product first.

A good example of the in-stock advantage model is Computer Literacy, which operates the CLBOOKS.COM Web store (Figure 5.4). It is successfully competing against Amazon.com in one specific segment of the book market by offering a much higher availability of in-stock computer books. Anyone who has ever had an urgent need for a computer book would understand the advantage of next-day delivery. Amazon has responded to the pressure put on by CLBOOKS.COM and Barnsandnoble.com by building two warehouses—one on the West Coast and one on the East Coast—to help it fill orders more quickly.

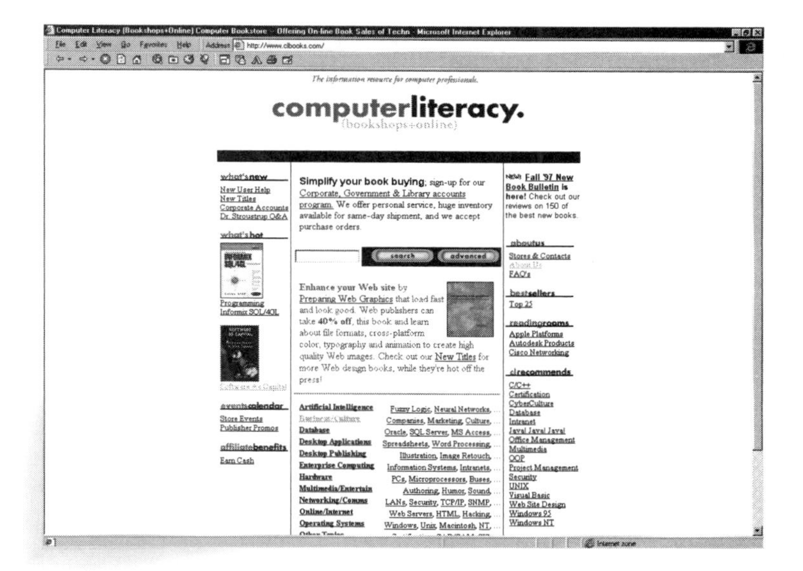

FIGURE 5.4
CLBOOKS.COM sells computer books and stocks over 25,000 titles ensuring its shoppers that most books can ship the same day.

Content Attraction

The content attraction model is implemented by many sites and raised to an art form by others. The theory is that compelling content will lead to more site visitors and, eventually, more sales.

This model is often implemented when content-focused sites create online stores as an additional revenue stream to supplement advertising and site subscription income. Sites using this model include CNET, which runs the online software storefront buydirect.com, and Online Game Review's OGR.COM, which also runs an online game store (Figure 5.5).

The key to this model obviously is strong content. While many stores offer content as an appetizer, content-based stores make it their centerpiece. Since the development of good content can be costly, so too can the deployment of this particular model.

You might also find customers who are concerned about a conflict of interest if, for example, you review a product as a publisher and sell it as a merchant. Thus it is important to make a clear distinction between what role your store plays in your content decisions.

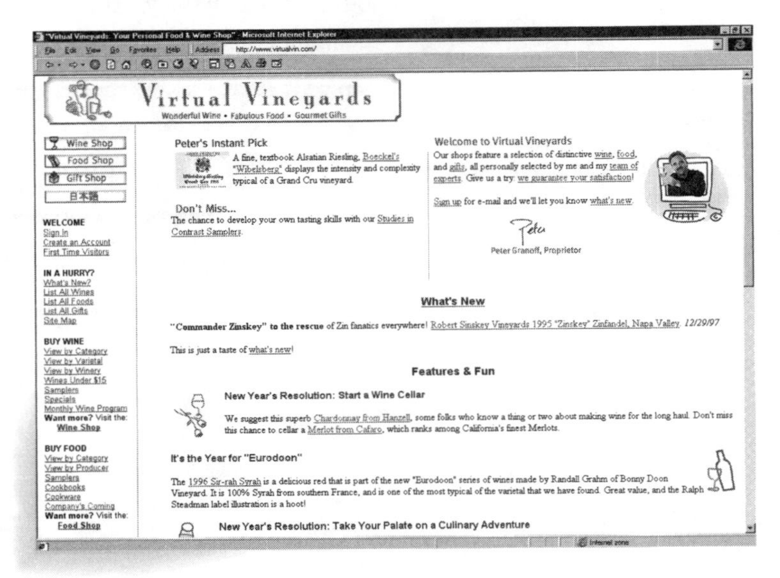

FIGURE 5.5
Some major sites like Virtual Vineyards attract people with content (such as this site's recipes or wine tasting notes) in the hopes of turning them into paying customers.

Online Associate

The online associate model involves one store (the closer of the sale) that relies on a network of associated sites to find customers and lead them to the sale. The associated sites receive a royalty for the sales they help generate.

Many stores use this as a supplemental model. It is, in essence, the franchise model of cyberspace. Amazon.com, with its Amazon Associates program, is the most visible user of this model. Realizing that a number of Web sites referred to or recommended books, Amazon.com offered those sites an easy way to cash in on that content. By embedding a specific code in a link, an associate can link a book title to the corresponding order page at Amazon.com. The program now has more than 10,000 member sites and has instigated similar deals with a number of online bookstores.

Effectively implementing this model depends on a number of factors. A store must be able to sell products at a high enough margin to afford to offer a percentage to associate sites. It also needs the infrastructure capable of providing a high level of service (Amazon.com is able to handle thousands of requests simultaneously). Finally, the primary company must be capable of aggressively signing member sites. In short, the key to this model is a strong set of links between member sites and the store. If a more capable site were to lure away associates, the host would not only see a drop in its sales, but also an increase in its competitors' sales.

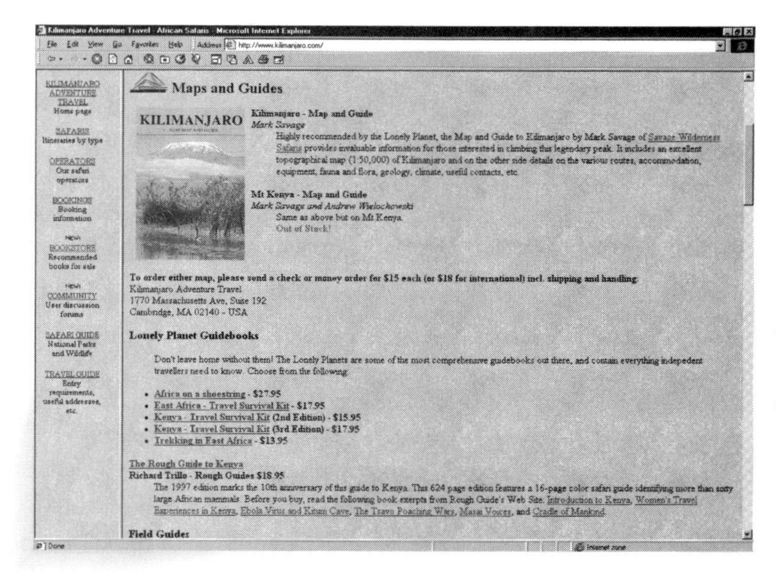

FIGURE 5.6
Kilmanjaro Tours organizes mountaineering trips and now has a bookstore business as an Amazon.com associate store on its Web site.

Price Busters

The lowest price model has existed since the dawn of time, so it is no surprise to see it being used on the Internet. Customers want low prices. What makes this model so interesting is how the Web can be used to eliminate some of the costs incurred by retailers and other companies. These savings can then be passed on to customers. For example, Tronix competes against retail stores that sell games, yet it has a fraction of the rent and much lower inventory costs. This can be used to offer lower prices and attract customers.

It is also vitally important to remember that offering the absolute lowest price is not necessarily the best model to use. A price-based business model tends to attract buyers who are looking solely for the lowest price. These customers will constantly look for the store with the lowest price, no matter how little that difference is, while ignoring all other factors. Therefore, if you compete solely on price, you stand to lose to the next low-price store that comes along. This means your margin will remain as thin as possible and you will find it difficult to implement the items that take time and money to develop such as online content or community.

Shopping Clubs

Shopping clubs, which also are becoming popular in traditional retailing, offer outstanding prices and other discounts in exchange for a yearly membership fee. Price clubs use the profits generated by membership fees to offset their low product margins.

Theoretically, a club with 250,000 members each paying a $40 annual membership would have $10 million to use toward lowering prices. The trick is attracting members.

The biggest problem with shopping clubs comes during their infancy. The member discounts must be substantial enough entice people to become members. However, non-member prices will not be attractive enough to lead to many non-member customers. Therefore, shopping club owners will generally have to sweat out minimal sales until there are enough members to create revenue through membership fees and membership sales.

You also have to be sure that member prices remain lower than those of non-club stores, otherwise there is no point in joining.

What some stores do is avoid creating large price differences on all items and instead offer other advantages to membership such as longer warranties or special product selection. Some stores offer deep discounts only on certain staple items while earning most of their profits in other areas, hoping that customers buy the less-discounted items in addition to the more attractively priced items.

In any case, the goal is simple: build repeat customers who return again and again because getting a return on the membership fee keeps them from considering competitors.

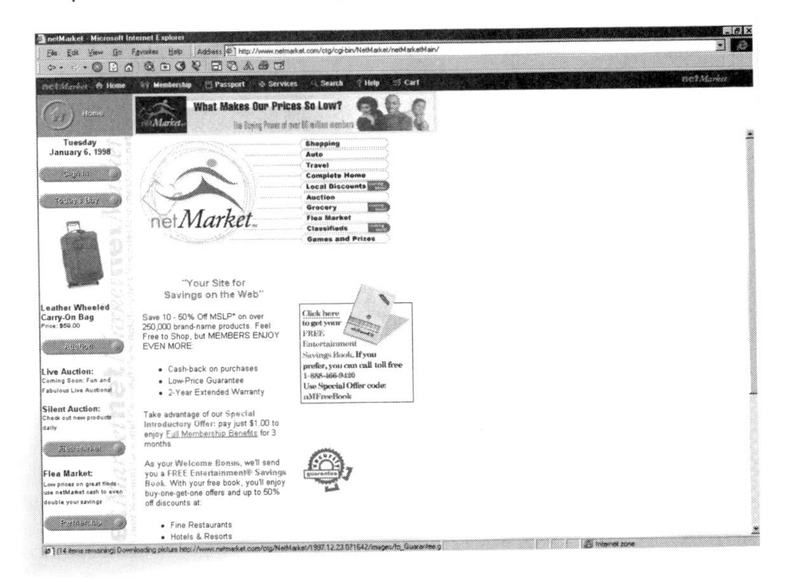

FIGURE 5.7
Affinity marketing giant CUC runs Netmarket.com one of the largest online shopping member clubs.

Sales Lead Generators

A sales lead-generating model is more about selling customers than it is about selling products. This model works best with big-ticket items such as cars. The customer asks the lead generator for information on the availability of a certain product and the lead generator sends the customer toward the most useful supplier of the product. For example, Microsoft's Carpoint uses this model. Carpoint not only negotiates a bounty for successful automobile sales, but also charges a fee to join and belong to the service. Car dealers pay nearly $3,000 per month to belong to the site.

Sales lead stores—like online associates—need exceptionally strong links to the dealers with which they work. The success of these networks rests primarily on having a large number of partners and users.

Community-Oriented

The success of the community-oriented model is based on developing sales through the creation of a tight-knit online community. Customers are compelled to purchase products because they want to reward the creation of a sustainable community of interest. Customers are additionally drawn to the community because of the subject matter.

For example, a comic book shop can create a viable online community that supports various discussions and online events that focus on the comic book universe. Not only do these activities generate participants who are apt to purchase comic books, but the interaction between the participants and the store creates a bond that leads to loyal, lifelong customers.

Narrow Interest

The narrow interest store rides a small niche that is only viable on the Web to success. The only competition comes from other Web stores.

An owner of a narrow-interest store usually shares a specific interest with his customers. These stores often stock items that are custom-made or that are only available through non-traditional means such as auctions, personal buying trips, etc. Narrow-interest stores often cater to collectors or hobbyists.

Narrow-interest stores can often expand by implementing community-oriented features.

Intranet Stores

This is a very low-profile store model, but one that could grow as intranets (internal company networks that are run like Internet sites) become more popular. In order to control budgets and better account for various internal product use, companies may opt to build stores directly on their intranets. The site would work like any other Web store although it would only be available to company members.

The real opportunity lies in the possibility of intranet stores that are actually specialized storefronts run by external stores for a specific corporation. For example, an online software store could offer a specialized storefront allowing Intel employees to order products through the company's intranet. The competition would be for large Web stores to become the "official" store for the company.

Custom Construction

Custom construction stores offer customized items and take advantage of the ease with which customers can order those items over the Internet.

Through an interactive process, customers can customize a particular item. The key to this system is that, by using a database, a store can remember and apply certain traits to each of a particular customer's order.

For example, Disney's online store allows customers to create personalized Disney merchandise by adding names, birth dates, and other information to items. Phatcatjeans (www.phatcatjeans.com) creates custom hip-hop style clothing. Customers choose styles, colors, and other traits, and a seamstress creates the product.

The future is in sites that can remember custom information for repeated use. For example, Levi's has a system with which you can walk into a retail store and be scanned for custom-sized jeans. The potential is there for people to be scanned at a local facility and then offer that information to any clothing retailer who would accept it. Dell and Gateway—two huge direct manufacturers—have been successful by offering customized computer systems ordered via the phone or the Internet.

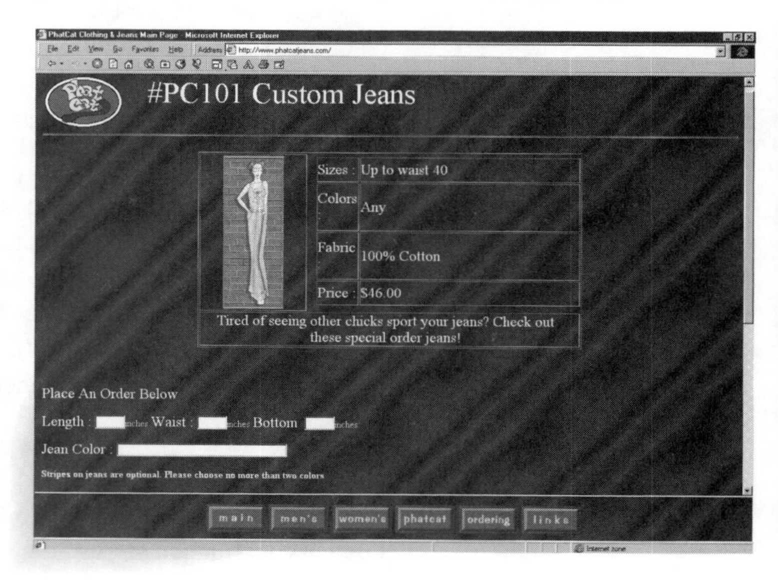

FIGURE 5.8
PhatCat Jeans lets you order custom styled clothing.

Which Model Works for You?

When considering which model to use, the most important thing to consider is how to unify the merchandise you want to sell with the customers you want to serve. The process you choose to implement entices people to shop with you and creates the energy that moves items out the door.

After you've decided what to sell and to whom to sell it, then and only then should you search for the model that brings these two groups together. If your intended customer base requires outstanding customer service, you would be better served by choosing the community model rather than an in-stock advantage model because your customers are more interested in service options than immediate delivery. However, if you sell readily available merchandise, a low-price model might work best.

The best way to select a business model is to become familiar with them and how they are being used on the Internet. As you investigate, you will notice how the most successful stores have perfectly matched their models to their merchandise and their customer bases. Not every site can work as an auction site and many can't operate as virtual brokers. This is not because the owners don't know how to create these stores, it's because they know that those would be unsuccessful models for their line of business.

This chapter has introduced you to 15 online store business models. In each case there are successful example enterprises on the Web. No single model is the best for every situation. In fact, many stores use one primary model and supplement that with certain aspects of other models. These customized models often work best.

PART II

Building Your Store

No matter what software package or process you select to build your store, there are some basics that all online merchants must understand. Part II covers fundamentals to philosophy, including how to launch your store, designing your store, stocking your store's virtual shelves, and creating compelling store content.

Part II Table of Contents

CHAPTER 6

Launching Your Online Store

Before you sell your first video game, pair of boots, or Lear jet online, you'll have to do plenty of work. The work will have nothing to do with the Web, your online presence, or selling, but it will lead to that. However, as many business advisors will tell you, the early decisions you make concerning your business setup can be the most essential.

You have to choose a name (no kidding!), probably find a lawyer, decide on the type of business (S-Corp., limited liability, sole proprietorship, partnership, etc.), get a tax identification number, find an office if you choose not to work out of your home, get insurance, etc. Tack a few more et ceteras on there if you'd like. You'll probably need them.

Get the point? Actually setting up the business can be more work than selling your product. And as you spend time doing it, you won't be doing business. However, if you simply stay organized, stay focused, and work through the long to-do list, you'll eventually reach your goal of becoming the owner and operator of an online store. You will have setbacks and you will get frustrated. Work through it.

Once you're ready to launch a store, you'll face another critical piece of work. Assuming you've done all the legal work and have your business entity set up, you will experience the hardest part of online anything—setting up the services and initial accounts you need to properly develop an online presence.

Surrounding these key tasks are several other startup items including obtaining phone service, setting up merchant accounts with the right credit cards and banks, and forming relationships with the distributors you'll order products from. We cover it all here in a simple step-by-step process. Although you will want to go out and quiz other professionals—especially a lawyer and an accountant—we've tried to simplify the process as much as possible. The good news here is once this stuff is done, you'll never have to do it again. And if it's done properly, you'll save thousands on headache remedies later on!

That being said, let's launch.

Selecting a Name

Chances are, if you're going into business, you've been thinking about it for awhile. And if you've been thinking about it for awhile, you've mulled over some names. Although choosing a name can be one of the most fun, creative aspects of the setup, it shouldn't be taken lightly. Your name is how your business will be identified. For example, you probably don't want to call your store Overpriced Junk unless you're selling antiques to people with sharp senses of humor.

When deciding on a name for your business, think in the long term. This name will be plastered on the entrance to your Web site which, hopefully, thousands of Net travelers will visit daily. Make your business name easy to remember and short. "Rubbereyes!" (made famous by the AT&T commercials) is better than "Ultraviolet Eye Shields Made of Flexible Material." Both names say the same thing, but the first name is far easier to remember and a bit more fun. And if your product is rubber sunglasses, fun is what you're selling. On the other hand, if you're selling surgical equipment, you might want to stay away from something like "Scalpels R Us." A serious product needs a serious name.

Before the name Tronix was arrived at, Joe played with a few other names. Once you present a name to a lawyer, the lawyer will do a local and national name and title search to be sure it's legally available. If there is a distinguishing appendage to the name—such as Acme Moving Co. vs. Acme Manufacturing Co.—you'll likely be able to keep your name.

Joe's Take: *I presented my lawyer with the name Title Wave. He ran a national search to see whether Title Wave had been copyrighted. Guess what? It had. So my fabulous, witty company name was already someone else's, which brings up a somewhat obvious but important point: if someone has a company with a name you want, you can't have it. It doesn't matter if you're selling video games in New York and the other is hawking surfboards in San Diego, unless they've chosen Title Wave Board Shop as opposed to Title Wave Video Games. Back to the drawing board.*

I then opted for playing with the theme of my business—electronic entertainment—and came up with Entertronix. The lawyer searched for it, another week went by, and once again I was disappointed to hear that Entertronix was copyrighted as well. Next I tried Tronix Multimedia Inc. Thank goodness it was available. Eventually we shortened it for the Web site, and now we're simply known as Tronix. One strong word, plain and simple, easy to remember—and fits quite nicely on our main page.

TIP ▸ ***Have a list of alternative names for your business ready in case your top choice is unavailable. You may think you have something unique, but you might be surprised how many people are thinking along the same lines. If you don't have some backup names, you may find your launch delayed.***

TIP ▸ ***Finding a lawyer is easy; finding a good lawyer a bit less so. The amount of experience your lawyer has will vary depending on how much you can afford to pay him or her. Depending on where you live, you can get a good lawyer with some relevant experience for $100 an hour. But no matter how much you can spend, find a lawyer who is experienced working with small, new businesses and who can do everything you need from a name search to advising you on contractual matters. If your goal is to eventually grow your business past a one- or two-person operation, you'd like to have a lawyer who has helped clients do that rather than having to find a new lawyer a year or two down the road. Lawyer's aren't hard to find; chances are you or a member of your family know one. But don't choose a lawyer just out of convenience, choose one who can provide the services you need and who will be able to answer your questions at a moment's notice. A lawyer with the support that is available at a mid-sized or larger firm is a plus, but be sure you won't be your lawyer's last priority. If you or someone you know doesn't know a qualified lawyer, ask some small business owners in your area if they can recommend one.***

Choosing a Legal Entity

As you're chasing down a name you should also be deciding what type of business structure you will have. A number of good business manuals available in any bookstore can give you an idea of what certain structures provide and what they don't. We suggest again that you find a lawyer, not only to advise you on what type of business best fits your needs, but also to take care of the paperwork. Most lawyers provide these services for a reasonable price (in the neighborhood of $500, possibly less) with the hope that, as your business grows, so will theirs.

Joe's Take: *A lawyer will also give you the simple paperwork needed to apply for a tax identification number. Unless you absolutely can't afford it or would rather do a pile of grinding work yourself, a lawyer is worth it. Obviously those people who can't find anything nice to say about lawyers never tried to start a business.*

TIP ▸ ***You may have seen those do-it-yourself incorporation kits. A few of these are even online (Figure 6.1). Although these kits offer a cheap way to set up a corporation or limited liability company, they rob you of the first chance to interact and set up a relationship with a lawyer and an accountant. And though it's true that you can pay 10-20 times more to incorporate with the help of a lawyer and an accountant, you're really getting much more than a simple incorporation. You're building relationships that will hopefully last as long as your business.***

The following is a brief rundown of the various business choices and what they provide. To avoid getting bogged down in the technicalities of the various choices, we stick to the basics. Your lawyer should be able to point you in the right direction.

Subchapter S Corporation (S Corp)

Most small companies are Subchapter S Corporations (S Corp). This type of entity gives you many of the benefits of a standard Subchapter C Corporation but is advantageous for small businesses because income passes directly through to the shareholder and is subject only to personal income tax.

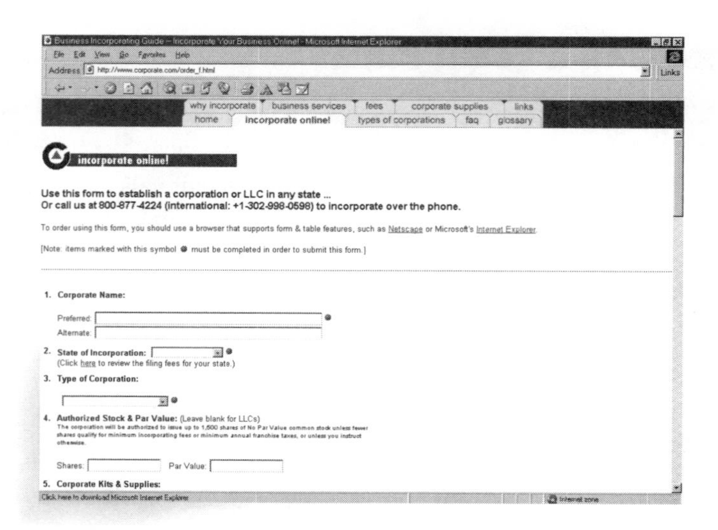

FIGURE 6.1
One of a number of online incorporation services.

An S Corp is limited to 35 shareholders—more than enough for a small business. Each shareholder must be a U.S. citizen or a resident alien and must also be a person, which rules out many foreign individuals and entities. An S Corp is not allowed to own more than 80 percent of another corporation. Certain types of businesses—insurance and financial companies, for example—can't be S Corps.

Most of the tax issues for an S Corp are the same as those of a Limited Liability Company (LLC). If you decide an S Corp is the best method of business—which is likely for a small start-up—get some good tax advice from an accountant.

Subchapter C Corporation (C Corp)

Subchapter C Corporations (C Corps) are full-fledged corporations that can retain earnings over the course of time and are independent taxable entities. When a C Corp earns income, it must pay corporate tax. If you, as a shareholder, want to receive the remaining income after corporate taxation, you receive a dividend and must pay personal income tax on that money. In other words, the money earned by a C Corp is taxed twice—at the corporate and personal levels.

Sole Proprietorship

In a sole proprietorship, a single individual operates as a business, either under his or her own name or by filing a fictitious business name statement. Except for filing a fictitious business name statement, no government filing or minimum tax payment is required. You work on your own, hire people as necessary, and deduct your business expenses from your state and federal taxes. If you do hire people to help you out, you'll need to file Form 1099 at tax time stating how much you paid out so the IRS will be aware of your employees' income. The major drawback of a sole proprietorship is that the owner is personally liable for all of the business' financial commitments.

TIP ▸ ***If you plan on doing business as a sole proprietorship, you may need to file a DBA (Doing Business As) certificate to denote the name of your business. This is a local law issue that you should check with your lawyer or accountant. The cost is pretty minimal everywhere, but look into it before you go around town promoting yourself under a company name that isn't on your bank account or checks.***

General Partnership

Being a partner in a general partnership is much like being a sole proprietor—each partner is personally liable for the obligations of the business. The partners are taxed as individuals, reporting their share of the partnership's income and their share of the partnership's expenses. Forming a partnership doesn't require any legal formalities or government filings. The issues surrounding partnership are much more complicated than doing business on your own.

Limited Partnership

The limited partnership insulates liability of the limited partners from losses of the partnership, yet is taxed as a partnership. However, the limited partnership has some serious drawbacks. At least one of the general partners is fully liable for the losses of the partnership. To avoid this potentially devastating liability, that partner is often a corporation. This creates a problem with the IRS, which requires a corporate partner's net worth to be at least equal to 10 percent of the total contributions of the partners to the partnership. Also, a limited partner must be truly passive and is not allowed to participate in management of the partnership.

Limited Liability Company (LLC)

A limited liability company (LLC) insulates your personal assets from creditors or in the case your business is sued. In other words, if someone breaks his leg in a fall from a defective mountain bike you shipped and decides to sue you, you don't have to worry about the plaintiff taking your house.

The LLC gained popularity in the mid-1980s when it was ruled that an LLC could be taxed as a partnership. The popularity of the LLC comes from the fact that it offers limited liability but has the tax status of a partnership, so it is taxed only once. LLCs do not have the same restrictions as S Corps. The owners can be any type of entity—not just individuals—and there is no maximum number of members. LLCs do not restrict how the owners' rights to money or liquidation proceeds are divided. LLCs can also own subsidiaries. Unlike general partnerships, the management of the business is not restricted to owners of the business; the owner can either manage the company him or herself or appoint management. All of the members can be involved in the business without the risk of personal liability.

However, forming an LLC requires more cost and effort than other types of companies. Owners are typically required to sign an operating agreement establishing such terms as the voting rights of members and the sharing of profit and losses.

TIP ▸ ***We've given you the basic background here on what the different operating entities are. However, you should consult a lawyer and accountant before making the ultimate choice. One thing to especially educate yourself on is how to maintain the corporation or LLC in order to retain its limited liability. You must be aware of a host of paperwork and filings and stay on top of them to keep the status of your corporation.***

A Tax ID and Resale Certificate

Every business and store has to obtain at least one if not *two* key tax numbers. Your accountant and lawyer should be able to help you.

Tax ID number

The federal Tax Identification number is what identifies you to the government for all tax-related purposes. It may also be called an Employer Identification Number or EIN. If you are a one-person operation running on a very small scale, you *can* just claim income on your social security number, but we don't recommend that at all. To get a Tax ID number, just download form SS4 (Figure 6.2) from the FedWorld web site at www.fedworld.net or ask your accountant or lawyer for it. Fill out the form and call the IRS number to apply. The number is constantly busy but if you keep calling during the day, it shouldn't take you more than an hour or so to get through. The operators there will step you though any questions you may have and at the end you'll be given the number. Send in the completed form when you're done.

TIP ▸ ***The Tax ID or EIN number is also the number a bank will require you to give it in order to open up a business checking account.***

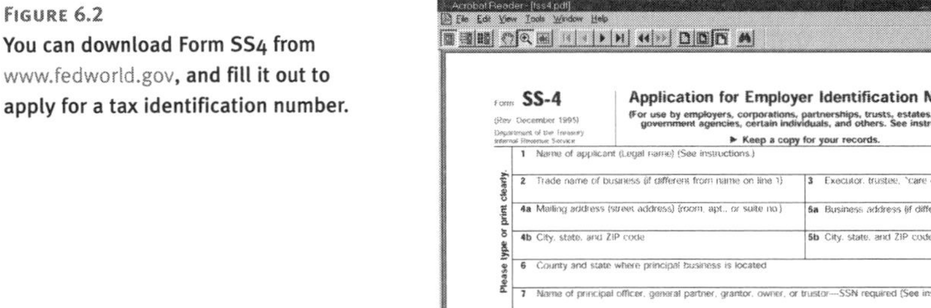

Acrobat Reader - [fss4.pdf]

File Edit View Tools Window Help

Form **SS-4**
(Rev. December 1995)
Department of the Treasury
Internal Revenue Service

Application for Employer Identification Number

(For use by employers, corporations, partnerships, trusts, estates, churches, government agencies, certain individuals, and others. See instructions.)

▶ Keep a copy for your records.

EIN

OMB No. 1545-0003

Please type or print clearly.

1 Name of applicant (Legal name) (See instructions.)

2 Trade name of business (if different from name on line 1) | 3 Executor, trustee, "care of" name

4a Mailing address (street address) (room, apt., or suite no.) | 5a Business address (if different from address on lines 4a and 4b)

4b City, state, and ZIP code | 5b City, state, and ZIP code

6 County and state where principal business is located

7 Name of principal officer, general partner, grantor, owner, or trustor—SSN required (See instructions.) ▶

8a Type of entity (Check only one box.) (See instructions.)
☐ Sole proprietor (SSN)
☐ Partnership ☐ Personal service corp.
☐ REMIC ☐ Limited liability co
☐ State/local government ☐ National Guard
☐ Other nonprofit organization (specify) ▶ (enter GEN if applicable)
☐ Other (specify) ▶
☐ Estate (SSN of decedent)
☐ Plan administrator-SSN
☐ Other corporation (specify) ▶
☐ Trust ☐ Farmers' cooperative
☐ Federal Government/military ☐ Church or church-controlled organization

8b If a corporation, name the state or foreign country (if applicable) where incorporated | State | Foreign country

9 Reason for applying (Check only one box.)
☐ Started new business (specify) ▶
☐ Hired employees
☐ Created a pension plan (specify type) ▶
☐ Banking purpose (specify) ▶
☐ Changed type of organization (specify) ▶
☐ Purchased going business
☐ Created a trust (specify) ▶
☐ Other (specify) ▶

10 Date business started or acquired (Mo., day, year) (See instructions.) | 11 Closing month of accounting year (See instructions.)

FIGURE 6.2
You can download Form SS4 from www.fedworld.gov, and fill it out to apply for a tax identification number.

Resale Certificate

The second number you need is a Resale Certificate. This is a local tax certificate that is handled differently in every state. It can cost anywhere from $20 on up. Contact your state department of revenue for more information (many are on the Web) and they'll explain where and how to get one. The certificate, which you will need to send to distributors and have on hand for inspection, entitles you not to pay tax on any items you purchase that are either products you will resell or go into the products you will resell. In other words, you don't have to pay tax on flour whether you are reselling it as flour or are using it to bake the cakes you're reselling. It's also the ID number you use to submit your sales tax receipts to your state tax department.

Working Out of an Office

You've got a name. You've established your corporate entity. And you've decided to move into an office. You could run a mail-order operation of small size directly out of your home, but there are a number of reasons not to do that. Simply put, homes are not offices. Homes are great for people who might do light, professionally oriented work, but they're terrible for people with tons of visitors or any employees. You may be restricted by zoning laws against operating an office where your home is. It's tough to deduct home-based expenses, and it's very tough for merchants and distributors to seriously deal with a home-based operation. They'll wonder how committed you are to the business if you're constantly being interrupted by a screaming baby in the background or your daughter's boyfriend beeping through on call-waiting. Certainly you will want to work from home occasionally, but it's no way to permanently do business. That means moving to an office, and that opens another sizable, but manageable, can of worms.

Choosing an Office Space

Selecting an office involves common sense. You're working online, so you don't have to worry so much about location. You don't need foot traffic to sell your stuff, so you should be able to get a reasonable rent. But before you go looking, figure out exactly how much you can afford in monthly expenses and how high an office is on your list of priorities.

If You Just Can't Afford an Office

If you absolutely can't afford an office to start, you can work out of your home, but bear in mind that it's much tougher. This means setting aside a portion of your house or apartment *for work only.* Try to keep work and your personal life separate or you will soon find you have no personal life. The sooner you can get into an office, however small, the better. Working outside your home allows you to keep work at the office and your life elsewhere. If you don't own your home, check with building management about using the apartment for work. They may not care for the idea of incoming and outgoing boxes on a daily basis, especially co-op buildings where more restrictive rules may apply.

As you look for an office, think functionality. With a minimum of clients visiting you, you don't need the sweetest space in the city. You should think about air conditioning (to keep your computers and yourself from breaking down) and whether heat and electricity are included in the rent. How much will it cost for phone service and, if available, a high-speed cable modem or T-1 service? If you're on the Internet a lot, and you most likely will be, a higher speed connection can save you an hour of work a day and is worth the slightly higher cost.

Insurance

There's no question you'll need insurance to cover theft, fire, and other events that could damage your equipment and inventory. If you think "It will never happen to me," it will happen to you. Would you consider not insuring your family, your car or your home? If you decide to blow off the cost of insuring your equipment and inventory, it's like failing to insure all of those personal things. If you lose your equipment due to a fire or some other calamity, you may well lose your business. And losing your business will certainly affect your ability to pay your rent or mortgage and your car payment and, more importantly, your ability to provide for your family. Insurance really isn't an option, it's a must.

Depending on your lease, you'll probably also need limited liability insurance to cover any visitor who may be injured in the office. This can generally be provided in a package by the company with which your equipment and inventory is insured. The cost of the insurance depends upon the value of the insured property, so we'll refrain throwing out any definite figures. A ballpark figure is several hundred dollars a year. Remember that your ballpark might be three times as big as ours.

You also must address the health insurance needs of yourself and any employees. Again, health insurance is something you really should have. If you don't think so, go out and do something simple like break an ankle and then pay for it out of your pocket. If you are married, you should compare the cost and benefits of purchasing your own insurance with getting on your spouse's policy. That will depend on your spouse's policy and whether or not his or her employer provides spousal coverage.

Whether or not you provide health insurance to an employee is up to you during the early stages of business when any employee will likely be less than full-time. If your business continues to grow, providing a comprehensive benefits package is a way to attract quality employees.

Then there is worker's compensation insurance to cover employees injured on the job. As a corporate officer, you have the right to waive worker's compensation insurance for yourself, but you'll need to provide it for your employees. Contact an insurance company, tell them what you need and they'll take care of you. You should comparison shop, however.

Phone Service

No business is a business without phone service. A number of options are available to consider.

How Many Phone Lines Do You Need?

Most small to medium sized businesses can probably get by on between three and five lines to start. Try to figure out as closely as possible how many lines you need; too many is a waste of money, and too few will force you to soon waste time and effort upgrading your system.

Your main line will include one number that, when busy, will roll over to the other lines until one is free to ring. You'll also need to order a separate single line for a fax machine and you may opt to order an additional voice number as a "private" line. This unlisted number is great in case you get a rush of customer calls and want to provide a separate number for distributors, critical customers, and other close associates.

JOE'S TAKE: *Actually the number of lines you need is easy to figure out. You need at least two lines for customers, an additional one that can be shared between the fax machine and credit card terminal, and a fourth line for Internet and e-mail. I use that line as a private number also. When I first started, in order to save money I ran the Internet, fax, and credit card terminal off one line. As I grew, I quickly added another line to allow me to keep the Internet connection up all day rather than constantly logging on or off every time I needed to use the fax machine or get a credit card authorization.*

Which Long Distance Provider Should You Choose?

Depending on how much long distance calling you're going to do, this can be a very important decision. Even after you make it, the small business market is so cutthroat you can be sure that you'll receive repeated solicitations to change your long distance service. Without going into the details of the dozens of plans that are offered, you should make some calls to all the major providers (AT&T, MCI, Sprint, and Worldcom) and see what rates per minute they'll give you. There are so many plans you need to be proactive in your search. You should be able to get a discount plan for between 10 and 13 cents per minute. If you're going to make a lot of overseas calls, take into account how the combined rates will work out.

TIP▸ ***Many small resellers of long-distance service exist. These companies buy minutes in huge bulk quantities and resell them to smaller companies. The biggest problem with resellers and other smaller providers of long-distance service is, well, service. As a store owner, any time someone can't reach you is lost business. It may make sense to avoid the lowest rate for the assurance that you've got top service and quality.***

JOE'S TAKE: *The problem with an 800 number is too many people may call you and waste your time. The barrier of being charged for the call is strong enough to keep little kids and general inquiries down to a minimum. If I were to get a toll-free number at all, I'd only give it out to my best customers. However, if sales grow to a substantial point a toll-free number may be a plus. If you do go with a toll-free number that isn't international in scope, don't forget to publicize your regular phone as well. And remember—when you're small every penny and every second saved counts.*

Should You Get Voicemail?

Many smaller stores will need to get a voicemail system. Using a voicemail box that is available directly from the phone company can save time and, because it's fast and digital, it sounds good and works flawlessly. A typical voicemail box addition to your main number should run about $20-$30 a month. Call waiting works well for small office solutions, but no customer is going to want to be interrupted by another call (as opposed to being placed on hold).

Should You Invest In an 800/888 Toll-Free Number?

Due to intense competition, the ability to add an 800 or 888 toll-free number is actually fairly inexpensive. Both MCI and AT&T offer toll-free number service that you can order for $5 a month if you use them as your long distance provider. The number actually rings through to your regular business number line and when answered you pay a 12 to 13 cents a minute flat rate during the call. Bills come separately. Overall, if you think the toll-free service will increase your business beyond the cost of providing toll-free service, then it's certainly a key item to have.

What Phone Hardware Will You Use?

You've got a bunch of lines ordered and coming in but nothing to use them with. You need to get phone equipment. If you only have two or three lines coming in for customers and aren't going to need more than yourself and one or two other people to answer calls, then you can just go to an office store and pick up some quality two- or three-line phones. If you've got more than three lines, then you'll need to install a phone system. A phone system isn't as expensive as you might think, but if you really expect your company to grow it's best to get a solid system that can be easily upgraded to handle more lines.

You'll also need to hire a technician to install this for you. Many technicians in the phone book install and sell systems. Ask about used systems or leasing if you want to cut costs.

TIP ▸ ***For a fax machine, get a plain paper fax or risk searching far and wide for fax paper.***

Joe's Take: *I like Hewlett-Packard's fax machines; they're priced nicely, they use plain paper, and the supplies for ink are easy to find. I also recommend getting really good phones no matter how extensive your system is—simple two-liners, like I did, or a complete system. There's nothing more frustrating than cutting corners on phone equipment and then getting a static filled call or a broken phone a month later. Reliable Internet and phone service are your lifeblood, so don't fool around with them.*

Acquiring a Merchant Account

Without a merchant account to accept credit cards, you'll only be able to accept CODs (cash on delivery) or money orders and checks paid in advance. No merchant account, of course, is a major disadvantage, especially since most customers would not thrill to the idea of sending money to a not-yet-established, online firm. If you don't get credit card orders, you're almost dead in the water.

CODs are fine, but your courier will charge you an additional fee which you'll pass on to your customer. In an age of modern-day shopping, most people purchasing mail-order goods want to whip out their credit card, make their purchase, and have it delivered to them in a timely manner, especially when they have their eye on an item but don't have the cash on hand to pay for it immediately.

Getting the equipment and approval to accept credit cards will be one of your biggest startup challenges. First you'll need to convince a merchant bank to accept you. This involves a credit check and telling them a bit about your business. It's important to have done all the other paperwork and account setup before you go see these people. Everything you can do and show that proves you're going to be a credit worthy and capable reseller is considered before they let you take cards. In addition you'll need to acquire some equipment to communicate and get approval for cards. Finally you may opt to find a vendor which will help you process card numbers via the Internet.

To find out more about accepting credit cards, see Chapter 14.

TIP ▸ ***Check locally in the yellow pages to find a listing of merchant card service providers in your area. Card service providers vary from state-to-state, although a few major national players are out there. Ask your accountant, too—he or she may be really helpful. If worse comes to worse, just call a few local stores until some owner or manager can help you out.***

Joe's Take: *Getting a merchant card account was one of the toughest things I had to do. The Internet was still fairly new when I applied. At the same time, these card service providers are very wary of mail-order only businesses—to say nothing of Internet-based ones. Be careful and thorough in explaining to the salesperson what you're going to do. If you're going to generate any sort of in-store traffic, let them know that immediately; emphasize it , because it's a big plus. Make sure you go to them once you've gotten a lot of your other aspects in place: an office, your business entity, phones, etc. The more bona fide you are the better. Be prepared to get rejected at least once. Line up a few different card providers to talk to.*

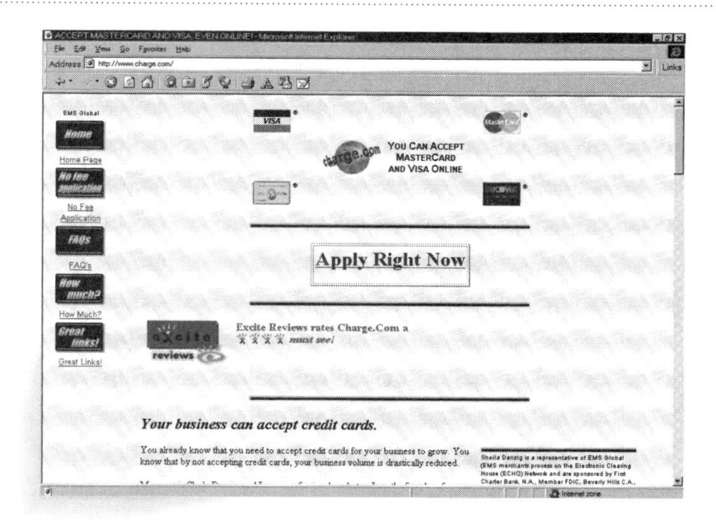

Figure 6.3:
This is a Web site offering a merchant account service.

Setting Up with Distributors and Vendors

If you're going to sell items over the Internet, in all likelihood you'll be reselling items rather than selling original items you produced. That means one of the biggest start-up challenges will be building a list of distributors and vendors which will provide you with the items you want to resell.

Building a list of distributors and vendors is very hard work. First, you'll have to identify the distributors and vendors. Turn to the Internet and your local library. Look for trade-oriented magazines and Web sites as well as vendors which specifically make the items you want to stock. From there you'll need to work the phones a bit and find out the names and numbers of the distributors to work with. If a vendor goes direct you may want to deal with them that way.

Armed with some basic research there are three key ways to find the names and numbers of distributors you can use:

- **Call vendors of the products** you want to stock, ask for the channel sales person, and get the names of the distributors they use and their numbers.

- **Find the names of distributors** in trade publications for the industry—you'd be surprised how many simple industries have one or two trade magazines.

- **Attend trade shows** for the particular industry, where you're bound to meet vendors and distributors.

Once you have a list of distributors and vendors (and their products), you're halfway through. You'll have to try and set up an account to order from and perhaps submit an application. They'll want to see your reseller's certificate and get of your Tax ID number as well—no sense talking to them until you have those items in place.

Most distributors, regardless of industry, want to deal with stores which will provide a constant stream of large orders and that have good credit. If you're new to the business, chances are you'll have to pay up front for quite a while before a distributor will offer you terms and credit. In addition, prepare for some setbacks if you don't convince them you're going to order a decent amount (simply ask what they consider a minimum year's worth of orders). When dealing with vendors directly it will be the same thing. Sometimes, with very small vendors, you can get terms because of the risk they may drop out of sight. In the end, it's a hard-work, straightforward process. Find distributors and vendors, negotiate the ability to order from them, maintain the relationship, and stay on good terms. Repeat this over and over until you have enough distributors and vendors lined up to keep you well stocked with everything you want to carry.

Joe's Take: *Having worked for a leading video game store prior to founding Tronix, I was lucky to have set up many personal relationships and reputations with top distributors in my industry. This situation made it very easy for me to avoid credit checks and applications. In some cases, with importing and foreign-based distributors, I had to work hard to get on their good side, but essentially it was a process of paying first and getting the items I wanted afterwards. As you develop a solid relationship with these distributors, the requirements will probably become less strict. All I can say is never make a distributor mad at you, be patient when first finding and talking with distributors, and always let them know you expect to be placing big orders and moving lots of product. They're not into small-time distributors—they make money on volume.*

The Miracle Solution: Web Hosting

August is a relatively soft month for retail in the video game business, so if there was a good time to concentrate on hooking up with a new provider, this was it. Everything needed to be right this time and, as it turned out, a "Web hosting service" stood out as the optimum plan.

A Web hosting service is just that. It hosts Web sites on its server and provides common webmaster tools such as CGI templates, mailing lists, and even a shopping cart feature, to enhance any Web site. Depending on your needs, you can choose from a number of different plans. The Web hosting service provides a specific amount of storage space per plan. You can start off with a basic plan and if your hit count (the number of people visiting your site) increases beyond your current plan, additional charges are applied to your monthly fee. The company always warns you ahead of time and encourages you to upgrade your plan. You save money by renting a larger block of space, rather then getting hit with overage charges on the less expensive plans.

So, what about e-mail, the newsgroups, FTP services, and Internet access? Simple—you can keep, as in Tronix's case, a reliable AT&T account. Tronix is still using AT&T WorldNet for its basic Internet needs while still working with the Web hosting company. It was comforting to visit a Web hosting service's own Web site and see the multitude of large business and retail sites that were also using this same service. With the amount of big-name companies using this organization, it's highly unlikely there will be any problems.

TIP ▸ ***Choose a large, well-known corporation as your Internet Service Provider. Because your business depends on the Internet, make sure you choose an unlimited use, monthly flat rate plan (usually $19.95). If we're talking AT&T, MCI, or even CompuServe, it's highly unlikely you'll run into problems. You also can log on throughout the country with a national provider—a plus if you travel a lot and don't want to deal with things like telnet. Seek out a professional Web-hosting service to station your Web site on its servers. It's their primary business, so there should be little or no problem. In the world of electronic communications, nothing is perfect, but this combination has eliminated any nightmares Tronix had dealt with previously. Taking care of your customers and getting orders out on time should be your business's primary concerns, not worrying if your service provider didn't pay their rent.***

Joe's Take: *A domain name is very important. I like Tronix because it doesn't take much effort to type in and it is easy for my customers to remember. For a while, I had a site that wasn't using a straight domain name system and when I switched over from that to tronix.com it made a huge difference in traffic. When you're thinking of a name for your store, think also of a domain name.*

Registering Your Domain Name

Chances are your Web hosting service will help you secure a domain name for your Web site. The base cost of acquiring a domain name from the Internic service which assigns them is $100 for two years of registration. Expect to pay more for it to be handled by your Web hosting service, but in some ways it's worth the extra $50–$100 for them to do it for you.

You will want your own domain for many reasons, the biggest of which is that it will give you a more professional-looking store and a Web brand name to promote. You will be taken more seriously and your customers will find you more easily if your URL is www.greatstore.com than if it is www.isp.com/~yourlogin/yourstore/.

When you register a domain name you will be able to use it for two years, after which you can renew it for another cycle. Sometimes you'll have to use a different name than your business name, especially if it's already taken or perhaps too long. For example, if you were going to call yourself the Digital Camera Store, you might already discover that www.digitalcamera.com is taken. Time to come up with a different name. Or if your store is John Smith's Outdoor Equipment you might want to choose a shorter domain name, such as www.jsmithequipment.com.

Domain names are registered with a special clearinghouse that everyone must use. Called the Internic (located at www.internic.net), it maintains the registry of all the names on the Internet. When you want to see if a name is already taken, just surf over to the Internic and use the Whois search engine to see if a name is already taken.

You must search the Internic, not the Internet, for names. Many times, a name will be taken but a site using that name isn't up yet. Simply checking the Internet and finding there was no site does not guarantee that the domain name is available.

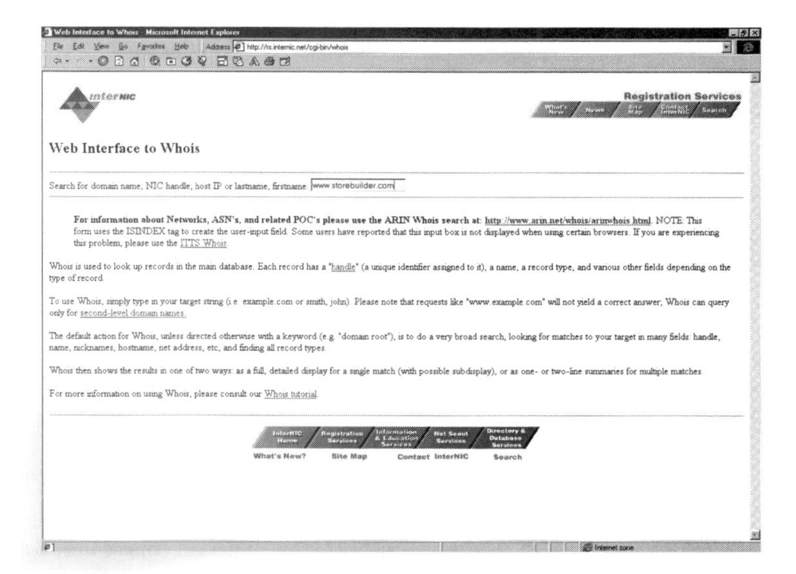

FIGURE 6.4
You can register your domain name at www.internic.net.

Why Not Use a Specialized Merchant Server or Set Up Your Own Server vs. Simple Web Hosting?

Many people starting stores might consider setting up their own server as part of their store launch. After all, with your own server you'll have more control. The problem with that is two-fold. The cost of purchasing your own server is at least $4,000–$5,000 for a good machine. Then you still have to get access to the Net set up with an ISP. Running such a server on anything but at least a fractional T-1 line is impossible, and the costs of running it on that fractional T-1 will be substantial (figure about $400–$600 a month depending on the exact circumstances.) That's why the majority of sites are hosted on some other company's server.

One other possibility you might have heard about is that of being housed specifically on a specialized server for stores, something like an online mall. Many new Web hosting companies are launching servers based on either Open Market's Web server product or Microsoft's Merchant Server. The problem here is that those services make their money on charging you more for access to these servers and they're more bent on reselling you all sorts of specialized database and merchant services add-ons. In some cases you are also required to purchase a license, which can set you back another $1,000–$2,000.

As you'll see and discover for yourself, smaller scale stores are better off keeping things simple. Although everyone hopes that some easy-to-use solutions come along, most of the commerce-server products we've seen are far too complex and pricey. As Tronix proves, you don't need anything more than a few basic CGI scripts and ultra-reliable Web hosting to pull off a successful store.

However, if you have a larger store, perhaps getting thousands of hits a day, and you're ringing up sale after sale, then you may need a more robust solution. In the software appendix of this book are listed all the major commerce server products with descriptions. These are best suited for the top five percent of stores. If you do go this route, the best recommendation is to hire a qualified commerce-server consultant and perhaps a full-fledged development person to set it all up.

Once your merchant server is up and running, you will need to either be trained by the consultant or hire a part-time to full-time administrator to run the server. If you need help finding these types of professionals, a well-run and decent sized ISP should be able to guide you in the right direction. Or you can call Open Market, Microsoft, iCat, or Netscape for a recommended consultant for their commerce-server solutions. You'll find their phone numbers in the software appendix.

Choosing the Right Software

All online stores are Web sites and Web sites need tools to help with development. As a store owner, you might decide to hire a firm or bring in an individual to develop your Web site. But this book is also about keeping costs down and flexibility up. Even if you get a good price for site design and development, there may be times you just want to put up a shot of a new product or change a price. If you're doing it yourself, you'll need good tools as much as you'd need them for more extensive development. That being said, here's what you'll need. Information on where to find these items is included in the software appendix at the back of this book.

Browsers

The most important piece of software any Net business needs is a Web browser. Since you are now going to deal with people viewing and using your own site, we recommend that you download the two top browsers: Netscape Communicator and Microsoft Internet Explorer.

Although you may have a personal browser preference, you'll find large groups of users viewing your site using the other browser. Because each browser has some slight differences in how pages are displayed, it's important that you be able to test any site designs or changes with both browsers to make sure there aren't any problems for users of either browser.

E-mail and Newsgroup Reader

A crucial aspect of any online store is the e-mail and newsgroup reading software you use. Make sure whatever package you use can filter incoming messages, manage large e-mail lists for newsletter mailings, and has a good address book for contact management and collecting a store mailing list that includes e-mail and traditional mail addresses. Eudora and Claris E-mailer are two excellent cross-platform e-mail packages.

Both Internet Explorer and Netscape Communicator also have good e-mail products you might consider using. On the PC side, there is also the popular Pegasus shareware e-mail package that has a lot of high-end features useful for mailing lists and filtering (see Figure 6.5). More will be covered on e-mail usage later in this book. For now, your assignment is to get a good e-mail application and learn how to use the incoming-filter features as well as how to construct contact lists in the address book segment that all of these programs have. Among the newsreaders, Free Agent and News Xpress are good products.

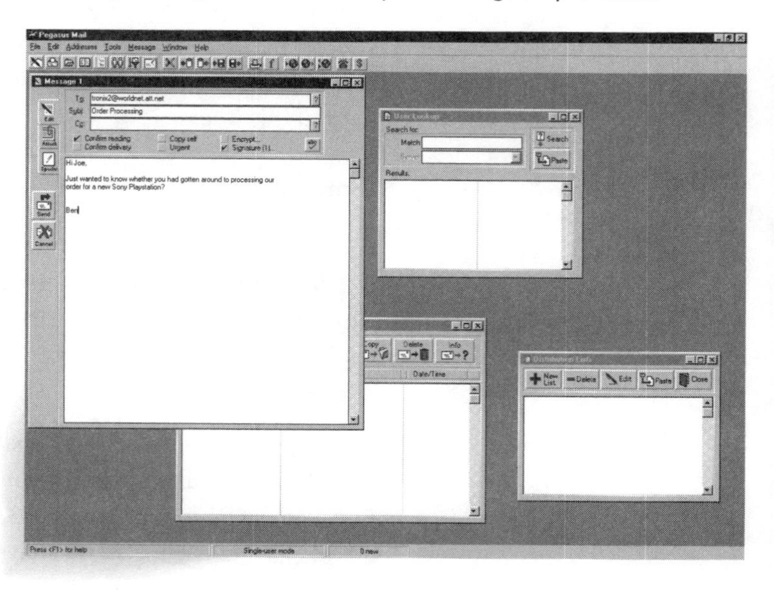

FIGURE 6.5
The Pegasus e-mail program.

FTP (File Transfer Protocol) Program

In order to upload new files to your Web site, you'll need an FTP program. If you're working on a PC, CuteFTP is the popular program (Figure 6.6). For Macs, Fetch is the most highly recommended FTP program.

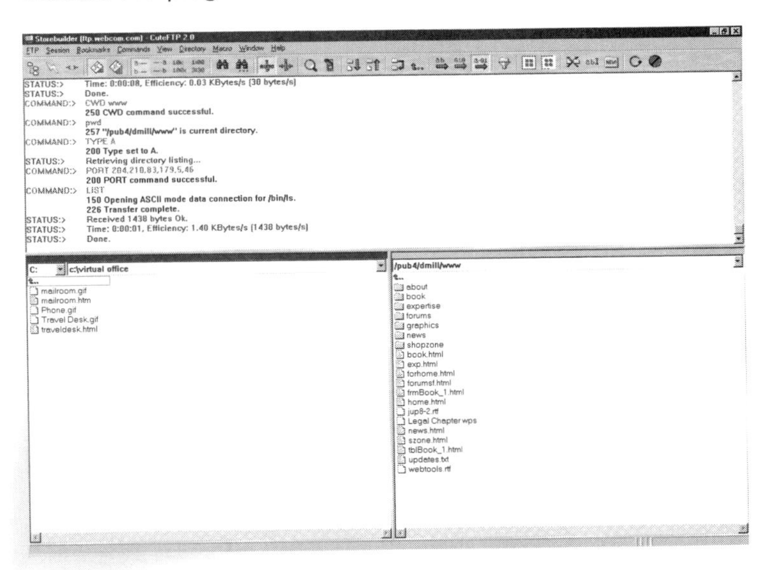

FIGURE 6.6
CuteFTP program in action.

HTML Editors

There are two types of HTML editors available: those that have graphic, visual, layout-type interfaces, often called Web authoring tools, and those that are specialized text editors. Ideally it would be great to have one super editor to recommend, but there isn't one that performs both functions undeniably well. The best solution is to get a visual editor to work with at first while you spec out the look of pages, tables, and so on. Then, when you have pages roughed out, you can switch to an HTML editor to clean up the code, add form items and scripts, plus periodically update items on your pages.

Visual Design Editors

There are a number of good visual Web editors out there. These are a few that are both easy to use and not terribly expensive.

Claris Homepage (Mac, Windows) is a nice, lower-end visual editor that even beginners will find excellent. Both Netscape Communicator and Microsoft Internet Explorer browser products include visual editors that are decent, especially considering the price. At the pricier end, you'll find GoLive CyberStudio, NetObjects Fusion, and Macromedia Dreamweaver.

HTML Code Editors

There are a number of HTML code editors available via shareware on the Web. The following four are the most highly recommended editors you can get. On the Mac, the entire Web editing community swears by BBEdit from Bare Bones Software; its advanced text-editing features make it a joy to use. On the PC side, three editors are worth mentioning. Homesite (Figure 6.7) from Allaire is an excellent product with lots of bells and whistles. Web Edit from Luckman Interactive/Nesbitt Software is also widely used, as is Hot Dog Pro from Sausage Software of Australia.

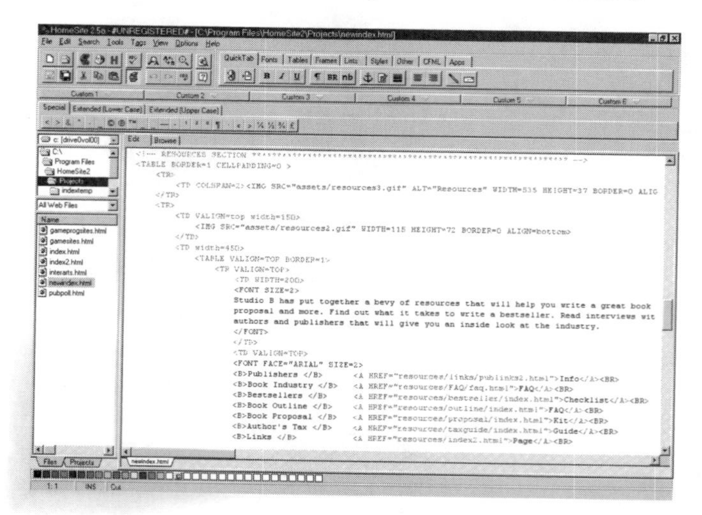

FIGURE 6.7
HTML editor in action.

Graphics Equipment and Imaging Software

Everyone needs to get some graphics onto their pages. They can be as simple as a scan of a product catalog or as complex as a full-page advertisement.

A good place to start is with a scanner—not an incredibly expensive one, but something that can scan an entire 8.5x11 page and that features 24-bit color depth. Hewlett-Packard, Umax, Microtek, and Agfa are quality manufacturers with solid models priced from $300–$1,000. Another image acquisition tool you might want to consider is a digital camera. Depending on what your store will be selling, a digital camera can be a really handy tool to have around for producing pictures of your merchandise. If you do decide to get a camera, get one that produces pictures at a resolution higher than 640x480. Several cameras, all listed under $1,000, produce better than 640x480 resolution. They are Kodak's DC50, and DC120 cameras, Olympus' 300L, and Cannon's Powershot. Over time expect many manufacturers to offer cameras that provide great resolution.

TIP ▸ ***When buying a digital camera, make sure you get the power supply the camera needs if it isn't included in the package. If you use batteries exclusively, you might end up spending a small fortune when you could just plug it into a wall if you have the power supply. Also get a decent tripod and good editing software. A tripod will help you take immeasurably better photos, and because camera images frequently need processing help (better than the free software products they typically include), you'll want to get a package like Photoshop to enhance the imagery.***

You should also acquire some decent image editing software. Chances are, something came with your scanner, which you may find useful (or not). Fortunately a number of good products, both shareware and commercial, are worth checking out.

You'll need a number of good tools for editing scanned photos and producing simple items like a nice logo, some graphical bullets, or colored backgrounds. Adobe Photoshop is available for both PCs and Macs and is one of the most popular programs going. At around $550, it's a bit expensive. If this is out of your price range, there are a couple of shareware products to consider. Paint Shop Pro for Windows by JASC is an excellent program and costs under $50 (Figure 6.8). Mac Paint is a low-end shareware package on the Mac, but it is not nearly as good to Photoshop as Paint Shop Pro are. Graphic Converter from Lemke Software is now very comparable to Paint Shop Pro. Photoshop, however, is the best product out there.

Once you've got a good scanner (and perhaps a camera) and an editing package, there isn't much more you need. Yes, you could go wild and buy all the fantastic art packages in the world, but that's a personal (and financial) decision. With the products we just mentioned, you can scan in any item, crop it down, do a little processing on it, and have it up on your site in a matter of minutes.

FIGURE 6.8
Paint Shop Pro in action.

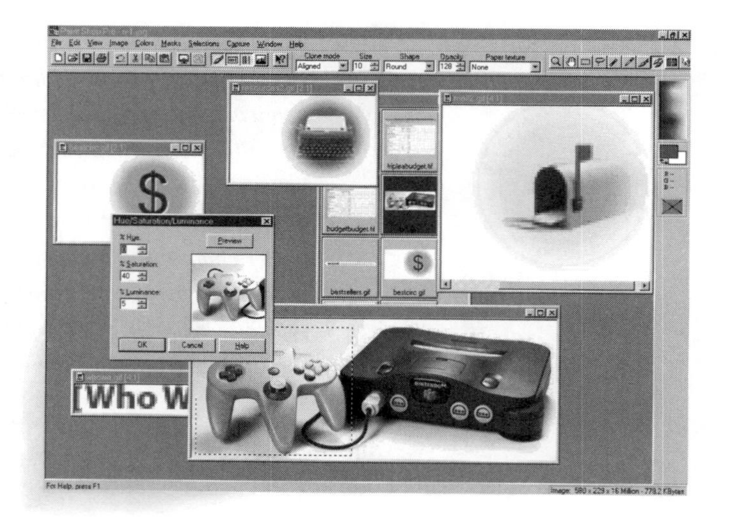

Other Software

Most of the software mentioned here relates to the tools you need to get online, send e-mail, and design and post Web pages. However, since this is the launch phase, you'll want to get a few other products.

Point of Sale Program

You may want to take the time now to get a good point of sale program. Point of sale programs are really designed for traditional stores, but they're great for mail order or Web stores as well. These programs let you enter inventory, print out an invoice, calculate sales tax and shipping, and provide sales reports at the end of the day, week, month or year.

JOE'S TAKE: *Fancy systems will eventually come along and combine traditional point of sale reports and processes with a Web-based store, but they'll be expensive and cumbersome until they're tried and tested. I continually find that by using a good point of sale tool offline, I'm able to assure myself that I've got a good product. In addition, because a large portion of your store's sales will come in as straight phone, fax, or e-mail orders, you're not going have the benefit of every order being automated through the Web site . That's reason enough to use a separate POS program to track sales information. The reports and other advanced features are quite important to analyze my stores success.*

Shipping and Tracking Software

All of the major shipping products and services are covered in Chapter 17. Be sure to check it out and get all of the services and software in place before you launch.

QuickBooks

What small business doesn't use this great program? As a store owner, you'll be writing checks for products, services, employees, and more every week. QuickBooks from Intuit makes it very easy to track expenses, cut checks, and compile the necessary tax records right from your computer. It's inexpensive, too.

America Online and CompuServe

Depending on your needs, you might want to consider America Online and CompuServe. Although their terms-of-service (and common netiquette) prevent you from blatantly posting ads for your store, you may find some online forums in which you can offer your expertise, find out about new products, or join communities that can bring potential customers to your store. AOL and CompuServe have more than 10 million members worldwide. You should at least check them out to see if there are some useful areas.

Joe's Take: *When I first started my store, I was on CompuServe's gamer forums a lot (in fact I was an early Sysop for them). While I didn't post obvious ads, people there eventually realized I had a video game store, and I got plenty of orders from those members without being the least bit intrusive or destructive to the forum.*

Wrap Up

We covered a lot of ground here and much of it seems to have less to do with actually building your store than you might have guessed. The next chapter covers more, but before you head off to it, think for a moment. Right now you might be trying to launch too quickly. The moral of this chapter is to get everything set right the first time.

As the story about Tronix shows, you can have a lot of problems if you jump in without much thought. If you do not consider every detail before launching your store, you may be bitten by a shaky ISP, a weak phone system, a clueless lawyer, etc. The best thing you can do during launch phase is take things slowly. Make sure you're fully ready to launch even before you upload your first pages to your site. Take the time to compare services and products and experiment with the software. Get into your space, make sure all the phone lines work, and spend the time making sure your distributors are 100 percent behind you.

When you go on the Web you don't have a lot of room for error. If you slip for just a second—your phones go out, your Web service goes down, your distributors won't ship you something, anything—you're going to have to do some scrambling to keep your customers.

If one customer has a bad experience or can't reach you, they might tell hundreds in a scathing post on a newsgroup. Check those newsgroups to find out what people think about your store and use that information to get better. Taking your time helps, watching the bottom line is key (far too often Web business burn through capital for no reason), and keeping things simple is paramount. The only time you've got to make mistakes, think things through and work out the kinks is before you broadcast to everyone and anyone.

Customers on the Web don't wait for you to fix things, and competitors will pounce on you faster than piranha on a drowning cow. That's why you need everything perfect the first time.

CASE STUDY

Getting Internet Service: A Horror Story

Now that everything is coming together, it's finally time to get the basic Internet site service put together for your store's launch. Starting up an Internet account is an adventure all its own, and not necessarily a fun one. When Tronix opened in 1994, the Web was still young, and the number of Internet service providers was limited. Net providers of yesterday were usually small firms that charged users by the hour, unless they paid a premium price for unlimited usage.

Without some basic knowledge of UNIX, it was almost impossible to explore anything the Net had to offer. There were no fancy Web browsers or Windows-based, mouse-driven, front-end Internet applications to shield the user from UNIX commands. After joining a service, you would simply get some basic applications to get you started, and a bunch of technical instructions on how to use functions such as e-mail, the file transfer protocol (FTP), Usenet newsgroups, and other Internet applications.

At that time, CompuServe was a total pleasure to use with its combined system of e-mail, forums, and file libraries, all available to the user with a simple sign-up procedure. In comparison, the Internet concept was difficult to grasp because nothing was neatly integrated.

When Tronix first started, we dealt with a major Internet Service Provider (ISP) on the scene—one of the first to offer a user-friendly way to gain access to most of the best features using an integrated, Windows- and Mac-based interface. It was possible to click around the Net, send and receive e-mail, download software, and explore thousands of newsgroups, all from the same interface. The most exciting discovery, of course, was the ability to see what the World Wide Web was all about.

As Tronix progressed through its first months, the Usenet newsgroups, in which people discuss a common interest, emerged as a good way to reach people. Knowing that everyone in a particular newsgroup had an interest that somehow related to Tronix, it was possible to do some minor advertising—just a few lines of text and a phone number. It started phones ringing and word of mouth did the rest. It was no overnight miracle, but business began increasing a bit with the addition of this new client base. After viewing some basic business Web sites, it became obvious that the next logical step for Tronix was to become an online store.

After spending enough time on the Net, you begin to realize the advantages and shortcomings of the service provider you chose. Tronix's ISP did not offer a service to help us start our own Web site.

We kept our account active anyway, just to access the newsgroups and take on the small number of e-mail orders. There weren't many options to start one's own Web site at the time, but Tronix eventually found a local service provider that offered full Internet access along with the ability to rent out space to host a Web site.

After Tronix's first Web site was up and running, business began to significantly increase, and links to the Tronix site began to spring up. But as the months passed, problems began to arise with the service. There was an increase in downtime, which usually means your service provider is doing maintenance, or something is not functioning properly on its end. This is, of course, the most frustrating scenario for any Web store owner—especially if your entire business relies on 24-hour access for your customers. Potential customers who visit your site for the first time only to see a message stating the address is not valid or the URL is not connecting, will think they've hit a dead link and might never return. Your current customers might even conclude that you went out of business! Not having Web access is like having people drive to your retail store, only to find it closed with no explanation. No e-mail is like having the phone company shut off service. No newsgroup access is like not having a TV, newspaper, or magazine to find out what's happening in the industry.

It became apparent that Tronix's service provider was a small, unorganized firm. After a series of announcements explaining why the Web site wasn't working on various days and apologies for not replying to e-mail in a timely fashion, it was time to find a new provider. Time was spent transferring the files which made up Tronix's Web site to a new host, tracking down customer e-mail addresses (which fortunately had been retained by the mail program), and sending out hundreds of "We've Moved" alerts, along with new e-mail and Web site address. There was no easy way to reach every customer, so it was necessary to keep the old account active for a few months so traffic heading to the old site could be redirected by a simple link.

Months passed, and more and more people found out about Tronix. The customer base had become quite large when the new ISP went down a few times and once again time was spent explaining to customers why they couldn't access the site. This began to happen more frequently, with explanations from the provider ranging from "we're installing new hard drives" or "we're changing phone companies because we're unhappy with our current service," to the oh-so-familiar "we're down for some minor maintenance."

Case Study, continued

During the course of 1996, everything ran fairly smoothly. Tronix made a name for itself, orders continued to increase and, in August, our ISP became non-operational and its phone was disconnected. Phone orders still came in, but the majority of orders came through the Web.

During this chaotic period a disk came in the mail from the communications giant, AT&T. It was a simple Internet start-up kit, announcing that AT&T had joined the ranks with other big guns to provide easy-to-use Internet access without spending a fortune. With one inexpensive flat rate, AT&T offered a basic Net package. It offered access to the newsgroups and, more importantly, e-mail. It took just one night to get up and running with AT&T.

Tronix's other account eventually came back on-line after a ridiculously long wait. It was having financial problems and the Web site would continue to be inaccessible.

CHAPTER SEVEN

Joe's Template For Store Site Design

Now that you have the grunt work wrapped up, it's time to have some fun while moving toward the goal of having your store up, running, and taking orders. The process of creating your Web site is similar to setting up a traditional store. You'll have a chance to exercise your creative muscles and you'll also need to spend some time researching other stores. There's no need to reinvent the wheel—or the store. Hopefully you will have some unique ideas of your own, but don't be afraid to check out other Web sites to see what works and, just as importantly, what doesn't. Combine that knowledge with your own ideas to build a functional store with sizzle.

This chapter is designed to help you create and construct your online store through simple HTML pages and some hard work, without spending a fortune. We'll point you toward some useful technical resources and give you some ideas about building a site that works for you and your customers.

Developing Your Own Web Site

HTML is the basis for developing text for display on the Web. As a store-owner, you should learn the basics of HTML. Learning HTML and creating Web pages is much easier than most people realize. However, there are some advanced HTML items and idiosyncrasies that can drive even HTML experts batty. Because it's easy to learn the basics but difficult to master HTML, you should keep things simple.

This book is not an HTML course. It assumes you have already learned the basics of HTML and how to use one of the many available HTML editors. If you haven't done this, here are a few tips for HTML and Web site production.

Get a Good HTML Tutorial and Reference Guide

A variety of Web sites offer tutorial information, and both Netscape and Microsoft maintain excellent reference guides you can print out. Table 7.1 includes information on several good books and Web sites that provide all the HTML education material one could want.

TIP ▸ ***When first learning HTML, don't bog yourself down learning every single command, because HTML has dozens and dozens of codes to master. However, you'll only use about 20 or 30 of them repeatedly. Table 7.2 is a list of the major HTML codes and items every store-owner should know.***

Table 7.1 HTML Resources

HTML Resource Books	HTML Resource Web Sites
HTML Sourcebook: A Complete Guide to HTML 3.2 and HTML Extensions by Ian S. Graham. Published by John Wiley & Sons. ISBN: 0-471-17575-7. List price: $29.95.	***Learning HTML 3.2 by Examples*** by Jukka Korpela. www.hut.fi/~jkorpela/ Clear reference and teaching source for HTML 3.2.
Using HTML: Special Edition by Tom Savola, Mark Brown, John Jung, Bill Brandon, Robe Megan. Published by Que Corp. ISBN: 0-789-70758-6. List price: $49.99.	**Microsoft HTML Reference** www.microsoft.com/workshop/author/newhtml/default.htm Describes HTML in an easy to understand reference, including those tags and extensions specific to Microsoft Internet Explorer.
HTML for the World Wide Web, Second Edition: Visual QuickStart Guide by Elizabeth Castro. Published by Peachpit Press. ISBN: 0-201-68862-X. List price: $17.95.	**Netscape's Documentation Site** developer.netscape.com/library/documentation/index.html Link here sends you to a list of documentation, including HTML provided directly by Netscape.
	HTML 3.2–4.0 Site www.w3.org/TR/WD-html40-970708/appendix/changes.html This Web page details the changes that will be made in HTML when it goes from the current 3.2 release to the upcoming 4.0 release.

Table 7.2 HTML Codes Every Store Owner Should Know

The basic text formatting tags	<B>, <I>, <U>, <H1>-<H6>, <FONT>
Positioning, paragraph and spacing tags	<CENTER>, , <NO BR>, <P>
Table tags	<TABLE>, <TR>, <TD>
List tags	<UL>, <OL>, <LI>
Form tags	<FORM>, <TEXT>, <TEXT AREA>, <SELECT>
Basic document tags	<BODY>, <TITLE>, <HTML>
Graphics and line tags	<IMAGE>, <HR>
Linking and anchor tags	<NAME>, <A HREF>, <A HREF="MAILTO:">

Learn to Write HTML at the Source Code Level

Using a Web page designer like FrontPage or Claris Homepage is a way to avoid learning HTML. Although these products make creating Web pages as easy as using a word processor, they don't eliminate the need for HTML knowledge. You will often need to modify HTML code directly. It's best to start learning HTML at the code level and then begin using an editor, modifying its generated code as needed.

The biggest problem with Web page creation programs is that results can vary when you view them in a browser. Complex tables and frames absolutely require source level editing.

It is fairly easy to write HTML directly. All you need is a simple text editor such as Notepad or an HTML editor, which is a specialized text editor for HTML coding. These are covered in Chapter 6.

Learn the Basics of Graphics Preparation

As you begin building your site, you'll need to prepare graphics for the Web. It's relatively easy once you have a graphics editor, which are also covered in Chapter 6. You'll be primarily concerned with three key graphics file formats: JPEG, GIF, and Animated GIF. Table 7.3 covers the basics of these formats and the reasons for using them. Table 7.4 includes some good Web sites and books concerning graphics for your Web pages.

TABLE 7.3 COMMON WEB GRAPHICS

Format	Description
JPEG **Best Used For:** Digital photos or large pictures of products. **Not So Good For:** Graphics with text, small logos or graphical buttons.	JPEG (Joint Photographic Experts Group) was created by a software developer consortium. This ensures that JPEG will remain a royalty-free file format. JPEG uses what graphics experts call a "lossy compression format," which means it will degrade the overall quality of the image to decrease the size of the file (99 percent of the time the loss is not noticeable). The compression feature of JPEG graphics makes them great for displaying digitized photos of products containing millions of colors. Most graphics on the Web are in the JPEG format. JPEG files can be saved in two variants: regular JPEG and a derivative known as Progressive JPEG. When Progressive JPEG files are created, the data is arranged so that the graphics are displayed as they are loaded. The graphics are initially very blurry but become progressively sharper as the data is loaded.
GIF **Best Used For:** Logos, text, graphical buttons, items which need to be irregularly shaped via transparency. **Not So Good For:** Photos or any graphic with more the 256 colors.	GIF (Graphics Interchange Format) was originally developed in the mid-1980s by the CompuServe online service. At the time, modem speeds of 9,600 bps or less were common. GIF was intended to provide a way to compress graphics so that they could be transported more quickly via modem. When the Web began to grow in popularity, GIF was adopted by Internet users as a standard graphics file format. GIF's strength is that it is pixel-perfect rendering. Unlike JPEG it is not a "lossy" format, making it good for logos, text and other graphics which aren't photographic in nature. GIF's biggest drawback is that it is limited to displaying just 8-bit graphics (256 colors). Extremely small, digitized photos don't look very good when rendered in the GIF format. GIF also offers a format, called GIF 89A, which lets you set one color of a graphic as transparent. Transparent GIFs are useful for creating graphics that let the background shine through.
Animated GIF **Best Used For:** Animated logos, displaying multiple shots of the same product.	Animated GIF is a specialized graphic file format that contains multiple graphics in the same file. It comes complete with information that denotes the time to wait before showing the next frame and whether it should loop the frames repeatedly. Animated GIFs are fairly easy to create with the programs mentioned in Chapter 6. They're great for adding liveliness to your page. Store-owners can create an Animated GIF that cycles through different shots of the same item or cycles through various items but with different colors. Again, the drawback is the 256-color limit.

TIP ▸ ***Free Web graphics sites are constantly going up and moving around. We've listed three of our favorites in Table 7.4, but you should consider regularly searching for new ones through search engines and indexes like Yahoo!, Lycos, or Hotbot.***

TABLE 7.4 WEB GRAPHICS BOOKS AND WEB SITES

GRAPHICS RESOURCE BOOKS	GRAPHICS RESOURCE WEB SITES
Designing Web Graphics by Lynda Weinman. Published by New Riders Publishing. ISBN: 1-56205-532-1.	**Jelane's Free Web Graphics** www.erinet.com/jelane/families/ An excellent, well-organized and very useful collection of free Web graphics including buttons, e-mail icons, and 256-color designs.
Designing Web Graphics 2 by Lynda Weinman. Published by New Riders Publishing. ISBN: 1-56205-715-4.	**Xoom Software** xoom.xoom.com Bullets, backgrounds, bars, icons and much more, all free for the taking.
Coloring Web Graphics by Lynda Weinman. Published by New Riders Publishing. ISBN: 1-56205-669-7.	**Amazing Free Stuff Pages** www.123go.com/drw/webs/graphic.htm This site which covers all the best free stuff for Web people has a very good—and up-to-date—list of some of the best free graphic sites on the Web.
GIF Animation Studio: Animating Your Web Site by Richard Koman. Published by O'Reilly & Associates. ISBN: 1-56592-230-1.	
GIF Animation Web Magic With CD by Shammus Mortier. Published by Hayden Books. ISBN: 1-56830-353-X.	
Web Graphics Tools & Techniques by Peter Kentie. Published by Peachpit Press. ISBN: 0-201-68813-1.	

TIP ▸ ***A great source of commercially available Web clip art is Photodisc. It markets a bunch of different graphics and CD-ROM collections available for sale on the Web site and through its catalog. Check out www.photodisc.com for more information.***

Learn the Basics of FTP Transfer to Place Files up on Your Web Site

Chapter 6 lists some of the popular FTP programs. FTP programs are what you use to send your Web pages, graphics, and other items directly to your Web site. Using an FTP program like CuteFTP or Fetch is fairly simple. If you're a novice, turn to the technical support person at your Web hosting company.

Using a Database-Backed Approach

Some store-owners use a database approach to create their sites. Price lists and products are commonly produced using database-backed systems. Often-changed items such as price, quantity, and new items can be quickly added by updating the underlying data. For all the benefits of this approach, there are a number of drawbacks to consider. The biggest drawback is that a database approach will require you to have a more complex Web site. This means you might need to hire someone to do your site development and you'll be a little more restricted in how you'll be able to display items. However, updating items will be easier.

You'll also need to have a developer create a custom Java or CGI approach to extract information from the database and then display the items in HTML on a Web page. Some hosting services will charge more for sites that use custom Java or CGI applets on their server.

If you're going to have several hundred items and numerous day-to-day price changes, then a database-driven Web site might be your best option. However, if you're going to have fairly static pricing and only a couple of hundred items or less, then maintaining a good set of HTML pages will keep things simpler and cheaper. If you want to create a database-driven Web site, you should talk with a capable Web site developer. There are also some store-in-a-box solutions like Viaweb and Check Out to make it even easier. However, these solutions tend to trade flexibility for ease-of-use.

The focus of the rest of this chapter is on straight HTML-created sites. Many of the tips are useful for those of you taking other approaches.

Constructing A User-Friendly Web Site

You can approach the structure of your Web site in many ways. The creativity and functionality of your site will determine, to a large extent, how well you compete in your particular market.

You'll want your customers to be impressed the first time—and every time—they visit. You'll learn how to maintain a streamlined site that is informative, easy to navigate, and does not burden the customer with unnecessary fluff. Whatever your formula may be, make sure it gets right to the point. The Tronix Web site is streamlined and easy to use.

Depending on your host, your rental fee may increase with the amount of space allocated for your site. Keeping your site lean will keep your monthly costs down. The entire Tronix site can be stored on a 3.5-inch floppy disk, which is a good source for backup. You can have 10 backups on your hard drive, but if something goes wrong (computer virus, hard drive failure, etc.), you'll always be covered. It's also great for transferring information between your office computer and home.

Here is how the Tronix Web site is structured:

- **Home page:** Also considered the main page, and the entrance to your virtual store.
- **Price lists:** Individual price lists, each with its own page, categorized by product line.
- **Shipping:** Information about shipping, the couriers you use, and their sample rates.
- **Specials:** A page dedicated to items on sale or weekly specials
- **News/Reviews:** An optional page that gives your site a friendlier, more informative atmosphere.
- **Order Form:** A secure form for handling your incoming orders.
- **What's New:** This page can be used to announce new products or Web changes.
- **Company policy:** Can also be considered a "before you order" page.
- **Common Questions:** This optional page can be used to answer frequently asked questions.

Home Page

Your home page (Figure 7.1) is the gateway to your business—the first page a customer views when accessing your site. It's the equivalent of a traditional store's window display. When you visit any store in the real world, the window display consists of various items, store hours, types of payment accepted and, in many cases, specials or close-outs. This is parallel to what happens in a cyberspace store, without the necessary finances for a sign, an awning, a locksmith, an alarm system, the replacement of damaged window panes, etc.

Your home page should contain your mailing address, telephone and fax numbers, hours of operation, and the types of payment accepted. For plastic payment, you may want to include small credit card logos, which resemble the decals adhered on the front window of any walk-in store.

You also might want to include additional images or logos for some of your top items, new arrivals, specials or sales. Don't overwhelm your customers with these. You want your customers to focus on those few items you're trying to move. You should also include dates when your business is closed (vacation, holidays) and, of course, your store's spiffy logo.

FIGURE 7.1
Tronix's home page.

Your Logo

One of the first elements involved in creating your home page is your company logo. There are a number of versatile graphic design programs that allow you to create a logo from a simple input of text. For the Tronix logo—and just about every other graphical item on the site—we use the powerful Adobe Photoshop and a fine shareware product called Paint Shop Pro. You should place your logo on the top half of your home page so that it will be one of the first objects your customers see.

Design your logo so it stands out but is not overly imposing; be aware of the color depth and size. The larger the logo in both size and in color count, the larger the file size. You should avoid creating a logo that loads slowly without a state of the art Internet connection. Apply this rule to all pages involving graphical images such as icons, visual enhancements, or photo images.

Joe's Take: *I've visited many sites where the company logo covered almost 50 percent of the home page and left me waiting...and waiting...and waiting for the page to load. I thought, if this is any indication of how the rest of this site is going to function, I'm not going to waste my time.*

TIP ▸ ***Take a good, long tour of other company home pages. This will usually trigger ideas of your own, and will allow you to sample the good, the bad, and the ugly. At each stop, ask yourself whether you would like to explore that company's site further or jump ship immediately. Take note of what you like and what you don't.***

Background Color or Patterns

Choosing a background color or pattern for your Web site may not sound like a tough decision, but your site will scream "UNPROFESSIONAL!" if you use clashing colors. Observe the backgrounds of other professional sites and you'll notice the classier sites tend to stay away from flashy colors or tiled backgrounds. With all the graphic options available today, you're still better off keeping things clean and simple. Solid backgrounds in light colors work well. Dark backgrounds can also be interesting, provided you have some artistic ability.

Black is Tronix's current background color of choice, particularly for a home page. White is also easy to work with, and no matter what color your foreground elements are, white will never interfere. Tronix has also used white in the past.

TIP ▸ ***Keep the color and theme of your site consistent. After you decide on a main page background color, think about the rest of your site. Keeping the pages all the same color is always a safe route, but varying the colors with shades will add flavor.***

Frames

Many Web sites are conformed to *frames*. Frames are independent panels that can change information or remain stationary with the same content no matter which part of a Web site you are exploring. The most common use of frames involves utilizing a main window to display the links that will lead visitors to various parts of your site. This stationary panel is present on each page, so navigational links remain visible and never have to reload. Most browsers support frames, but it does depend on the individual accessing the site. Some customers might be using older browsers or one of the newer, dedicated black boxes such as WebTV or Sega's Net Link, which originally did not support frames.

If you decide to use frames, make sure you also provide a duplicate set of navigational links (either text or button-style) on every page so your "non-framed" audience can get around. If you don't design your site to accommodate everyone, you will lose potential customers.

Image Maps vs. Individual Buttons

When designing your main menu of choices, decide whether you want to use generic text links, individual buttons, or an image map. Straight text links are the easiest to lay out, but a good set of icons always looks more inviting. It's a lot more fun clicking on visual objects than simple text. Navigational icons (Figure 7.2) simply add more flair to any Web site.

Image maps are a great alternative to independent buttons, especially if your site has numerous links. Having an image map load one sheet of choices can be faster than waiting for individual buttons to load one-by-one. Image maps are more complex to develop, and if you decide later to add a new category to your inventory, you'll have to design an entirely new image map to include any new pages.

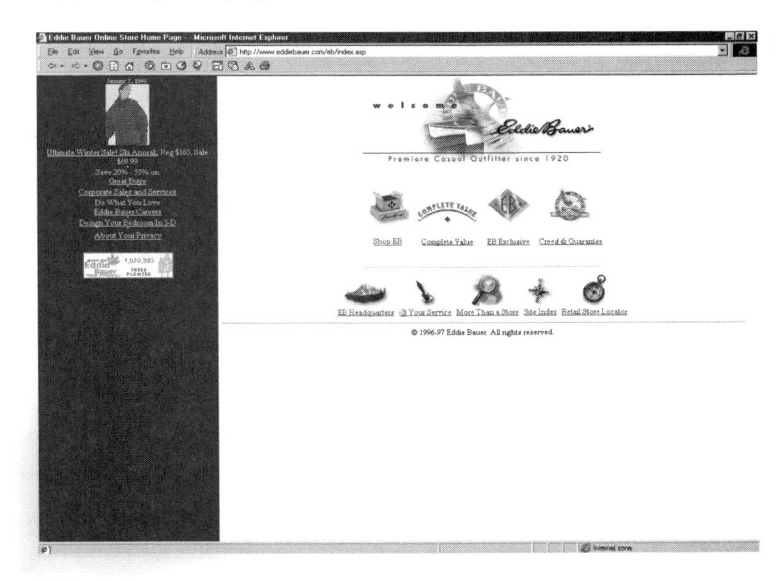

FIGURE 7.2
Navigational icons.

JOE'S TAKE: *Whichever graphical approach you choose for your main navigational panel, keep the objects small, and watch your color count. You want your customers to enjoy their visit and not be locked in a standstill by a slow-loading panel of options. I've visited many sites where the Webmaster spent a lot of time developing fancy rendered buttons, but I never stayed long enough to appreciate how talented he or she really was. A customer can't do a thing until she sees the menu. It's like going to a restaurant where the waiter doesn't arrive at your table until you've been seated for 20 minutes.*

Font Choices

Keeping your fonts similar in style and size on all pages is aesthetically pleasing and gives your site consistency. Main header information should be larger and bolder than your body text, and your fonts should be universal. That way text will display similarly on every browser no matter which computer the customer is using. Some fonts look great on a word processor, but not on a Web page. The same rule applies for different browsers. For example: small copyright text on the bottom of a page running under Netscape may be unreadable using Microsoft's Internet Explorer. Text that is too large could scare away customers.

TIP ▸ ***If you want fancy headers for your site but want to avoid using rare fonts, then render the headers as GIF graphics and use those. The downside to the flexibility of using really neat fonts is that every time you want to change the text or add a header, you're going to be toiling away in your graphics program.***

Hit Counters

A hit counter is an optional little CGI script that indicates how many people have visited a particular page of your site. Usually these gadgets look like an odometer. Tronix has a counter displayed on the main page and, although it's not essential, it has been a handy little add-on in determining the average of my daily traffic. You can put one on every page if you're interested in knowing which pages are getting the most attention, but that tends to be a bit showy.

Specifying Compatible Browsers or Resolutions

Design your site so that it works well with all resolutions. People use different computer configurations, from low-end to high-end, from PCs to Macs to UNIX boxes and even Amigas. Large text or graphics in high resolution will be enormous in the lower resolutions. Small text in low resolutions could become illegible in high resolution, and screen shots can become too small to appreciate. You can add a note to your main page specifying which resolution you modeled your site around but that forces customers to conform to your personal preference when, in fact, you should be catering to them.

TIP ▸ ***The best way to tackle the Web site resolution problem is to do all your modeling in a medium resolution. After you get some text and images on a sample page, save your work. Now fire up a browser such as Netscape or Internet Explorer, load your sample page, and flip between all of your computer's capable resolutions to see the results.***

In addition to using different resolutions people use different browsers and different versions of the same browser. Although these browsers try to maintain the same look, there are differences, often in the rendering of tables and spacing. Netscape Communicator is pickier than Microsoft Internet Explorer in terms of how tables are rendered. Have both browsers available on your machine to test pages. Ask regular customers or friends with different versions of browsers to periodically check out your site and let you know if something isn't working right.

TIP ▸ ***As HTML progresses, make sure you don't get too far in front of your customer base. While new tags or features may seem useful to adopt because of their functionality, many customers might not have downloaded the browsers that can render these new tags. When Netscape first added frames as a feature, many sites jumped to use them only to hear the screams of users who couldn't use the site as a result.***

Accessible, Consistent Links

Your main page is the hub of your store. Every major link involved with a customer's visit should be immediately accessible from the home page. Have you ever walked into a department store looking for a simple item and found one of those obscure maps or had to deal with a frightened information booth clerk surrounded by a gang of rabid customers? Don't let your home page resemble this.

Your major home page hyperlinks should take your customers to price lists, shipping information, company policy, a "what's new" page, your on-line order form, and anywhere else they need to go. Other important links may include any specials or sales (if you want them separate from your price lists), a page for any news or reviews related to your business, and a page for common questions and answers about your company. It's also important to include your e-mail address, so customers can send you mail if they have further inquiries, general comments, or advice.

Once you decide where and how your links will appear on your home page, carry this layout over to every page on your Web site. This consistency will make it easy for your customers to navigate your site.

TIP ▸ ***Customer feedback is incredibly important. Read and reply to their comments and suggestions, as it could have a great impact on the way your site turns out. You'll get valuable Web site tips from customers, some of whom will be experts in fields such as graphic and Web design. You needn't make changes to your Web site in response to every negative comment or good idea. But if more than one customer makes a similar suggestion—positive or negative—it's likely worth looking into.***

Price Lists

It is imperative to keep your price list page (Figure 7.3) clear, uncluttered, and fully functional. This is an informative page with one purpose—letting your customers know how much everything costs. Customers need to be able to find the product they want and immediately get the price without any further effort.

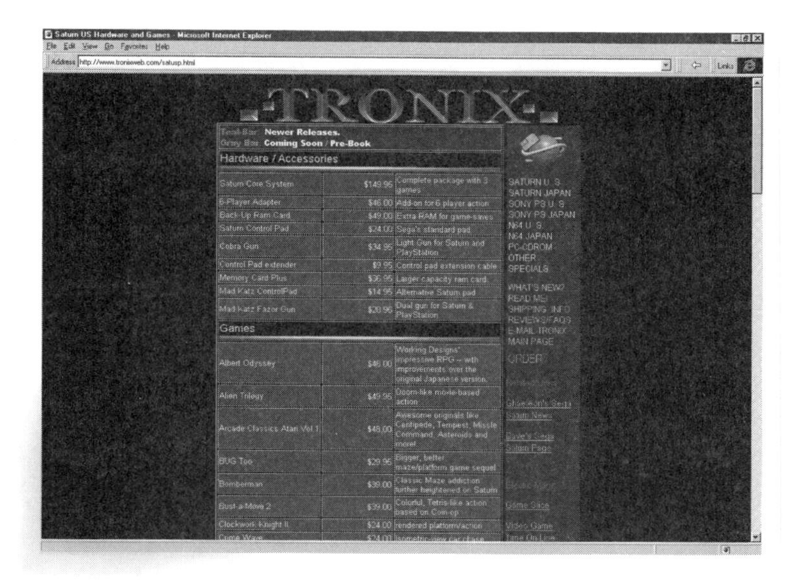

Figure 7.3
Tronix's price list.

One issue that will arise is whether you should list an item without a price. Depending on what you're selling, you may not know the price of an item until you get it in stock. When Tronix first opened, it used to post TBD (To Be Determined) for unpriced items. However, customers want a price and the lack of one might lead customers to believe you're either out of the item or the price is so high you don't want to list it. In the end, a solid price is best.

Joe's Take: *At first I used TBD as an excuse to list upcoming items and bulk up my stocking lists. It was pure filler and made it look like there were titles in stock that actually weren't—especially when the Nintendo 64 had just shipped and there were only two or three games available. Later, people got confused about TBD and I got so many calls and criticism I dropped TBD as a policy. Eventually I got better at setting prices.*

Using Tables

Tables work best with price lists because your content is organized in rows and columns, all perfectly aligned to your preference. The versatility of tables allows you to add or delete rows as your inventory changes. A good layout to use is a three-column setup. The first cell of a row contains the name of the item, followed by the price, which should be properly aligned to the right so all decimal points are vertically justified. The third cell should include a brief (one line) description of the product.

You can add columns depending on your line of business. You may want to list an item's color, style, dimension, and whether it's in or out of stock. You can even include a small icon that is linked to a screen shot of the item. While tables keep price lists organized, they're a bit of a hassle to update. A WYSIWYG HTML editor is best suited for quick table updating. Once you become familiar with HTML, you can easily load the page into any HTML text editor and do it manually.

If you study the HTML layout of your price list pages, you can see where each item and its related information starts and ends by the accompanying table-related tags. You can keep a template of one complete row on a simple text editor such as Microsoft Notepad as long as you save it as text only. If you need to add a new item to your price list during a busy day, you can fill in the item, price and description like this:

```
<TR>
<TD><FONT SIZE="2" FACE="ARIAL"> Item goes here </FONT></TD>
<TD ALIGN="RIGHT"><FONT SIZE="2" FACE="ARIAL"> Price goes here </FONT></TD>
<TD><FONT SIZE="2" FACE="ARIAL"> Description goes here </FONT></TD>
</TR>
```

Then copy and paste this section directly where it's needed.

Tables take a bit longer to load up then straight bodies of text so don't make your tables too large. If a particular line of products that you sell contains many items, you may want to consider splitting the tables onto a few pages, rather than having a customer wait for a huge price list to load. Just be sure you make it obvious the list continues onto other pages by adding additional links as needed.

Organizing Various Categories

Categories should be separated logically. How many types of individual products will you sell? How many product lines do you have? Will they all be similar but from different manufacturers? Ultimately, you want your customers to find what they are looking for without having to bounce from page to page. Before you lay your tables out online, plan them out on paper. If your inventory consists of jewelry you might want to separate your products by types—earrings, broaches, necklaces, rings, bracelets, etc. Or you could have separate price lists for different manufacturers or designers. If your inventory is small, you could separate it more simply—gold on one page, silver on the other.

TIP ▸ ***You can link Web sites relating to your products right on your price lists. Customers may want to learn more about the product before making a purchase. Keeping some handy links off on a side bar will provide access to further information.***

Highlighting Your Newest Items

When new releases arrive, it's easy—and a good idea—to make them immediately noticeable against your previous stock (Figure 7.4). After you enter the new items into your tables, you can change the cell's color so an entire row is highlighted. Using good color combinations, customers can immediately spot the new items on your price lists. Other possibilities are highlighting just the text color, changing the font to bold face, or adding an icon that says "New" to the left of the item listing.

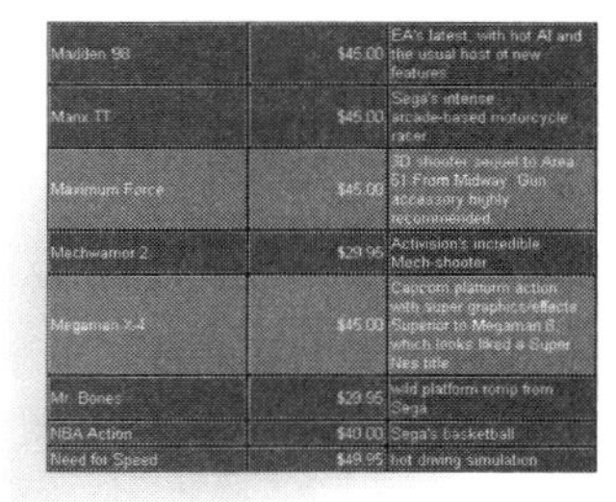

Madden 98	$45.00	EA's latest, with hot AI and the usual host of new features
Manx TT	$45.00	Sega's intense arcade-based motorcycle racer
Maximum Force	$45.00	3D shooter sequel to Area 51 From Midway. Gun accessory highly recommended
Mechwarrior 2	$29.95	Activision's incredible Mech-shooter
Megaman X-4	$45.00	Capcom platform action with super graphics/effects Superior to Megaman 8, which looks liked a Super Nes title
Mr. Bones	$29.95	wild platform romp from Sega
NBA Action	$40.00	Sega's basketball
Need for Speed	$49.95	hot driving simulation

FIGURE 7.4
New items are highlighted on the price list.

There are many Web sites with interesting public domain icons, such as pointing arrows and animated "New" symbols. If you don't like what's out there, design one yourself. You can even develop your own fancy icon which represents new stock; just be sure to address its meaning by adding a legend to the top of your price list.

Using JPEGS with Your Price List

Adding digitized shots of products to your site gives the customer an idea of what the product looks like. Depending on the size of your inventory, you can add photos for every item you sell, or just selected titles you feel customers would enjoy viewing. With a good scanner or digital camera and an image-processing program like Adobe Photoshop, you can save your images in JPEG format and link them to your items in a number of ways. You can have a page specifically dedicated to items that have digitized shots or you can turn the item into a link directly from the price list.

JPEG images shouldn't be too large or you will try your customer's patience. Tronix processes all of its images through Adobe Photoshop using an 800x600 resolution. Finished products are reduced to a maximum of 250x250 pixels. With this size, you can have about four images on one screen without bogging down the transmission. The ease with which an item can be scanned depends on its size and shape. CDs or computer games work fine, but your business may be dealing with much larger items. Scanning a Tiffany lamp or designer beach ball would be quite a feat. This is where a camera or a digital camera can come into play. See the sidebar on digital cameras for more information.

TIP ▸ ***There's always a way to get a scanned image of an item on a Web site, no matter the size. Start by looking at the packaging. Does it contain a picture of the item that can be scanned? Ask your supplier if they have any promotional materials or empty packages you can use. Of course, if you have a camera, you can simply take a sharp photo of the actual product.***

Digital Cameras

Storeowners who have products that can't fit on a scanner are increasingly turning to digital cameras to create product shots. Digital cameras are especially popular with real estate agents. The great thing about digital cameras is that they reduce the time between taking a photo and placing it on your Web site. If you use a conventional camera you've got to get the film developed and then scan the resulting photos. A digital image can be transferred immediately into your computer. A digital camera also gives you immediate feedback about the photo. Here are some tips on using digital cameras to create product shots for your store:

Get a camera with 640x480 or better resolution

Most of today's cameras create pictures of 640x480 or better resolution. Several manufacturers have created cameras that sell for less than $1,000 and provide 1,024x768 or better resolution. The higher the resolution you can afford, the better. Although you'll reduce it to a 250x250 or smaller resolution, your goal is to reduce from the highest quality photo possible. The standard resolution for graphics on the Web is 72 dpi.

Get the power supply for the camera

Digital cameras eat batteries for lunch. If your desired camera doesn't come with a power supply, get one. The more you're able to draw power out of an outlet instead of from batteries, the more money you'll save.

Shoot in front of a backdrop

Most product shots will display best and be easiest to edit if they're photographed with a plain background such as a white foam board. Once you've shot the item you'll be able to cut away all the shadows and other background and improve the image and its sharpness.

Get lots of light—daylight works best

Digital cameras love light. Low-light conditions are terrible and even artificial light isn't great. If you can, shoot in daylight conditions.

Fill the viewfinder with the item you're shooting

Since you have a finite amount of pixels per photograph, make the most of them. Don't try and frame the background around the object since you'll eventually cut it out in a paint program anyway.

Top Sellers

Hot-selling items can have their own spot on your price list or even your home page. You can create a "Top 10" list that can be changed on a weekly or monthly basis. You can post this right on your home page or add it as a small side link above your price lists.

Shipping

Your shipping page should contain all the necessary information so customers can get an idea of what fees they will be paying in addition to their purchase. You should include a list of available couriers, your shipping cut-off times, and any e-mail and phone order deadlines you might have. The main part of the shipping page should be your sample rate chart. For a far more detailed discussion of your shipping page, refer to Chapter 17.

Specials

Sales and specials are great ways to unload older stock. Many times your own distributors will be facing the same situation and will offer you a reduced price to get rid of stock. You don't necessarily have to buy their slow-moving titles, but you can combine them with your own sale items and bring them into stock when a customer places an order. You can also theme your sales around holidays, such as a Fourth of July sale or after Christmas specials. The specials (Figure 7.5) should be presented in the same format as your regular price lists. You can highlight your newly reduced items as you did your new releases. If you have any specific rules about your sale items, such as "all sales final," display this information above your price list. Another way to advertise specials is on your standard price list. You can simply add a sale icon next to the reduced title, highlight the entire row with an alternate color, change the color of the typeface to red, etc. Another option is using a font strike-through that displays a slash across the original price with your lower price added underneath. Offering periodic sales can easily expand your customer base.

News and Reviews

You can also set up a page with news and/or reviews (Figure 7.6) related to your products. Depending on the nature of your business, you can post your own personal reviews of particular products, and even devise your own rating system. Articles of interest might be press releases or general industry news. If you find information about your products on other Web sites, you can add small articles with embedded links that lead to those sites. This page might also be a good place for rumors—information you heard through the grapevine about upcoming products. However, be careful what you post and always consider the source.

Figure 7.5
A page of specials for Tronix customers.

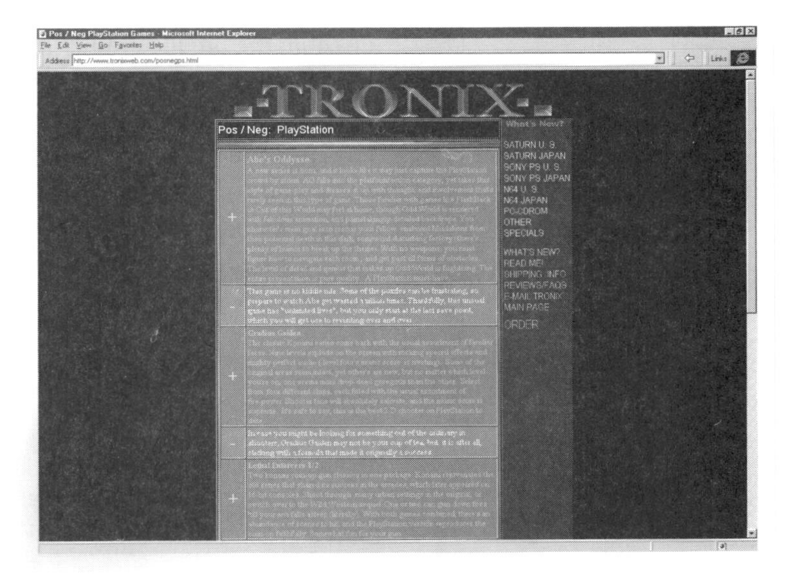

Figure 7.6
Tronix's news/reviews page.

Having a page of news or reviews is a bonus for your customers. It separates your business from the many generic cyberstores and shows that you care about your customers and the products you're selling. This area of your Web site will also complement your store by giving it an informative atmosphere. People will turn to your site as a resource and many of them will become customers. In Tronix's case, it's not uncommon to see newsgroup postings referring to the informational aspects of the site. (For more on using the newsgroups to build your customer base, see Chapter 10).

Review Honestly

If you plan on posting your own reviews about products, be honest with your audience. If you give a 5-star rating to a loser item that's been sitting in your inventory for ages, you'll lose your credibility. And if you hand out fawning reviews to all of your products, customers won't be able to differentiate between the truly outstanding and the hype. After buying a couple of mediocre products because of top-notch reviews, people will stop believing what you have to say. Instead, tell your audience it's not the greatest product and put it on sale. You can always discount the product, rather than having a customer purchase it after reading glowing (and embellished) reviews on your Web site. It's better to lose a few short-term bucks than your long-term reputation.

TIP ▸ ***Keep reviews short. Lengthy content on the Web gets tuned out. Short paragraphs that get to the point quickly work better.***

Order Form

When Tronix first came into existence, credit card transactions on the Internet could be frightening. Many customers either called by phone or took the risk of sending all their information through standard e-mail. Tronix has never encountered any hacker-related problems, but the chance of someone breaking into the service provider was always something to worry about. Customers were warned that sending their credit card information through e-mail was not safe, but many of them continued to use this method. International customers were the most common users of this method of payment because of the time difference or the fact that they simply didn't want to make an expensive overseas phone call.

As the Internet matured, online stores and shopping malls premiered at a startling pace and the Internet became a viable tool for commerce. (For details on secure transactions, see Chapter 14). New customers inquired about safely sending credit card information to Tronix. They didn't want to call or fax long distance, and they weren't comfortable sending their credit card information through e-mail.

As customers became more interested in placing credit card orders, it became necessary to build an online order form, which can be one of the most difficult additions to your Web site. Tronix's Web hosting service supported Secure Sockets Layer (SSL) and offered simple template forms for its clients to download and experiment with. There were three parts to this kind of form:

- **The form itself,** which contains all the fields to be filled out by your customer.
- **A simple ASCII text page,** which contains all the customer information that is extracted from the form and immediately sent to your e-mail address.
- **The "Success" page,** which is invoked after your customer submits the form. It's basically a follow-up page with final notes to the customer and, of course, a courteous thank you comment.

Your secure, online order form (Figure 7.7) should be accessible and easily identifiable on every page of your site. You can have a small icon separate from your other links, or you can keep it uniform along with your order categories. Whether you prefer a button, icon, or straight text hyperlink, it makes sense to give it a color that stands out from your other links. This is the one link that will present your customer with an order form, which should ultimately produce a sale.

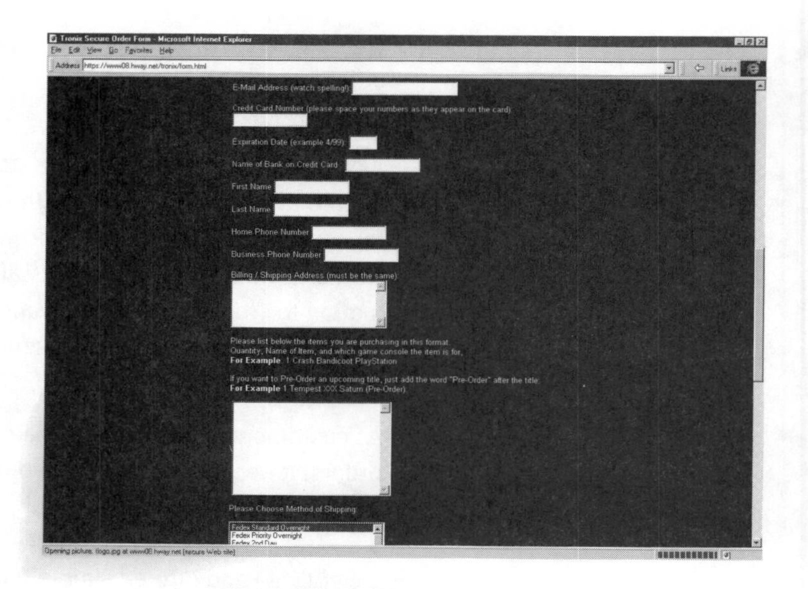

FIGURE 7.7
Tronix's order form.

Required Fields

The order form should be carefully designed and must include all the required fields needed to process your customer's order. It's essential for a solid online form to include the following fields:

Personal Information

- First Name.
- Last Name.
- Middle Initial.
- Home Address or Business Address.
- Home/Business Phone Number.
- E-mail Return Address.
- Credit Card Type.

- Credit Card Number.
- Expiration Date.
- Name of the Issuing Bank of the Credit Card (for Visa and MasterCard).

Order Information

- Item(s).
- Quantity.
- Color/Size/Style (if applicable).
- Shipping Choice.
- Submit and Reset Buttons.

Optional

- Fax.
- Phone number of credit card issuing bank (for Visa and MasterCard).
- COD.
- Pre-Order.

Field Construction

Fields should have enough space to fit all the necessary information. For instance, an expiration date usually consists of five characters: the month, a slash, and the year (05/99 for example). The credit card number field should provide enough room for all the spaces in between the groups of digits. Spaces count as characters, so if you only leave your customer enough room for the credit card digits, you'll find the process of entering the credit card number into your point of sale program much slower and with more chance of error. Look at the difference:

No spacing:	4121444455552222
Proper spacing:	4121 4444 5555 2222

Also, leave plenty of extra room in the name fields. You need to accommodate Patricia Wojechowski as well as Ed Ott.

Provide Specific Instructions

Emphasize the importance of filling out every field carefully and correctly. If a name or address is incorrectly entered, it could lead to a customer's order sitting in a shipper's warehouse until the mistake is corrected. If a customer incorrectly types his or her credit card number, your authorization terminal will simply throw it back at you and you'll have to contact the customer for the correct information. This will slow down the order and will be especially frustrating if the customer chose an overnight service and was expecting to receive a package the next morning.

TIP ▸ ***If you notice a customer is using a Visa or MasterCard and neglected to include the name of the issuing bank, immediately contact the customer and obtain that information. Failing to include the bank name might simply be an accident or it might mean the customer only had a stolen number but no card.***

Optional Fields

There are various optional fields to consider. If you honor CODs, you can add this as a check-off box after your credit card fields. Some customers will ask whether they can pre-order an upcoming item that hasn't been released by the manufacturer. You can add a check-off box for pre-orders, or have the customer type "Pre-Order" next to the item in that field.

Some mail order companies will only ship to the card holder address that is on file with the issuing bank. Following this rule will limit fraud. After you establish a good relationship with a customer, you can consider shipping products to alternative addresses, such as a business or a relative's house.

Define Policies Clearly

Before your customer clicks the "Submit" button, you should clarify how the order will be handled. For example:

- When and how the customer will be contacted (e.g., during business hours, before a certain time, in the evening, the following day, by phone or email?).
- Additional fees (e.g., handling, taxes).
- Options for out of stock orders.
- The deadline for orders.
- When the customer will be billed.

Whatever rules your company has established, make sure they are posted clearly so the customer is aware of them *before* placing an order. You can have this information explained directly above your order form, or provide a separate page for your company policies. Encourage your customers to read this information.

Success!

After a customer submits an order, he or she should be presented with a "success" page. The success page is simply a final note that shows the order was submitted correctly. You can post your thank you and perhaps reiterate a few important factors (like when they'll be contacted). You can finish this page with your address, phone number and hours of operation within your time zone. This is a good final reminder, because there are plenty of international customers who don't realize they're submitting an order early in the day, while you're in bed dreaming about being a rich and famous online retailer.

Updates

An "Updates" or "What's New" page (Figure 7.8) is a must-have, especially for sites that are constantly under construction with new items or changes. For retailing, it's essential to keep your customers up to date on any new happenings in your business. As new products are brought into stock, you'll want your customers to know what they are and when they arrived. Updates for special announcements such as a sale, a price change, a highly requested restock, or any key cosmetic changes to your Web site can be easily found on one page, separated by the date the event occurred. Rather than having separate pages for new items and Web-related updates, it might be more convenient to combine the pages and minimize the need for page hopping.

How important is an update page? You have an active group of customers who check out your site every day, yet without an update page those customers can't tell whether anything new is going on unless they hunt through the various pages of your store and fall upon a new release. If they aren't the kind of person to hang around long, they'll never know whether you just received something they've been looking for. It would be a mistake to make dramatic Web modifications without letting your regulars know about it. It would be like walking into your office one morning and finding that the night maid reorganized your desk without telling you where your calculator ended up.

Date Your Updates

After you complete the day's updates, add a notice to your home page telling people when the site was last updated. There's no need to post uneventful updates, such as a background color change on your price tables, a new font you decided to use, or a new parakeet named Jake in the office.

Tronix has confined all updates to one page labeled "What's New." Interestingly enough, this page has the highest hit-count on the Tronix site. The page consists of a clean table format, separated by month and broken down by the dates on which updates were made.

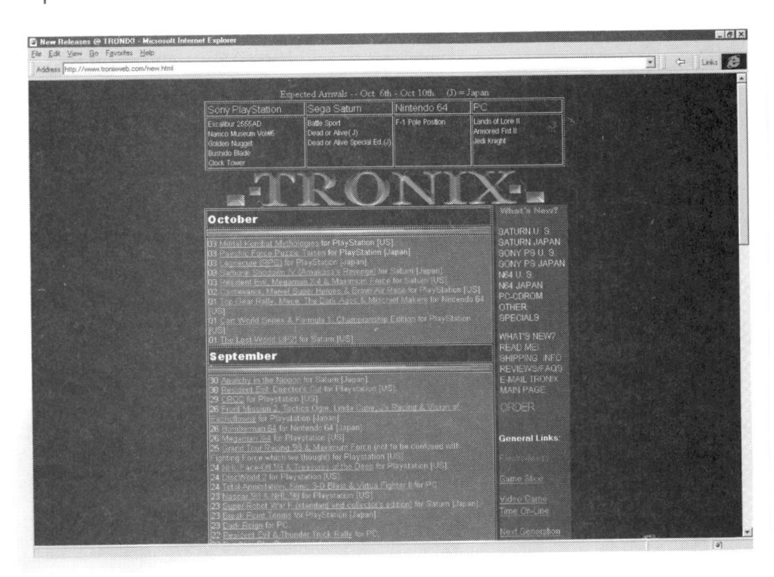

FIGURE 7.8
Tronix's "What's New" page.

TIP ▸ ***Link each announcement to its respective page. Customers should be able to jump right to the page or specific area of a page to get more information on the newly announced item or update. Remove all outdated information. Customers are more interested in what's new, not what arrived in stock or changes you made six months ago. The three most recent months are plenty.***

Company Policy

Every retail business has a company policy or set of rules governing transactions; your cyberstore should be no different. It is extremely important to list all of your policies to avoid misunderstandings between you and your customers. Think about what your customers need to know before purchasing an item and present it clearly. It will save you a lot of headaches and even a possible lawsuit.

What you include on your company policy page (Figure 7.9) will vary depending on your type of business. Some of the information you should include:

- Return policy and refunds.
- Warranty details.
- Payment.
- Credit card issues (theft or unauthorized use).
- Bad checks.
- Refused CODs.
- Rules on special orders.
- Cancelled orders.

TIP ▸ ***If you're unsure about what to include in your company policy statement, check out some other mail-order sites like L.L. Bean or Eddie Bauer to get an idea of how they present their policies.***

FIGURE 7.9
Tronix's company policies.

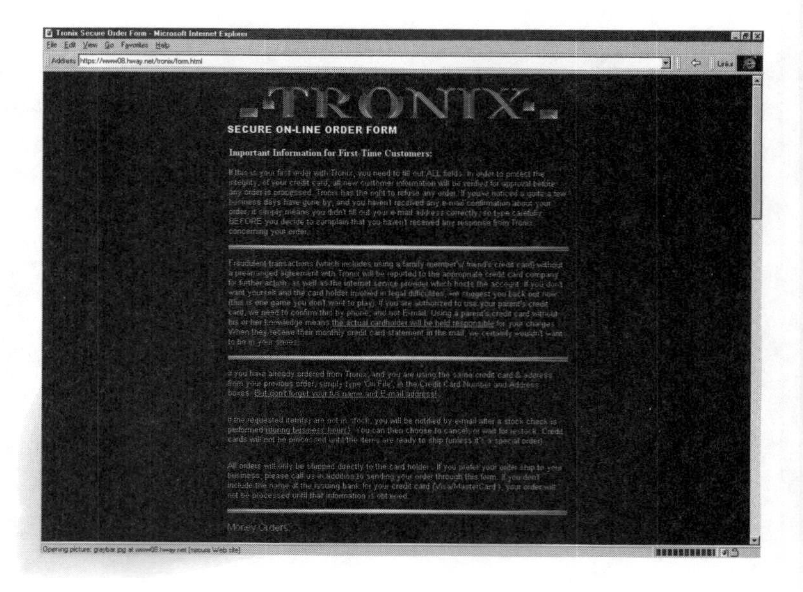

FAQ

As your store grows, you'll answer more e-mail than you can imagine. Some of it will turn into a sale. Customers may ask simple questions that you don't have time to answer. A good FAQ (Frequently Asked Questions) page (Figure 7.10) can help weed out some of the repetitive inquiries. A simple question and answer layout works best. For example:

> **Question:** Why are your DaVinci wine glasses so much more expensive than the other brands?
>
> **Answer:** Because they are imported from Italy, and the rest of our wine glasses are made in the United States.
>
> **Question:** What is the best time of day to place an order to ensure it will be processed and shipped that same day?
>
> **Answer:** If placing an order by e-mail, it's best to send us your order the previous night, or before 3 p.m. that day. For further information, please visit our Shipping Page.

TIP ▸ ***A good idea for an optional page is one that includes customer compliments. If your customers, especially first-time visitors, can see how happy your other customers are, they will have more confidence in your service and feel better about making a purchase.***

Content for All Pages

There are a few things you should include on every page, including a copyright notice to discourage competitors or users from stealing graphics or review content. You can also include your phone number, address and store hours on every page. Not everyone will come in the front door. If you have this information at the bottom of every page, you'll never have a customer searching in frustration.

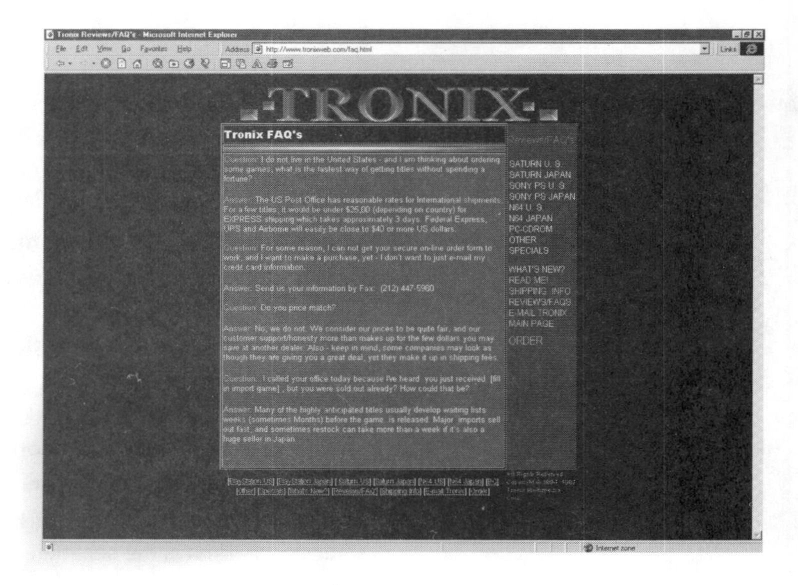

FIGURE 7.10
Tronix's FAQ.

Another thing to have is a small e-mail link to you or your Webmaster with a message on the bottom in small type "Site problems or comments <EMAIL>." If someone notices a dead link or a problem with your page or site you'll quickly get feedback. The easier you make it to give feedback, the more of it you'll get.

Viaweb Store

Many businesses hire an individual or a company specializing in Web development to design and maintain a Web site. The initial cost to have a company build and design your Web site can be quite high and you'll have to pay a weekly or monthly fee to keep it maintained. One company, Viaweb, has been successful helping online stores get started at a reasonable cost.

Viaweb Store is a combination of an authoring tool and a hosting service. There is no start-up fee. Stores selling up to 20 items pay $100 a month while those selling up to 1,000 items pay $300 a month. You don't need to know any HTML—you simply enter the necessary information (names, prices, and other information about your products) and it takes less than a minute to add a new item.

You build your store on Viaweb's server using a point and click interface. All you need for software is a normal browser and Viaweb serves your finished site. Orders are accepted securely using the Netscape Commerce Server and you can retrieve orders from Viaweb's server. You can change your site or retrieve orders whenever you want.

Viaweb says its Viamall is serving more than 3.3 million page views per month, or about 23 million hits. Viamall orders are running at more than $450,000 per month.

On to Inventory

Absorb as much useful information as you can as you build your Web site. Refer to this chapter and the resources we have provided and also study as many Web sites and stores as possible. You never know where you'll find a neat design idea or a new wrinkle to keep customers surfing back to your store.

The key to building a strong store site is balancing flair and functionality. While you want to keep your site simple, quick to load, and easy to navigate, you don't want to make it dull. The more you learn by reading and studying other sites, the easier it will be for you to find this balance.

Now that you know how to get your site up and running, it's on to Chapter 8. We'll show you how to stock your shelves and keep product moving while maintaining a reasonably small inventory.

CHAPTER EIGHT

Stocking Your Store

One of the great things about owning a Web store is that no one needs to see how, where, or what you actually stock. On the other hand, it can be difficult to initially find cooperative distributors and/or producers to work with. The size of your business, its financial stability, your cash flow, and your confidence in the salability of your products are among the factors that determine the size of your store. To top it off, the idea of a Web store can be a bit frightening to distributors who aren't as impressed by or as educated about Web retailing as you are.

Many Web merchants have successfully minimized their risk by keeping inventory as small as possible. They then rely on speedy distributor turnaround or patient customers. As customers place orders, the store receives the needed products from the distributor or manufacturer and ships them. Although the store appears to have a large stock, in fact it is primarily paying for pre-sold items. This can backfire if the order is for a hot item and it is impossible to get the item in the customer's hands when he wants it. Often a next-day order needs to be in stock to satisfy customer demand. In that case, knowing what items to stock is very important.

In most cases, Web stores follow the 80/20 rule. They stock the 20 percent of available products that they expect 80 percent of the customers to regularly order. Remaining products are special orders. In this model, knowing which products are worth stocking and which ones aren't is crucial to your store's success. Until you have a good handle on that, the smaller the stock you can carry, the better.

TIP ▸ ***Superior knowledge of which products will sell and the ability to soothe a customer while you await the product's arrival will help you as a Web retailer. Losing sales due to inventory misses draws the ire of any retailer. As customer inquiries begin to roll in, keep track of what people are asking about. Keep a small stock of the most popular items.***

Getting Product

The first stage of stocking your store is acquiring items. Some of you will be selling products you make, but most of you will exclusively or partially sell items made by other companies. This requires you to win support from these companies or individuals.

Building Relationships with Manufacturers, Distributors, or Yourself

Unless you are building the products yourself, you'll need to build comfortable relationships with manufacturers and distributors. It is not always easy to win their confidence. A lot of work goes into establishing the type of successful relationship that will benefit your business.

First you must decide where and how you will obtain your merchandise. Will you work directly with the manufacturer or go through a distributor? Depending on the type of merchandise you're selling, you may be able to use both. Either way, you'll find advantages and disadvantages.

Working Directly with a Manufacturer

Working directly with the manufacturer usually means paying less because you eliminate the distribution middleman. You should also be able to get new products on the same day a distributor would, rather than waiting for the distributor to receive the items from the manufacturer and then re-ship the items to you.

However, many manufacturers require a minimum order, which works against the goal of minimizing your inventory. As you grow and become more financially solid, a manufacturer's minimum order might not be a problem. But early in the life of your business, a minimum order might be enough to dissuade you from working directly with a manufacturer. Look closely at the numbers. Does a manufacturer's less expensive price outweigh the drawbacks of having to order more of a product than you would like?

Joe's Take: *I would like to work directly with Sony or Nintendo and acquire a discount level close to what my distributors have. While that sounds like an ideal situation, if I tried to order a dozen or so pieces of a product, I might get laughed off the phone. Large corporations like Sony, Nintendo, or Sega have sizeable minimum requirements—we're talking triple digits. The companies that order such large quantities are generally distributors. Not every manufacturer will impose a steep requirement on an order. If you are considering working directly with a manufacturer, your best bet is to call and talk to someone in the new accounts department.*

The other reason to work directly with a manufacturer is that it could be the only way to get the product. Many small artisans or companies create products that only are available directly from them. They have their own way of approving vendors and may also require money up front more often. Typically the smaller the direct company, the less formal the vendor program will be. It will take a bit more work to set up a proper supply system with them.

TIP ▸ ***Maximizing availability is sometimes more critical than ensuring the best price. That is why you should open as many channels to a product as possible and use the best option when you need it. For example, just because you can get a product from a distributor at a lower price doesn't mean you shouldn't consider opening up a direct line to the manufacturer as well. If you have a crucial sale to make, you may find working directly with a manufacturer when a distributor is out of stock can be a sale-saving option regardless of the higher cost per unit.***

Working with a Distributor

Finding the right distributors may be more suitable than working directly with a manufacturer. An established distributor can sometimes offer a better deal than the manufacturer. Distributors are generally able to order large quantities directly from the manufacturer, which leads to an unbeatable discount. An even bigger advantage to working with distributors that you don't have to deal with large quantities. Most distributors allow any size order. There's no need to worry about keeping a large inventory, and non-moving products will be the distributor's headache, not yours.

TIP ▸ ***When first working with a distributor, let it know that you're serious about your business and put together a decent-sized order for your initial purchase (unless you are ordering very expensive merchandise). If you can afford it, ordering a dozen units of a $20 item will make a better impression on a distributor than ordering two or three.***

Defective Items and Stock Balancing

When establishing an account with a distributor (or a manufacturer) make sure you ask about stock balancing and defective items.

Stock balancing allows you to return slow-moving stock toward the purchase of newer stock, as long as it is done within a reasonable amount of time. Returning defective items should be no problem, but like your own store, distributors and manufacturers will grant this exchange only through a certain number of days. This can be critical to your business. Even small businesses use a point-of-sale and inventory program to keep track of in-stock merchandise that needs to be sent back for stock balancing.

Stock balancing is a great, no-risk policy, but very few distributors offer it. You're more likely to find stock balancing offered by the manufacturer. However, as you build a strong relationship with your distributors, they may occasionally allow you to return some slow-moving stock, especially if it is something they can use in their inventory.

TIP ▸ ***Be careful when ordering the same product from multiple distributors. Be careful not to return three pieces of a product to a distributor from whom you initially only ordered one.***

***Joe's Take:** Like traditional stores, you can run specials on your Web site to move dead stock. I post specials on my home page to move those last remaining titles. Remember to make specials stand out like they would in a retail store display. Some stores send out weekly specials via e-mail to registered subscribers. You can also bundle items together, offering a chance to get a slower moving item for a deep discount when a customer orders another item.*

Setting Up an Account

To set up an account with a distributor or manufacturer, you will have to submit your Tax Identification Number and possibly a retail certificate and fill out an application. On the application, you'll have to provide information on how long you've been in business and about your business bank account. You'll also be asked to provide a list of current or previous business relationships. If you're just starting out, your list of business contacts will either be short or non-existent. Don't panic. The primary reason for the list of business references is to help the dealer decide whether or not you qualify for special "net terms."

Net terms are like credit cards without the finance charge. For instance, a Net 30 account means you have 30 days from the invoice date to pay for the goods you ordered. In a perfect world, you have time to sell the goods, repay the distributor, and pocket the profit before the 30 days are up. Every distributor or manufacturer has its own set of rules. Some may have Net 15 accounts, and others may not offer any net terms. Unless your new distributor is related to you, it's highly unlikely you'll immediately be granted net terms, especially if your reference list is short.

Working without Net Terms

So how does a new owner of a mail order business get product without net terms? Meet your savior: C.O.D.

C.O.D (cash on delivery) means just that; whether your orders are delivered or picked up, you pay for your goods immediately. Early on, you'll need to get used to having cash, a money order, or a certified check ready to pay for your inventory purchases. Once you have established a steady relationship with your sources, you'll probably be allowed to pay with a standard company check, eliminating the annoyance of running to the bank for a certified check before your orders arrive. Paying by a company check is a pleasure because the amount is not immediately deducted from your account. Depending on your distributor's bank, how close he is to your business, and how quickly the check is deposited, you could have anywhere from two days to more than a week before the check clears, giving you a bit of time to turn over stock.

TIP ▸ ***If you have a low budget, be careful how much you order versus how much you sell. Ordering a few thousand dollars worth of inventory when you are only certain of a few hundred dollars worth of sales can be a disaster. Always leave yourself room for checks to clear with additional funds for overlapping purchases.***

TIP ▸ ***If you are the sole operator of your business, it's best to spend the $5 charge on C.O.D.s and pay for your goods immediately. This eliminates any bills hanging over your head (which can be overlooked during busy periods) and gives you a more realistic picture of your financial situation.***

Dell Computer's Virtual Inventory

Dell Computer is the master of the virtual inventory. The company, which is selling more than $3 million worth of items daily on its Web site, practices a very strict form of virtual inventory that not only lets it build customized computers but keeps its supply of parts and products razor thin. Orders come into Dell's store system and items are sent to manufacturing. The data on what parts are needed is fed into another system that automatically notifies nearby suppliers (suppliers must maintain warehouses of their own near Dell's manufacturing facility). The suppliers ship directly to Dell.

Dell rarely pays for parts that aren't almost immediately going into a computer upon coming through the door. For example, monitors aren't even on hand and instead are shipped directly from the manufacturer. Dell sends an e-mail notification to a freight company, which picks the package up from the distributor and brings it straight to the customer. Products no longer have to be shipped anywhere else first, which saves Dell money. Dell saves more than $30 per monitor order by having the monitor shipped directly to the customer.

Minimizing Your Inventory

In the early stages of your business, you certainly don't want to be stuck with excess, unneeded stock. Stock is basically money on hold, and unless you are starting out with a hefty, regular cash flow, excess stock simply eats up money. Instead of the money going in your pocket, it sits on the floor in a big box marked "Loser." It takes time to get a feel for what types of products will move fast and which ones will collect dust. When you're starting out, carrying the smallest inventory possible makes the most sense.

Almost every business starts slowly. You may not want to stock anything until you actually have orders coming in, especially if you're selling expensive merchandise. Minimizing your stock helps you pay your business bills and hopefully even pay yourself.

The Advantages of Being Physically Close to Your Distributor

Having your suppliers (distributors or manufacturers) located near your business is a nice bonus. It's also something you have no control over unless you want to relocate. If you work with three distributors and one happens to be nearby, consider yourself lucky. Having your source for stock nearby allows you to physically zip over and pick up whatever you need. This allows you to eliminate shipping charges and pick up products the same day they are ordered, and customers don't have to wait for you to special order their item(s). It also gives the impression that you have the items in stock, when in fact it's down the street at the distributor. The distributor's stock room becomes your own risk-free storage spot.

Setting up Pre-Orders with Longtime Customers

Pre-orders are the best way to get an overall picture of what sells, what doesn't, and how many units to order at the time of release. You should announce available pre-orders on your site. You can include your pre-order chart in your "What's New" section, above all the current releases, or above related price lists. If you have an exact release date, include it. If not, you can label it "coming soon" and list the month or week of expected release. Make sure your customers are aware if a release date is not exact.

Depending on the price range of your merchandise, you can take pre-orders in various ways:

- **Have the customer fill out** your online order form and notify him when the product arrives. If the customer is paying by credit card, let him know the card will not be charged until the merchandise ships.

- **Take a deposit** for the soon-to-be released products, especially if the item is one that might sell out quickly. However, bear in mind that customers sometimes are a bit leery of having money deducted from a charge card before they even see what they're getting. This method makes more sense if you are dealing with expensive items.

- **Set up an e-mail folder** for customers who don't want to commit to an order yet but are very interested in ordering the product at the time of release. When a customer is interested in a future release, you can simply add her name to the folder that is set up specifically for that product. When the product arrives, open your folder and send each customer an announcement along with the price. Using a simple cut-and-paste method, you can send the same information to each customer, without having to type up the same letter for each e-mail inquiry.

TIP ▸ ***Customers who make a commitment by filling out your online order form should receive their products before those who simply express an interest in the product. Make this clear to your customers by posting it on your site.***

Drop Shipping

A drop shipment is sent directly from the distributor to your customer's door, eliminating the extra step of having it shipped to you first. Many distributors don't offer drop shipping, but it's worth your while to ask.

Advantages of Drop Shipping

Time. That's what drop shipping provides.

Your customers don't have to wait for their orders to go from the distributor, to you, to them. This not only means your customers get their orders more quickly, but it also decreases the time you have to spend packing orders and getting them shipped. If your distributors happen to be just around the corner, drop shipping is somewhat of a luxury. But if your distributors are far away, as will be the case in many situations, drop shipping can be a time-saving option.

Disadvantages of Drop Shipping

While drop shipping sounds like a comfortable process, it isn't perfect. Drop shipping places the responsibility on your distributor, which isn't necessarily a good thing.

Your distributor could process the wrong address, ship the wrong item, or commit any number of mistakes that will become your responsibility to fix. If you prefer to have a hand in every aspect of your business, as most small business owners do, you'll probably want to limit the amount of drop shipping you do. That way you won't have to fumble for answers or make excuses for someone else's mistake.

Also, with drop shipping you are also at the mercy of your distributor in terms of the shipping method. You may prefer to offer one option, but your distributor may only offer another.

JOE'S TAKE: *With my distributors close by, I haven't needed to drop ship on a regular basis. Even if you don't plan to use drop shipping, you should know whether your distributors offer it in case of emergency. If a distributor forgets to include an item in a shipment, I can simply have it drop shipped from the warehouse.*

Virtual Product Fulfillment and Inventory Management

One way to create an even simpler stocking system is to outsource as much of the stock-to-fulfillment process as possible. To do this you can find a fulfillment company that warehouses inventory, accepts your orders, packs the boxes and arranges the shipping as ordered. You pay fees or percentages of the order. This is a great option for stores that want to keep their focus on the Web site development and not the daily grind of product inventory.

However, this approach may be more expensive in actual dollars than if you did it yourself–you gain efficiency for a price. Product fulfillment companies are available now, and expect to see even more as e-commerce grows.

Some companies run fulfillment operations that are industry specific while others are cross-industry. You won't have direct control over any of your warehouse operations, so if customer service and fulfillment isn't of the quality you expect, you'll have to work with the company to develop a solution.

Another aspect of outsourced fulfillment is tight coordination with a shipping company. For example, FedEx offers a service called FedEx VirtualOrder. Customers visit your online catalog, which resides on a FedEx secure server, search for the products they need, and submit orders. FedEx then automatically assigns order-confirmation numbers and transmits orders to a FedEx Merchant Access Unit housed on your site.

Once the order is confirmed, a shipping label can be generated and the product is tendered to FedEx for express delivery. Inventory control is automated by a warehouse that does the picking and packing. FedEx, via virtual order, is automatically on hand to pick up the package and ship it. A high level of coordination with this set-up could leave you without any inventory management to deal with other than a few spreadsheets.

If you are interested in checking out fulfillment companies, a search on the Web using keywords like **product fulfillment** can get you started in the right direction.

Keeping a Sale When You're Out of Stock

You will receive orders on almost a daily basis that you can't immediately fill. When you receive an order, check the availability of the item. If you don't have it in stock, contact your distributors or other business sources. If none of your sources has the item, find out when it will be in. Contact your customer as quickly as possible. By following up on an order in a timely manner, you are letting the customer know she is dealing with an organized, caring company. Give the customer the option to wait for the order or cancel.

Here's an example of an e-mail Tronix sends in this case:

> Thank you for submitting your order with Tronix. Currently, we are out of stock on the item(s) you requested, but we should have restock by the end of this week. If you would like to wait for our restock, let us know and we will fulfill your order when the shipment arrives. If you prefer not to wait, then feel free to cancel this order by letting us know.

Most customers (especially regulars) are willing to wait for restock. During the interim, you can update them on the status off the order. This gives the whole process a personal touch and makes it less frustrating for the customer. The key to keeping a customer's order active is good communication and honesty.

TIP ▸ ***When a distributor tells you the restock of an item will occur on a given day, it is not always wise to pass this information back to your customer. If your distributor's order is late, you'll find yourself once again e-mailing the customer with additional bad news. It's best to give your customer a general time frame, rather than a solid date.***

TIP ▸ ***Many online merchants such as Dell are learning that they can help shape demand on the Web through a variety of tricks, like home-page placement or suggestions to interested callers. This way you can steer people away from out-of-stock items. People won't know something is out of stock if they never order it.***

Knowing Which Items Are Hot

You should know better than anyone which items are going to sell and what ones aren't. If you don't, you probably won't be in business very long. There are a number of ways to stay on top of industry trends. You can read trade and non-trade magazines, stay on top of the relevant newsgroups, and do your best to attend consumer and trade shows. You should also visit the Web sites of the company whose products you are selling. Calling a company that has a product you want to sell and asking for names of distributors is the easiest and fastest way to get hooked into the network of distributors serving a particular store type.

Magazines

You would be hard-pressed to find an industry that doesn't have a trade magazine. You would also be hard-pressed to find a successful merchant who didn't at least scan that industry's trade magazine. If you aren't sure what your industry's trade magazine is, go to a search engine on the Web and look for information on your industry's trade association.

Trade magazines will not only keep you up to date on particular products but also on issues effecting your business.

Newsgroups

Usenet newsgroups are a great way to spread the word about your store, as we discuss in more detail in Chapter 10. They are also useful for learning more about your customers, their tastes, their buying habits, and their preferences.

The more active you are in posting to newsgroups, the better. But even if you aren't constantly involved in newsgroup discussions, it's a good idea to poke your head in and see what people are talking about. For example, if you sell ski equipment there's a good chance a skiing-related newsgroup will have a number of posts and responses about the latest technology. If everyone is raving about a particular new binding, you should expect high demand.

Trade Shows

Trade shows, if they are good ones, can be your best source of product information. The only drawback is that there is a very good chance that attending one will require some travel. So, on top of the cost of attending the show, you'll also have to pay for a hotel, meals, and possibly even airfare. You'll also wind up spending at least a couple of days away from work. Although most of your expenses can be used as tax write-offs, the lost work time is not recoverable.

That said, attending a good trade show is usually worth the time, effort, and money required. Besides the fact that they provide networking opportunities, trade shows also allow you to check out the latest products. You'll almost certainly be able to gauge the popularity of new products simply through your own judgment and through the buzz among the show attendees.

Web Sites

Checking out a company's Web site (assuming it has one) should provide you with all the information you need about a product, how the company is marketing it, and how important it is to them. If a particular item receives minimal attention from its own company, you can expect the public's interest will be similar. On the other hand, if the company is promoting a new product all over its Web site, you can bet the company is very serious about getting that product out to the public.

Importing

Because of the vast amounts of information available on the Internet, importing has become a growing market there. Anyone with Internet access who wants to purchase hard-to-find items such as imported goods will likely check the Web. Selling rare items and imports can add sales and set you apart from those businesses that don't.

Importing products is not as easy as setting up an account with a domestic dealer. You must first find your source for imports; a good place to begin is right on the Web. There are many import wholesalers with their own Web sites, so using a good search engine should send you in the right direction.

Joe's Take: *You can have your exporter bill to your own shipping account (whether it is UPS, FedEx, or Airborne). And if you plan to use various distributors overseas on a regular basis, your shipping representative may be able to give you a special discount, depending on frequency/volume.*

Conducting business with foreign companies usually involves wire transfers of money to the company's account or, in some cases, using your own credit card. If you plan to do business with foreign wholesalers, there are a few things to remember.

Working with Import Distributors

Much like domestic buying, when importing you can either work directly with the producer of the products you are selling or with a distributor. Most of the issues are the same as when using a domestic distributor, as we discussed earlier in this chapter. Using a distributor can eliminate some of the headaches, including the issue of returning defective items. Distributors will be in no hurry to exchange slowly moving imports.

Researching Overseas Companies

Most companies with Web sites are legitimate, but you should check out international companies by making a few phone calls to the host country. Make sure the company's address and phone numbers are listed.

If everything appears legitimate, you can go a step further by checking around to see if any of your competitors have dealt with the company. If you can't find anyone who has, you should be cautious.

The reason to be careful when dealing with foreign companies isn't because they are any more likely to scam you than domestic companies are. But if you do get ripped off internationally, it will be much more difficult to recover your losses.

TIP ▸ ***If you just get e-mail from a company claiming it has goods that you should be interested in selling, be cautious. If there is no legitimate contact information, Web site, or knowledge in the industry of the company, take a pass.***

Paying Customs/Duties

When you place orders overseas, you are responsible for paying any import taxes on the products. United States customs will charge you a percentage of the total cost of the imported goods.

When ordering overseas, it is actually more sensible to place large orders since both the shipping and taxes can be absorbed into your prices. For example, if you order $1,000 worth of product, shipping costs $75, and customs adds another $125 in taxes, you are paying $200 above the cost of the goods. If your order contains 50 pieces of an item at $20 each for the $1,000 total, you could easily spread the shipping and tax costs over the 50 pieces for an additional charge of just $4 per piece.

Wire Transfers

Wire transfers can be done through any bank, but it is less of a hassle if it is done through your own bank from your actual account. Wire transfers require all bank information from the recipient, such as branch name, address, and routing number. Overseas companies generally require advance payment, at least early in a relationship.

Wire transfers can take anywhere from a week to two weeks depending on the countries involved. Your bank will charge you a fee (usually $15–$20) for this service. You also need to know whether the foreign dealer accepts Untied States dollars or the currency of its country.

If you are dealing in foreign currency, you must consider the exchange rate. Obviously your bank will let you know what the exchange rate is with a particular country, but if you want to check daily exchange rates, a good resource is the Olsen and Associates Currency Converter (Figure 8.1) on the Web. The O&A Converter (www.oanda.com/cgi-bin/ncc) allows you to easily figure out the exchange rates among 164 countries. It is updated daily.

FIGURE 8.1
The O&A Currency Converter provides exchange rates for 164 currencies.

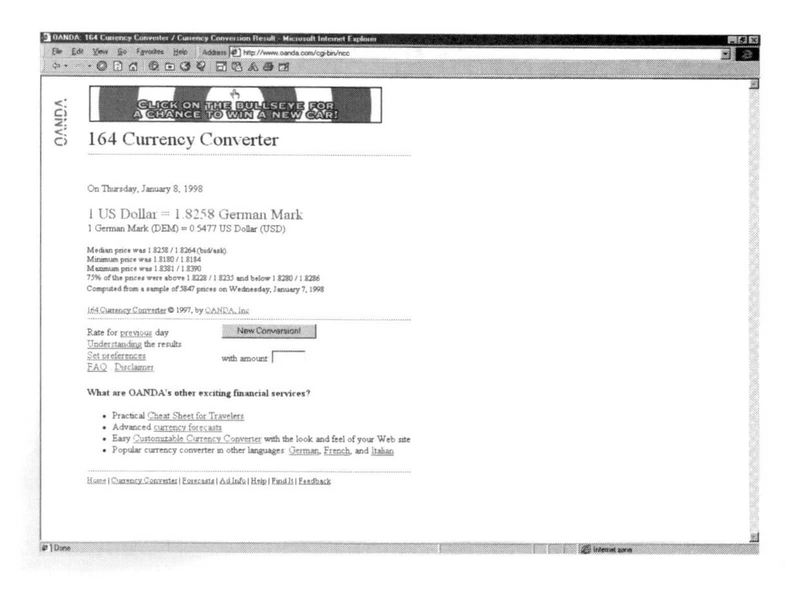

Build Long-Term Overseas Relationships

A good, long-term relationship with an overseas exporter can work to your advantage, especially after a continuous stream of successful business transactions. In some cases, a foreign distributor might improve the terms of your business relationship. For example, it might ship advance orders and allow you to pay later. This saves on the cost of wire transfers and cuts down on the paperwork involved.

Defective Items/Returns

Rules for returning defective items vary. Make sure you know which of your overseas suppliers accept returns and which don't. If one does accept returns, you must also be clear about shipping charges. Not only must you ship the defective item back, you also need to have a replacement shipped. Does the exporter pay for both shipping charges? Neither? Just one?

As with all other issues, know the quirks of the individual company you are dealing with.

Getting Big By Keeping It Small

The most important thing to take away from this chapter is that you should work with as little inventory as possible and as necessary. Inventory is risk. Unsold inventory is your unusable money. The more effectively you minimize your inventory, the better. And the more inventory you must stock, the more confident you need to be that it will eventually sell.

Now on to Chapter 9. We'll talk about how to create great Web content without spending a fortune or slaving for endless hours over your computer.

CHAPTER NINE

Creating Retail Content Without Spending A Fortune

Anyone can put price lists and order forms up on the Web and call it a store. That would be like a clothing store stacking its items on the floor and sticking someone behind the cash register to ring up orders. Neither works. Nothing to attract customers, no help for them, and before long no store.

As an online retailer, unless your prices are far less than those of the competition, you need something to attract customers to your site and to keep them coming back. The content you provide (news, reviews, product descriptions, pictures, etc.) can be done to fit your budget. Few businesses have the revenue necessary to license and maintain the enormous state and national park database that outdoor clothing and gear giant L.L. Bean provides its customers. What good content does require is a little time and creativity, the ability to write coherently (you needn't be Ernest Hemingway), and in some cases the help of your loyal customers.

Content is an educational service to your customers and yourself. The difference between making a sale or not often comes down to education. The customer's confidence in a product is related to the amount of knowledge the person has about that product. A site with good content leads to better-educated consumers and, therefore, customer confidence. That means sales.

If you can prove you are knowledgeable about your products, your customers are more likely to keep coming back for more information and buy more products. They'll enjoy their shopping experience more than if they just pop on, order, and leave.

To provide good content, you'll have to stay on top of current trends in your industry. It will take a little work, but that work will ensure you remain on top of new products, technological advances, etc. The more you know, the better your store will be. And the better your store, the more customers it will have.

Informational Content

Tronix was among the first online video game stores to provide informational content for its customers. We started with simple reviews, a news column on industry happenings, and reports on the annual E3 (Electronic Entertainment Expo) video game trade show. A review also doubled as a fairly detailed description of the particular game.

At that point, with only one or two new releases each week, it was easy to stay on top of the reviews. Now, with video games a $6 billion to $8 billion a year industry, it is impossible to review every new release without hiring people to do it. As the technology improves and people come up with more content ideas, the amount of content on most Web stores has improved and increased dramatically. How much time you spend on content will depend on your budget. If you're a one-person operation, the amount of time available for generating content will obviously be less. Don't ignore it, however. No matter how much time you spend answering the phone or packing boxes, always set aside some time to create content. A good time to do it is at night or on the weekends at home, where customer phone calls won't disturb you.

Depending on what you're selling, there are a number of informational content options for you to consider.

Product Descriptions

This is the most basic content that every store needs. Obviously you can't just post price lists that say things like "Table: $100," "Chair: $75." What kind of table? A coffee table? Dining room table? End table? Diaper changing table? A chair could be anything from a cheap wooden seat to a luxurious recliner.

The more specific the product description, the less likely you are to have customer complaints about your merchandise. Back to the wooden chair: if you provide the type of wood, the dimensions (including back height), the color, and whether or not it has arms, it's less likely a customer will call with a complaint than if the description says simply "oak chair." If your description specifically states that the chair has no arms, someone won't assume that it does.

Depending on what you're selling, you can be very creative with your descriptions. Don't overdo it where it isn't necessary. If you have an online hardware store, the only reason to describe a selection of nails as "three inches of solid, sparkling steel, flat on one end, sharp on the other, and as tough as, well, nails" would be for a laugh. Which, come to think of it, isn't a bad idea.

Some items lend themselves better to flowery descriptions than others. Decide which category your products fall into and go from there.

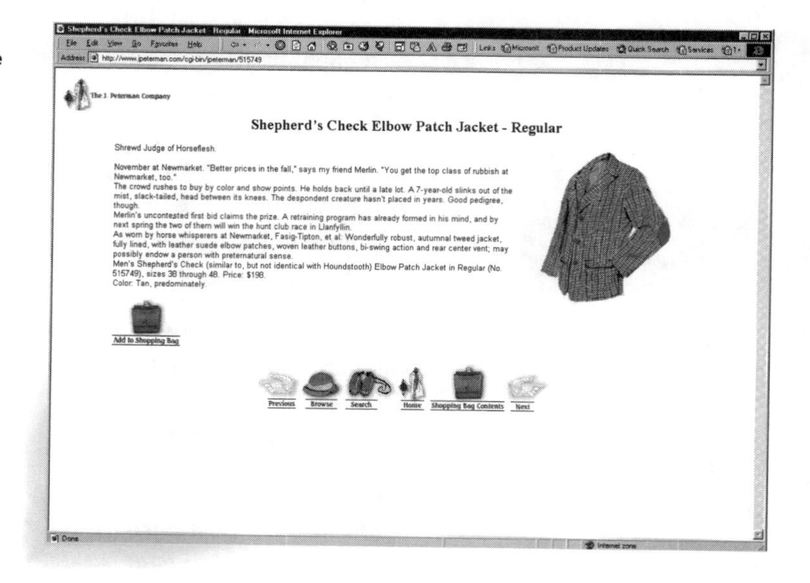

FIGURE 9.1
The J. Peterman catalog utilizes creative product descriptions to grab the attention of customers.

TIP ▸ ***Before you unload the lavish prose, make sure the facts are covered. After a spectacular description of a shirt, the customer shouldn't be left wondering "Is it long-sleeved or short-sleeved?"***

Photos and Graphics

The best way to add some spark to your product descriptions or any other content area is with photos or graphics. Just about anything can benefit from a photo, whether you're just scanning in a music CD cover, including a screen shot from a piece of software or using a digital camera to take a picture of a surfboard. However, when considering graphics, don't forget bandwidth issues.

TIP ▸ ***The more graphics on a page, the longer the page takes to load. Don't just slap up graphics and photos. Instead take the time to optimize them and make them both attractive and quick to load.***

If all of your products can benefit from photo representation, feel free to go wild. If none of them does, don't completely avoid it. Even a boring picture can be used to break up text here and there. However, a bunch of boring photos is a bunch of boring photos and will only clutter your page.

For more on adding photos and graphics to your site, see Chapter 7.

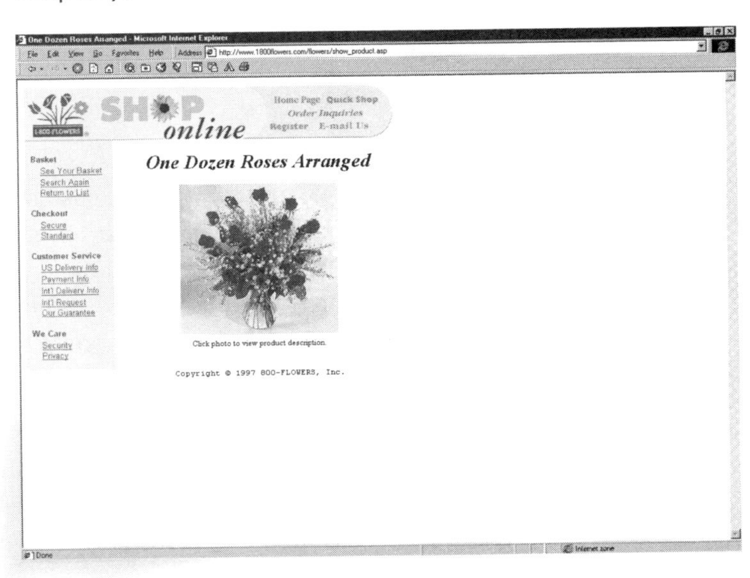

FIGURE 9.2
1-800-FLOWERS offers a necessary photo of its arrangements.

Joe's Take: *Pages and pages of text can get boring. A good combination of photos, graphics, and text can be very eye catching. When Tronix first started, we didn't have photos. Once we started using them, I saw our hit ratio go up. People started saying they had seen a really great picture of something on the Tronix site and people would come to check it out.*

Web Content Color

One key aspect of graphical content is color. It is difficult to ensure that the red you put on your Web site is the same as the red that the user sees through a browser. Monitors, JPEGs, and other items all contribute to the fact that what looks one color at design time might look slightly (or very) different when someone views it on a monitor.

How do you eliminate this problem? It's not easy. Many sites run disclaimers that tell users that the colors on the screen may not be truly representative of the actual color. In short, don't match the house paint via the Web!

However, a few solutions will help minimize the difference between the actual color of a product and what is displayed on the Web. The first thing to do is work on optimizing graphical content for the Web as it relates to color.

FAQ

An FAQ (Frequently Asked Questions) is becoming standard on most sites. FAQs provide an easy way to answer questions about your business, how it works, how to order, how navigate the site, and more without constantly responding to e-mail. A good FAQ should eliminate simple questions from your e-mail bin. Don't be afraid to update your FAQ if you get a good question from a customer that isn't answered there.

Your FAQ should include information about the products you sell, how to order, what credit cards are accepted, what secure transaction system is used, and where to find specific information on your site. You needn't give a complete answer to a question if the answer can be found elsewhere on your site. For example, if one of the questions is "What are my shipping options?" you can say what companies you use and direct the customer to your shipping page for specific information. Otherwise you'll end up with an FAQ that's as big as the rest of your site.

You can also use an FAQ to provide information about the history of the company, your guiding principals, and other more personal information if you so choose. Be sure to cover the basics first.

TABLE 9.1 20 GOOD FAQ QUESTIONS

HERE IS A GOOD LIST OF STARTER QUESTIONS FOR AN INTERNET STORE'S FAQ:
What payment forms do you accept?
What shipping companies do you use?
How late can I order for next day delivery?
What is your store's contact information?
Do you allow walk-ins? Can I visit your store's location?
How long have you been in business?
What is your sales tax policy?
Are items insured in transit?
What are your live operator hours?
Do you match or beat prices?
Do you have a mailing list?
Can I set up an account?
Do you accept bulk or distributor orders?
Can I special order items?
Is your Web order form secure?
What do you do with my contact information/e-mail?
What is your return or exchange policy?
Do you accept orders by fax?
Do you accept and fulfill international orders?
Can I submit articles or reviews for your store?

News

Including news on your site is helpful for both you and your customers. If you're going to spend time creating content beyond product descriptions (and you should), a news section is a good place to start. A good news section contains brief, timely items that are related to your store and of interest to your customers. You can also include product features or other features that are related to your customers' interests. You can get information from the companies you deal with, industry trade magazines and newsletters, and simply by keeping your eyes and ears open.

Obviously any good storeowner will want to stay on top of the happenings within her industry. Knowing that you need to keep updating your store's news page will force you to be informed about your industry or else look like a fool. A news page is especially important in release-sensitive businesses such as music, books, movies, or, in the case of Tronix, video games. Being able to post advance word and release dates for highly anticipated products like Thomas Pynchon's next novel or R.E.M.'s next record is a plus for you and a service for your customers.

If you do a thorough job collecting news, you can become a source of information—not just a store—for your customers. Your customers will consider you trustworthy if you consistently provide timely, correct information and will visit your store more often. If you prove to be the best place for information on your industry, word will spread and you'll probably find swarms of potential customers arriving at your site.

TIP ▸ ***If you really like to write and can find the time to do it, you can even expand your news column past the confines of what you're selling. For example, if you sell surfboards, snowboards, skateboards, and related gear, you don't have to limit your news to product information and technological advancements. Your customers will probably be interested in some of the top performers in each sport and the results of recent events. In this case, you might even want to mention when the new records by Pennywise and NOFX (two popular bands among the board crowd) are coming out.***

The amount of news available in your industry on a daily basis and the amount of time you want to spend on a news column will dictate how often it is changed. If you're selling software, you could change your news column daily. Other industries will only produce enough news to warrant a monthly. It might take some time to figure out how often you should update your news column.

Don't make the mistake of promising a new column each week only to find you don't have enough time or news to support it. Cutting back from a weekly to a monthly will send a negative message to your customers. Instead, start conservatively and when it becomes apparent you have enough news and time, you can hit your customers with a message like "Due to popular demand, Pete's Pepper Pit will provide gardening news twice a month rather than just monthly!" Your customers will be pleasantly surprised and realize you really care about what you're doing.

Your news column will be a reflection of you and how much you care about your customers and your business. Assuming the prices are comparable, most people would rather buy from someone who is truly passionate about her products than someone who is just trying to make a buck. This is a chance to prove that person is you.

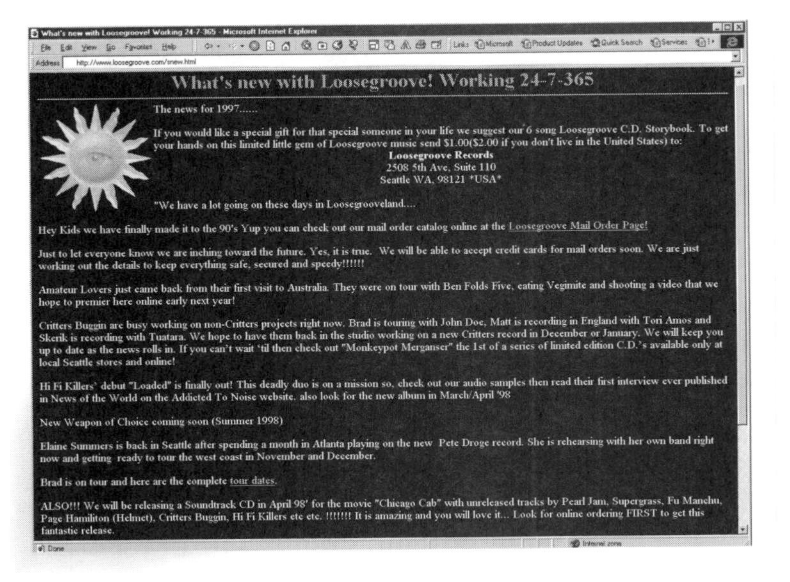

FIGURE 9.3
Loosegroove Records keeps customers informed about its bands' new releases and tours.

TIP ▸ ***Once you've decided when you're going to update your news, stick with that schedule. Your customers will hopefully be excited to read each new column, and if it isn't there when it should be, they'll be disappointed. If a major piece of news ("Gates sells Microsoft, buys fishing boat") breaks before you plan to change the news, you should update the column with that news without removing anything else. Archive the last few news columns for customers to refer back to.***

Reviews

Here's where content gets tricky. Many of you will never have to worry about it because not every type of product is conducive to a review. But if you are planning to do reviews, our advice is to be honest. That's where reviews can be a problem. Not everything you have is going to be good, especially if you're selling entertainment medium like games, books, music, and movies or products like software.

Reviews, even negative ones, are very important for many online stores. Traditional stores hand out negative reviews all the time by not stocking items. You just don't see the review. However, many online stores actually have an incredible amount of virtual shelf-space and could list thousands of products without actually stocking them. A negative review allows you to stock a complete inventory while steering customers away from products you think they shouldn't buy.

An honest, positive review is the best thing you can hope to write. It will help sell the item, it won't upset anybody, and assuming the product really is good, it will reinforce your honest image.

Joe's Take: *If you have to write a bad review, that doesn't mean you have to really rip the thing apart. In my case, I might risk offending the company or the distributor to the point of affecting my business. As an extreme and unlikely example, where would Tronix be if I completely trashed a Sony game and Sony decided it didn't want me selling it's products anymore?*

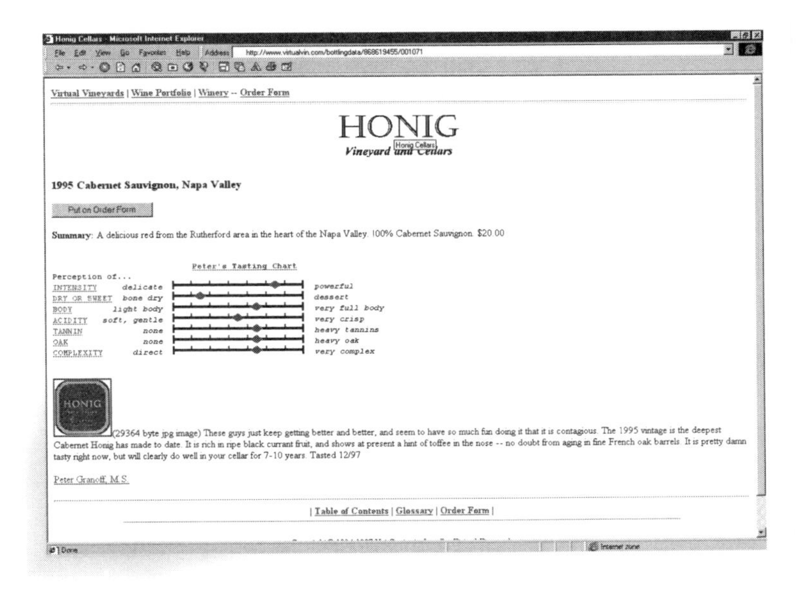

FIGURE 9.4
Virtual Vineyards' taste chart helps customers select a wine that fits their preferences.

Since you'll never have a reason to write a dishonest, negative review, the toughest thing you'll have to do is write an honest, negative review. Never write a dishonest, positive review. Never. Your customers will realize it, the word will spread on the newsgroups and you'll be branded a liar and a scam artist. If you don't want to write a negative review about a product, just don't write one at all.

Sometimes you can't avoid writing a negative review. If you have been doing them all along and a much-hyped product comes out, you can't just ignore it because it fails to live up to expectations. People will notice and it will make you look bad. In fact, you can make a negative review work for you.

Honesty is an admirable trait and not one always associated with business people. When writing a negative review, you should be able to convey the message that the product is lousy without using inflammatory language. In other words, you can say something stinks without saying "This stinks!" If there are some positive qualities to the product, mention them. You can actually gain more sales than you lose with a negative review.

JOE'S TAKE: In the video game industry, reviews are a good way to kill two birds with one stone. As you're reviewing a product, you're also telling people what the game is all about so it can double as an in-depth product description. Reviews were the first pieces of content we added to our site and it really brought in a lot of customers. At the beginning it was easy to review every product because there was only one or two new releases a week. Now it's nearly impossible. Some of the products reviewed early on just weren't very good and we had to grin and bear it by writing an honest, negative review. Those reviews were important because it was the first indication that we were honest. The customers thought we must be alright if we were willing to give a bad review to something we were selling. It's great when you here someone say a review you wrote was right on the mark.

Guest Columns

Guest columns are great for a number of reasons, not the least of which is that someone else writes them. They also put another face of expertise on your store. If you know someone who is capable of adding to your site's content without asking for a lot of (or any) money, you would be crazy not to use them. A lot of people will be willing to write about a topic of interest simply for the fun of it.

If you want to add a guest column to your site, run through a list of friends or business acquaintances who might be willing and qualified to help you. One or the other won't work. If they're qualified but not really enthusiastic about it, every column will involve your begging and pleading for a mediocre piece of content that arrives two weeks after you wanted it. If they're willing but not qualified, the column isn't going to add anything to your site. Instead, you'll spend a lot of time polishing garbage and finally having to break it to the columnist that you no longer need his services. However, you should be able to find at least one or two people with the time, inclination and expertise to help you out.

Once you've found someone, you should sit down and discuss a number of potential topics that she can cover in the coming weeks or months. It's your store, so you want to have control over the content, but don't be a dictator. This person is doing you a favor. Provide a list of topics you want covered and ask for the columnist's input. She'll have plenty of ideas if she really is qualified. Before long you should have a number of potential columns.

As the columns run, bring up any potential problems so the same mistakes aren't repeated. Keep the lines of communication open and, as with product reviews, don't get nasty if a column doesn't cut it. Work together with your columnist to correct the problems. Eventually she'll get a better feel for what you want and the process will flow smoothly.

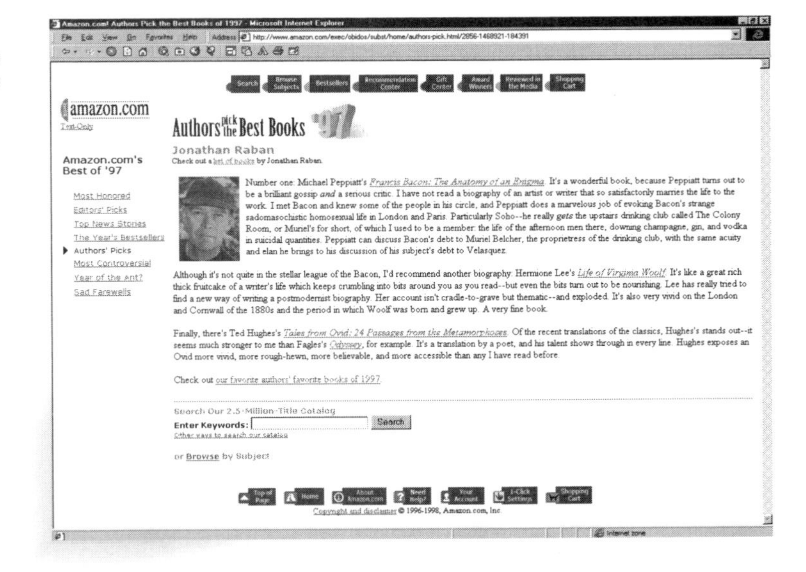

FIGURE 9.5
Amazon.com helps readers select books by providing guest recommendations by authors.

TIP ▸ ***Don't get into the situation where you're constantly scraping for ideas and your columnist is rushing to finish something at the last second. Keep a list of future column topics and the dates on which they will run. In a perfect world, the columnist will even be able to write ahead so there will never be any deadline panic for either of you. With the pressures of running a business, that's the last thing you need.***

Newsletters/Mailing Lists

Many stores and Web sites distribute an e-mail newsletter to users who request one. A newsletter provides your customer with information that is available without visiting your site. Receiving a newsletter might spark a customer to return to your site when he otherwise wouldn't.

A good e-mail newsletter is generally one to two pages long and contains URLs linking people directly to the wares you are discussing. It should also include specials and other newsworthy information about your store. Avoid sending out your newsletter too often or packing it with too much information. Chances are, the customer doesn't want to spend two hours reading it.

You can operate a newsletter two ways. You can simply collect e-mail addresses and then use your e-mail program to bulk mail your newsletter. Some packages automate this process somewhat, but it can get a bit messy, especially as the number of customers climbs. But the more automated way to do this is to run all your bulk e-mail through what is known as a *listserver* service.

A listserver is a program that can be used as a bulk e-mailer or as a mailing list. You can set up your own listserver, but some stores would be better off outsourcing such work, freeing up time and bandwidth. If you run your newsletter through a listserver service, you simply send it once to a special e-mail account and the service forwards the newsletter to every subscriber on the list.

Another way to use a listserver is to operate a discussion mailing list with it. Users subscribe to the listserver and, once on the list they can post a message that is then replicated and sent out to other members of the list.

TIP ▸ ***One of the better listserver services is Skyweyr's Skylist, which is located on the Web at www.skyweyr.com.***

The key to a mailing list discussion is to keep people talking and interacting with you as a moderator. This is very time-consuming, but it is a good way to keep in touch with very frequent customers and provide them with special content and services.

JOE'S TAKE: *I participate on newsgroups so frequently that a mailing list would be overkill for me. Concerning newsletters, I initially liked operating one for Tronix, but it became difficult to commit the necessary time as Tronix grew. If you start a newsletter, commit to a small number of issues and work to increase the frequency. The worst thing you can do is start a newsletter and then dump it or cut back on the frequency and the content. How would it look if you produced a weekly newsletter only to cut back to monthly? Contrast that with offering a quarterly newsletter and then, as you get better or bigger, increase the frequency.*

Links

Links to other sites can provide even more information for your customers. Be clear that you are sending them to another site. You don't want to be seen as taking credit for someone else's work.

You can either group all of your links together or include them in the text of an article. Anything mentioned in an onsite article, any company you deal with, or any site you think your customers would enjoy that is somehow related to your business are good prospects for links. For more on links and links exchanges, see Chapter 11.

Don't worry about sending people off to another site never to return. Many sites worry that linking a lot to other sites is going to create a virtual sieve that will drain customers before they decide to purchase something from you. Although this may happen with a few customers, the majority of links that stores provide should be to further educate your customers.

Databases

One of the best types of content to offer on a site is a database. While many sites offer an interesting database simply by listing their products with descriptions (CDNow's database of music titles is interesting in and of itself) many sites have found that offering a searchable database of information is a good draw. As we mentioned in Chapter 3, L.L. Bean offers a searchable database of state and national parks—something buyers of its outdoor gear and clothing would be very interested in.

The strength of database content is drawn from the ability to search for a lot of entries in a number of different ways. For example, the Internet Movie Database (www.imdb.com) lets you search movies by actors, title, director, crew, date, rating, and more. The database also has thousands of entries, which is what makes it so appealing. The online video store Reel uses this database.

Constructing a database and displaying it on the Web requires more work than just putting up pages. Your site hosting company or an independent consultant should be able to guide you through it. Before you can display it, you need to construct it. Start by seeing if there are any pre-existing databases that you can license. It will probably be less expensive than keying it in yourself.

TIP ▸ ***Some of the best uses of database content on the Web are ones which let users add to it. While you will have to edit and validate these customer entries, it can be a good way to build up the database while offering a piece of interactive content on your site. For example, the Amazon.com database catalogs book reviews submitted by patrons.***

TIP ▸ ***If you decide to provide your own information for a database, you should still hire a database consultant to develop it. If you want to save money by keying in the data yourself that's great. Unless you have experience building actual databases, you should meetwith the database consultant who will help you spec out the field lists and other features of the database.***

Database content can be a big draw to your site. Most stores will have a product database people will enjoy, but others are finding that databases of content related to the product line can draw people to the site and keep them coming back.

Figure 9.6
L.L. Bean not only provides a database of park information, but also offers instruction on a number of outdoor activities, including how to choose a fly line.

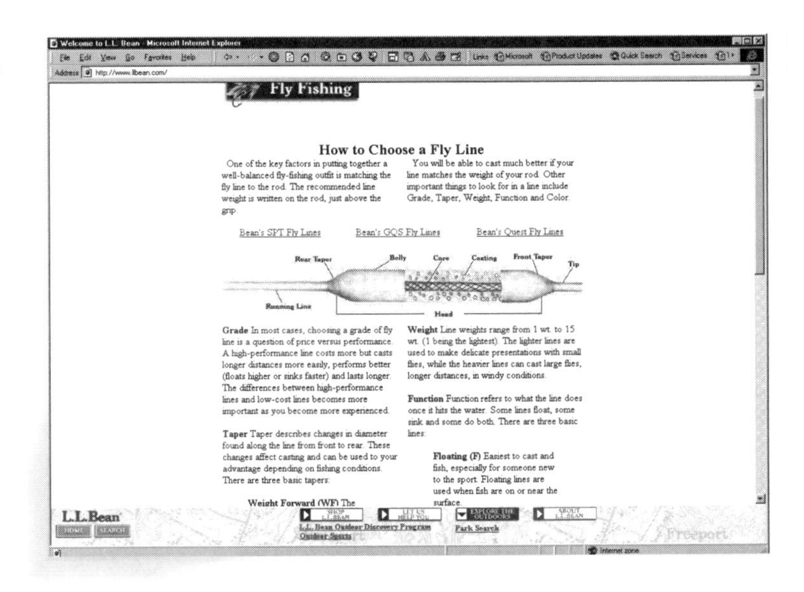

Testimonials

You know your store is fantastic and so do your customers. But not everyone who visits your site for the first time will be immediately aware of your outstanding customer service, honesty and all-around greatness. So tell them. Better yet, let your customers tell them.

A page of customer testimonials can be far more effective than your bragging. If you do your job, you will almost certainly receive e-mail from satisfied customers. They may write to tell you how great your prices are or how their shipment arrived exactly when it was supposed to. If you receive some particularly complimentary letters, ask the writer if you can post it on your site for other customers to see. If the writer is that enthusiastic about your store, he'll probably be happy to help.

When posting testimonials, try to cover a wide range of issues. Five letters about your incredibly low prices will have a customer thinking "I get the point!" Instead, include letters that show your store in a positive light in all areas. You needn't post every positive letter. Hopefully you'll receive so many that you would need a separate Web site to do so.

Not all the testimonials have to be fawning reviews of your store. For example, a good testimonial might come from a person who was originally shipped a defective product or received it a day late. A quick, hassle-free credit might draw a positive letter. Posting a letter like this lets your customers know that you are human and occasionally (though not often!) things go wrong. When that happens, they can count on the problem being rectified in a timely fashion.

Assuming you have enough to choose from, keep the testimonials fresh by replacing them every few months. If people keep seeing the same testimonials for a couple of years, they might start wondering if anyone is still sending them in.

TIP ▸ ***A good testimonial doesn't have to come directly to you. You might see a newsgroup post that you'd like to include. Try e-mailing the person a message like "Thanks a lot for the kind words about my store. Would you mind if I put it on my testimonials page?" You'll probably get an affirmative response.***

Customer-Generated Articles and Reviews

The more you involve your customers, the better. If you let it be known that customer input is encouraged on your site, you probably won't have any problem getting some content from the most loyal of them. Once you've gotten to know a customer reasonably well through e-mail and phone conversations, you can ask her if she'd like to contribute to the site. You can offer a free item or to pay the person in exchange for her services, but she'll probably help out for free.

Remember that all the content on your site is a reflection of you and your store, so you'll have to keep a close eye on what your customers are submitting. Unlike guest columnists, who should have an amount of expertise and some writing experience, your customer contributors will probably just be fans of your particular product. Therefore, you'll probably do a lot of editing and might even decide not to use some submissions. If you decide not to use something a customer has submitted, break it to them gently and give them some constructive criticism. Nobody likes to be rejected. Don't compound the problem (and lose a customer) by being mean.

Joe's Take: *Once one person writes something for you, you'll probably have others asking to do so. They see somebody else's name on your site and think "That's cool, I wonder if I can write something." Many of Tronix's reviews are done by customers.*

Interactive Content

Providing information for your customers is the basic level of content. It keeps your store from being nothing more than a big price list and gives people a reason to visit your site other than simply to buy something. Interactive content goes a step further, giving your customers something to do on your site.

Contests

Contests are a nice sporadic feature for your store. Not only are contests a great way to attract people to your site, you can have them as frequently or infrequently as you like. Some larger stores like CDNow and Amazon.com have regular contests for the simple reason that they can. Giving away merchandise or gift certificates each week is no big deal. For you it might be. That doesn't mean you should avoid contests altogether. You'll probably find giving away a small amount of merchandise or gift certificates to be worth it. If you find you can afford a regular contest, you can schedule them around holidays, monthly or even weekly.

Contests are easily done via e-mail. You can post a question or questions on your home page with an e-mail link for answers. Depending on how much you want to give away, you can either hand out a prize to the person who submits the first correct answer or to the first five or so people with the correct answer. Once you have a winner or winners, post the answer and a congratulatory message on the home page for the winners.

If you have enough in your budget to run ten contests a year, you might consider having a couple of "Contest Weeks" each year. When the word gets out through the newsgroups, you could have people flocking to your site every day for a week in hopes of winning. Some of these people will certainly be new visitors who won't stop at answering the question. They'll probably browse your store and, if they like what they see, you'll end up with a group of new customers.

Questions

Obviously the question should be easy enough for someone to answer but difficult enough to make it challenging. If the answer is available somewhere else on your site, let people know that to encourage them to look around, just don't tell them exactly where it is. Ask questions that are related to what your selling or to news related to your business. For example, if the Rolling Stones are on a highly publicized concert tour, a music store might want to ask a question about the Stones, such as "Who is the oldest Stone?" (A: Drummer Charlie Watts).

Prizes

Which leads to prizes. A question about the Stones should reward the winner with the new Stones record. But there are a number of things you can give out. Hot new items are sure to get people rushing to your site. You can also use contests as an alternative to specials to get rid of old stock. If you have a product that just isn't selling, why not give it away? You're not losing much, although giving away mediocre products won't be nearly as good an attraction as handing out something new and sought-after.

Probably the best prize for a storeowner to give away is a gift certificate. You can give out small gift certificates in the hopes that people will use them toward more expensive products. However, if you do this you run the risk of irritating your customers. If you are concerned with building a strong relationship with your customers (and you should be), give out a gift certificate that's hefty enough to buy something without chipping in another $20 or so. If someone uses a gift certificate for a free item, he might buy something else, too.

Polls

Polls are easy to do and a good way to get your customers involved with your store. The key to a good poll is asking a timely question that likely will draw a balanced response. Provide two or three answers for respondents to check off. The answers should tell you quite a bit about your customers. For example, the online music magazine "Addicted To Noise" has a question of the day which asks readers their opinion on a timely issue related to popular music. When it was announced that the relatively young Pearl Jam would open some concerts for the not-so-young Rolling Stones, Addicted To Noise asked its readers which band would put on a better performance. The fact that 67 percent of respondents voted for Pearl Jam is an obvious indication of the age of the e-zine's readers.

You can even use polls to help you decide what to stock. If you're selling competing products, a poll that indicates an overwhelming amount of support for one over the other might push you toward stocking more of the favored item.

Chat Rooms/Message Boards

Chat rooms and message boards can get your customers communicating and visiting your site on a regular basis (see Figure 9.7). Be forewarned. Depending on your customers, there can be a lot of work involved.

The key thing about chat rooms and message boards is that they exist within the Web page. Users don't have to fire up an extraneous product like NetMeeting or a Usenet reader to participate. In addition people usually have to be at your site to participate, thus making them a good draw. Message boards and chats can also be great content builders. Host a chat with someone relevant to your store and then post a transcript later for people who missed it. You should also cull message board answers for FAQs and other areas of your site.

FIGURE 9.7
The Racing Store provides gifts and a chat room for auto racing fans.

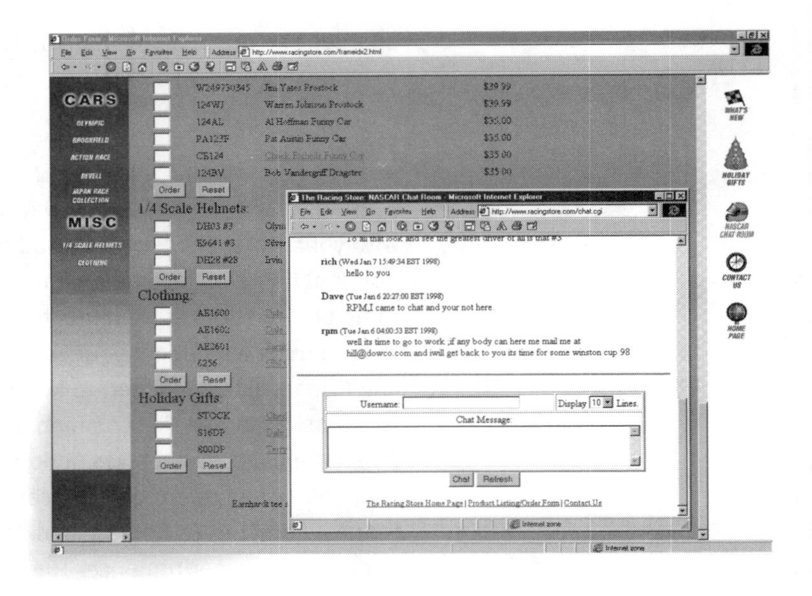

Chat rooms and message boards are also great for providing customer service. Many sites are installing these items to cut down the number of customer phone calls. Instead of picking up the phone, users can just go to a chat room to find an answer to their question.

The downside to this all is the amount of work chat rooms and message boards require to maintain. Message boards need to be watched for errant or even libelous posts. You also need to answer questions quickly so people can get an answer in the next 24 hours or sooner. With chat rooms, you'll need to monitor and mediate chats with guests to make sure things run smoothly.

Another concern is cost and installation. Chat rooms and message boards require the installation of some server side components and the cost of such programs is not cheap. Top-notch Web bulletin boards can run more than $1,000. Chat servers can cost thousands as well. While pricing should steadily drop, strongly consider the cost vs. return before you decide to offer them.

Joe's Take: *Chat rooms or message boards can lead to a lot of work. You might spend a lot of time editing out lousy comments and you have to make sure things don't get too nasty. Someone might post a message that really rips a product, and you're liable because it's on your site. One of my competitors, who is now out of business, had a message board and he had to deal with a lot of obscenities on it. If you're considering a message board or a chat room, keep in mind who your customers are and figure out if you're going to have to spend hours editing posts.*

Web Boards

A Web board is a Web page-based system that allows users to write and post messages to your site. This is a great way for customers to share experiences and news about your store's products. It's also a way to hook them into your site. As a moderator you can answer questions on the board and post more information that may help people decide to buy a product.

There are several major Web board products a store can implement. Details are included in the Resources section of this book.

Joe's Take: *I don't have a Web board on the Tronix site but I'm intimately familiar with them from my days as a CompuServe SysOp. Boards are great community builders but they're difficult to manage. If I were to do one for even a minimally busy site, I would consider paying someone (or swapping merchandise) to manage it.*

Multimedia Content

Digital video, audio, and full-fledge programs are the kings of the content hill. However, while many sites want to offer more than just text or graphics, users can't always access it due to low bandwidth connections or poor implementation by the site itself.

As the Web matures, multimedia content will become more important so you should stay on top of the technology. Store owners need to approach multimedia very carefully. While the content potential of multimedia is quite dazzling, it is easy to get tripped up and spend a lot of time and money on content that doesn't help boost sales. To get the most out of multimedia content, make sure it is integral to your stores wares (for example, using RealAudio clips of music you're selling).

When it comes to multimedia content there are several types to know about. Table 9.2 is a summary of the four key categories.

Table 9.2: Multimedia Content

Content Type	Description	Key Issue
Downloadable Audio/Video	As opposed to streaming, these higher quality files must be downloaded entirely before they can be listened to or watched.	Much better quality in terms of playback, but even "small" files can be 400K–3MB in file size, creating a long download.
Streaming Audio/Video	Audio or video content is sent from the Web site to the user in near real-time, offering quick access to these types of files.	Almost always requires special server software to accomplish and, in the case of video, is nearly unusable by users accessing via modems.
VR Photography	Specialized graphics files which render a complete 3D scene or object crafted from stitched together photographs.	Files can take a while to download.
Multimedia Programs	Categorized also as software content, these are full-fledged programs, Java applets, or Shockwave programs which integrate graphics, text, audio, and sometimes video into an interactive application.	Costly to produce and often requires programming knowledge.

It is important to identify how a store can use these technologies to produce interesting content for its Web site.

Downloaded Audio or Video: QuickTime, AVI Files, AIFF, and WAV Files

QuickTime and AVI files are the main digital video formats for computers, although you will also come across MPEG files from time to time. AIFF and WAV files are two of the most often used digital audio formats on the Web. Although the quality is high, these files need to be downloaded almost entirely before a user can digest them. An upside is that you need no special server software to offer these files to your users.

AIFF and WAV files are too large to use for long, speech-length applications, but can be effective in offering a 20–30 second preview of a song, or some other item that could benefit from an audio preview.

Digital video using QuickTime or AVI files, is great for showing items that are kinetic in nature (see Figure 9.8). That includes anything from movies and video games to robotic toys and sculptures. However, video files eat up server space. Additionally, a 1.5 MB video file can take a 28.8 modem as long as 15 minutes to download. While the quality is higher than streaming video formats, the immediacy for all but the fastest surfers is non-existent. Your use of video clips should be judicious.

Video files are best used only after other content types have been used with the particular item. They are better for higher-end items where educational content is paramount and people might value a long download in order to make a more informed purchase.

And if you want to include video on your site, don't use streaming video. The quality is simply unacceptable.

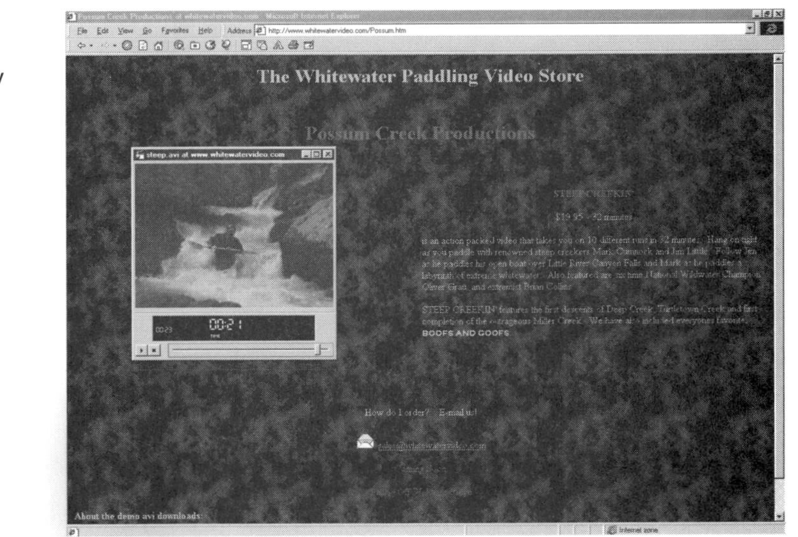

FIGURE 9.8
The Whitewater Paddling Video Store allows customers to preview videos by using AVI files.

Streaming Audio and Video: Real Audio and NetShow

Although there are other streaming solutions such as Xing and VDO, Real Networks' Real Audio/Video and Microsoft's NetShow formats are the dominant forms. In fact, NetShow is a distant second. As we mentioned, streaming video has nearly no relevance to stores because of the poor quality. However, streaming audio content is quite good and can be very useful for stores.

Music stores are a natural for Real Audio content, which streams audio over the Internet in real time. However, useful Real Audio content isn't just for music sites. For example, you can provide audio interviews with people your customers are interested in, or audio commentary for your products. Many browsers are distributed with the Real Player directly, so plenty of people have access to it. It's also fairly easy to develop content for it.

The problem with Real Audio or NetShow is that you need to be with a Web host or have your own server with Real Audio or NetShow installed. There aren't many hosting companies offering this yet and owning your own server is expensive. The cost should eventually drop, and these two formats will become more widely used.

Virtual Reality Photography

Virtual Reality (VR) photography is becoming more popular among store sites. As of this writing there are three dominant types of VR photography. The two most common are Apple's QuickTime VR and BlackDiamond's Surround Video (see Figure 9.9).

These two technologies allow you to take multiple pictures of an area and, after stitching them together, provide a 180–360 degree photo of an image. Users viewing the image can use a mouse to navigate the scene. This makes VR photography great for large spaces such as real estate or for the insides of cars (which is what Microsoft's Carpoint.com uses it for).

QuickTime VR also lets you create object movies. By photographing all around an object, you can create a 360 degree scene. Surround video doesn't offer this feature, which is great for all kinds of objects.

To create VR photographs you need two things—a camera (preferably digital) and a "stitcher" program, which lets you put the pictures together into the final product. PhotoVista from LivePicture is the best stitcher currently on the market. For 3D object photographs, you must use Apple's own stitcher as well as a special "object rig," which lets you position the object and rotate the camera around it. Rigs are also made for taking panoramic 3D shots as well. The best rigs are made by a company called Kaidan, which is listed in the Resources section.

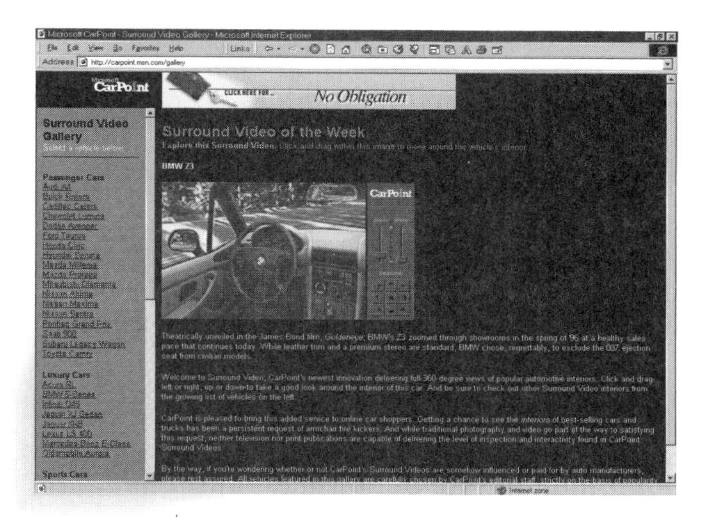

FIGURE 9.9
Microsoft's CarPoint uses Surround Video to help customers explore an automobile's interior.

Software Content

Software content could be programs that users download from the site. These could be more advanced, multimedia looks at products offered by the store or, in the case of stores that actually selling software, demos of the products.

It might also be a custom program or shareware that is of use to your customers. For example, a store catering to gardeners might offer an entire download of utilities and software that is of use to gardeners. A camera store might offer downloads of popular shareware or demo software that helps with digital images.

There are several ways to offer software content to your users:

- **Build custom software.** This is an expensive route, but if you have a large base of customers and have competition it can be worthwhile. The best thing to do is to tie the software directly to the store itself. For example, the gardening store might make a custom version of garden planning software that, at the end of the program, would place an order directly from the store for the seeds and other items needed to create the planned garden.

- **Offer access to relevant shareware or demoware.** There are lit erally thousands of demos and pieces of shareware that you can offer as a download. Make sure it is directly relevant to your site's customer base. Don't just offer a download for the sake of offering it.

Some shareware software comes with very strict license rights to redistribute the software. Don't ever assume that it's fine to distribute shareware.

If you plan to offer shareware, consider the strains on bandwidth it can cause. Find out what the total transfer allowance is from your Web hosting service. There might be a limit before you run into an extra fee. Keep in mind how quickly a 6MB download can eat up bandwidth if it's downloaded 200 times a month.

- **Link to relevant shareware or demoware.** Simply linking your customers to the relevant shareware or demoware is less taxing on your own server. Find the relevant link to a page on one of the bigger shareware Web sites like Jumbo.com, Tucows.com or Download.com and send users to it.

Getting into the software content business—especially custom software offerings—is a very expensive proposition. While the advantage of a custom program might give you an edge over your competition, it should only be done if it's nearly critical to the success of your store. Here are two types of software content being used by stores.

Shockwave

Shockwave is a catch-all name for multimedia Web content created using the programs of Macromedia, a leading multimedia tools company. Almost every Web surfer has come across some sort of Shockwave program.

Shockwave's true power lies in its ability to deliver multimedia oriented programs directly on a Web page with relative ease. However, even with recent developments, this type of content can take a while to download over normal phone lines.

Shockwave files are created with Macromedia's Director program. Most sites employing it don't create Shockwave files and instead rely on one of the thousands of freelance Director programmers available for such work. On Macromedia's Web site (www.macromedia.com) you can even search a database to find the name of a local Director programmer for your site.

Java

Java applets are a major way to deliver software oriented content directly on a site. For example, instead of having that garden planning application written for download, you might have it as a Java app that runs directly off a Web site when the user loads it.

Again, as with other forms of software content most storeowners will need to work with a contract programmer to design and develop the program.

Tips for Generating Good Content

Anyone can generate content. Good content separates the wheat from the chaff, the contenders from the pretenders, and in some cases the businesses from the out-of-businesses. What is good content? To some extent it can be defined like good art—"I don't know, but I know it when I see it." Or is that obscenity? Anyway, there are a few guidelines that will keep your content strong. But remember, it will be your creativity that takes your content from the simply good to the truly great.

Be Accurate

No matter how creative you are—if you're wrong, you're wrong. Having incorrect information on your site is no way to build a community of loyal customers. While many customers will shop at your store simply for the prices or the convenience, many will choose you over your competitors because of your knowledge and passion about your industry. If you continually post incorrect information, your credibility will suffer and so will your business.

Sometimes you will simply be presented with incorrect information, which is why attribution is important. If you run an online sporting goods store and a sneaker company tells you its new line will be out in time for Christmas, attribute the information to the company by writing, "According to XSneaks, the new Joe Shmoe basketball shoe will be out in time for Christmas." Then, if the sneakers are not available, the misinformation is on XSneaks, not you. This way, if an irate customer calls screaming, "You said the Joe Shmoe shoe was going to be available by Christmas," you can tell them it was XSneaks that said that and hopefully give the customer an explanation for the delay.

TIP ▸ ***Of course there will be times when you* are *wrong. If the mistake is yours, admit it. There's nothing worse than someone trying to blame a mistake on someone else. For those rare instances, immediately remove the incorrect item and add a correction to your news page. That should keep customers from deluging you with phone calls and e-mail to point out your mistake.***

Consider Your Customers' Needs

You'll probably have all kinds of information you want to share with your customers. Do they need it all? Probably not. As a store owner, you should have little difficulty figuring out what your customers need to know and what they could care less about. Because it's important to you doesn't mean it's important to them.

For example, feel free to provide personal information in your FAQ if it emphasizes your experience and expertise in your field or helps your customers identify with you a bit more. They will probably feel better about shopping at your site if they know there is a likable person behind all that HTML. However, you needn't burden them with a rambling tale about how the tragic death of your cat has left you emotionally scarred since childhood.

Keep news, contests, and polls related to what you sell or to related topics that you know your customers will find interesting. For example, posting daily professional sports scores on a sporting goods site might not have anything to do with selling sneakers, but it will probably be of interest to your customers. Posting sports scores on other sites might cause people to wonder, "Who is the jock running this place?"

As for product descriptions, include as much technical information as needed. If you're selling computers, simply saying, "It has a bunch of memory and is really fast" won't cut it. On the other hand, unless you're selling quality craftsmanship, you needn't tell your customers how the jeans you're selling were stitched together.

Be Innovative

Our philosophy is, "Don't be afraid to fail, just don't do it too often." That could be rephrased as, "Take chances, just not stupid ones." However, since stupid is in the eye of the beholder, you probably won't know that an idea is a bad one until after you've tried it. Considering the very competitive nature of your business, you need to set yourself apart from the field. One way is by consistently providing content that isn't available elsewhere. It might be an entirely new content area, or it might just be a fresh way of presenting information.

How do you do this? Know your business, know your customers, know what's out there and spend time thinking about how you can be different. What would you like to see if you visited a store in your market? More often than not, what you want to see will be what your customers want to see.

Innovation is simply thinking more and thinking better than everyone else. The more you think about your content, the better the chances you'll come up with something truly interesting and unique.

Keep it Simple, Stupid

Being innovative is the key to breaking out on the Web, but the other key is not biting off more than you can chew. It is very hard to dig yourself out of a hole on the Web, so don't try everything at once. Some very advanced content concepts have been covered here—but not all are recommended for people who don't have the resources or the knowledge. Instead, most people should keep things simple.

The power of the written word is going to stay strong on the Web for some time. Some of the best store content is similar to what you find on the Tronix Web site—nice pictures, simple blurbs, and an occasional review. If you keep things well written and consistently publish interesting content, people will respect your content far more than if you set up the most amazing chat room and have all sorts of custom Java programs tied into a killer database, none of which works.

Once you've mastered getting content up on a regular basis, you might go for something fancier. The key to how fast you grab at more complex content ideas is watching what your competitors do. If you feel that some other store's content is outstripping yours to the point that your losing sales because of it, it's time to upgrade your content. Until then—or until you really have the ability to pull off something fancy, we encourage you to stick with simple articles, JPEGs, and reviews.

Beat the Competition

If you find yourself constantly checking out your competitors' sites and saying "What a great idea!" then you're not beating the competition and you're not being innovative. When you have a great new content idea, don't sit on it. Chances are somebody else will have it up before you do.

If Appropriate, Use Humor

Take your business seriously, but don't take yourself too seriously. Some products don't lend themselves to humor, but if yours do, you should use it. Humor and other types of asides can work well on the Web to make something that seems very "virtual" like your store have some emotion and attitude that other physical stores try to convey.

If you plan on poking fun make sure and direct it toward yourself rather than outward. In the era of political correctness, any joke you might tell could lead to an avalanche of e-mail or even calls to boycott your store.

Give Honest Reviews

We've been over this, so we'll keep it brief. Don't lie. When your mom said, "Honesty is the best policy," she was right. If you refuse to print a negative review, remember something else Mom always said: "If you don't have anything good to say, don't say anything at all." Just don't lie.

Update Regularly

Keeping the same content on your site month after month is like having no content at all. Eventually, your customers will have seen it all and they're not about to re-read it just for the heck of it. This doesn't mean you have to redesign your Web site every week.

As you look at your site and the information therein, ask yourself if you are bored with it. You'll probably become bored with your site more quickly than customers will simply because you'll have to look at it every day. However, when you can't stand to peruse your own site, it's time to spice it up. New graphical touches or different uses of color are nice, but you should be just as concerned with keeping the information fresh. Change it as often as you can without making it impossible to keep up with everything. Here's where a "What's New" section is a big help. Your customers can immediately find out where you've made updates without searching the entire store for something new.

Joe's Take: *I spend an average of one hour a day generating content. I do a redesign every six months. A major overhaul of the Tronix site takes about 30–40 hours. When you see the same thing every day, you get sick of it. You have to go with the times. As the technology advances, you advance your Web site.*

Essential Gravy

If the price lists, order forms, and overall functionality are the meat and potatoes of your online store, the content is the gravy. However, your site will consist of pretty dry meat without at least a dollop of gravy. The key is finding the right amount so that your site is plenty tasty without giving your customer a heart attack. If you have the time, pour on the content. Just don't forget about the meat and potatoes.

If you're not too hungry, move onto Part III: Promoting Your Store. This includes information on finding your customers, promoting your store on the Internet, a guide to advertising, and how to do international sales.

PART III

Promoting Your Store

Build it and they will come—assuming you promote it. Launching an online store and simply waiting for flocks of customers is a recipe for failure. Part III shows you how to find customers, how to promote your store on the Internet, where, when, and how to advertise, and how to attract the important international market.

Part III Table of Contents

CHAPTER TEN

Finding Customers Online

You're site is finished. You've got inventory. You're ready to do business. What else do you need? Well...customers. No customers, no income, no store and you're back where you started. By now you realize that getting your store off the ground is going to take some work. That includes attracting customers; they aren't going to just show up. In fact, enticing customers to visit your Web site might be even more difficult than drawing them into a traditional store. However, there is a much larger pool of customers from which to draw, and, with a little planning, effort, and diligence, you can make a large number of potential customers aware of your store.

This chapter will give you some ideas about how to find and attract people who are interested in whatever you are selling. We'll show you:

- How to find customers on the Usenet, mailing lists, and online forums.

- How to post messages that will make people aware of your store while not being intrusive.
- How to spread the good word about your store.
- What not to do.

Making Use of the Usenet

Usenet newsgroups are basically bulletin boards dedicated to a particular subject and used by people interested in that subject. You can find newsgroups dedicated to almost any musical act, actor, actress, sport, hobby, or other interest on the planet. People post messages to one another discussing, for example, the upcoming Pearl Jam tour, the latest Julia Roberts movie or the chances of the Green Bay Packers winning another Super Bowl. You can also find newsgroups frequented by people who might be interested in shopping at your store. For example, if you sell skateboards, you could find potential customers at alt.skate-board. If you have a music store specializing in alternative rock, there are dozens of spots like alt.fan.pearl-jam, alt.fan.nirvana or alt.fan.nin.

There is always a percentage of worthless bandwidth and inappropriate or offensive postings, but most posts are interesting, informative and useful. You can skim through endless debates, helpful hints, product announcements, shameless plugs, and the ever-popular flame wars, in which a posting instigates an avalanche of passionate, contrary opinions.

An online merchant can gain a plethora of potential customers by working the newsgroups. You can also learn more about your customers and the industry in which you are working. The more time you can spend scanning the newsgroups, the more you are likely to learn.

There are also specific newsgroups, usually referred to as marketplaces, aimed at users who are interested in buying and trading items. This is where it's safest to post small advertisements without getting flamed. Outright ads in *these* groups are welcome—elsewhere they are not. In most cases, your best advertising will come from being visible and dragging along your implicit advertising as you gain notoriety for being informed and helpful. You can keep your store plugs to a minimum and still gain plenty of exposure. There is sure to be a newsgroup related to whatever you're selling. For example, if you sell a special shampoo for a horse's mane, you probably won't find any newsgroups dedicated to horse shampoos. However, you will certainly find groups that cater to horse enthusiasts. Any number of members could be interested in your product. Many times before you post you will want to search the entire Usenet. You can also search for any references to yourself or your products. To do this you need to become an expert at searching newsgroup posts. There are several ways to do this.

Finding the Newsgroups of Your Customers

To search for particular newsgroups, you can start with specific keywords before branching out into more general categories as necessary. The key is to experiment with various words and combinations, varying the generality and specificity. If your search is too specific, you may find nothing. If it is too general, finding the most useful newsgroup among the hundreds of possibilities could be just as difficult.

Returning to the example of the horse shampoo salesman, he could do a search for **Thoroughbred** or simply **horse**. He may even try shampoos, but could spend an entire day scrolling through all the possibilities, most of which will be geared toward human hair. How about a search for **animal shampoo**? As you tailor your search, a subject relevant to your business will show up. Join the groups you think can help you add customers or learn more about your specific industry.

There are a number of sources to help you find relevant newsgroups. Three of the easiest and most effective are Deja News (www.dejanews.com), Hot Bot (www.hotbot.com), and New Bot (www.wired.com/newbot). Deja News (Figure 10.1) is the best of the three for finding newsgroups, simply because that is the site's only function.

Deja News

Deja News is a search engine specifically geared toward finding the newsgroup you're looking for. There are a number of ways to do searches depending on the information you have and that which you are seeking.

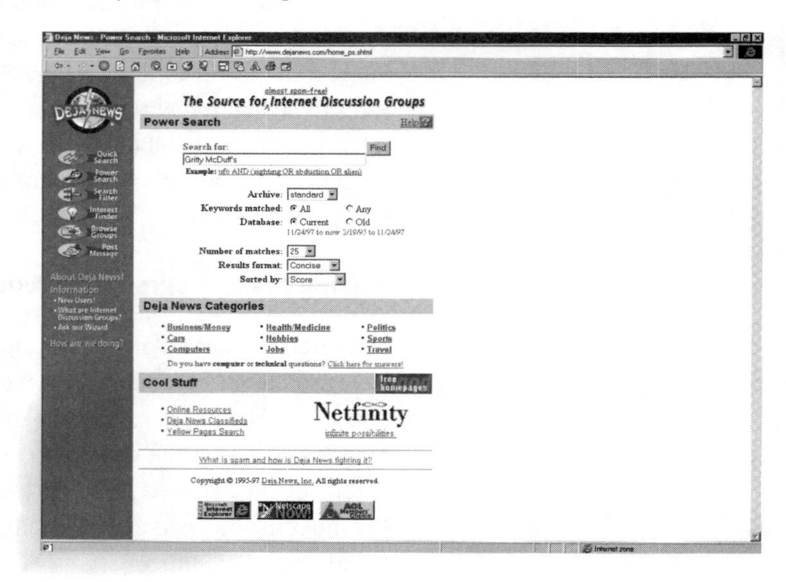

FIGURE 10.1
Deja News is specifically geared toward finding and searching newsgroups.

Quick Search

The Quick Search asks you to enter a specific question or topic and responds with a number of possible newsgroups to visit. Results are listed beginning with the most recent posting and include a subject line, the newsgroup and the author.

If you click on the author's e-mail, Deja News provides an author profile. The profile includes the number of postings by the author and where they were posted. You can then read any previous postings.

Click on the subject line to open the document. Once you have opened the document in any search mode, you are presented with a number of new options. You can move to the next article or the previous article or, by clicking on "Current Results," move back to the list of postings. Clicking on "Post Message" allows you to do just that. Finally, you can view the thread of the posting back to its origin.

Power Search

Start the Power Search by entering a keyword or keywords and choosing a match option of "all" or "any" and a database search of "current" or "old." You can then choose the number of matches (25, 50, or 100) and the results format (concise, detailed, or threaded). The concise format provides the same results as the Quick Search. The detailed format offers a slightly longer subject line. The threaded format follows the thread of related postings.

Power Search allows you to sort by score, date, author, newsgroup or subject.

Search Filter

The Search Filter helps you refine your searches by filtering on a message field. Enter a group (i.e. **alt.tv.x-files** or ***x-files***), search for a particular author, and/or choose a subject (i.e. **Gillian Anderson**). Select a date range (i.e. **From: Sept 14 97 To: Sept 15 97**) and click on Create Filter.

This will give you a number of documents, which in this case was 69. Click on the number and you will be given a list of the documents. In this case, it was rabid fans of "The X-Files" celebrating Anderson's Emmy Award for Best Actress in a Drama.

Interest Finder

The Interest Finder searches for newsgroups by topic and rates each group with a percentage of confidence that the topic will be discussed in that newsgroup. For example, an Interest Finder search for **Michael Jordan** returned a 99 percent confidence rate for rec.collecting.sport.basketball, a 23 percent rate for rec.collecting.sport.baseball, an 18 percent rate for rec.sport.basketball.pro, and a surprisingly low 7 percent for alt.sports.basketball.nba.chicago-bulls.

Browse Groups

Browse Groups lets you search for groups by hierarchy and gives examples of top level groups such as news., biz., comp., talk., sci., or misc. For example, clicking on news will lead to a number of options such as news.software. Choosing news.software will provide more options, such as news.software.misc, which will lead to actual postings.

Deja News Categories

This provides a number of categories to search. The primary categories are business/money, cars, computers, health/medicine, hobbies, jobs, politics, sports, and travel. Each category is divided into subgroups. For example, clicking on sports will result in football, basketball, baseball, etc. Choose a subgroup and search, read, or post.

Cool Stuff

Cool Stuff brings you to Newsreader Software, Deja News Classifieds, and Yellow Pages Search. The Newsreader Software provides the opportunity to download three different pieces of software. @ccess News 1.01 is a newsreader and mail client for Windows 95/NT. @ccess Mail 1.01 provides more features than most Windows 95 e-mail programs. Virtual Access Professional is an advanced newsreader and mail program for those who are confident with newsgroups and need killfiles, crossposting and other advanced functions.

Hotbot

At Hotbot, you can chose to search the Web or Usenet News. Enter a keyword or phrase and search for all the words, any of the words, the exact phrase, words in the title, the person, links to this URL, and the Boolean expression. You can have your results returned with full or brief descriptions or just the URLS.

Newsbot

Newsbot is most helpful when searching for news stories on the Web. For example, you can enter **Microsoft** as a keyword and find all the stories dealing with Microsoft that have appeared on the Web in the past six, 12, 24, or 48 hours. If that time frame isn't enough, you can go back three days, four days, seven days, or indefinitely. You can use Newsbot in the same manner to search for newsgroup postings.

Other Newsgroup Engines

Two other sites may also be of interest to you as you search for newsgroup information.

The University of North Carolina's Sunsite hosts a newsgroup searching engine that lists newsgroups based on various interest topics. It also can search and list associated FAQs and other interesting information. Check it out at sunsite.unc.edu/usenet-i/search.html.

Another great site is called Tile.Net and is located at www.tile.net/tile/listserv/index.html. This site lets you search for names of newsgroups and topical mailing lists.

Usenet Software

When you apply for an Internet account, your package will usually contain a Web browser, an e-mail client, and a newsreader. One of the finest newsreaders is actually the one integrated with Netscape's Web browser as well as the one that comes with Microsoft's Internet Explorer suite. Both are easy to use, but not as extensive as some of the stand-alone products on the market. If you are already familiar with the relevant newsgroups, you can simply add them to your Netscape or Internet Explorer setup.

The more powerful, independent newsreaders usually offer a broader range of features. There are several major newsreaders available for Mac or PC, many of them shareware.

Anawave Gravity has won a slew of awards, has a number of features unavailable almost anywhere else, and costs $29.95. Visit the Anawave Web site at www.anawave.com for a downloadable version and more information.

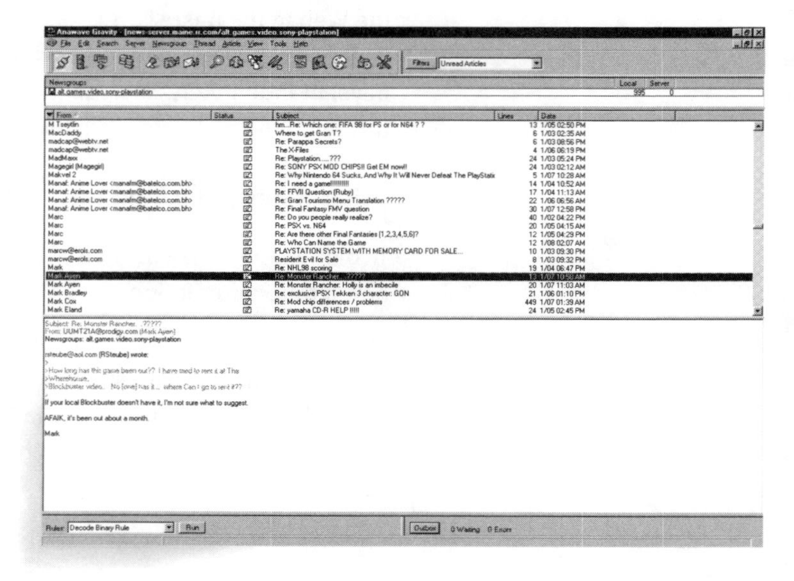

FIGURE 10.2
Anawave Gravity is an award-winning newsreader.

You might also check out NewsWatcher, which is freeware and also has received good reviews. It is available at charlotte.acnes.nwu.edu/jln/progs.htm.

Using Mailing Lists

Another great place to find customers is mailing lists. Mailing lists are a little different from newsgroups because they foster discussion through e-mail rather than on the Usenet. These lists require direct subscription in order for someone to participate. Users send an e-mail to the list and include a command in the body or subject line of the message which initiates the subscription.

Members receive messages posted to the list by other members and the discussion commences.

The subscription and delivery method of discussion is what makes mailing lists interesting for several reasons. Since list members must seek out and choose to subscribe to the lists, they tend to be more deeply involved in the subject matter.

TIP ▸ ***Many mailing lists are privately moderated and unreceptive to advertising. Using the participatory approach is best. Study the instructional message you'll receive after subscribing—it will generally contain the rules of the newsgroup. Sending a note to a moderator can help facilitate good will.***

Mailing lists can generate dozens, if not hundreds of messages. Often the best thing to do is subscribe to the "digest version" of the list. This combines the day's messages into one daily message or several delivered at key intervals during the day. You can also deliver private messages to other members. Be careful. There are few things more embarrassing than sending what was intended to be private message to the entire mailing list.

TIP ▸ ***Since even small mailing lists can quickly lead to a pile of e-mail, we suggest you use a separate account or filters on your e-mail to handle the inflow. Otherwise, you may be overwhelmed by mailing list messages co-mingling with direct customer e-mails.***

You should also know how to get off a mailing list. When you subscribe, keep the instructions to issue an "unsubscribe" message to the list. Write it down, put it in a notepad file—just don't lose it. If you can't figure out how to get off, you'll end up feeling like Michael Corleone—"Just when you think you're out, they pull you right back in!" Actually, you'll just have to post a message to the moderator or the list asking how to get off.

Many mailing lists are actually sponsored by advertising. When you subscribe to a list, find out if the list is supported by advertising. While the participatory method can be good, many offer a much more direct route to customers through advertising, which is often inexpensive and quite focused. A good way to approach advertising on a list is to become a participant before actually buying advertising. This will let the members know that you are helpful, knowledgeable and open for business.

Joe's Take: *Mailing lists are great places to find customers. However, keep in mind that these are moderated far more closely than newsgroups and you should participate frequently. This means a lot of work to produce useful information and join lively debates. I suggest working just one or two lists at a time. Since members tend to stay on mailing lists, you can work one for several weeks before moving on to another.*

Using Online Forums

Online forums are similar to newsgroups; the primary difference is that forums have one or more moderators to oversee all the messages. Moderators watch for offensive material such as harsh language, subjects that stray from the forum's topic, and advertising. CompuServe, America Online, and Prodigy have their own forums that are formed and maintained by SysOps (System Operators). If you have a membership to any of these services and try to use a forum for advertising, your message will be deleted. Depending on the service, you will be warned not to try it again. After a couple of warnings, you may have your membership revoked.

As with newsgroups, people generally join forums because they share common interests, not to get pounded with advertisements. Suppose you joined a music forum and found a section dedicated to The Beatles. While scanning various messages trying to find the name of a particular song from *Sgt. Pepper's Lonely Hearts Club Band*, you wind up wading through record store advertisements which claim to have every Beatles album at unbeatable prices. Most subscribers would be annoyed, especially in a world where you can't eat dinner at home without being harassed by telemarketers.

If you plan on "invading" one of these online services, you should contact its customer service department, which will guide you to the proper places for advertising. You can also search around yourself. Every online service has its own search engine. Perhaps you can find a forum that has a section dedicated to buying or trading items. Let the SysOp know your intentions, and find out if it's acceptable to advertise there.

TIP ▸ ***Online forums ironically have been slow to develop on the Web itself but you soon you may start to see more pop-up. Nerdworld (www.nerdworld.com) is one site beginning to implement a strong message forum type presence. As Web based forum software gets better and easier for sites to deploy you may begin to find yourself with tons o services to check in on. Watch the Web engines, newsgroups, and Yahoo! for deployment of Web based online forums as well. Unfortunately each one will operate differently, and have its own moderation rules. As you spread out to these forums be sure to take the same cautious approach you would within more established forums like those found on Compuserve and AOL.***

Finding the Online Forums of Your Customers

CompuServe, AOL, or Prodigy have areas where you can find forums by entering keywords.

On AOL, you simply call up the keywords function, type in a keyword and hit search. You can also go to the Directory Of Services, which is accessed through the program menus or through keyword **DIRECTORY**.

You can access Compuserve's index of forums by selecting the GO function and typing in the keyword **INDEX**.

To find an index of Prodigy's bulletin boards check out the Member Services.

Software for AOL, CompuServe, and Prodigy

Getting the software for America Online, CompuServe, and Prodigy is easy. If you haven't received AOL software in the mail, we have to question whether you actually exist. To get in touch with AOL call 1-800-827-6364 or visit www.aol.com.

CompuServe can be reached at 1-800-848-8990. To get the software, go to world.compuserve.com/cs/csfaq.asp and click on the indicated phrase in the first question. Prodigy software is available at www.prodigy.com.

Rules and Tips for Posting

So you've figured out where you need to post messages—now what? How do you approach this group? Do you go in full-force and advertise you business name surrounded by a border of asterisks—the equivalent of a theatre marquee? Do you post your entire inventory with prices, hoping to lure people to your Web site? Those are definitely aggressive approaches, but if you're in an area that is not defined as a buying or trading group, you could be in for some nasty responses. Before you start posting the first thing that comes to mind, consider the following tips.

Stick to the Topic

When posting in the newsgroups or forums, stick with the topic. Just because you are selling hand-held electronic chess games, doesn't mean you should promote this in any video game group like Nintendo or Sega. Those people will certainly let you know you've entered the wrong territory. If you want to post information about your products, try to find newsgroups that are geared toward buying or selling. If you find newsgroups that are general discussion areas for the types of products you sell, pay close attention to them. Of course, members of these types of newsgroups are there to share information, and are not fond of getting inundated with ads.

TIP ▸ ***Think before you post. With a number of potential customers watching, you don't want to make a fool of yourself. If an individual makes a worthless post, the consequences are no worse than the other newsgroup members thinking the person is a dork. As the representative of an online store, you can cost yourself credibility and customers with an uninformed post. Most newsgroups have a large number of regulars, so if you make a bad first impression, you'll certainly be remembered.***

Keep Promotional Posts Subtle and Simple

An accepted and effective approach is simply becoming active in the newsgroups—posting your opinions and taking note of what others have to say. If you can subtly include the fact that you own an online store related to the newsgroup, you'll likely have people inquiring about your store without having to shove it down people's throats.

After you become a familiar presence you can be a bit more forward. For example, if you sell items like baseball cards, toys, or other premiere sensitive items, you can begin to post simple "what's new" messages. If you participate in many discussions without trying to sell people anything, they usually won't mind these brief, informative posts. When you post information like this to a group try to take a "journalistic" approach—be informative and unbiased. Don't try to sell the item, just talk about it.

If you're going to post an ad, it should be something small and simple. You can use a header like "New @ Tronix." Potential customers can see a list of what's new and, of course, a date in the header will let them know when the ad was posted. You can simply list your newest arrivals with a trailing line of text, which lets people know how to get further information. Your signature can contain all the rest of the pertinent information (e.g., store hours, site address, phone). Most newsreaders today recognize hyperlinks, so your site address can simply be activated right from the message, leading readers to your site.

Here are some sample messages that we would post to two newsgroups related to Tronix customers—the Sony PlayStation newsgroups and the general video game marketplace.

Message begin:

To: rec.games.video.sony,rec.games.video.marketplace
NEW AT TRONIX: 4.22.98

****
Tomato Brawl
Knights from Hell (2 CDs)
Spider Mountain
For more information, visit our web site at:
http://www.tronixweb.com

TRONIX http://www.tronixweb.com
PlayStation * Saturn * Nintendo 64 * PC * Imports
Hours: M-F, 10-5 EDT. 212.447.5980
No-Nonsense Mail-Order for the Serious Gamer

Message end

The information is simple and there are no prices, which can flag your post as a flagrant advertisement. If you post pricing, you might draw responses like: "I don't think your prices are that good" or "I got that item cheaper somewhere else, so stay out." If potential customers see the prices in the newsgroups, they may not bother to see what else you carry.

If you have items you want to post for a special sale, you can follow the same format as above replacing "New" with "Sale." Sales are usually more acceptable as everyone is always looking for a good bargain. They're also a great way to bring in new customers.

TIP ▸ ***Keep your signature down to about four lines of text. Large signatures tend to aggravate users.***

What to Respond to and What to Avoid

Replying to the proper messages becomes a talent after awhile. When you own an online store, everything you post in the newsgroups becomes an immediate reflection of your business. As you thread various topics, you might see people asking about where to find a certain product. You can join in with a reply and mention your business, as long as it's done in a way that does not look like a desperate grab for customers.

For example:

[user@somewhere.net] Hey, does anyone know where I can find those new infrared Bose desktop speakers?

[you@somewhereelse.net] They should be available at most stores by now, but if you're having trouble finding them, we just received some stock a few days ago. Our web address is in our signature.

Notice the approach. Don't push your store down the user's throat. Give the person options. Another post that's ideal to respond to is a question someone may have about a product. If the question relates to an item you carry, and you're familiar with it, you can reply with a small review. For example:

[you@somewhere.net] The translucent CD holder you are referring to unfortunately holds only 40 discs and it's not that convenient to get at your discs once it's full. I've had those in stock, but the newer model X holds a lot more and is designed with better spacing for easier identification of your discs.

With this type of response, you are helping a consumer make a better decision while simultaneously setting up a pointer to your business.

The types of postings that are best left alone are complaints about other stores or those by disgruntled users who like to go online just to whimper or find fault. Replying to someone's complaint about a purchase from a store with "You would have had a better deal had you come to us" does not solve a person's problem. It simply makes him or her look unintelligent and makes you look arrogant. While it could grab some attention and maybe even some customers, it also sets you up as a perfectionist—which you better be after a post like that. It also is a blatant invitation for flames and looks incredibly self-serving.

Responding to an Attack

If a customer goes public with a complaint about your store, reply publicly and personally with concern and ask how you can remedy the problem. This will show your customer that you are interested in the problem and others will take notice. For example:

[user@somewhere.net] I went looking for a bootleg tape of Phish's "Great Went" concert in Limestone, Maine, and Phred's Phishing Hole doesn't have it yet. Can you believe that? I'm never visiting that site again.

[phred@somewhere.net] We have to apologize for the lack of a "Great Went" tape at this point. We actually had a copy, but the sound quality was so poor we didn't feel it would be fair to make it available. We're working on getting a tape we feel comfortable distributing, but until then..."We will sell no Phish before its time!" We're sorry for any inconvenience and thanks for your patience.

You can also take your disagreement into a private exchange, but always remain civil. If you privately call your nemesis a moron, there's always the chance your tirade will be made public by the recipient. Never post anything you don't want revealed publicly.

Joe's Take: *Posting in the correct newsgroups without overdoing the advertising was a great way to get the word out about Tronix. As I scanned the Net, I came across a number of newsgroups with topics that were associated with my line of business. The products I currently carried (or planned to carry) were discussed openly, so I jumped right into many of these topics, answering questions, and posting informative information (small capsule reviews of games or release dates in my case). I didn't post any ads, other than my automatic signature file which was basically four lines of store information (company name, Web site URL,* *office hours, phone/fax number, formats carried). After a number of postings, the e-mail started to roll in. It ranged from simple inquiries to actual orders. Between the simple link to my site in my signature, and a hearty dose of intelligent posts, Tronix began to form a name for itself. Forums and newsgroups each have something to recommend them. With no monitors, anything goes on Internet newsgroups. It also means they are less organized than online forums. A topic about the best digital cameras on the market can suddenly turn into a feud about presidential candidates. For storeowners, newsgroups do have an obvious advantage over online forums. If a topic labeled "what online shop carries a good assortment of DAT movies?" is posted, you can jump right in and give them your movie store URL without worrying about the deletion of your reply by a SysOp. If you have good customers who frequent the forums or newsgroups, they'll usually jump in and recommend your service. I had the opportunity to be a SysOp for one of CompuServe's popular video game forums and had to weed out any advertising I came across myself. You can imagine what it was like, owning an online business selling games, reading questions about where to find a certain product and not being able to refer people to Tronix. If you were a regular member you couldn't get away with it, so being a SysOp and attempting to direct someone to your Web site was a big no-no.*

Other Ways to Spread the Good Word

Posting in newsgroups or online forums is a great way for you to get the word out about your store. This self-generated content can promote the image of your store and yourself. If done correctly, potential customers will soon realize that you have the products they want. Just as importantly, you can promote yourself as knowledgeable and easy to deal with. Once you have built up a base of loyal customers, they will do much of the work for you with strong word-of-mouth. Their positive posts can be used to endorse your business and, in some cases, customers might even go out of their way to help you succeed.

Monitor and Cull Posts to Promote Your Store

Reading the newsgroups should be a daily routine. Once you've decided which newsgroups will be your permanent hunting grounds, run through a quick scan every day and keep your eyes out for any topics that you think would benefit your retail business. Most newsgroup readers will allow you to mark a particular thread so you can follow its progress as people reply to the topic. Decide when it's best to join in and offer information that will benefit both the group and your store.

Getting Customers to Help Online

In the early days of your business, your primary method of advertising will be through your own periodic posts. As time goes by, individuals who are satisfied with your service will surely make reference to your store to others in the group. The great thing about the Internet is how fast information spreads. One happy customer's comment, whether it is in a newsgroup or Internet Relay Chat (IRC), can lead new customers to your Web site. Newer customers who decide to give your company praise will bring in even more.

Unfortunately, not every customer you correspond with will be active with the newsgroups or IRC, but of course the traditional word of mouth can be just as effective. From time to time, customers who purchase items from your store and receive shipments on time and in perfect condition, will usually send you e-mail comments about how they've enjoyed your service. When you feel comfortable enough with them, you might want to make a subtle suggestion that they mention your place. For example:

Customer: I really like your store. I have purchased a number of products from you and I just want to say you have a wonderful service!

You: Thanks again for your business and the much appreciated feedback. Since we're fairly small right now, it would be great to get the word around a bit so we can grow and keep providing great service. Perhaps you can mention my place if you see other people looking for similar products?

The key is to make them feel like they have a stake in your store's survival—if they love your store and service enough, they'll want to make sure you don't have to scale back your operation or go out of business.

What Not To Do

We've tried to give you an idea what to do when searching for customers online. Nearly as important is what *not* to do.

- **Don't knock the competition in your postings.** It makes you look unprofessional and could backfire. No one is perfect (including you) and chances are if you rip someone, they'll find a way to rip you right back.

- **Never overdo your posts.** One small post several times a week is plenty. Excessive posting will almost guarantee you writing something that can garner negative feedback.

- **Be careful when posting about new items.** Do you actually have them in stock? A lot of companies jump the gun to grab an audience on a new item not yet in stock. Think about the people who will contact you by phone, especially if you don't have an 800 number. Long distance callers will not be happy when they find the item is not yet in.

- **Stay away from those UPPER-CASE ASSAULTS.** You can use upper-case letters here and there, but an all-upper-case advertisement on the net is like an annoying television commercial with a screaming salesman. It also makes you look inexperienced with the Internet.

- **If you want to get your message out to a number of related newsgroups, be careful when you cross-post.** If you are selling baseball cards, there's no need to plug your shop through 30 different baseball-related newsgroups. People often join many similar groups, and you don't want them running into the same advertisement everywhere they look.

- **By all means, do not plug or push anything** that is related to your business in a newsgroup that has nothing to do with your business.

- **Don't come across as biased** and don't get into feuds with anyone in the newsgroups. If you disagree with someone's opinion on a specific topic, it's best to stay out of it.

- **Don't post high praise about your store** while trying to keep your affiliation secret. Savvy net users will immediately associate your e-mail address with your Web site and you'll look like a dishonest fool.

- **Avoid posting large price lists in newsgroups,** especially those not set up for buying or trading. This is what your Web site is for, so there's no need to force-feed your inventory to other users.

- **Chat rooms** are generally a waste of time unless you are the guest.

An Easy, Personal Way to Reach Customers

It's extremely easy to find potential customers online. Not only are participants in newsgroups and online forums readily reachable, they are generally passionate about the subject. If someone consistently participates in a newsgroup dedicated to mountain biking, you can be sure she'll be interested in hearing a bit about xtremebike.com's selection of suspension forks. The more you participate, the more people will get to know you and your store.

Using the newsgroups and online forums is a personal way to reach your customers unavailable anywhere else. To ignore the newsgroups and forums is to ignore your customers. If you find the relevant newsgroups, follow this chapter's posting tips, and remain dedicated to becoming a contributor to the online community, customers will almost certainly follow.

That said, it's on to Chapter 11, we're we'll show you how to promote your store on the Internet.

CHAPTER ELEVEN

Promoting Your Store on the Internet

You have the greatest online store on the Web. Your content is second to none. Your graphics sizzle and pop. Your prices are unmatched. So you sit back and wait for customers to flock to your site, spend gobs of money, and pay for your yacht. Well the Web isn't an "if you build it they will come" field of dreams.

You know your store is outstanding. Now you have to let everyone else know. There are some obvious ways to promote your store on the Internet: submitting to search engines, finding quality links, setting up bounty programs, having your store included as part of an online mall, buying advertising on the Web and off, and being involved in newsgroups and mailing lists. In Chapter 10, we focused on how to get the most out of newsgroups and in Chapter 12 we'll give you some tips for advertising—online and offline—on a small budget. Here we will cover search engines, links, bounty programs, and malls.

This chapter focuses on what you can do on the Web to promote your store without spending a cent or an overwhelming amount of time. Creating an informational atmosphere, as discussed in Chapter 9, will give people a reason to repeatedly visit your store, but you have to get them there initially. That's what this chapter will help you do.

Search Engines

If you're on the Web and aren't sure where to find some information, what do you do? Go to a search engine. You're not alone. And when you get that first list of 10 options, how often do you feeling like looking at the second 10? The following 10? Not often and neither does anybody else. It is of the utmost importance to be among the first 10 sites listed by a particular search engine.

Rather than get bogged down in the technicalities of how search engines work, we'll give you a little background and then get on to what really matters—how they can work for you. If you're interested in more details about how search engines work, we strongly recommend reading *Getting Hits: The Definitive Guide To Promoting Your Website* by Don Sellers, published by Peachpit Press. Actually, we recommend it for anyone with a Web site.

Automatic Submission

There are a number of search engines to choose from—far more than you're probably aware of or will ever use. If you don't want to take the time to submit your site individually to each search engine, there are a number of automatic submission sites that do the work for you. You fill out one form and the service does the rest. However, different search engines use different methods of ranking sites, and automatic submission does not allow you to tailor your submission for the quirks of each particular engine. Your automatic submission might get your site listed in the first 10 by one engine and 150th by another.

If you really don't have the time to submit to individual engines, automatic submission is a good alternative. Then, once your business is off the ground and you have a bit of time to catch your breath, you can re-submit to the engines with which you would like to improve your ranking. Make sure the particular engines understand you have already submitted automatically and you are updating your listing.

Yahoo! (www.yahoo.com) has a list of automatic submission sites you should check out if you're planning to submit your site automatically. One of them is Submit-It.

Submit-It

www.submit-it.com

Submit-It is arguably the top automatic submission service on the Web. Submit-It (Figure 11.1) includes announcement services and traffic-driving services. Submit-It Online announces your Web site with your choice of 400 directories. Submit-It Free submits your site to 20 search engines, including all the big ones.

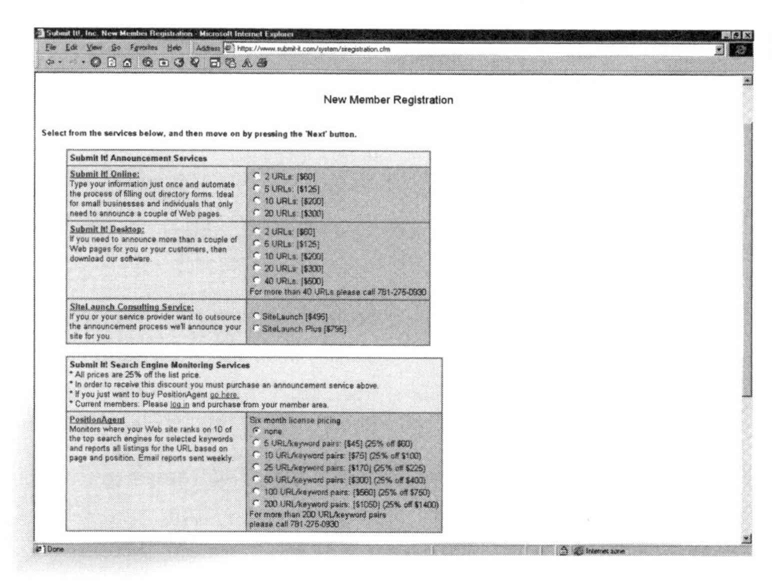

FIGURE 11.1
Submit-It's announcement and search engine monitoring service.

Submit-It also offers a number of paid services to help maximize and track your site's ranking. You can also get free information about the latest methods for driving traffic to your Web site.

Individual Submission

Many search engines will find your site without out your even submitting it. However, he who hesitates is lost. Go find the search engines on which you want to be listed rather than waiting for them to find you. Most of the major search engines provide you with an easy method of submitting through a link from their front pages to their submission pages.

As we have already mentioned, search engines work differently so you need to tailor your submissions to each engine. While some search engines have "spiders" (information retrievers) that will dig through and index your entire site, others will only index the main page or one level deeper. Learn as much as possible about the particular search engine to which you are submitting before actually doing so. This chapter includes some basic information on some of the top search engines. The Web sites of the engines also have much of the information you need.

Maximizing Your Ranking

Search engines are changing constantly and we'll emphasize again that they all have their own idiosyncrasies. If you are intent on getting your site ranked appropriately, pay particular attention to your submission. This doesn't guarantee anything, however. No matter how good the engine, they are all dependent on the searcher.

Search engines aren't perfect, either. You might be the top source on the Web for a particular item and wind up with a poor ranking. This imperfection works both ways. You might just as easily wind up with a surprisingly high ranking.

There are a few things to think about that will apply to some search engines but not others: depth of search, meta tags, keywords, title, word repetition, word placement, text and page design, and number of external links.

Depth of Search

As we mentioned, some search engines send out spiders that dig through entire Web sites. Others dig a bit, but not into every page of a site. And others do no digging at all. Most search engines will let you know how much of your site you need to submit. If a search engine doesn't have a spider that will follow links throughout your site, you need to submit each page individually.

Meta Tags

Meta tags are pieces of information placed in the head of an HTML document. Although the information is not displayed by Web browsers, it can be found and recognized by some information retrievers. Not all search engines recognize meta tags.

The key to writing a good meta tag for your store is in optimizing the tags to get the best impact for your site. Don Sellers' book is a good resource for learning more about the peculiarities of each search engine. Another helpful resource is the Meta Tagging for Search Engines page located on the Web at www.stars.com/Search/Meta/Tag.html.

The Tag Structure

Two types of meta tags need to be considered in relation to search engines—description and keywords. A description meta tag allows you to include a brief description of your site that will appear when your site appears as the result of a search. If you fail to include a meta tag description, as many sites do, your search summary will be the first portion of text on your site, which might not be descriptive of your site at all.

Here is the basic structure:

```
<META NAME="KEYWORDS" CONTENT="KEYWORDS">
<META NAME="DESCRIPTION" CONTENT="DESCRIPTION">
```

And here is an example that might be used for a store, like Tronix, that sells computer and video games.

<META NAME="KEYWORDS" CONTENT="Video, Games, Game, CD, CDs, Cartridges, Store, Shop, Tronix, Sony, Sega, Nintendo, Computer, Joystick, Gamepad, Imports, Mail, Order">

<META NAME="DESCRIPTION" CONTENT="Tronix is the place to find all your favorite video and computer games from all over the world. Sony, Nintendo, Sega specialists with great prices, imports and fast delivery.">

That covers the basic structure of meta tags. You can avoid writing them and learn how to tailor them for some specific search engines on the Meta Tag Builder Site which has a fill-in form that will builder an HTML header all set with the optimal tag information. The Meta Tag Builder Site is located at vancouver-Webpages.com/VWbot/mk-matas.html.

Keywords

Keywords are the words someone might use while doing a search for a site. Defining your site's keywords is essential and difficult. You need to come up with the words someone is most likely to use when looking for your site. Those words might not be the same as the ones you would use. Sellers has a good tip in his book. He suggests gathering a group of friends, colleagues, and potential site visitors and having them generate the keywords for your site. Think of any variation of those keywords and once you have a list of as many as 30 keywords, have the group rank them in importance and descriptiveness. Use the top two or three words in your title, headings, text, and meta tags.

Title

Even without regard to search engines, your page's title should be as descriptive as possible. Most search engines display the title of the page in the results and use the title words heavily in their ranking of sites. Having an accurate, descriptive title for all pages—not just your home page—is essential.

Word Repetition

Originally, word repetition was an easy way to increase your site's ranking. Since then, many search engines have actually reversed things and begun penalizing sites with flagrantly unnecessary word repetition. Still, others use word repetition as a criteria for high-ranking.

Word placement

As we have mentioned, word selection in the title is essential. Also keep in mind that many search engines place a greater emphasis on words located near the beginning of the page, making this word selection very important also.

Text and page design

If you don't include any text on a page, the spiders won't be able to read it. Spiders also are unable to read text that is embedded in a graphic, so don't embed too much of your text.

Also, remember that some search engines don't recognize meta tags and instead take the early part of a page's text for the summary. Make sure that text will work well as a summary in a search result.

Number of external links

Some search engines use the number of links from other sites to yours to determine your site's popularity and then use popularity as part of the ranking process. The feeling is that the more popular a site is, the more links there will be to it. This factor makes working to get links to your site doubly advantageous.

Submitting to Specific Search Engines

Now that you have a general idea about what search engines look for, here are a few of the top search engines and some keys to submitting your site to them. Most of the sites have an icon for adding URLs and will step you through the process.

TIP ▸ ***Many search engines and indexes like Yahoo! (shopguide.yahoo.com) are actually setting up separate areas that index online merchants specifically. As more of these specialty search engines pop up make sure you target listings among them specifically.***

AltaVista

www.altavista.digital.com

At AltaVista, click on Add/Remove URL and submit just the main page of your site. AltaVista says its crawler will follow links through the entire site. AltaVista asks that you use meta tags.

Even if you don't submit your site, AltaVista's crawler will most likely find your site if there are external links to it.

Excite

www.excite.com

Excite uses artificial intelligence to discern your site's dominant theme. Check to see if your site has been found by Excite and, if not, click on Add URL. Excite doesn't use meta tags. Using descriptive phrases near the top of your pages will help Excite's artificial intelligence rank your site correctly.

Hotbot

www.hotbot.com

Hotbot is HotWired's search engine. It is supposed to update every two weeks and advises that if any other indexed site is linked to yours, it will find you. Submit each page's URL once and limit submissions from the same domain to 50 in a 24-hour period.

Hotbot supports meta tags and focuses first on keywords in the title, followed by keywords in meta tags, and frequency of keywords in the text.

InfoSeek Ultra

ultra.infoseek.com

InfoSeek does not accept automatic submissions and you must submit each page of your site separately. If you want to submit more than 50 pages, they should be sent through e-mail rather than be submitted directly on the site.

InfoSeek says it chooses only the most relevant and valuable sites and that an inappropriate site definition or spamming can lead to exclusion from the index. InfoSeek Select sites are chosen from the index by InfoSeek's editors based on editorial value, traffic, and the number of external links to the site. You should use meta tags of 200 characters or less.

InfoSeek suggests you use a highly descriptive title, include a meta tag description, create meta tag keywords that contain comma-separated phrases, and use an assortment of synonyms that accurately describe the site. Attempting to boost your site's relevance by overusing keywords may result in a lower score or omission.

Lycos

www.lycos.com

Lycos says its spider will dig through your entire site and that you will show up on a Lycos search two to four weeks after submission. You should definitely use meta tags with Lycos.

Lycos ranks sites based on keywords used in the title, in high-level headings, and in text near the top of the page. Page popularity also improves the ranking while word repetition will be penalized.

WebCrawler

www.webcrawler.com

WebCrawler indexes every word on your site up to 1MB of text. You needn't submit keywords or categories. The keywords under which a page will be found in a WebCrawler search are the words on a page.

WebCrawler provides a few tips that it says will ensure your site a deserving index. WebCrawler suggests using a uniquely descriptive title because it gives slightly more weight to titles than text or meta tags. Use short meta tags for keywords and a description/summary, but avoid over-repetition. Make sure the main page describes the site fully.

Spamdexing could get your site eliminated from WebCrawler. Separately submit the URLs for the home page and the main subsidiary pages, but not for every document.

Yahoo!

www.yahoo.com

Submissions to Yahoo! (Figure 11.2)are controlled by people. Before submitting to Yahoo!, you have to select a category and then narrow it down to subcategories. Once you have selected a specific category for your site, click on the Add URL icon. If you have already submitted a site and want to make a change, select Change Form.

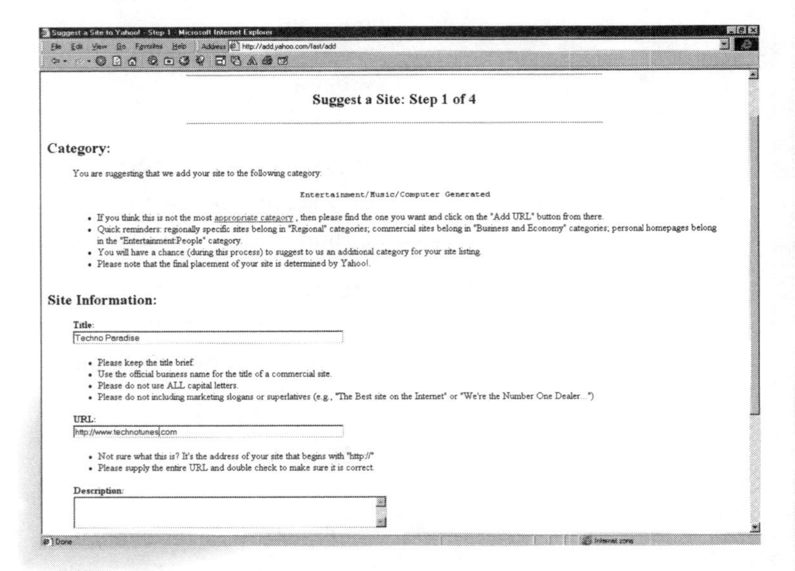

FIGURE 11.2
Step One of Yahoo's submission process.

Before you begin the submission process, Yahoo! suggests you read its information on how to suggest a site and its detailed explanation about how to find a category for your site. You should search Yahoo! to confirm you are not already listed and confirm that you clicked on Add URL at the appropriate category for your site.

You will then be asked to provide a title, URL, and brief description (25 words or less) of your site. Meta tags are not allowed and Yahoo! asks that you do not use phrases like "The Best Site On The Internet" in your description.

You are then given the option to provide other category suggestions and time-sensitive information (if your site is going up or coming down on a particular date). Yahoo! also asks for contact information.

More Information About Search Engines

In addition to Don Sellers' book, there are a few places you can learn more about search engines and how they operate. As search engines continue to evolve, it's a good idea to stay on top of developments by checking Search Engine Watch (calafia.com/webmasters/).

Search Engine Watch includes a number of categories. The most useful (for storeowners) is the Webmaster's Guide to Search Engines. This guide explains how search engines find and rank Web pages with an emphasis on what Webmasters can do to improve how search engines list sites. The Search Engine Watch's Status Report provides insight on how search engines perform in different areas and gives choices based on popularity and technical performance. The Search Engine Resources section is a collection of links to search engine related sources.

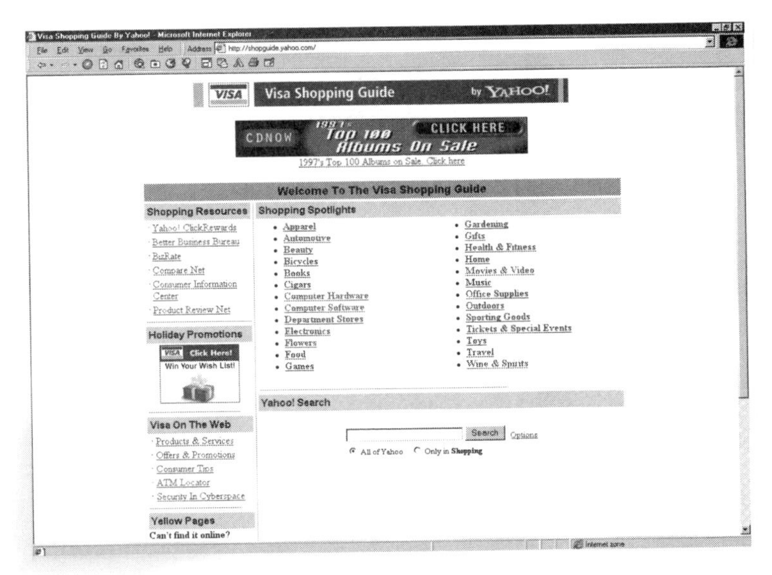

FIGURE 11.3
Many search engines, such as the Visa Shopping Guide by Yahoo!, direct potential customers toward Web stores.

Links

No matter how good your site is, not everyone will find it through one of the search engines. The inherent imperfection of search engines can lead potential customers to other sites. Don't despair. Search engines aren't the only way to draw customers to your site. Another common way for people to find your site is through a link on another site. Of course people aren't just going to link their Web sites to yours for the heck of it. You can pursue links through exchanges and other incentives.

You can get links from other sites that are likely to be visited by your customers, topic-specific link pages and directories, award sites, or announce sites. You can shoot for a low number of well-researched, high-yield links or you can try to links from every site under the sun. While a competing store is unlikely to link to your store (would you?), it isn't unheard of.

Wide-Spread Links

The more links you have out there, the more likely someone will stumble across your site. As anyone who has done any Web surfing can tell you, it's amazing how quickly you can get from a site on one topic to another on a completely unrelated topic. It's like the game "Six Degrees Of Kevin Bacon" which claims that everyone in Hollywood is no more than six people away from having a relationship with the actor. (For example, John Travolta to Bacon. Travolta starred with Samuel L. Jackson in "Pulp Fiction." Jackson worked with Bruce Willis in "Die Hard With A Vengeance." Willis is married to Demi Moore. Moore and Bacon were both in "A Few Good Men").

So it often goes with links. You might start at a site dedicated to classical music and within a few links wind up buying a new filter for your swimming pool. Trying to get links from a wide variety of sites operates on the idea that few people are so dull that they only have one topic of interest. However, it's unlikely the proprietor of Ted's Fine Crystal will be interested in linking to Lucy's Death Metal Dungeon.

The broader the appeal of your store, the more likely you are to benefit from widespread linking. When we say broad, we don't necessarily mean your store has to be selling everything from dining room furniture to athletic shoes. It simply means you need to be selling something that a lot of people need. Clothes have an extremely broad appeal. Everybody wears them (unless you want to get locked up). Video games have a much more specific appeal. Be honest when evaluating your site's appeal.

Even stores selling a specific type of product can stray from that area when looking for likely links. For example, if you sell swimming pool maintenance products, you can find customers all over the place. Or at least wherever people with enough money to afford a pool might shop.

Assuming another site operator thinks it's worth her while, she'll link to your page if you link to hers. If you plan to go for a large number of links (and therefore offer a lot of links), you should organize them on a links page.

Staying Specific

Rather than shooting for links from every site that is remotely related to what you are selling, your time might be better spent looking for a smaller number of links more likely to yield a better return. This takes a little more research and thought, but will be worth your while.

Even if you are going to go for as many links as you can, you should still do enough research to guarantee you have at least a few high-quality links. This section should help you do that. If you are to the point of running an online store and scouting out links, you are certainly aware of a number of sites on which you would like to be linked. Start here.

Contacting Similar Sites

As you move toward setting up your own store you will probably spend some time looking at sites of similar interest. If you haven't already done so, bookmark the best sites you see. When you're up and running, contact those sites with which you would like to be linked.

The best way to contact a prospective site is through e-mail. If you can't find an e-mail address on the site, you should find the Webmaster and slap him upside the head, actually. But since we don't condone violence and slapping the Webmaster upside the head won't help you get a link, you can try "info@" or "webmaster@" or "postmaster@" followed by the domain name.

Use the word "link" in the subject line to differentiate your e-mail from the rest. Keep your message brief. Tell the recipient what your site is all about, why you think a link would make sense, and give him the URL so he can check out your site for himself. Chances are he'll want a link from your site in return.

Link Exchanges

Link exchanges can be done on a barter system with similar sites. While looking for links, you'll almost certainly encounter a Webmaster from a more established site who will look down his nose and ask "What's in it for me?" You should have an answer for him. Being linked to by any site is a good thing, but not everybody is going to be quick to hand out a link. Stress the fact that your customers will be people who will also want to visit his site. Flattery might get you somewhere, too. Tell the Webmaster that, while you hope some of his visitors will link to your site and eventually become customers, you're sure they'll still return to his outstanding site. In other words, he'll gain some of your visitors and lose none of his own.

If you can't get him to link to your site, you may still want to link to his for the benefit of your customers, assuming the site contains some useful information. Although it's not legally required, you should get permission. Don't try to pass off an external link as a link to another part of your site unless you happen to be a sneaky, conniving, little weasel. In that case you can go right ahead!

Joe's Take: *I wouldn't recommend pushing a link with every Web site out there. At the beginning, a lot of Tronix customers had Web sites and they approached me about swapping links. They were doing me a favor by sending potential customers to the Tronix site.*

LinkExchange

LinkExchange (www.linkexchange.com) works as a free advertising exchange agent between sites. By joining LinkExchange (Figure 11.4), you display banners for other members and they do the same for you. LinkExchange screens all sites and does not accept those that display inappropriate content.

Members determine where they want their banner ad to be shown by selecting one or two categories in which they want to be listed. A rating system and filtering technology help ensure that banners on your site are appropriate for your audience and that your banner is displayed on sites that will potentially help your site the most.

Surf Point is the LinkExchange directory. Simply categorize your site for inclusion. LinkExchange can offer the service for free because of the support of Friends and Sponsors. Friends and Sponsors receive additional services for a fee.

Surf Point lists more than 100,000 sites, including about 5,000 shopping outlets.

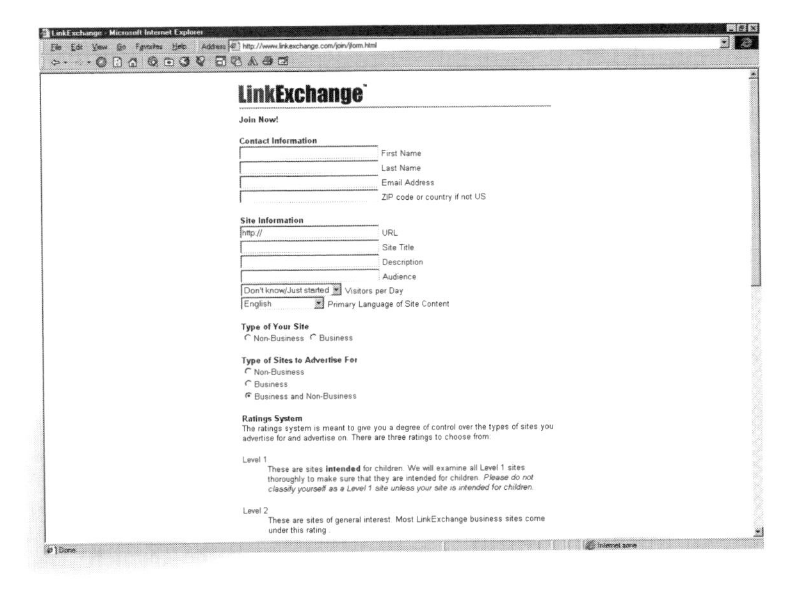

Figure 11.4
LinkExchange's sign-up form.

Friends and Acquaintances

As was the case with Tronix, you can look to friends, acquaintances, business associates, and even customers to link to your site. Chances are they'll be immediately receptive to your inquiry and if you're having a hard time getting links, this is a good place to start.

Customer sites are usually good selections assuming their sites and your store have the same topic. If you buy products from a small manufacturer or craftsperson, she'll probably be happy to send customers to your site where they may well buy more of her product. The more of her product they buy from you, the more you'll buy from her.

Award Sites

There are a number of award sites that can be beneficial in two ways. After you have exhausted the sites that you are familiar with and before you go diving into a general search engine hoping to find something useful, check out a few award sites. Obviously getting honored or obtaining a link from one of the actual sites should be a boon for your business. However, only a fortunate few sites are so rewarded and not many of them are online stores.

Even if your site isn't honored, award sites can guide you toward some of the outstanding sites in your field. Although inclusion on an award site doesn't guarantee a site to be spectacular, there is a better chance you will find high-quality links here than you will by using a general search engine.

Here are five of the top award sites and one to avoid.

Cool Site of the Day

cool.infi.net

Cool Site of the Day is the granddaddy of award sites, which probably explains the overwhelming use of the word "cool" when it comes to describing Web sites. So what's cool? Cool Site of the Day is, well, pretty cool itself. If you want to see its definition for cool, click on What is Coolium?

CSotD says it receives between 400 and 600 submissions a day. You can submit a site by sending the URL and a description to cool@infi.net. You can also check out the Still Cool archives, Iso-Topically Cool (news), and rate the day's selection on the Cool-O-Meter. Cool!

By the way, CSotD has an opinion of Web sites that include pictures of the Webmaster: Not cool.

Lycos Top 5% of the Web
point.lycos.com/categories/index.html

Lycos provides a number of categories (even one for shopping), each of which has links and descriptions of what Lycos considers the top 25 sites in that area. Of course you'll probably have your own ideas (especially if they don't add your site).

You can submit a site for inclusion on Lycos' search engine by clicking Suggest A Site, entering the URL, your e-mail address, and the topic of the site. Lycos' site reviewers pick the top sites.

TooCool
toocool.com

TooCool links to Today's Winner and past winners. There are 17 winners each month rather than a new one each day. Submit a site at Leave A Link. Enter the URL, the title (40 characters maximum), and a description (254 characters maximum).

ProjectCool
www.projectcool.com

ProjectCool, rather than existing just as an award site, is a resource for Web developers. The Developer Zone provides help for Web developers. Peoplesphere is a forum for Web developers. Future Focus provides essays and features on Web-related issues.

Sightings is where you can not only check out past ProjectCool winners but Submit A Sighting. ProjectCool says it is looking for great use of the Web as a medium, quality content, and well thought out design. Don't bother with a list of links, a sales brochure, adult material, or crime glorification. Online stores must provide a lot more than a list of goods to have any hope of inclusion. And if you're selling porn or brass knuckles, don't bother submitting your store to ProjectCool.

Netscape What's Cool

home.netscape.com/home/whats-cool.html

Netscape's What's Cool (done by Yahoo!) not only provides a list of what it considers cool Web sites, but also has links to other award sites such as Yahoo, Project Cool, and The Useless Pages.

The Useless Pages

www.go2net.com/internet/useless/

Try not to wind up here. They say any publicity is good publicity, but the sites on The Useless Pages are just that—useless. Actually they have one use—to make people laugh. If you see your site listed on The Useless Pages next to The Web Page Of Solitude, Chicken Hunting: An Introduction, or Jason's Desk Inventory, it's probably time to rethink your strategy. The Useless Pages offers some extreme examples of what not to do. It's also very funny.

Announce Sites

Announce sites are directories of new Web sites. They are yet another way to get your store noticed. Keep in mind, these are only temporary listings, otherwise most of them would have to take the "New" out of their names.

Netscape's What's New

netscape.yahoo.com/guide/whats_new.html

Netscape's What's New includes a handful of the day's new Web sites and also archives its listings for the past week. There's also a Category of the Day, a Site Spotlight, and links to other collections.

There's allowance for submission of sites for inclusion.

What's New Too

newtoo.manifest.com

What's New Too is a user customizable announcement service that says it is updated daily and posts new sites within 36 hours of submission. What's New Too does not filter or limit the kinds of sites that are posted. Personal home pages, informational text files, and product announcements all are welcome.

Today's Sites lists and links to all sites added to the directory within the last 24 hours. The Custom form allows you to create a personalized Today's Sites page and get lists of new pages that fit your parameters each day. Users can also search the directory by date.

To submit a site, click the Add icon and provide your site's title, URL, and category, the name of your organization, your geographic location, a site description, and contact information.

Nerd World What's New
www.nerdworld.com/whatsnew.html

Nerd World's What's New lists sites under either Leisure or Knowledge. Find the category to which your site should belong and submit your link. Nerd World suggests businesses include a company name, street address, city, state, zip code, phone number, and fax.

Nerd World gets more than one million views per month.

Web-Oriented Online and Offline Media

The amount of online media dedicated to the Web seems to grow every day. If you feel you have a truly unique or compelling Web store you should consider putting together a press package and getting it to some of the top Web-oriented online and offline magazines.

There are a number of magazines listed in the Resources section of the book that you should consider contacting. One that we feel the need to mention now is Internet Shopper (for more information see Resources). If you can get a positive mention in this magazine, you should dance a jig. There will also be online and traditional magazines related to your specific industry. For example, if you sell rock and ice climbing gear, you should do whatever you can to get mentioned in magazines like *Outside*, *Men's Journal*, and any more specific magazines.

Here are a few tips for putting together an inexpensive media kit.

- **Use company letterhead.** If you don't have any, get some. Include your company's name, logo (if you have one), mailing address, e-mail address, phone number, fax number, and Web address. Also include the name of a contact person.

- **Include an honest description** of your site, what you sell, what special services or content you provide, how long you've been in business, how well your store is doing, and why it is of paramount importance that the particular magazine's readers be made aware of your site.

- **Don't use terms** like, "Hands down the best Web site of its kind." Don't use exclamation points! Be reserved, yet confident. Read, re-read, and then have a friend who writes well edit your press release. No mistakes. No typos. No outlandish claims. When reporters or editors see a press release that screams like a used car salesman, they cringe. Then they throw the release in the trash.

- **Now that you know not to be obnoxious, sell your site.** Everyone who reads your release should say, "This sounds pretty cool" and check out your site.

- **Don't worry about mailing** out enormous press kits to every magazine remotely relevant to your site. Chances are you are on a slim budget and won't be able to afford printing and mailing dozens of bulky, glossy press kits unless you know you are going to get a fantastic response. And you don't know that.

- **If possible, send the information to a specific person.** Of course you have to make sure you send it to the *right* specific person. If that information is readily available, a phone call should get the answer you need.

- **Follow up with a phone call** about a week after you think the package has arrived. It's easy to reject a letter or e-mail. If an editor or reporter thinks your online store is unworthy of a mention in her magazine, make her tell you so.

Link Pages and Directories

Link pages and directories—much like award sites—are not only good places to be linked from but also valuable searching grounds for potential links.

InfoSpace

www.infospace.com

InfoSpace is a leading directory and content aggregator on the Internet. InfoSpace includes an E-Shopping category that groups some of the world's biggest stores into a number of categories. L.L. Bean, CDNow, Barnes & Noble, Eddie Bauer, Land's End, and Amazon.com are among the stores that you can find via InfoSpace. Getting listed next to these stores certainly won't hurt your business.

InfoSpace also attracts potential customers to its site with content offerings such as Yellow Pages, White Pages, and city guides. There is also a Business Guide that helps people find your businesses Web site.

InfoSpace offers three options for listing, including one free. The Hot Site business are the first ones listed and is limited to just 10 per category. The Priority Sites are listed next and costs $99 a year. Free Sites are shown after sites in the top two levels and include a brief description and a link to your site.

Webscout

www.webscout.com

Webscout asks you to select a category (Arts, Business & Investment, Computers, etc.) and then a subcategory. Each subcategory has 15 or 20 links with a short review of the site. You can also search the reviews for a particular subject.

Webscout's SuperSearch allows you to select a search engine from a pop-up menu and search by keywords. You can also nominate a site for inclusion, but Webscout says the site better be "very cool" (there's that word again!).

Beaucoup
www.beaucoup.com

Beaucoup can help you find a search engine for your specific needs. Pick a category and you'll get a list of links to a number of topic-specific search engines. You'll have to spend some time trying the various engines as not all are created equal.

Bounty Programs

The bounty program is one of the best and more innovative ways to promote your store. As mention elsewhere in this book Amazon.com's bounty program has over 10,000 member sites. That's a lot of links and it is all done by people who actually seek out Amazon.

You can set up a bounty program as well, but before you rush out to start one consider the needs you must fulfill in order to run a successful bounty program:

1. You must be able to properly provide good fulfillment because people linking to your site as bounty members will quickly drop links to stores that provide bad service.

2. You need to have a way to quickly account for sales by each bounty member. Amazon does this by having associate sites include a code in their URL that lets the Amazon.com server know specifically who sent the surfer over for the sale. Sales are then written to a database which at the end of the month adds up the total sales and writes out checks. Obviously this would require some good technical infrastructure on your part.

3. You need to sell a product that will have a successful enough appeal that people will already be out and about talking about products your selling. One reason Amazon's bounty program works so well is people on their sites are constantly discussing books. Now your appeal doesn't have to be as wide as book but as a rule you shouldn't start a bounty program for things that aren't being discussed on Web pages very often.

In addition to those three key items you need to be able to promote your bounty program. While many times customers to your store will be good chances for signing on associate sites, you won't want to rest the growth of your bounty program to a page that sits on your site. Get up and surf! Find sites—homepages, and fan sites are the best that are in whole or part dedicated to the same interests or products that your store is. Send the Webmaster or site producer email explaining your program and its benefits and let them know about how to join.

TIP ▸ ***The big sites on the Internet are actually forcing stores to pay up front in some cases or pay bigger bounties than normal for signing on to a particular bounty program. Depending on the site and its reach this may be necessary expense. Not every site will have this power but don't be surprised to see it.***

What you want to accomplish with a bounty program is to get people recommending products you sell first and then provide the link specifically for that product. The more links provided from one site the better. That means they're recommending more and more products for people to buy. You can accomplish your goal by educating your member sites.

For example, Amazon.com sends out a newsletter to members. You can also supply bounty members with other goodies such as news on upcoming products (so they'll prepare links to them). You can even provide templates and graphics for their sites. In short, treat them as part of your sales team and shower them with information and tools that make it easier to be part of your program.

Malls

Not surprisingly, there are hundreds of online malls. Since online stores all exist on a shopper's computer, a mall doesn't provide the same advantage of convenience that a traditional mall does. However, it does give a merchant a chance to be included on a mall that is home to thousands of other stores. Being listed with other popular stores might attract customers. If you have the best prices in your category, comparison shoppers might end up buying your products.

Advantages of Online Malls

The major advantage of an online mall is promotion. Many stores on the Internet have stand-alone sites and also join online malls. Operationally, some stores join malls to gain access to server space and commerce technology.

Successful Internet malls become destination sites. People turn to online malls for the same reason they turn to search engines—they can easily find what they are looking for. For example, someone might start an online mall called fishingstuff.com and, instead of selling everything on their own, they might sell "mall space" to hundreds of stores that sell products to fishing fans. This could include boating equipment, fishing rods, lures, etc. At the same time, a boating store that is registered with this mall could also exist as a standalone store.

There are also temporary malls that are built around holidays or special promotions and regional malls.

Disadvantages of Online Malls

Many online malls have requirements such as rent or certain style points you need to follow. Premium malls such as AOL's Shopping Channel can be expensive. It is key to track sales and visits that are due to your presence on an online mall. If you aren't earning a return on your investment, stay away.

TIP ▸ ***Unless you really think there is a compelling argument avoid malls that want exclusivity to your presence. Malls are in promotional terms just another gateway to your store—why would you choose just one and thus shut yourself off from other excellent mall opportunities?***

Some Top Online Malls

Cyberspace malls, much like traditional malls, are not created equal. Here are some of the biggest that, if you are considering placing your store in a mall, you should look into.

Internet Mall

www.internet-mall.com

You thought the Mall of America was big? The Internet Mall (Figure 11.5) has 27,000 merchants and stores and has won more than 30 industry awards. Headquartered in California, the Internet Mall was incorporated in November 1996 and developed the Order Easy Secure Electronic Commerce Server.

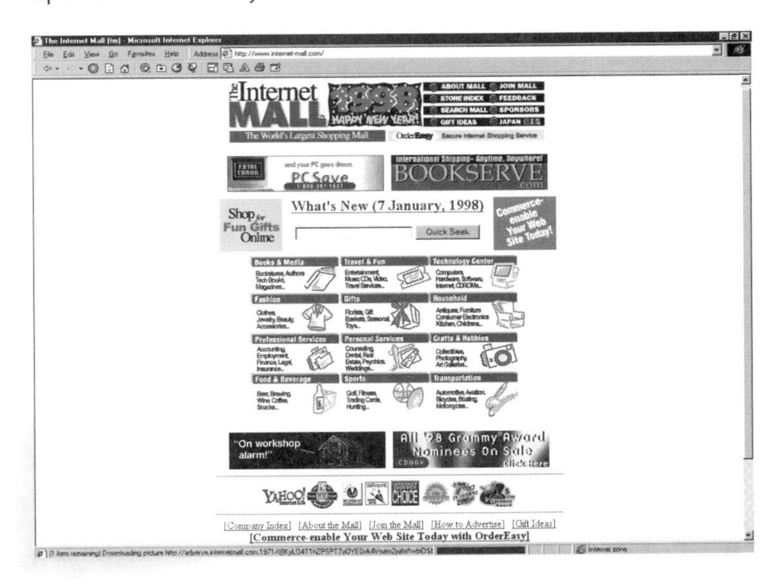

FIGURE 11.5
The Internet Mall's home page.

Order Easy can commerce-enable your site no matter what type of operating system, Web server, or Web host you are using. The back end system is managed and stored by the Internet Mall, which provides you with product SKU (Stock Keeping Unit) database server, shopping cart system, shipping and tax module, and secure transaction server. As a merchant on the Internet Mall, you don't have to worry about managing an electronic commerce system. Transactions are taken care of, you just take orders and ship products.

The Internet Mall's search engine searches on your title and description to find exact matches, making your keyword selection very important.

To become a merchant, you select from a list of 12 "floors" (Books and Media, Technology Center, Professional Services, etc.) on which you want your store to be listed. You then pick the appropriate department and submit your business name, description, URL and e-mail contact. Charges vary.

iMall

www.imall.com

iMall launched in January 1996 and has gone from 150,000 hits per month to nearly 17 million hits in August 1997. There are more than 1,000 stores located at iMall and merchants chose from 12 categories in which to be included.

iMall provides merchant clients with order tracking and compilation services that can be sent to the merchant via e-mail on a daily or weekly basis for final processing and expediting. iMall uses a secure server and the Cybercash system for online transaction verification and processing.

Unlike the Internet Mall, you must first contact iMall to get information on becoming a merchant. E-mail your business name, address, phone number, and e-mail address to info@imall.com.

America Online Shopping Channel

www.aol.com/netchannels/shopping.html

The AOL Shopping Channel is host to some well-known retailers such as Eddie Bauer, 1-800-FLOWERS, The Sharper Image, and Starbucks. That's because inclusion here costs the kind of money that only established retailers can afford to spend. However, you should keep an eye on AOL's rates. If you ever have an enormous enough advertising budget (and we sincerely hope you do), AOL and it's 10 million or so members is a nice market.

CompuServe Electronic Mall

mall.compuserve.com/mall/index.stm

Some of Compuserve's online stores include JC Penney and Sports Illustrated Insider Authentics.

If you want to be considered for listing on The Electronic Mall, CompuServe asks that you submit a proposal. You'll need to include the following:

- What information and online experience do you want to deliver?
- What are your target markets? How will you generate interest in the site?
- What other media can be used to reach this market? What is your business plan?
- What would your area include? Goods for sale? Messaging? Chat?
- Is your product or service for the U.S. market?
- Is there anything that is time sensitive?
- Does a prototype of your product exist on the Internet?
- How often will the information need to be updated and who will be responsible for updating?

Never Underestimate Promotion

Can you imagine where Madonna would be without the power of promotion? She'd be little Madonna Ciccone, the marginally talented singer down at the corner bar. Now, thanks to constant image changes, well-timed controversies, and a knack for getting her name in the news, she's one of the most famous people on the planet. No matter what you think of her musical ability, Madonna is a marketing genius. You should hope to do as much.

No matter how great your store is, it isn't going anywhere without a little promotion. Promoting your store correctly on the Internet can bring you countless visitors without ever spending a cent. The right search engine placement or the right link could help vault you past all your competitors. However, expert promotion probably isn't going to save a lousy store from an early death.

There's nothing like a little free advertising. However, you'll probably wind up spending money on advertising eventually. Now that we've showed you how to promote your store without spending any money, it's on to Chapter 12: The Storeowner's Guide To Advertising. We'll show you how to get the most for your advertising dollar.

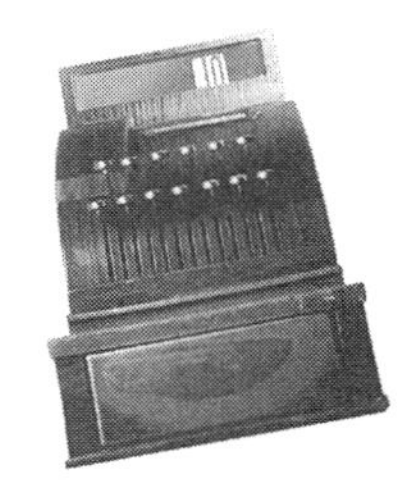

CHAPTER TWELVE

Advertising

Advertising is a key element for your store's success. In fact, when some of the largest Web stores went public or gained additional financing, one of the primary reasons was so they could spend more money on advertising. With so many Web sites in existence, advertising can be the most effective means of spreading the word about your store.

When planning an advertising campaign, it is important to get the most return for your dollar. There are a number of options to consider, both on the Internet and in traditional media such as radio, newspapers, magazines, and direct mail. This chapter is intended to help you weigh all of your advertising options, both on and off the Internet. We'll cover when, where, and what to advertise about your store.

When and What to Advertise?

Before you worry about where to place advertisements, you should decide when and what to advertise. An advertising agency—even a small one—can be helpful. But before you pick up the phone (and your checkbook) to get the expert advice of an advertising agency, consider some of the following tips.

When Should I Advertise?

As you prepare to launch an advertising campaign, you must also prepare for the added attention your store will receive as a result. One of the biggest advertising blunders you can make is to advertise your store only to have new customers arrive at an unfinished site with a non-functioning order system and major items out of stock. In that case you have simply advertised that your store is not worth patronizing.

Many Web stores don't advertise until the site is sufficiently ready to handle the influx of browsers and the operations system is able to deliver the kind of quality customer service that turns first time buyers into repeat customers.

Don't advertise too early. Build your store, get the kinks worked out, and gently test the advertising waters until you are prepared to widen your campaign.

What Should I Advertise?

The more comprehensive the site, the tougher this question is to answer. It may take a variety of messages to convey the feeling of your store. However, there are two critical messages to deliver—that your store offers advantages because it is on the Internet and that your store is somehow different (and better) than the competition.

The first message differentiates your store from the other types of stores you are competing with, from retail locations to mail order catalogs. To convey this message, you need to illustrate the advantages of online shopping. Customers can place orders at any time without having to deal with pushy salespeople. Regular customers receive immediate notification of new product arrivals. Your site offers search capabilities that make accessing your unsurpassed selection very easy. Anything that shows the customer how smart it is to shop on the Web is worth mentioning.

Although the first message is directed at people who may not have considered shopping online, the second is aimed at attracting people who may already be shopping online but haven't yet found your store. In this case, you must identify the advantages of shopping at your store rather than a similar store whether it is the fact that you have better prices, more shipping options, the best customer service, etc.

You should also use advertising to establish your store's brand identity. This often involves nothing more than delivering a direct message containing your Web site address and brief, memorable image of your store. For example, Amazon.com spends much of its time reminding millions of people of the Amazon.com URL and convincing customers that it is "Earth's Biggest Bookstore."

Where Should I Advertise?

Once you have a handful of solid advertising concepts, it is just as important to advertise in the right place. It is important to understand that just because your store is on the Internet, the Internet is not necessarily the best place to advertise. While the Net is certainly a fine place to advertise, Internet stores also place ads in trade magazines and in newspapers, as well as on radio. However, we've never seen a television advertisement other than the listing of Web addresses for major catalog companies or retail chains.

Online

Online stores will naturally find customers through online advertising. Customers can click on a banner ad and instantly be transported to a store or a page with an item ready to be bought. The majority of online company advertising takes place online. We'll cover exactly where to advertise online later in this chapter.

While there's no reason to avoid online advertising altogether, it is important to understand that spending all of your advertising money online is also not the best answer. You should reserve a good portion of your budget for advertising through more traditional media.

Newspapers

Newspapers offer online stores a medium to advertise in a certain geographic location. Because newspaper readers tend to be more affluent, educated, and older, advertising with newspapers can help you target a nice demographic niche as well. In addition, many newspapers have added regular sections dedicated to Internet and technology news and lifestyle. People also turn to newspapers to find the latest sales. All of these factors make newspaper advertising a solid choice.

Rather than focusing on large daily newspapers, small weekly, alternative, and university papers can provide a less expensive outlet with readerships that fit into basic online user demographics. The best way to purchase ads for these newspaper outlets is through advertising networks that run your single ad across the country among their participating newspapers.

TIP ▸ ***Many college students have disposable incomes, computers, and fast and free Internet access via their university account. Most universities publish student newspapers that are generally funded by small ads that are placed by local business owners. According to statistics, the average college newspaper is read by 62 percent of the students in its market. Ad syndicates can help you place ads in these papers. This is often done at no cost to the advertiser since they are commissioned by college newspapers to represent them to advertisers. Some well-known college advertising syndicates are shown in Table 12.1.***

Table 12.1 Key College Newspaper Advertising Syndicates

American Passage Media 100 West Harrison, Suite 8-150 Seattle, Washington 98119-4129 800-359-6676	**AllCampus Media** 26 Castillion Drive Santa Barbara, California 93117 805-968-8007 ext. 165
Cass Communications 1800 Sherman Place Evanston, Illinois 60201-3769 708-475-8800	Collegiate Advantage 617-262-3734

Alternative newspapers have evolved tremendously since the counterculture publications of the 1960s. The Association of Alternative Newsweeklies has 87 members and a collective readership of more than 13 million.

More information on alternative newspapers is available from:

The Association of Alternative Newsweeklies
Helene Seisel, Administrative Director
1201 E. Jefferson, Suite A-260
Phoenix, AZ 85034
(602) 229-8487

You can obtain a membership roster, which includes addresses, telephone numbers, and staff information, as well as helpful circulation and demographic data from this organization. Another to contact is:

Alternative Press Center
P.O. Box 33109
Baltimore, MD 21218
(410) 243-2471

This organization produces the quarterly *Alternative Press Index*, a selection of articles indexed by subject.

Magazines

When advertising in magazines, concentrate on publications that offer readerships with a natural interest in your store's offerings. National magazines such as *Time* or *Newsweek* are a waste of time unless you have established a major category store such as Amazon.com.

TIP ▸ ***Many magazines have begun to research their readerships' tendency to be computer owners and online users. Before you consider buying magazine advertising, see if they have this information. If you sell gardening tools and only five percent of a particular gardening magazine's readers are online, advertising in that magazine is probably not worth the effort.***

JOE'S TAKE: *Many monthly magazines cover the Internet—in fact almost too many. Most of these magazines print a list of Web sites to visit in every issue. They may have a theme or feature article along with a list of Web sites that best cover the particular category. If you happen to have an outstanding Web site, you might find your store listed. Much to your surprise, you may gain a new group of customers who found your company in a magazine. It happened to me and was a pleasant surprise.*

Radio

Until Web TV becomes more prevalent, television and cable advertising for all but the biggest online stores is a waste of money. However, radio advertising can be a useful secondary advertising avenue. Radio can target an audience more precisely than television. More importantly, many people listen to the radio while at work where they actually have their only means of accessing the Internet. Amazon.com and CDNow.com are two prominent online retailers currently advertising on the radio. Table 12.2 shows some areas that could provide the highest return on your radio advertising dollar.

Table 12.2 Top Internet Using Metro Areas

By Absolute Numbers	By Population Percentage
1. New York	1. San Francisco
2. Los Angeles	2. Washington
3. Washington	3. Seattle
4. San Francisco	4. Boston
5. Chicago	5. New York
6. Boston	6. Chicago
7. Philadelphia	7. Philadelphia
8. Detroit	8. Dallas
9. Dallas	9. Los Angeles
10. Seattle	10. Detroit

Source: September 1997 "Local Information On The Net" by Scarborough Research, Arlen Communications Inc. and Find/SVP.

Cable/TV

If and when some Internet stores begin to advertise on television, they will probably begin on cable. Cable provides a better method of matching special interest advertisements with related programming. For example, a sporting goods store could advertise on ESPN, while a record store might chose MTV. As online competition increases and markets mature, cable will become a viable outlet and will signal the ascent toward national television advertising.

Direct Mail

Direct mail, although often overlooked, is a great way to advertise a product or service. The catalog industry is the most obvious user of direct mail. Since the Web store industry is closer in style and workings to catalogs than it is to actual retail stores, direct mail can be a good advertising outlet.

Where Should I Advertise on the Internet?

Conventional wisdom says you should place much of your advertising on search engines and on the top 20 Web sites. However, as the Web grows and audiences become more widespread, advertisers will move beyond the major areas and explore alternative sites. In many cases, niche sites will return the highest number of interested customers per impression.

Classified Advertising Sites

The Web is rapidly becoming a leading source of classified advertising from newspapers around the country. While classifieds are usually used to advertise used equipment and other items on the Web, it is also a good place to advertise in general. Not only can you probably advertise your store via a classified ad, you can also purchase banners that appear in various classified sections.

Classifieds2000

www.classifieds2000.com

Classifieds2000 (Figure 12.1) provides advertising across multiple categories through some of the Web's most visited sites. The company advertises more than $500 million in goods and services weekly and more than 2.1 million users access the listings database.

The Classifieds2000 Network gives corporate advertisers the chance to achieve the results of a targeted campaign along with the brand-building benefits of a broad-based campaign. Some current and past advertisers in the Classifieds2000 Network include Saturn, *Consumer Reports*, Pennzoil, Yokohama Tire, Progressive Casualty Insurance, Warranty Direct, Intuit and Auto-by-Tel.

Customers select a category, then a sub-category, a price range, and a sales channel. This leads the customers to a list of items, with prices and a phone number. Customers then click on a desired item and receive a description. Categories include computers/software, vehicles, general merchandise, and opportunities/services. Each category has numerous sub-categories.

One buy places ads into a targeted Classifieds2000 category within search engines such as Lycos, Hotbot, Web Crawler, and other sites like BigFoot, NetAddress, Tripod, Nerdworld, AT&T, and TechWeb.

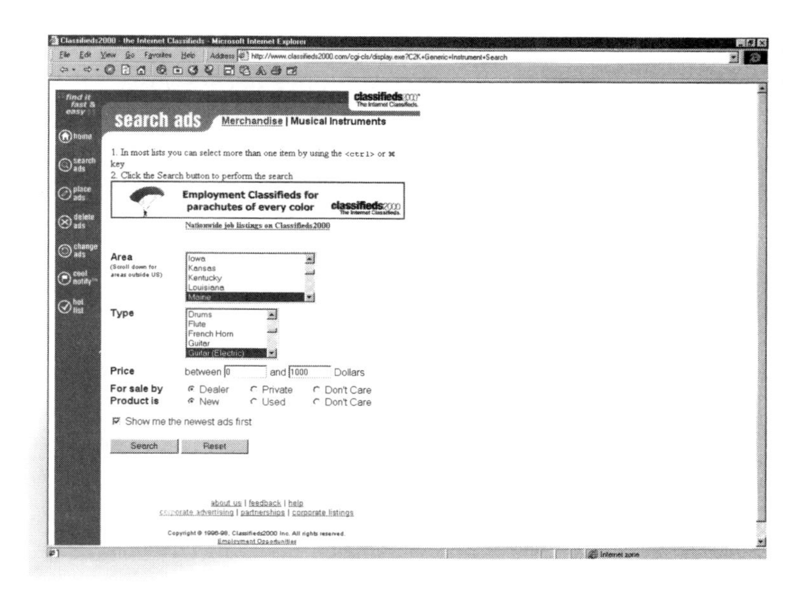

FIGURE 12.1
Classifieds2000 helps customers locate items based on preferences such as type, location, price range, and so on.

Ad-One Classified Network

www.adone.com

Ad-One Classified Network allows customers to search classified databases of more than 500 publications in North America. One buy allows the advertiser to place ads in these publications.

New Century Network

www.newcentury.net

NewsWorks is a service of New Century Network, a national network on the Web consisting of more than 130 affiliated Web sites operated by major newspaper and media companies. The network sells national advertising on behalf of the affiliates, creates Web sites that direct readers to content on affiliated sites and provides syndicated content and technology tools to the affiliates.

NewsWorks was developed and is funded by a nine major media companies: Advance Publications, Cox Newspapers, Gannett Co, the Hearst Corporation, Knight-Ridder, The New York Times Co., Times Mirror, Tribune Company, The Washington Post Co. NewsWorks Affiliate Network Packages and Banner rates run from \$20-\$40 per 1,000 impressions (CPM). Banner advertising rates are \$35 CPM for less than 500,000 impressions, \$32.50 for 500,000 to 1 million impressions, and \$30 for more than 1 million impressions. Advertisers can choose as much or as little of the network as needed.

AdQuest Classifieds

www.adquest.com

AdQuest Classifieds collects classified ads from nearly 600 publications throughout the United States. AdQuest also provides Internet services, including Web site promotion, through links on AdQuest's site. To place an ad, contact one of AdQuest's member publications directly and your ad appears on the AdQuest site. The site has a list of member publications, most of which are small newspapers or advertisers. It breaks its classifieds into nine categories, each of which is further divided into subcategories.

Advertising Networks

As advertising on the Internet expands, so too will the role of advertising networks. Information on a number of advertising networks can be found on the Web site of Mark J. Welch, a California attorney and consultant in the area of banner advertising networks. Part of his Web site (www.markwelch.com/bannerad/) is dedicated to advertising networks, brokers, and representatives, and in some cases includes evaluations and warnings about potential scams.

DoubleClick

www.doubleclick.net

DoubleClick offers a number of Internet advertising solutions and generally represents large sites.

DoubleClick Network (Figure 12.2) is the company's flagship product. It consists of seven categories of interest and more than 70 sites. The network of sites is coupled with the company's DART targeting technology. Online reporting lets advertisers know how their campaign is performing and what types of users are seeing and clicking on their ads.

DoubleClick International allows advertisers to reach users in more than 80 countries with one buy and one contact. Advertisers can also conduct campaigns in local markets and can target users in their own language.

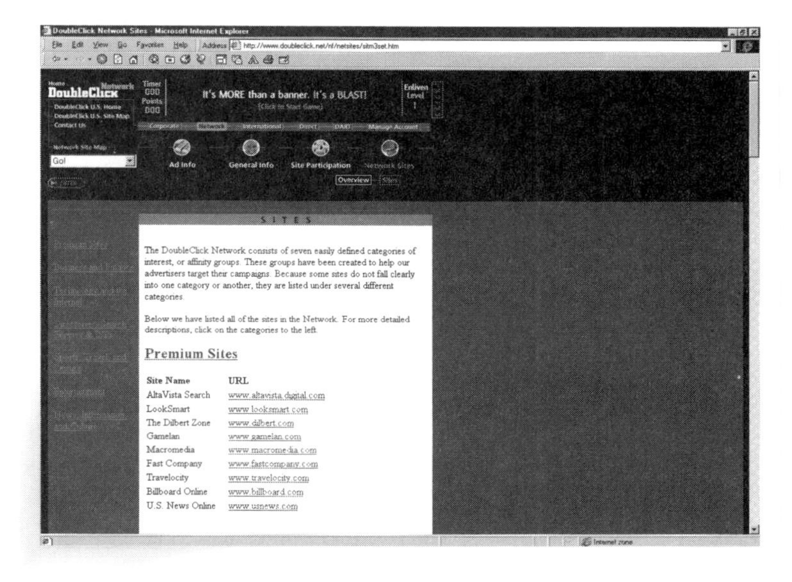

Figure 12.2
DoubleClick Network includes nine premium sites.

AdKnowledge

www.focalink.com

ClickOver, Inc. and Focalink Communications merged in the fall of 1997 to form AdKnowledge. Focalink brings its MarketMatch and SmartBanner products to the new company and ClickOver offers ClickWise and ClickWise Pro.

The ClickWise and ClickWise Pro ad management system for Web publishers has served over a billion online ads since launching in March 1997.

Burst Media

www.burstmedia.com

Burst Media directs advertisers toward sites on which they should consider advertising. Burst has had some rather high-end clients but represents sites of various sizes. Burst collects information about the content of its members' Web sites and the demographics of the sites' visitors with the goal of providing the best results for advertisers and members.

FlyCast

www.flycast.com

FlyCast's AdAgent provides desktop access to an open network of Web sites. AdAgent can execute both traditional up-front buys and spot buys.

Link Ad Exchanges

As your store gains popularity, you will correspond with other Web merchants and Web site operators, many of whom will offer to exchange advertising links. These simple links can lead to new customers. Although links from non-related sites can lead to new customers, you are more likely to gain customers when exchanging links with a site of similar interest. If you specialize in greeting cards, there is always a chance that a visitor to a comic book related site will also be interested in greeting cards. However, a Web site that is dedicated to designing Christmas ornaments is more likely to send customers your way.

The amount of hits a particular site receives is another important factor to consider when exchanging links. It is better to have a link from an unrelated site that receives thousands of hits a day than one that, although related to your site's offerings, is rarely visited.

Some Web sites will offer to link to your site for a small fee. You should certainly investigate the opportunity closely before making an agreement. Study the offering Web site. Does it provide information that will attract customers to your link? How many hits does the site receive? If the site has a hit counter, watch it for a week. Is it spinning like the odometer on the vehicle of a salesman or does it remind you more of the little old lady from Pasadena? Does the site appear to be well maintained or is it one of the many offered free of charge by an ISP?

The more link exchanges you acquire, the better the chances you will win new customers. Don't be afraid to initiate link exchanges.

You can easily find related sites by using a search engine and offer link exchanges to the sites that impress you the most.

Sites that offer link exchanges might also be worth advertising on. However, consider that most sites using link exchanges are personal homepages with a fairly small amount of traffic.

For more on link exchanges, see Chapter 11.

Advertising Directly on Small Sites

Depending on your store's focus, you might want to reach the audiences of narrow-interest sites. There are many excellent, small sites that reach a significant amount of people but have little or no advertising. On these sites, you can reach out to an interested audience for far less money than would be required to advertise on sites like Yahoo!, ClNet, or Hotbot.

Joe's Take: *Some neophyte Web sites looking to increase their exposure offer free banner advertising. If the Web site takes off, you'll already have had an advertising seed planted and will benefit from the deal in the long run. The hope of course is that you will see the benefit and maintain it at a cost later on when the site's audience has grown.*

While Joe's advice is to look for free direct banner ads, that isn't always feasible. Here are some things to remember when working with small sites:

- **Approach the site directly** and suggest they post your ad. Your offer should include both a duration and a price—we suggest three months duration and a price of about $50–$100 per 1,000 visitors. Be aware that site counters and logs can be made to look more impressive than they really are. Make your offer a take-it-or-leave-it proposition.

- **Assuming you reach an agreement** on terms, supply the site with the banner(s) and links and track their compliance. Checking 10 or 15 sites every day can be time-consuming. To make this process easier, bookmark the sites and visit them periodically to see where your banner is positioned and how well the site is doing.

- **Check those logs** to find out which sites are sending visitors your way. Each visitor is worth between 50 cents and $2 in average sales. After you have an idea of how many visitors each site is sending you, what each site is averaging you can try to re-up at the rate that equals the number of site visits.

Advertising on small sites can be a painstaking process because many of those sites are maintained by part-time operators. Some disappear quickly will prove to be worthless advertising outlets. But many special interest sites can be extremely useful if you take the initiative and monitor your advertisements and their returns.

Advertising on Search Engines

Search engines are among the most popular sites on the Internet. Because they are the crossroads of the Internet which users often visit several times during one surfing session, search engines collect major advertising revenue. Search engines offer a variety of ways to purchase targeted ads, some of which are worth discussing here.

Keyword Purchasing

Advertising on search engines is effective not only because they are among the most viewed sites on the Internet, but also because potential customers can be targeted by purchasing ads that will be displayed whenever a user enters a certain keyword. For example, a store selling baseball cards can purchase an ad on a search engine that will be displayed whenever someone enters a related keyword.

Cluster Groups

One keyword often isn't enough. A storeowner can purchase a suite of related keywords, commonly called *cluster groups*. For example, a gardening store could buy a cluster group of keywords related to gardening (**gardening**, **planting**, **horticulture**, and so on).

Domain targeting

Domain targeting allows you purchase ads that are only shown to certain domain types. For example, if you sell video games (like Tronix) you could purchase ads that are targeted only at .edu domains because of the high percentage of students (who make up a high percentage of video game players) that surf from .edu domains.

Search engines are amazing advertising tools given their sheer volume of users and the means by which they can target your ads. They are often the first place advertisers consider when they begin advertising. However, before you order search engine advertising, do the following:

- **Do everything you can** to get good positioning within the engine's listings.
- **Make sure that you are capable** of making a good-sized purchase because volume counts—$3,000–$5,000 or more a month should provide good visibility if targeted precisely. Stores that sell more commodity-style merchandise may need to spend more.
- Familiarize yourself with all the options. Ask the sales staff to walk you through them step-by-step.

Not All Search Engines Are Created Equal

In May 1997, online store provider Viaweb released the results of a study that compared the amount of money spent by online shoppers who used different search engines. Per capita spending varied surprisingly among search engines, differing by as much as a factor of three. The study was used to show how different search engines can be in terms of yielding results and to hype the ability of Viaweb's store products to track the amount of money made from various search engine visitors.

The study examined more than one million visitors arriving at 132 sites during a 120-day period from mid-December 1996 to mid-April 1997. Viaweb's tracking tools showed that traffic from search engines generated an average of 17 cents per visitor in online sales, with individual search engines ranging from 10 cents to 31 cents. Table 12.3 summarizes Viaweb's findings.

It is important to remember that this data was found at the beginning of 1997 and the Web is growing rapidly. Experiment and look over your logs and customer reports to see which search engines work best for you.

Table 12.3: Viaweb Search Engine Sales Lead Studies

Source	Visitors	Sales	Sales/Visitor
Excite	226,321	$ 26,478	$ .12
Infoseek	217,448	26,170	.12
Webcrawler	179,551	17,943	.10
Yahoo	170,522	53,553	.31
Altavista	164,369	37,067	.23
Lycos	24,895	5,302	.21
Hotbot	16,917	2,513	.15
Total	1,000,023	$ 169,026	$ .17

Joe's Take: *If and when your budget allows, look into advertising with better known companies that have major Web sites. Larger, well-established companies will of course have much higher advertising rates than average, independently owned Web sites. For example, I sell video games, but advertising with a major video game manufacturer such as Sega, Sony, or Nintendo is simply too expensive. I choose to advertise online with a popular video game magazine. The fee is more than that of an average Web site, but it is far lower than the same ad printed in the hard copy version of the magazine.*

How Much Should I Advertise?

There are entire books dedicated to advertising. Although we can't cover it all here, one popular advertising strategy involves a burst of advertising followed by quiet period and then a second burst. Research has shown that a highly visible advertisement made available over a concentrated time period not only gets the message across, but people also recall the advertisement long after it is no longer being run.

TIP ▸ ***People see a lot of banner ads on the Internet. Buying a high frequency of ads in a short time frame will help you break through the clutter.***

Burst advertising works especially well for companies with limited advertising budgets. It also provides the opportunity to make a big splash and then mold that attention into customers during the quiet period.

How much advertising you do often depends on timing. For many stores, the majority of sales come at certain times such as Christmas, back-to-school season, or perhaps a time specifically related to the market (fishing equipment in the spring, ski equipment after the first snowfall). By focusing your advertising budget on these time periods, you can target customers who are eager to buy.

Joe's Take: *Video games are popular Christmas gifts, so that is an obvious time for me to unleash some advertising. However, I also consider advertising based on new product arrivals. If your store might have hit products throughout the year, consider advertising around the time of these major releases. Most customers won't wait until Christmas to buy the latest game, software, book, or music CD. If you have a hot item in stock, let everyone know.*

Banner Ads

Banner ads are the most popular form of advertising on the Internet. Although many advertising experts talk about moving "beyond the banner," it will be some time before that happens. Any advertiser on the Internet needs to be familiar with ad banner characteristics.

Creating Banner Ads

Once you know what, where, when, and how often to advertise, you must create a banner ad (Figure 12.3a). The first Internet ads were simple banners that sat frozen on a Web page, usually at the top and/or bottom. Animated GIF banners followed. As Web technology has improved, the options have increased. Now it is not uncommon to see banner-sized Java applets and interactive Shockwave ads. Other new options include ads containing HTML forms with drop-down lists (Figure 12.3b) or image maps that allow users to select a specific part of an ad to trigger a response. This style of ad can be effective for merchants who want to list all of their departments or some of their items in an advertisement.

Once you have decided how you want your ad to perform, your wisest option is to hire a design firm familiar with Internet advertising creation. Unless you possess the design skills necessary to create a good-looking advertisement, you may otherwise end up with an unattractive banner that wastes your advertising budget.

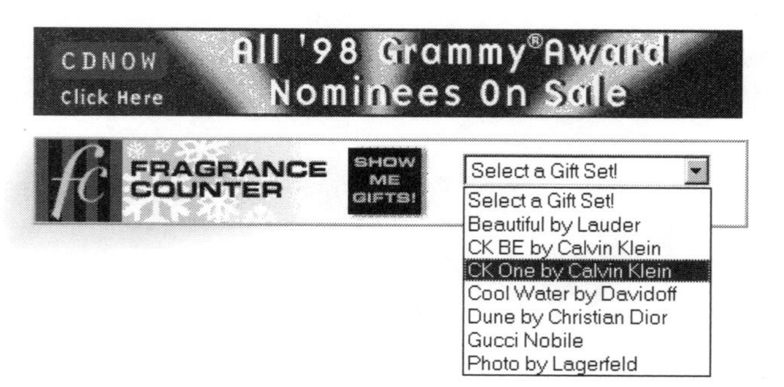

FIGURE 12.3
A standard banner ad (a), and a banner ad with an embedded selection list (b).

Standard Ad Sizes

In 1996, the Internet Advertising Bureau and CASIE (Coalition for Advertising Supported Information and Entertainment), two groups that work to develop Internet advertising standards, announced what it calls voluntary model banner sizes (Table 12.4). These standard banner sizes are meant to give developers and advertisers a set of dimensions around which to design. The most common size is 468x60 pixels, which is used in about 75 percent of banner ads.

Although use of the size standards is voluntary, many sites accept ads only in these sizes.

Table 12.4 CASIE approved banner ad sizes

Size	Type
468 x 60	Full Banner
392 x72	Full Banner with Vertical Navigation Bar
234 x 60	Half Banner
125 x 125	Square Button
120 x 90	Button #1
120 x 60	Button #2
88 x 31	Micro Button
120 x 240	Vertical Banner

Calculating a Return on Your Investment

In calculating your return on advertising investment, you should first develop an *expected* return on investment. You can then measure the actual return and gauge the difference to determine whether or not your advertising campaign met, fell short of, or exceeded expectations. Using the accepted averages of click-throughs and purchases, the resulting formula looks like this:

Number of Impressions * Average Click-Through Rate * Average Customer Turnover * Average Sale Net = Expected Return

- **Number of Impressions** is the amount of impressions you purchase.
- **Average Click-Through Rate** is the current average percentage of users who click through banners. Current statistics seem to place this at around 3.5 percent on average.
- **Average Customer Turnover** is the percentage of new visitors expected to become customers. The high end of this statistical range is 5 percent.
- **Average Sale Net** is the average net profit earned per customer order.

If your store earns an average of $5 per customer order, it is easy to develop an expected rate of return on an advertising buy of 200,000 impressions:

200,000*.035*.05*$5=$1,750

According to the formula, you should expect approximately $1,750 in near-term new sales as a direct result of your advertising efforts. If your campaign cost $6,000–$12,000, it would not seem to be worth the effort. However, if each of your new customers made several purchases over the course of the year, you might earn your money back. And if you created a campaign that did slightly better and sold items at a somewhat higher profit, you could speed your return significantly. It could take a year or more of well-done advertising in conjunction with other efforts (promotional work, good customer service, and a compelling inventory) before you can build an active customer base through advertising. This is why most stores wait until they have achieved some success over a period of time before making large advertising buys.

Advertising almost never offers an immediate return on investment; on the Internet it can take a while for your ads to settle in and provide the customer base you need. However, using the above formula can give you a rough idea of whether or not your advertising is effective. If, after spending significant amounts of money, you are not receiving a good return, you might need to adjust your strategy. Don't panic if, after the first week of a six-week campaign, your results are negligible.

Do it, Mix it, and Maintain it

Cyberspace is already crowded and it isn't going to get any easier to rise above the din. Not only are Web stores seeing more direct competitors, but the sheer volume of sites vying for attention makes it difficult to make an impact. Good promotion will only take many sites so far. That is where advertising comes into play.

Don't put all of your advertising eggs in one basket. Not everyone uses the same search engine (the most-used, Yahoo!, is regularly used by an estimated 45 percent of the Web's population) and there are plenty of useful, non-Internet advertising media. Successful advertising campaigns are often multi-media in nature, combining ads on a variety of sites, search-engines, and non-Internet media to create a highly visible mix.

Once advertising pays off, don't desert it. Advertising isn't a quick-fix means of grabbing customers. It's something you should continue to use once it works. Advertising not only attracts new customers, it reminds previous customers of your presence.

In addition, it may take a year or more before someone clicks through on a banner. Sites that advertise don't go dark for long. Once they have created a successful mix, they maintain it as an integral part of their overall business operations.

CHAPTER THIRTEEN

International Sales

Making an international sale and shipping the package overseas involves a bit more work than completing a standard domestic order. However, the extra work will pay off handsomely in terms of an increased customer base. The Web makes your store a global entity the moment you launch. Even if you don't want international customers, you're going to get them.

Domestic customers have access to U.S. products through local stores, mail order catalogs, and of course online stores. Foreign customers who aren't planning a trip to the United States need to gain find access to American mail order houses. Ordering through a catalog involves finding the company's contact information, sending away for the catalog, waiting for the catalog to arrive, placing the order by phone or mail, and waiting for the order to arrive. Other overseas shoppers must rely on friends or family to purchase goods when they are visiting the United States.

However, international customers have immediate access to and direct contact with American retailers through online stores. They also have the shipping options laid out in front of them and don't have to worry about dealing with long distance phone calls and operators who barely understand their language.

This chapter will step you through the process of accepting and fulfilling an international order and will show you how important your overseas customers can be. The processing of international credit card orders is covered in more detail in Chapter 14.

Processing an International Order

While some aspects of processing an international order are the same or identical to processing a domestic order, there are a number of differences. Although the process of completing the invoice is the same, shipping a package involves a few extra steps, which we'll take you through.

International Shipping

After your sale is processed, there are extra forms that need to be included with foreign shipments. These are an absolute requirement from the big shipping companies like FedEx, UPS and Airborne Express.

Customs Form

One form that is required by every shipping company including the post office is a customs form. The customs form required by the private couriers is contained in a clear plastic pouch and attached to the outside of the package. The form contains a list of all merchandise enclosed, the value of each item, and the shipper's signature.

FedEx provides its own separate customs form while UPS and Airborne will just want three copies of the original invoice packed together with the airbill. All packages containing merchandise pass through a customs house for inspection and collection of any dutiable taxes. If you neglect to include the required information and the shipping company accepts the package without noticing the absence of this paperwork, the package will be held up in customs. Customs will inform your customer that the package cannot be released until an invoice stating the contents and their value is received.

When your customer informs you of the problem, you will have to fax or mail the missing information to the customs house. You should fax this information. Otherwise, your customer will probably end up waiting at least another week for the package.

If this situation ever arises, quickly grab your customer's bill of sale and fax it as soon as humanly possible. This will not be a pleasant experience for either you or your customer.

TIP ▸ ***Simply put, don't forget your customs paperwork!***

Joe's Take: *You won't get any lecturing from me. I've done it twice. Ouch. The post office customs form is slightly different and the easiest to complete. It's a small green sticker that adheres to your packages. You can go to the nearest post office and ask for Customs Form 2976. Keep a stack of them on hand as your international business begins to flourish. Before you put the invoice inside the package, fill out the form and slap it on the outside where it is easily seen before you head off to the post office.*

Flat Packages

Usually when sending flat letter packages (magazines, catalogs, etc.) through any of the private courier services, there will be no need to fill out any customs forms or triple invoices. If you are required to include a customs form on a flat letter package, then simply write "Documents, No Commercial Value" in the contents field or check off the corresponding box. Documents of no value are not taxable and can go through without being taxed.

Express Mail, Global Air Mail and Standard Air Mail letter packages shipped through the post office still require a green form. Again, you can simply write "Documents, no value" on the form.

The Airbill

When filling out an international airbill from a shipping courier, be sure the total value listed on your sales invoice corresponds with the amount on the airbill. If the package is lost or damaged it will be insured for the value listed on the airbill.

Express Mail packages from the post office are automatically covered up to $500, but Global and Standard Air Mail packages are uninsured. If you want to insure an item sent in this manner, you must fill out an additional form and pay an additional charge. You can simply transfer this charge to the customer unless you are feeling particularly philanthropic.

Promoting Your Store Internationally

The Internet is a massive global community. Whether it is through newsgroups, e-mail, or Internet Relay Chat (IRC), people from every nation are connected with one another. Once your domestic customers begin praising your business in the newsgroups or on the IRC, word of mouth reaches Internet users all over the world. A kind word can be seen as easily in Belgium as it is in New York.

If a customer halfway around the world has a good shopping experience at your store, he will probably recommend your business to others in his country—and to the rest of the Internet community.

There are a number of ways you can make yourself known on an international level. Look for international Web sites that are related to what you sell. Just access a search engine and use names of countries or words like **international** in combination with the names of some of your products. For example, Tronix could use the words **Germany video games** to search for game-related sites based in Germany.

Once you have found a relevant site, you can e-mail the Webmaster or whoever is responsible for the site and inquire about advertising or swapping links. Since people are more apt to hear about small companies from their own country and therefore visit those Web sites, this is an ideal way to promote your store in other countries. Assuming you advertise or link on a well-respected foreign site (why would you do otherwise?) you will gain immediate respect through your association with the site.

If you have enough money in your advertising budget, you can look around for some relevant foreign magazines and newspapers in which you might be able to advertise. You should be able to get some contact information from one of your foreign customers, a foreign Web site with which you have a relationship, or by searching the Web or domestic magazines.

As far as searching the Web, you can simply add the word "magazines" to the type of search we discussed when looking for Web sites. You should also check out some of the larger bookstores and magazine/news shops that might feature an international section.

When you do begin to gain international customers be sure to ask them how they found out about your business. Many of Tronix's international customers found the site through newsgroups, links on smaller product-related "webzines," personal home pages, and major search engines. This will give you a better idea of how they are ending up on your doorstep and where you should focus your international promotional efforts.

Joe's Take: *I've seen my international business grow in a pattern. I started out with a few customers from Germany and the Netherlands, and within a few months I noticed an increasing number of new customers from those two countries. Shortly thereafter, I received my first orders from Japan, Brazil, France, Canada, and Israel. Within a few weeks, I had many new clients from these same countries.*

TIP ▸ ***When supplying information about your Web site to the many search engines available on the net, it is essential to include in your company description that you ship worldwide, and/or specialize in exporting products. You should also try to become involved in newsgroups that not only deal with your particular type of store but also those that are dedicated to imported products or foreign countries.***

International Telecommunications

The majority of your international customers will use your online order form or standard e-mail to place orders so they can save on the cost of expensive phone calls. International phone orders will be rare.

If you feel that it is important enough to your business, you can order international toll-free service, which is offered by both AT&T and MCI. You might want to offer this service only to your most loyal international customers.

With AT&T, the same toll free number you use domestically can also be used international. There are a number of options available, all of which are described on the AT&T Web site (www.att.com). Among the options are AT&T Direct 800 Service, AT&T Toll-Free Service, and AT&T Universal Freephone Service.

MCI International Toll Free Service offers call routing, call termination, and network management services. For more information, visit the Web site (www.mci.com), contact your nearest MCI branch office or call 1-800-988-9294.

Credit Card Orders

Just as with domestic orders, international credit cards need to be verified. Credit card fraud is not just an American phenomenon.

Verifying an international credit card can be a more time-consuming process than verifying a domestic card.

You should ask the customer to provide the phone number of the issuing bank. If the customer can't provide the number, you'll have to contact your credit card merchant service to obtain it. Because of the time differences across the globe, you may not immediately be able to speak with a bank representative for an international verification. You'll also have to spend money on a couple of international phone calls.

It is more difficult to qualify for and receive a credit card in most countries than it is in the United States. While credit card fraud may not be as common as it is in the United States, it still exists. Be sure to set your requirements for international orders, spell them out on your Web site, and stick to them.

TIP ▸ ***One way to limit fraud is having all new international customers fax over a photocopy of both sides of the credit card, along with a utility bill showing the billing address. You can use this rule for first-time orders over a specific amount, such as $100. Some international customers may feel that faxing over their information defeats the purpose of using the Internet since they'll have to make a long distance fax. Let them know that this is the policy for first time orders and all future orders can be completed without faxing confirmation. You may lose a few customers who are required to meet these needs, but in the long run you will be less likely to get hit with a charge-back from your credit company. Charge-backs are tough to dispute, especially when you have accepted a fraudulent credit card order from overseas.***

Dealing With the Language Barrier

If you receive an international phone order, you may have to deal with a language barrier. A foreign customer who chooses to call will probably be able to speak at least some English. However, parts of the conversation, especially when it comes to foreign addresses, may be difficult to understand.

Politely ask them to spell out every letter in the address. Letters like "S" and "F," or "M" and "N" can easily be misunderstood over the phone. Be sure to read back the entire name and address to your customer. If necessary, verify every letter using simple phrases such as "S as in sick," "F as in Fred," "M as in Mexico," "N as in nice (or Nice!)," etc.

Internationalizing Your Web Store

When international customers visit your Web site, they should immediately feel welcome and be made aware that you export products. Add a noticeable line of text stating that you ship around the world. You can even add an animated GIF of a spinning globe above or below the text line. However, there's much more to creating a truly international Web site than that.

Translation

Many high-end Web sites even offer specialized versions for people in various countries.

Unlike the United States, where few people speak a second language with much facility, English is actually spoken as a second language in many countries. According to an OTEC On-line Consumers Study (March 1997), English is cited as the first consultation language by 55 percent of all European Internet users. If you sell technical products, chances are very good that your customers will speak English. In this case, you might want to simply create a foreign language summary page in order to be indexed in the countries you are targeting. Assuming you aren't fluent in the desired language or languages, you can either purchase the needed dictionary or hire someone to translate your page. The cost is generally less than $1 per word.

TIP ▸ ***There are a couple of places to find inexpensive translators—at local colleges and shopping on your Web site. As anyone who has attended college will tell you, college kids are always looking for a little extra money. Contact a local college's foreign language departments and ask if there are any students willing and able to give you a hand. You can also ask your international customers. Be sure that they know English well enough to do the job. If you find someone who can do the job, you can offer to either pay the person or give discounts or gift certificates to your store. However, if you are going to bother translating your site, make sure the translation is dead on. After the text has been translated, have it translated back into English to make sure it reads well. Otherwise, your foreign customers may read the text and come away feeling the same way you would if you found a site that greeted you with "This be my Web site. It are the most good on the Web if you are wanting the most coolest stuff."***

You might not be able to afford to either translate your entire site or translate into more than one other language. If you decide to partially translate your Web site, you need to decide what languages you will include and what parts of your site will be offered in foreign languages. For example, if you sell photography equipment you might decide to offer part of your site only in Japanese and German given those cultures' affinity for photography.

Since many of you may choose not to internationalize your site immediately upon its launch, when you finally decide to do so you should target the countries from which you have the most customers. Unless your customer base dictates otherwise, three important languages for Web sites to offer are Japanese, German, and French.

TIP ▸ ***Even if you can't afford to translate your entire Web site, you should plan to do so over time. Decide which pages are most crucial for your international customers, and which foreign languages are most used by your customers and start there. Eventually, you will have a truly international Web site so you can take advantage of the global scope of the Internet. In the meantime, you should keep the English on your Web site simple for the benefit of those international customers who aren't fluent in English.***

Where to Focus Your Translation Efforts

Which pages should you have translated first? Good question. Ask your customers. Assuming you have gained some international customers prior to translating your site, ask them what parts of your site they have the most difficulty navigating due to the language barrier. Are there one or two pages that would make the entire shopping experience more enjoyable if they were offered in your foreign customers' native language? Your customers should be able to provide valuable insight and will be more than willing to help—after all, it's to their benefit. Generally, instructional pages such as Frequently Asked Questions, shipping pages, home pages, and indexes are good places to start. Content may take longer and be more expensive.

TIP ▸ ***One way to internationalize some of your content is to combine narrative efforts with simple ratings and grades that are universally understood. For example, if you write a positive review for a product, add a numerical grade (1–10 or 1–100) or star rating that almost anyone can understand.***

Integrating International Pages

Many sites offer links to the international version on the home page. However, it's also a good idea to offer links on other key pages, especially if you have only translated a few critical pages.

TIP ▸ ***An outstanding reference for those wanting to take their Web store to a global level is*** **How to Build a Successful International Web Site** ***by Mark Bishop (published by The Coriolis Group, 1997, ISBN 1-57610-158-4). The book features techniques for creating a successful international online site, including how to create graphics in foreign languages, how to use Internet Web sites to market and conduct businesses domestically and abroad, and a discussion of European, Asian, and Unicode servers and browsers. Other highlights include Web translation services and products, multilingual Web browsers and editors, and import/export considerations. The book also has information on foreign language editors and helper applications designed to assist in the creation of multilingual Web pages.***

Is Translating Worth It?

In a word, yes. Since 84 percent of all Web pages are in English, there are a lot of potential customers out there suffering through English sites that they barely understand. If you can offer a site that is even partially translated into a few key languages and promote it in those countries, people may choose your site over your English-only customers. A customer from Germany or France or Japan is just as important as one from Kansas. In fact, foreign orders tend to be larger on average and the customers can be extremely loyal.

International Hosting

Many of the larger international sites are learning the importance of the server location. Customers accessing your site from Germany or Japan may have an easier time doing so if the contents of your site were available on a local (in relation to them) Internet server. You can do this by "mirroring" your site on another server in a host country. This creates a localized version of your content and can make it much easier for international surfers to get to it.

If you find your international customers complaining about slow access to your site, you might want to consider putting up a mirror site with a foreign host. Because of the cost, you need to consider if it is cost effective to do so. If you only have a handful of overseas customers, it probably isn't worth the cost. However, if a large percentage of your customers are from foreign countries and you feel you may lose them because of slow access, a mirror site may be necessary.

As the Internet grows it will clog up and bog down at times. The farther away a customer is, the more difficulty he might have accessing your site quickly. This problem can also occur in fits and starts. Traffic might flow smoothly one week, only to grind to a near standstill the next. Listen to your customers. Go with a mirror site in the country where you have the most regular customers and where they repeatedly have the most difficulty accessing your site.

There are a number of international domain services that you can find on a search engine such as Hotbot. For example, the international domain name registry NetNames (netnames.co.uk) handles overseas registrations in more than 200 countries. NetNames registers in every available top level domain in the world.

Finding a Web host in a foreign country is a matter of searching the Internet for "international Web hosting." You might also query Webmasters of sites in the host country for a few good recommendations.

Most countries have their own top-level domain and each country has its own requirements that must be complied with in order to use their domain. The fees and/or regulations are subject to frequent change. It is a common stipulation that the registering organization must trade, and have a presence in, the country of the registration.

Shipping Page

Divide your shipping page between domestic and international. You can have both layouts on one page, using a "jump to" link so international customers don't have to wade through tables of domestic prices to get to the section in which they are interested. You can also have separate shipping pages. If you decide to have a separate international shipping page, be sure to link to that page throughout your site.

When International customers fill out your order form, they'll be presented with a list of shipping options. Specify which options are for International orders. Foreign customers who are unable to read English very well might simply choose FedEx Priority thinking that they will get their product overnight for a very low price, when in fact they are choosing a domestic service. The Tronix Order form clearly separates FedEx Priority from FedEx International Priority.

- **Let your international customers know** they will be charged additional taxes by their customs house, which is separate from the charges that will be made by your company. Many foreign customers may be unaware of this, especially if they are ordering overseas for the first time. Unless you make them aware of customs charges, they may be upset by these extra charges and take their frustration out on you.

- **Do not internationalize prices.** Exchange rates fluctuate, so the price of a product on Monday might be inappropriate on Tuesday. Instead, maintain pricing in your home currency and let your customers do the conversion. You could offer a link to an online currency converter such as Olsen & Associates (www.oanda.com), which allows you to easily convert from one currency to another.

- **Be aware that certain kinds of appliances** or electronic equipment may not function properly, or at all, depending on the type of standard or electrical current used by a particular country. Research your products for compatibility with foreign issues such as electrical voltage and television, VCR, and telephone standards.

- **Information regarding these issues** should be posted on your site so your international customers will be well informed before they make their purchase. If in fact you do sell products that need an adapter, you'd be wise to offer them for purchase on your site as well.

Tips For Conversing with Foreigners Through E-mail

Stay away from English slang words and complex, idiomatic expressions. Your customer from Spain is more likely to understand "Your shipment will be arriving shortly," than " It'll be there in a flash."

Simplify your language, without talking down to your foreign customer. You may want to sound professional by using sophisticated replies in e-mail, but in this case, clever can be daunting.

If an international customer becomes impatient waiting for an order to arrive (particularly non-express orders), explain how packages can sometimes be delayed passing through customs.

The most difficult decision for a first-time foreign customer is usually shipping. Many times, you'll get orders from foreign customers who choose a very expensive means of shipping, which can turn out to cost more than the product itself. If you think the customer has made an uninformed shipping choice, feel free to point it out. In some cases, when a customer hears the price he might want to switch to a less expensive service simply because he didn't understand his initial choice.

If your foreign customer does not have a credit card, explain to her in e-mail that she can make out a bank money order or wire transfer instead. Give her all the details she needs, such as the total cost of the item(s), plus the shipping charge, and be sure to mention that the currency is U.S. dollars.

TIP ▸ ***If you receive e-mail in a foreign language, AltaVista has a translation service that is in beta testing. You simply enter the foreign text and follow the steps to translate it to English. You can also translate your English message into a foreign language. However, computer translation can be rather rough. It is expected that most search engines will eventually add this feature.***

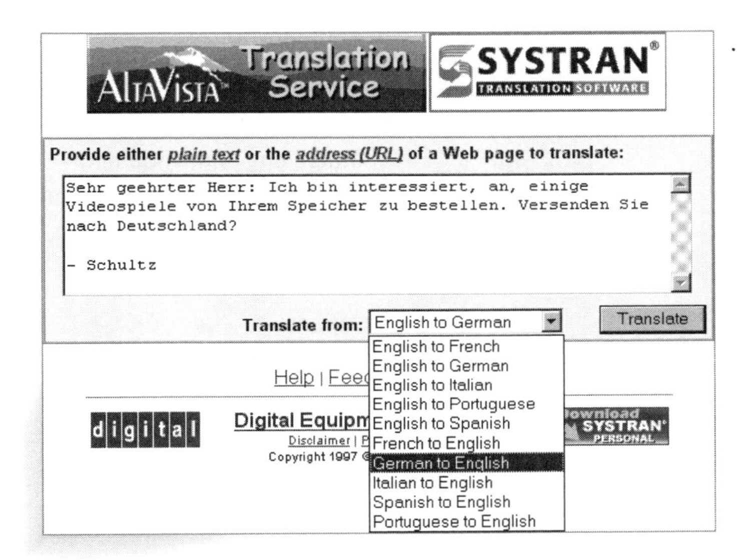

FIGURE 13.1
AltaVista's translation service in action.

International Access from Your Back Yard

Owning a Web store provides you with an opportunity to sell goods on a global level. While someone from London would probably never walk into a store like Tronix, that same person might well become a regular customer on the Web. While international sales can involve some unique issues, don't shy away from them. Selling internationally is another way to increase your customer base. The more welcome you make your international customers feel, the better the chance that they (and their friends) will become regular visitors to your store. The better you promote your store to international customers, the more will visit.

Being a truly international store will require some additional work. While you might not be able to completely translate your site for a number of countries, you should make the extra effort to gradually transform your site. There is a whole world of customers out there.

Next up is Part IV, which includes everything you need to know about selling and shipping. We'll fill you in on taking credit cards, spotting and catching online thieves, electronic retailing, and shipping.

PART IV

Selling and Shipping

You've learned how to build a store and attract customers. Now for the final step: completing and processing sales of all kinds and fulfilling orders. Part IV helps you identify and avoid online thievery. It also shows you how to handle credit card orders and how to get orders from your hands into your customers' hands.

Part IV Table of Contents

CHAPTER FOURTEEN

Payment Acceptance and Processing

As an online storeowner, the majority of your customers' orders will be paid for with credit cards, whether the customer calls with the information, faxes it, mails it to you, or enters it into your online order form. One advantage of shopping on the Web is the immediacy with which someone can have a product in her hands. Most people don't want to go through the process of getting a money order. They'd rather put the purchase on a credit card and get it over with.

Accepting credit cards improves your cash flow and reduces your costs. It can sometimes take 30, 45, or even 60 days after invoicing to receive payment from your commercial customers. By accepting credit cards, that time is reduced to two or three days. In addition to improving your cash flow, purchasing card acceptance eliminates the need to invoice your customers, thus reducing your administrative costs.

When you accept purchasing cards as payment, you avoid the cost of collection. Because you receive payment directly from the bank or, in the case of American Express, from the card company, you don't have to worry about possibly not getting paid.

However, a lot more goes into a credit card order than just punching in a number. Secure transfer of credit card information is an issue that has been addressed over the years. But to even accept credit cards, you must set up a merchant account with a merchant service provider or a bank. This chapter helps you find and be accepted by a merchant service, discusses the major credit card companies, gives you an understanding of Secure Electronic Transactions (SET), and takes you through a credit card transaction from start to finish.

Setting Up A Merchant Account

We covered the basics of merchant accounts in Chapter 6, but the information is worth covering in more detail here. Setting up an account with a merchant service provider or a bank allows you to accept credit cards as a means of payment. Without a merchant account to accept credit cards, you'll only be able to accept CODs, money orders, or checks paid in advance.

Not accepting credit cards severely hampers your ability to do business. Most people ordering products over the Web want to use a credit card. As credit card transactions become more secure, that percentage will only increase.

As we mentioned in Chapter 6, enabling your store to accept credit cards is one of your biggest challenges. A merchant service provider will not accept you simply because you want to open a business and accept credit cards.

To find a merchant service company near you, refer to the Yellow Pages under "Credit Card & Other Credit Plans—Equipment & Supplies." A company representative will interview you about your business plan and you will have to go through a credit check.

Before you meet with a merchant service provider, make sure you have your business set up, your bank account in order, a strong business plan, and a good argument for being accepted. Anything that shows you to be a capable and worthy reseller will help you.

However, you must understand that all Internet credit card transactions are placed in the highest-risk category (MOTO for mail order/telephone order or CNP for "card not present").

TIP ▸ ***Merchant service providers tend to be a bit leery of working with strictly mail order businesses, especially those existing on the Web. We're not suggesting you lie, but if there is any possibility of your store generating walk-in customers, emphasize that fact immediately. In fact, if you can do something to generate a small amount of in-store traffic you'd be wise to do so, simply to help you get a merchant account in place. As e-commerce becomes more prevalent, it will become easier for Web stores to get the same treatment as traditional stores.***

What a Merchant Service Provider Looks For

Merchant service providers want minimal risk. They don't want to work with a store that has an unfocused or non-existent business plan. They don't want to work with a business that will cease to exist in a couple of months. They don't want to work with a business that will be anything less than diligent about minimizing credit card fraud. And they don't want to work with a business that won't be able to pay its bills.

Merchant service providers, be they a bank or a service provider firm, want to work with businesses that will succeed. You know your online store will be successful. Now it's up to you to convince them.

Building an Argument

As we said, you need to have your business set up (have an employee identification number and a bank account) before you go looking for the ability to accept credit cards. Your argument should include a well-defined, realistic business report, and any supportive statistics about your industry and online retailing.

Statistics

Every research firm is predicting massive growth for the online retailing industry. You can check magazines (online and offline) such as *Internet Week* (techweb.cmp.com/internetwk/), *Web Week* (www.webweek.com), Mecklermedia's Internet.com (www.internet.com), or the IBM E Commerce site (www.hp.com/Ebusiness/toc.html) to find articles about the current state and projected growth of Internet business. If you don't find what you're looking for there, go to the sources themselves—Jupiter Communications (www.jup.com), Forrester (www.forrester.com), or International Data Corporation (www.idc.com).

Find statistics that support the argument that online retailing is a stable, growing industry and present those statistics in an organized manner. You needn't offer every statistic supporting your case, but you would be wise to refer to more than one firm that has come to the same conclusion. That will keep the interviewer from wondering if every other research firm is predicting failure for online retailing.

Crediting the firms will add weight to your argument. In fact, you might want to provide a copy of the article or the report from which the statistics were taken. You should also know a bit about the research firms you are using in case you are asked "What's Jupiter Communications?"

As you research your decision about what to sell online, you will probably come across a number of statistics that point you to your selected industry (computer games, snowboards, whatever). Use those statistics to show the interviewer just how solid your industry is. Some industries will be an easy sell—computer software initially sounds more impressive than video games. Pointing out that video and computer games are part of a multimillion-dollar industry should allay any concerns. Pointing out that the potential customers for a particular type of product are Internet users will further help your argument.

If you decided on your store's focus without researching the industry, now is the time to do so. Use your search skills on the Internet, check out an industry trade magazine, or go to the library (believe it or not, the Internet hasn't made them obsolete) to find the information you need.

Business Plan

Having a business plan is not only essential to the success of your business but will help you better explain your goals and projections to the interviewer. Your business plan needn't be a 20-page report, but it should cover your expenses, your sales and marketing plans, and your growth projections.

You should be able to back up your projections. Consulting with a similar store will help you. Your plan should be optimistic but realistic. Show the interviewer that you will begin making a profit immediately and that those profits will grow. However, don't claim that your store will be raking in $5 million a year just a couple of years down the road unless you have an extremely detailed plan showing how this will be accomplished.

You can open your business plan with a few paragraphs about what your business does, what makes it unique, what your goals are, and what needs to happen for you to reach those goals.

The rest of your plan should include a detailed accounting of your costs (many of your start-up costs will be behind you) and your revenue. You should explain how you arrived at your projected revenue and show that your business will survive even if revenue falls short. You should conclude by reinforcing the growth potential of online retailing.

While online shopping is growing, a merchant service provider might still be a bit hesitant to jump on your bandwagon. Show a plan to include walk-in customers, even if you know there will be very few. Explain that the reason many consumers have been reluctant to shop online is the questionable privacy. Then provide a brief, non-technical bit of information about the potential of Secure Electronic Transaction (discussed later this chapter) and existing security methods such as SSL and leave some literature. Don't dwell on the technical aspects of SET. Just explain how it will help online retailing grow.

Credit History

Although you probably will have been in business for just a short time when you approach a merchant service provider, any real numbers you can show will be to your advantage. If you've been in business for a month and are already selling well and paying your bills on time, this shows a business off to a good start and primed for an even better future. If you are off to a slow start, don't despair. Most businesses don't come flying out of the gate. Show that you are doing reasonably well for such a new business and emphasize how much business will improve when you can accept credit cards.

What a Merchant Service Provides

The most important thing a merchant service provides is access to credit card orders. If you are accepted, you will be able to lease a credit card processing terminal through the company for about $30 or $40 a month. Depending on your businesses needs, you can choose a point-of-sale terminal, computer software, or mainframe CPU-CPU connection for card processing. Once your have selected an option, processing an order is relatively easy.

Lowering Your Merchant Rates

Visa and MasterCard take between two and three percent of each sale and American Express takes even more. The merchant service provider or bank will give you the rates. As you begin to sell a higher volume, your rates will go down.

Your rates are also affected by the amount of fraudulent charges that are run through your store. In fact, too many fraudulent charges could lead to the revocation of your contract. Most credit card companies offer anti-fraud programs and advice that you should heed. For more on hindering fraud and online thieves, see Chapter 15.

Types of Payment and Acceptance

As a Web store, you can accept a number of payment types. In addition to traditional payment forms such as credit cards, checks, and money orders, customers may choose to pay through electronic cash or smart cards.

Electronic cash lets users send digital messages that act like currency to and from their accounts. Vendors can collect these messages and turn them back into a bank in return for their value. Unlike credit-card based systems, users are not advanced credit, and the goal is to enable ways for "micro-transactions" to take place. So while credit cards may handle payments of $10–$20 or more, electronic cash systems will be focused on items which cost less.

Smart cards allow users to store either e-cash, or digital verification information, which can be used to enable a transaction over the Web. Smart cards are not only for in-store transactions. Although smart cards can be used like debit cards for such transactions, they may also be used by customers who want to carry a portable digital certificate. This enables a user to transfer credit card and other e-cash information from any machine they are working at. Currently people who work at multiple machines must maintain separate certificates and/or electronic wallets.

A merchant can either process credit card orders through the Internet or by keying the information in through a terminal. A processing terminal, which you can get through your merchant service provider, is usually available on a two-year lease for about $35 a month. That will also get you a printer that allows you to get copies of your transactional information at the end of the day.

There are also a growing number of transactional software solutions available. The following are some of the companies, lists of their products, and contact information.

CyberCash, Inc.

2100 Reston Parkway
Reston, VA 20191
Phone: 703-620-4200
Fax: 703-620-4215

or

303 Twin Dolphin Drive, Suite 200
Redwood City, CA 94065
Phone: 650-594-0800
Fax: 650-594-0899
www.cybercash.com
E-mail: info@cybercash.com

CyberCash's CashRegister software enables secure, encrypted Internet transactions and the Wallet that allows shoppers to store their transaction information in one secure place. CyberCash also allows customers to make small payments with the CyberCoin service and use Internet checks with the PayNow service.

To begin accepting credit cards with CyberCash software, first contact your bank. You will need a merchant ID, terminal ID and other information before installing the software. After executing a service agreement and registration of the software, you can then download the software or have your hosting service do it. After generating the public and private key pair that encrypts and decrypts information, you can install CyberCash software.

CyberSource Corporation

550 S. Winchester Boulevard, Suite 301
San Jose, CA 95128-2545
Phone: 800-530-9095 or 408-556-9100
Fax: 408-241-9270
www.cybersource.com
E-mail: Go to Contact CyberSource at Web site

CyberSource specializes in secure electronic distribution of software and digital products over the Internet. CyberSource offers CommerceEZ, a service that is best used for straightforward product and pricing offerings and CommerceFLEX, which is for more complex commerce offerings such as shopping carts.

DigiCash, Inc.

2656 East Bayshore Road
Palo Alto, CA 94303
Phone: 415-321-0300
Fax: 415-321-0322
www.digicash.com
E-mail: info@digicash.com

DigiCash's ecash is a software-based payment system. Users and merchants open a bank account with a bank that issues ecash. The bank provides the merchant with the ecash Merchant Purse software with an account ID and password.

Ecash merchant software is used on the Web server. There are versions of the software for most of the platforms commonly used by Web servers. The ecash Purse is provided by the issuing bank for Windows 3.x, Windows 95, and Windows NT.

First Virtual Holdings, Inc.

11975 El Camino Real, Suite 300
San Diego, CA 92130
Phone: 619-793-2700
Fax: 619-793-2950
www.fv.com
E-mail: info@fv.com

First Virtual's transaction system involves the distribution of a VirtualPIN. The customer's credit card information is stored offline and when she makes a purchase with a VirtualPIN, she receives an e-mail message seeking confirmation of the order. The customer's credit card is not charged until First Virtual receives an affirmative response to the e-mail inquiry.

To sell using FirstVirtual, you need a private e-mail account, a bank account that accepts direct deposits through the United States Automated Clearinghouse, and a Merchant's VirtualPin.

GO Software, Inc.

42 West Montgomery Crossroad, Suite O
Savannah, GA 31406
Phone: 912-925-4048
Fax: 912-927-0214
www.gosoftinc.com
E-mail: sales@gosoftinc.com

GO Software's PC-Charge product enables businesses to process credit cards, ATM/debit cards, and check guarantee services on a computer. It automatically deposits the transaction amount into your bank account. PC-Charge was the first electronic transaction processing software system to be developed for Windows. PC-Charge is a Web control that resides on Windows 95 running Personal Web Server or Windows NT running Internet Information Server. PC-Charge ActiveX Payment Server acts as a bridge between IIS and PC-Charge that actually processes the transactions. PC-Charge is widely certified with all major credit card clearinghouses and will accept all card types.

ICVERIFY

473 Roland Way
Oakland, CA 94621
Phone: 510-553-7500
Fax: 510-553-7553
www.icverify.com
E-mail: info@icverify.com

ICVERIFY can process all credit cards with automatic draft capture into an existing bank account. The software supports more than 80 major card-processing networks. Direct access is available to Visa, MasterCard, American Express, and Discover for authorization and settlement.

InfoDial

22761 Pacific Coast Highway,Suite 101
Malibu, CA 90067-5908
Phone: 800-932-9311
www.infodial.com
E-mail: Go to Contact Us at Web site

InfoDial's Cashier allows real-time credit card authorization and supports most processing networks.

Major Credit Cards

Not accepting a certain type of credit card can mean losing customers. Visa, MasterCard, and American Express are the most popular. Each credit card company has its own rules and benefits. Here's a bit about Visa, MasterCard, and American Express.

Visa

Visa says it has more cards worldwide than the total number of American Express, MasterCard, and Discover cards combined. Visa's 525 million cards are accepted by more than 12 million merchants worldwide. In 1996, spending on Visa cards accounted for more than $410 billion in U.S. sales volume—more than American Express, MasterCard, and Discover combined. Retail purchases made with Visa cards are 15 percent higher than those made with checks and 193 percent higher than those made with cash.

Visa financial institutions typically pay merchants within 24 hours after deposit of sales drafts.

Visa has a number of risk-management programs and materials designed to help you decrease charge-backs, reduce fraud, and improve customer service. These programs include Card Verification Value, Educational Materials, Merchant Training, Merchant Forums, and Neural Networks.

Visa Purchasing can help you make purchase information available electronically to companies to help them comply with tax regulations, reporting requirements, and expense reconciliation.

For more information on accepting Visa, call your banker or 1-800-VISA-311, ext. 96 or go to the Visa Web site at www.visa.com.

MasterCard

MasterCard has over 200 million cards carried in the U.S. With MasterCard transactions, you receive payment within 24–72 hours, improving your cash flow.

Like Visa, you can contact your banker or MasterCard (914-249-2000) to learn more about accepting MasterCard. You should also check out MasterCard's Web site at www.mastercard.com.

American Express

Accepting American Express cards is different than accepting Visa or MasterCard, since American Express is a company unto itself while Visa and MasterCard work with a collection of lending institutions. For information on accepting American Express, go to its Web site at www.americanexpress.com or call 1-888-829-7302. To apply to accept American Express, call a customer service representative at 1-800-445-AMEX ext. 808.

American Express, like Visa and MasterCard, is involved in the development of SET protocol through its relationships with Microsoft, IBM, Netscape, GTE, and others as part of the SET technical advisory committee.

Processing an Online Credit Card Order

Credit card orders can be processed with payment software, which does much of the work but lacks the human interaction that can make a merchant feel more in control of the transaction. Or, the merchant can simply receive a credit card number, punch it in to a credit card processing machine and wait for verification of the number. However, that doesn't ensure that the card user is authorized. For more on that sticky subject, see Chapter 15. Once the customer has selected the item(s) she wants to purchase, she will be presented an order form that will include a list of items, their individual prices, shipping, handling, and tax charges, and a total price.

The customer either opens an on-screen electronic wallet and selects which credit card account she wants to use or simply types the credit card information into a secure online order form. Wallets are just now making it to customers as part of next-generation browsers. so they'll be little used for a year or more. See the sidebar about Microsoft Wallet for some understanding of about the client side application that more sites will interact with during credit card transactions.

Either through a wallet or an order form, the storeowner is made aware of the form of payment. In the electronic wallet system, the merchant responds to the electronic wallet, which verifies the merchant certificate and acquirer certificate.

The merchant can then determine if the message is authentic and has all of the order information. If the merchant is using automated processing software, the information is sent from the server to a clearinghouse, which checks the information with the issuing institution. If the card information is authenticated, it will be returned to the server, which logs the sale and sends an invoice and verification to the customer.

For the most part, credit card processing software will be sold as part of your server choice or, in the cases of some of the vendors mentioned in this chapter, sold as a plug-in for other server software.

If processing the card manually, the electronic slip and card number are encrypted and sent by the merchant to the merchant sends the information to his acquiring bank. The bank receives the encrypted information, decrypts the electronic slip, authenticates the cardholder certificate, and sends the card number out for authorization. The merchant receives the authorization response from the acquirer which, at the acquirer's option, may or may not contain the card number.

The merchant sends authorization status to the cardholder. If authorized, the merchant ships the goods or performs the requested services. The merchant receives payment from the merchant's financial institution.

Whether you use software or traditional processing methods is a matter of preference. While traditional processing affords you more hands-on involvement, it also requires more work. Software payment processing reduces the amount of work, the possibility of data-entry mistakes, and lowers transaction fees.

Microsoft Wallet

The Wallet allows customers to store and access payment and address information for online shopping. It allows customers to provide information without retyping it. Payment information is secured by password access and is integrated with the Windows address book.

The Wallet includes a credit card payment module that utilizes SSL-based security. It also provides an interface for development of additional payment protocols (including SET), and add-on payment methods such as digital cash. The Wallet also includes a protected storage area.

The Microsoft Wallet has a fully extensible, open COM architecture that supports additional payment methods and protocols.

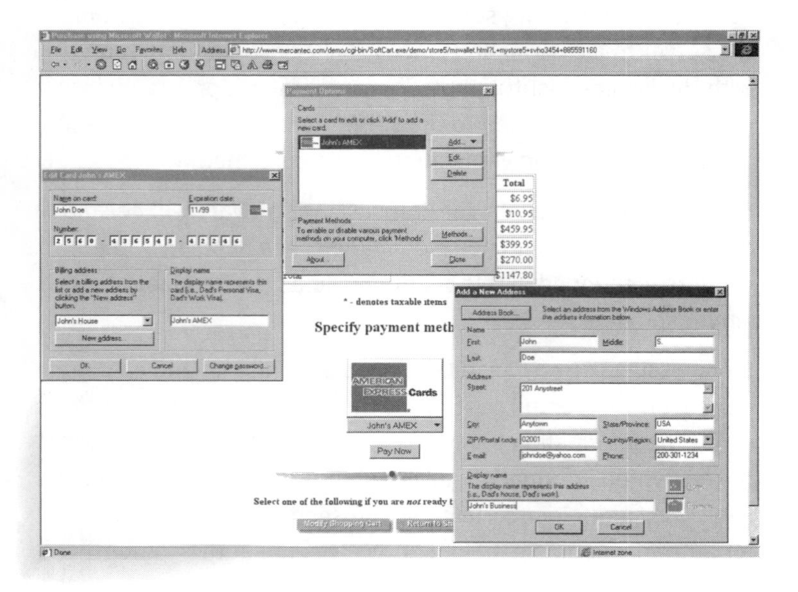

FIGURE 14.1
Microsoft Wallet in action.

Processing A Phone/Fax Order

If a customer calls to place an order, the first thing you'll do is collect credit card information—card type (Visa, MasterCard, American Express, and so on), card number, customer name as it appears on the card, expiration date, and issuing institution (Citibank, MBNA America, etc.). You should also ask if the person you are talking to is the cardholder. If someone is honest enough to say that he isn't, you should deny the order and report the card information to the credit card company. Even if a kid says that his mother let him use her card, deny the order. Only the cardholder is authorized to use the card.

If the customer can't provide an issuing institution, deny the order and contact the card company. That information is available on the card, and if someone can't provide that information, it means the card is not in his possession. That could mean a thief got the card number, name and expiration date, but failed to get the name of the bank. You can also ask for the bank phone number to further verify the card.

After you have taken the information and the order, you can call your merchant service provider, give them the card information and they'll pass it on to the issuing institution. You then call the issuing institution, give the card number and expiration date and check their billing address with the one you have been provided by the customer. With American Express, you simply call the company since it does not work with banks.

Once you have determined that the information you have received is legitimate, you can finish processing the order and ship the product. If there is something wrong, you can either call the person back to ask for clarification or wait for them to get back in touch with you. If the person has made an honest mistake in reading a piece of information to you, she will most likely call back when she doesn't get an order confirmation. If the person is a thief, only the most brazen will call back to ask, "Hey, where's my order?"

TIP ▶ ***To take things a step further, you can ask for a business address to ensure that the customer is not a child using a parents' card.***

Charge-Backs

And if you don't verify the information, this is what might happen—a charge-back. Charge-backs occur when someone sneaks a fraudulent credit card past you, the cardholder reports the problem, and the credit card company asks for its money back. Therefore you not only lose a piece (or pieces) of merchandise, but also the money you thought you had made from a sale.

Charge-backs are the reason for you to do whatever possible to limit credit card fraud. For more on fraud, charge-backs, and how to avoid them, see Chapter 15.

International Orders

Processing international orders is a little trickier than processing domestic orders. If the customer can't provide the bank phone number on his order form, you'll have to contact your credit card merchant service to obtain it. Because of the time differences across the globe, you may not immediately be able to speak with a bank representative to confirm the authenticity of a credit card.

One way to limit international fraud is by having all new international customers fax a photocopy of both sides of the credit card, along with a utility bill showing the billing address. Some international customers may feel that faxing this information defeats the purpose of using the Internet, since they'll have to make a long distance fax. Let them know that this is the policy for first time orders and all future orders can be completed without going through this process.

You may lose a few customers who are required to meet these needs, but in the long run you will be less likely to get hit with a charge-back from your credit company. Charge-backs are tough to dispute, especially when you have accepted a fraudulent credit card order from overseas.

Secure Electronic Transaction (SET)

Although Internet shopping has great potential, it will only begin to reach that potential when consumers are confident that online transactions are secure—that their credit card information can't be easily stolen by an unscrupulous hacker. There hasn't been an industry standard method of preventing fraud or theft of financial or personal information.

The development of Secure Electronic Transaction (SET) is leading to a single standard for safeguarding credit card purchases over open networks such as the Internet. However, SET has run into some problems. There are still technical difficulties to be worked out and, as of early 1998, SET had not become the industry standard. Its backers insist that SET will go to market in 1998.

The technology behind SET includes digital certificates—a way of verifying that a purchase is being made by a legitimate card holder—and will help customers shop safely, thus driving Internet commerce closer to its potential.

SET is designed to utilize technology for authenticating the parties involved in payment card purchases on any type of online network, including the Internet. SET is being developed by card companies such as Visa, MasterCard, and American Express, and technology companies like Microsoft, IBM, Netscape, SAIC, GTE, RSA, Terisa Systems, and VeriSign. By using cryptographic techniques, SET will hopefully make cyberspace a safer place to conduct business and boost consumer confidence in electronic commerce.

Digital certificates will be used to authenticate all parties involved in a transaction. Not only will merchants know they are receiving a legitimate credit card from its actual owner, but customers will be made aware that they are sending their information to an actual merchant, not some crook with a Web site. The developers of SET hope it will eventually make online purchasing as comfortable as using a credit card at a traditional store. The SET specification is open and free to anyone who wishes to use it to develop SET-compliant software for buying and selling in cyberspace.

The growth, both real and expected, in Internet usage has drawn attention to the potential lack of privacy. In cyberspace, the potential for fraud and deception is far greater. How is a customer to be sure that a Web site is not just an elaborate front for thievery? And how is a merchant to know that the person typing in credit card information didn't come upon that information illegally? For electronic commerce to flourish on the Internet, all parties must be able to verify each other's identities.

Digital Certificates

Digital certificates are the key to secure transactions and give both sides of a transaction confidence due to the presence of a third party, such as a credit card company, to verify information. For example, Visa or MasterCard provides digital certificates to the issuing institution, and the institution gives a digital certificate to the cardholder. Merchants also receive digital certificates.

When a transaction occurs, each party's SET-compliant software validates both merchant and cardholder before the exchange of any information. The validation takes place by checking the digital certificates, which were issued by an authorized third party.

The technology behind digital certificates is encryption. A message can be converted or encrypted into code using a *key,* which changes the message into a collection of characters that make no sense to an uninvited interloper. For example, a number might be replaced by the corresponding letter beginning at the end of the alphabet. In this case, 03412 would become ZWVYX. To decode an encrypted message, the recipient needs to have the key that unlocks the code.

The two most common forms of cryptography in use are Secret Key encryption and Public Key encryption. Public Key encryption is the key to safe electronic commerce.

Public Key Encryption

In Public Key encryption, each participant creates two unique keys—a public key which is available to all, and a private key which is kept secret from all. The two keys work together. Whatever data one of the keys encrypts, only the other can decrypt. If you want to send a secure message to a particular recipient, look up the recipient's public key and use that key to encrypt your message. The recipient then uses his private key to decrypt your message back to its original form. Even if the message is intercepted, the message can't be decoded without the private key.

Keys exist as series of electronic signals on personal computers or are transmitted as data over phone lines. The computer handles the encrypting and decrypting of messages. You don't have to do any of the work.

Underlying commerce software will be a layer of code that conforms to the new industry standard. This layer will use Public Key encryption to ensure that messages containing card numbers and other information are strictly confidential.

Digital Signature

Through digital signatures, Public Key encryption can also keep people from portraying others during online transactions. If you want to prove that you are, in fact, you, you can lock a message with your private key and the recipient can then unlock it with your public key, showing that you are the only person who could've originally locked the message.

This "digital signature" links the message with the sender. Only you will be able to use your card account over the Internet.

VeriFone Merchant Software

As Web commerce grows, software companies will continue to battle to provide for merchants. VeriFone offers an Internet point-of-sale solution called vPOS Merchant Software. Through VeriFone Exchange, VeriFone provides Internet developers tools and information.

The VeriFone Exchange delivers the technology and resources needed to deliver complete systems. Members of the VeriFone Exchange receive the latest vPOS development software and ongoing upgrades to create SET-ready Internet commerce sites.

Members also receive: complete vPOS documentation; a development guide; e-mail access to VeriFone's technical support staff; a copy of the VeriFone Internet Commerce Training Program; materials to integrate into sales presentations; communications on industry events and conferences; Internet commerce announcements; marketing opportunities; and the latest technical and business information.

Accept Credit Cards, But Be Careful

Not accepting credit cards is professional suicide. You have to do it. As Web retailing grows and online credit card transactions become more secure, the use of credit cards on the Web will continue to grow. You need to be prepared to grow along with it.

However, credit card fraud exists. If you accept a fraudulent credit card, chances are good that you'll end up stuck with the bill. The more you do to eliminate credit card fraud, the less money you'll lose to online thieves. Chapter 15 focuses on how to spot and catch online thieves, including those using credit cards illegally.

CHAPTER FIFTEEN

Identifying and Preventing Crime

As the owner of a corner store has to deal with kids pocketing candy bars, so too will you be forced to confront potential thieves. Rather than sneaking out of your establishment with something stuffed in their pockets, these thieves will try to use stolen credit cards to purchase merchandise. They'll hack into your site and wreak havoc like a vandal with a can of spray paint. They'll cost you time and money unless you protect yourself against them.

Merchants lock up their shops when they leave for the day. Your online store will be open 24 hours a day, seven days a week, making it necessary for you to keep everything as secure as possible at all times. The advent of Secure Electronic Transaction (see Chapter 14) will eventually help make purchasing products on the Internet a safe, enjoyable experience. There are also a number of things you can do to make the lives of thieves and hackers miserable. That's what this chapter is about.

A Variety of Crime

Before you prevent a crime, you must know what you are trying to prevent. There are essentially three kinds of crimes a Web merchant must be aware of—those that are perpetuated electronically, those that are order-related, and those that are directed physically at your place of business. Some examples of these crimes are listed in Table 15.1.

Table 15.1 Internet Store Crime Breakdown

Electronic Crimes	Order-Related Crimes	Physical Crimes
Hacker attacks to steal goods	Customer attempts to use invalid/stolen credit card	Inventory theft or damage
Hacker attempts to "sniff" credit cards or e-mail information	Child attempts to use parent's credit card	Stolen credit card records
Hacker attempts to steal credit card numbers and customer records	Customer tries to claim no order reception on good card	Computer equipment theft or damage
Hacker attempts to destroy or vandalize Web site		Vandalism
Viruses		

It is very difficult to completely eliminate the possibility of crime. However, there is plenty you can do to limit crime and, more importantly, to keep any crime that does occur from forcing you out of business.

Electronic crimes are those that occur when a "hacker" or electronic intruder attempts to actually steal from you by illegally obtaining information from your site or from your Internet communications. There are a variety of ways this can be accomplished. First and foremost, hackers can crack your site security and rifle through your data in an attempt to steal actual software (this is a common problem for electronic software delivery) or credit card records.

Hackers also sometimes attempt to gain access to a site and vandalize it by replacing files, deleting files, etc. They can also attempt to intercept and decode communications between you and your customers (a practice called "sniffing") in search of valuable information. Fortunately, hackers attack less frequently than many people think. However, as Web stores add value to attacks, more hackers will likely engage in theft rather than simple mischief.

Preventing Electronic Crimes

Four important practices will help you to prevent electronic crimes from occurring on your Web site. Follow basic Internet security practices; consult with either your ISP/Web hosting company or with a computer security expert about your site's security; utilize encryption whenever possible; and educate your customers about how they can protect themselves.

Basic Internet Security Practices

It is rather surprising how many Web site operators and Internet users fail to follow basic security practices. Some write down passwords on paper and hang them on the walls. Others repeatedly use the same simple password such as the name of a family member or a date of birth rather than choosing something unrelated to their personal life. The majority of hackers gain access because the victim has used a ridiculously obvious password.

Another problem occurs when a new employee is issued the same password as the person he replaced and the former employee supplies that information to a hacker. By avoiding these common mistakes you can close the common intrusions routes.

TIP ▸ ***Microsoft has a good, one-page document on creating passwords located at** www.microsoft.com/security/guide.htm.*

Another common problem is people not installing the proper security systems on their site and not keeping backup information in the case of criminal deletions.

Consulting with Experts

The best sources of introductory security are your technology partners. It only takes a day or so to make a few phone calls, read some manuals, or send some e-mail inquiries to cover all the basics. What you need to find is any configuration-tweaking help or information on any specific problems that your partners have encountered.

If you plan to run any specialized software for your Web store, be sure to review any manuals or documentation for security issues, instructions, and tips. Be wary of using software about which you have little documentation or that doesn't have a solid company behind it. Poorly designed or secured programs can expose the user to hacker attacks. If you are unsure about the security of your software, contact the vendor. If you fail to get the necessary security information, you may be the victim of an easily avoidable intrusion.

If you are working with an ISP or Web hosting company, find out what basic security measures it has in place. ISPs generally have decent security and cover the basics well. However, even the most professional ISP can be broken into. Still, you should listen to their recommendations, know what they can do to help, and understand their procedures should your site be attacked.

If you decide to run your own site, you must install your own security measures. This can be a daunting though necessary task. A good Web consultant can guide you through the basics. There are also computer security firms that offer higher-end help.

Finally, if you install a firewall or other security measures, those server software companies should provide some help and recommend consultants.

In most cases, implementing good store security involves knowing and installing all of the software security features available, having the names, phone numbers, and background of those who are responsible for protecting you from an attack (and helping you recover), and being educated about the security processes.

Utilizing Encryption Whenever Possible

Encryption is the key safeguard against many types of electronic crime and is a centerpiece of Internet stores. Encryption allows you to scramble information with a mathematical formula that is nearly impossible to decipher without the proper formula (known as a "key"). By using encryption to receive and transmit private and sensitive information, you can protect yourself against sniffers or programs that intercept Internet communications. If messages are encrypted, the programs can sniff all they want but won't be able to decrypt the stolen information.

Encryption is implemented by using technologies such as SSL (Secure Sockets Layer) and SHTML (Secure-HTML) with Web forms to protect their transmission to your server. Encryption can also be used in your e-mail package through a technology called S/MIME (Secure/Multipurpose Internet Mail Extensions). Encryption is discussed in more detail later in this chapter.

Educating Your Consumers

Securing your store involves your customers as well as yourself. Educating customers about Internet security involves three things.

Customers must first be educated about how they can best protect themselves. This can be easily done through a Store Security FAQ on your Web site.

You should also inform customers of the security measures you provide to ensure their privacy. Customers want to know how you will protect any personal, credit card, or demographic information they have supplied.

Joe's Take: *One way to educate users about security is to include that information on the order form. Much of the attempted crime at my site involves kids trying to their parent's credit card, so I remind them (and others) what that means. The Tronix order form includes the following message:*

> *"Fraudulent transactions (which includes using a family member's/friend's credit card without a prearranged agreement with Tronix) will be reported to the appropriate credit card company for further action, as well as to the Internet service provider which hosts the account. If you don't want yourself and the card holder involved in legal difficulties, we suggest you back out now (this is one game you don't want to play). If you are authorized to use your parent's credit card, we need to confirm this by phone, and not e-mail. Using a parent's credit card without his or her knowledge means the actual cardholder will be held responsible for your charges. When they receive their monthly credit card statement in the mail, we certainly wouldn't want to be in your shoes."*

You can also implement a WebTrust Examination (see sidebar), which is a certified audit of your Web site's ability to meet "a defined criteria for standard business practices and controls over transaction integrity and information protection." If you meet the criteria, you can display a button and information that informs customers of your strong security practices. According to research by WebTrust backers (including VeriSign), 75 percent of online users have a favorable impression of the WebTrust seal and half report that seeing the seal makes them more likely to conduct an online transaction at that site.

TIP ▸ ***To understand more about Web security, read The World Wide Web Security FAQ at www.w3.org/Security/Faq/.***

Implementing Encryption

To properly implement encryption, you must accept orders on a server that is equipped for encryption. Many Web hosting companies have special servers to allow for secure order forms. Be sure to discuss with your hosting service how to place a form and script the right submission program to implement secure placement on the server.

If you don't use a hosting company, you must the SSL and associated certificates on your own. That requires getting a compliant server (most major servers are compliant) and applying to a certificate authority such as VeriSign or Nortel Entrust for the digital ID necessary for compliant browsers to register your site as valid. (If you use a Web hosting company, it should have digital ID for the server you use.)

TIP ▸ ***If you use a Web host, you should note in your Security FAQ why the digital certificate isn't your own. Essentially certificates reside on the server and are the responsibility of the server owner. Therefore the certificate for your site will be assigned to the host.***

Obtaining WebTrust Certification

WebTrust is a service that was developed by the American Institute of Certified Public Accountants (AICPA) and the Canadian Institute of Chartered Accountants (CICA). Certified Accountant reviewers check your site and assess three critical principals:

- **Business Practices Disclosure:** The Web site owner discloses business practices for electronic commerce transactions and executes those transactions in accordance with its disclosed business practices.
- **Transactional Integrity:** The Web site owner maintains effective controls to ensure that customers' orders are fulfilled and billed as agreed to.
- **Information Protection:** The Web site owner maintains effective controls to ensure that private customer information is protected from uses not related to its business.

In order to begin the WebTrust process you must hire an approved accountant to implement the program. The specially trained CPA will go through your site and operations to see if they meet the developed standards. Once your site is certified, you are granted the right to obtain the WebTrust seal and place it on your site. Clicking on the seal will make the examination report and additional background on the program available to the customer.

CPA WebTrust VeriSign click here

Your site will be regularly re-visited by the CPA to ensure continuing compliance. VeriSign uses its technology to authenticate the seal, allowing customers to find out if a seal is real, active, and still in good standing.

You can find out a lot more on the AICPA WebTrust site at http://www.aicpa.org/webtrust/index.htm. There are more details about the criteria you must meet and how to implement the program.

While there are a number of things you can do to reassure customers of your security efforts, the WebTrust program adds the legitimacy of a CPA audit and brand identity. Your customers' responses will likely be worth the time and effort.

Ordering a digital certificate isn't difficult. Simply visit the order page of any major certificate authority, choose server certificate, and follow the instructions. The following lists are the major server certificate authorities.

- **VeriSign** (www.verisign.com): Leading Certificate Authority company on the Web.
- **Nortel's Entrust** (www.entrust.com): Certificate Authority run by major communications giant.
- **Thawte** (www.thawte.com): Another world-wide certificate authority located in South Africa.

After setting up your site with a digital certificate and a secure SSL server, you will need to develop a system to move information from the site to a form in which you can process it. The information also must be secure while it is in storage. Don't make the common mistake of e-mailing the secure form data back to yourself or of FTPing it off the server. Although the information has been moved to your server securely, e-mailing the information off the server or FTPing it down defeats the purpose of the secure form implementation. Sniffer systems can intercept the message in either case.

Instead, set up a secure directory on your Web site that is password protected. Then access the information in that Web directory via your SSL-enabled browser. You can also use a backend system that securely e-mails encrypted information to you. No matter which method you choose, remember to never allow retransmission of private data through unsecured means.

E-Mail Encryption

Encrypting e-mail is rather easy. Start by using an S/MIME compatible e-mail client such as one of the major offerings from Eudora, Microsoft, or Netscape and installing a certificate that can be obtained from one of the certificate authorities listed a few paragraphs back. The resulting configuration process, no matter which e-mail package you use, is also not complicated. While the process will vary from package to package, the instructions will certainly be available in the program's documentation or help file.

TIP ▸ ***Although the certificates do the same thing, you need separate certificates for your e-mail and your server (if you are running your own server).***

To send encrypted e-mail, your customers must also implement an encryption process. Although many will send credit card information through standard, unencrypted e-mail, it is wise to offer them information about encrypted e-mail. Certificates cost as little as $9.95 per year and are well worth the money when weighed against the potential loss.

TIP ▸ ***Include information in your Security FAQ about obtaining a digital certificate and using encrypted e-mail.***

For information concerning encryption for specific e-mail packages, check the help file, documentation, or Web site of your e-mail package.

Joe's Take: *When an encrypted message is sent to a user, it still appears in her e-mail box, which might not be particularly secure (if the computer is accessible to other people). Therefore you must be particularly careful about replying to e-mail that contains credit card or other personal information. The worst thing you can do is send a message with a complete credit card number included. Anyone nearby the recipient's computer could simply copy the card number off the screen; not all Internet-related crime is high tech.*

Credit Card Fraud

Unless you do something or sell something to tick off a hacker, credit card fraud will be the most common thorn in your side. Whether it is someone who ripped off a credit card number or simply a kid using mom's credit card to buy those CDs his parents refused to purchase, credit card fraud is an annoyance. If allowed to continue, it can be a financial disaster. Fortunately, it's also avoidable. It simply takes a little knowledge about what to look for and a lot of patience in verifying information to limit (and hopefully eliminate) fraud. When you realize that you not only lose merchandise, but usually the money from the sale, it becomes worthwhile to do everything necessary to thwart online thieves.

Verifying Information

Some software packages automatically verify credit card information for you. However, since many of you will not have such a system, you need to know how to verify information yourself.

Your online order form should be set up so that a customer is forced to enter all necessary credit card information—card type (Visa, MasterCard, American Express, etc.), card number, customer name as it appears on the card, expiration date, and issuing institution (Citibank, MBNA America, etc.). If you take an order over the phone, you should also ask if you are talking to the cardholder. Never accept an order by anyone but the card's owner.

Joe's Take: *American Express and other cards place four extra digits on their credit cards. These numbers don't show up on carbons nor are they read off the magnetic strip of the card. However, they are verifiable. These numbers are intended to make it more difficult to steal credit card numbers. By asking for these numbers in addition to the regular numbers, you can guard better against fraud. Check with your merchant services company and the credit card companies for more information.*

Don't process any order—online or by phone—that has incomplete information. If the order is placed online, the customer might have simply forgotten to enter a piece of information. You can either contact the customer about the missing information or wait for the customer to contact you. If a customer never contacts you again, you can be reasonably sure that the order was fraudulent. Why else would someone place an order and never call back when it failed to arrive?

TIP ▸ ***After you have taken the customer's information and order and your terminal has not issued a "Hold Card" order, you can pass the information on to your merchant service provider, which will contact the issuing institution. To further verify that the customer is using a legitimate card, check the customer's billing address with the issuing institution.***

Once you have determined that the information you have received is legitimate, finish processing the order and ship the product. Remember that you needn't repeat this process every time a particular customer places an order. Once a customer has established herself as trustworthy (two or three months of legitimate orders), you don't even need to ask for the card information. You can simply keep that information on file and allow her to place orders and direct you to use the same information.

Joe's Take: *After two or three months, if someone is still using the same credit card information, you can usually trust that it is legitimate. Fraudulent credit card use doesn't last long because once the actual card holder gets a bill, he'll see the charges, contact the card company, and the card will be cancelled. For that reason, you'll also see more fraud early in the billing cycle. The card thief will want to get the most use possible out of the stolen information before the owner learns of the problem.*

Recognizing Suspicious Customer Behavior

Credit card thieves will often tip themselves off—if you know what to look for. Although none of these activities guarantees that the customer is trying to pull off credit card fraud, they are all warning signs to proceed with caution.

- **Watch for a customer** who makes large orders without regard to size, style, color, or price.
- **If an international customer** wants the fastest possible shipping option, keep an eye open. International shipping prices are so prohibitive that most legit overseas customers will take a less expensive option.
- **A first-time customer** who places a large order and wants it shipped overnight should be treated with caution.
- **Don't believe a customer** who won't allow you to call him and insists on either calling you or communicating through e-mail.
- **Beware of different names** sending messages through different e-mail accounts.

- **If you get multiple orders f**rom the same person on the same day, the person will usually ask that you package the items together to save on shipping. If the person doesn't ask that the order be packed together, it's likely a fraudulent order.

- **If a new customer wants an order** shipped to an address other than the card billing address, deny the request. There's a good chance it's a fraudulent order.

- **The most common form** of credit card fraud is a child using a parent's card. If you get a big order for teen-oriented products, beware. Teenagers generally don't have credit cards and it may be a case of a youngster snatching a credit card out of dad's wallet and stocking up on those Sega games he couldn't get otherwise.

Examples of Credit Card Fraud

The most common type of credit card fraud you will encounter depends largely on the type of store you run. In the case of Tronix, which has a relatively young clientele, the most common form of fraud is when children use their parents' credit cards. If you sell adult-oriented products such as furniture, it is unlikely that you will face that form of fraud.

Joe's Take: *When Tronix first opened, I was very naïve. On one occasion, a person from Kuwait made an order for $300. I didn't do any verification because it was Kuwait and I didn't think it would be worth the hassle. Sure enough, it was fraud.*

Although I rarely receive fraudulent orders from international customers, on another occasion a guy from Poland said he was from a magazine and ordered $2,000 worth of software. He gave me a story about how he could only be reached by fax—and I bought it. I sent him his order and I never heard from him again. To further complicate matters, the charge-back from the credit card company came while I was on vacation. You only have 12 days to respond to a charge-back before they pull the money from your account. By the time I got back, I only had two days to respond. That's when I became really vigilant about verifying credit card orders.

Stores that sell computer equipment, stereos, televisions, etc. are also likely targets for fraud simply because those items can be resold. The same goes for jewelry. In this case, the thieves avoid the hassle of breaking into a house and loading up a van.

How Credit Card Fraud Affects Your Costs

Allowing a stolen credit card to be used at your store is similar to getting arrested for drunken driving—you lose in a number of ways. First, you lose the merchandise (your license). Then, you lose the money (the fine). Finally, you pay higher merchant rates (car insurance rates). Yes, checking and rechecking credit card information can be a hassle, just like hailing a cab or sleeping on someone's floor. But it's worth it.

The worst aspect of accepting a fraudulent credit card order is that the credit card company will almost always side with he defrauded card holder because that's where it makes its money. If you think that's unfair, imagine if someone stole *your* card information, piled up a couple thousand dollars worth of merchandise, and your card company said "Tough break." You'd be canceling your account and taking your business elsewhere.

Even if a child uses a parent's credit card without authorization, the credit card company will usually rule against you. The only chance you have is if the shipments went to the billing address. Don't ever be foolish enough to send merchandise to a college dorm or an address other than the credit card billing address. While college students might be a solid percentage of your customers, they tend to use cards of their parents or their own which are assigned to their home address. What you must do in this case is simply send the order to the billing address.

Joe's Take: *You might find people who try to soften you up with friendly e-mails before hitting you with a fraudulent order. I once had a guy submit a credit card order that completely checked out. He started with two games, then three, then five. He told me how much his kids were going to enjoy the games and told me a nice family story. One day I got a really big order from him, so I wrote back asking him how many kids he had and that I wanted to talk to him by phone. I called on a Saturday night and got an office. So I called back and quickly found out that it was a son using his father's credit card. We eventually set up a plan where I sold the (used) games at a discount and he got some of his money back.*

Merchant Education Programs

Credit card companies don't like fraud any more than you. Although the card companies will usually get their money (out of your pocket), it's a time- and money-wasting process for them to deal with fraud. It is in their best interests to educate you about how to limit credit card fraud. And it is in your best interest to listen. Here's what Visa, MasterCard, and American Express provide for merchant education programs.

Visa

Visa offers a Merchant Education Program with materials written for merchants to provide information about Visa policies, procedures, programs, and services. Contact your Visa merchant bank for industry-specific and card-specific information.

Visa's Merchant Best Practices area (www.visa.com/cgi-bin/vee/fb/merch/practice/main.html?2+0) on its Web site is designed to help merchants avoid fraud and implement best practices.

MasterCard

MasterCard launched the Address Information Management Service (AIMs) to help combat credit card fraud, especially when an item is shipped someplace other than the billing address.

AIMs is a fraud control system that allows direct marketers to instantaneously check the identity of any address. By providing immediate, on-line access to real-time address inquiries, AIMs enables catalogers, airlines, concert ticket agents, book and CD clubs, or Web retailers to stop suspected fraudulent acts before they occur. For more information about how AIMs works, MasterCard suggests you contact your acquirer.

For more information, check out the MasterCard Web site's Merchants area (www.mastercard.com/merchants/).

Internet Fraud Watch

MasterCard has also provided a grant to the National Consumers League to help launch the Internet Fraud Watch, which is intended to monitor, report, and prevent online fraud. The IFW is designed to assist local, state, and federal law enforcement agencies in gathering complaints about online fraud.

To check out the Internet Fraud Watch, go to www.fraud.org and click on Internet Fraud Watch. Reports of Internet and online fraud have tripled since the Internet Fraud Watch was launched in March of 1996.

The IFW, a project that operates in tandem with the League's National Fraud Information Center, received an average of nearly 100 fraud reports per month in the first seven months of 1997, compared to 32 per month in 1996. More than 3.5 million people visited the NFIC's web site from February 1996 to August 1997.

American Express

American Express' Small Business Exchange Web site (www.americanexpress.com/smallbusiness/) includes an Expert Advice area. You can read the Tip of the Month or the Guest Column, send a question to Ask the Advisor, or browse the previously answered questions in the Advisor Forum.

For more information on limiting credit card fraud, American Express suggests you call Interactive Customer Service at 1-800-297-1234 or write to:

American Express Company
200 Vesey Street
New York, NY 10285

Cooperating With Competitors

Although retailing of any kind is competitive, dealing with credit card fraud is one instance in which online storeowners often work together. Despite the fact that you will be competing for the same pool of customers, no one wants a customer who is really a thief. It is a good policy to share information with other stores within your industry on bad credit card users. If you warn your competitors about potential thieves, they'll probably do the same for you. No one wants to get ripped off and no one wants to see anyone else get ripped off.

Joe's Take: *A competitor once sent me a message about a bad order he had received. About an hour later the same person tried to place an order at Tronix. Fortunately, since my competitor had shared the information, I was able to immediately deny his order. You'll find that within your industry, small storeowners are willing to share this type of information. It helps everyone and hurts no one—except the perpetrators.*

CyberSource Turns Early Difficulties Into Business

CyberSource, a service provider for secure electronic distribution of software and other digital products, was initially hit hard by online software thieves. Now CyberSource runs a fraud clearinghouse for online merchants, where services include comparing a credit card sales request against a list of about 75,000 known online thieves.

CyberSource has developed the IVS fraud screen. In addition to real-time bank validation, every transaction is checked, analyzed, and cross-checked by Internet address, browser type, and more than 100 other validation factors to uncover potential fraud. For 50 cents a transaction, other cyber merchants can pay CyberSource to run a pending credit card request through this online model. For the same fee, CyberSource will compare the request against its 75,000-name fraud database.

For more information on CyberSource, see this book's Resources section or visit www.cybersource.com.

Physical Theft or Damage

Although it is probably the most uncommon form of crime that you will face, don't discount the impact that a physical crime can have on your store. Hopefully, you will never have to deal with a break-in or employee theft or damage. To minimize damage and prevent these types of crimes in the first place consider the following tips:

- **Use password protection** internally as much as externally. Not everyone needs access to credit card information or to the Web site.

- **Screen potential employees carefully,** especially if they will be working with sensitive information.
- **Institute a vigorous backup system.** This should include daily backups of sensitive data including the Web site's files, customer records, inventory, and credit card transactions. Store copies both on and off site in a secure manner.
- **Have a catastrophe plan in place.** Everyone should know what to do in the aftermath of a site crash or attack or in the case of site, inventory, or customer record theft.
- **Purchase** appropriate business insurance.

Although the security efforts of your business will focus on the Web side of operations, don't ignore the potential for real world theft.

Stop, Thief!

Most people don't steal. However, the ones who do can make life miserable for the rest of us. There's no need to be paranoid, but there is a great need to be careful. Unless you consistently verify credit card information and use the most secure transaction system available, you will be left open to fraud. The consequences of allowing fraudulent credit card use at your store pile atop one another. Not only do you lose merchandise, you also lose money and watch your merchant rates rise. In addition, other forms of crime can instigate disruptions that drive customers elsewhere.

Thwarting thieves requires a commitment to verifying credit card information and an eye for suspicious purchasing habits. It's also a good idea to follow the advice offered by the various credit card companies. They've seen every type of credit card scam imaginable and are more than willing to help you combat them.

This was kind of a downer of a chapter, but it was necessary. No one wants to lose their business because of a failure to combat thieves. With a little effort and a little thought, no one should.

With all of this nasty talk behind us, it's on to something a bit more fun—electronically distributed software. Technology now allows software to be delivered over the Internet rather than shipping out endless CDs, documents or other hard goods.

CHAPTER SIXTEEN

Electronic Software Distribution

Electronic Software Distribution is an alternative to the traditional distribution of software and other digital goods. Rather than mailing shrink-wrapped CDs, online retailers can save time and money while providing timely customer service by distributing software through ESD. This chapter will take the software vendors among you through the steps, benefits, and potential pitfalls of ESD. Although this chapter is certainly more useful for those of you who sell products that can be transferred over the Internet, non-software merchants may find some of the information interesting as well. Although some of you don't currently sell software, you never know when you might decide to add, for example, a piece of software on bike repair and maintenance to your online bike store. If that day arrives, you might want to employ ESD.

Benefits of ESD

Everyone involved in software sales—including the customer—can benefit from ESD.

Customers will find ESD more convenient and timely. No longer will the customer have to pay shipping costs and wait for a CD to arrive before installing the software. Delivery is immediate. Nearly as important, in many forms ESD will save customers the agony of having to deal with that pesky CD shrink-wrap, sticker, and little metal thing.

ESD also makes subsequent upgrades easier to receive. Software purchased via ESD can be easily upgraded over its life by the vendor or developer.

ESD also tends to include a try-before-you-buy component that allows users make a solid decision that they want they want the software, thus reducing returns.

If you not only sell software, music, or documents but also produce them, ESD offers lower delivery costs and a direct avenue to market for new products or upgrades. ESD is used by many of today's software companies to get their products to market. Rather than deal with the regular problems of the traditional retail channel, companies such as Borland, JScape, Sun, and RealAudio are setting up software-based stores right on their corporate Web sites.

For software merchants, ESD provides an even more extensive list of benefits. ESD allows merchants to eliminate physical inventory and the associated costs, risks, and headaches. The lack of associated inventory also allows the online merchant to offer a wider variety of products.

Selling software through ESD also allows the merchant to cut packaging time and get products to customers anywhere in the world immediately. A store offering ESD to its customers has an advantage over one that doesn't; what customer wouldn't prefer to receive software immediately and without having to pay shipping costs?

While modem speeds and growth of high-bandwidth will hinder ESD somewhat, it is expected to become the most dominant form of software delivery.

Types of ESD

There are several styles of ESD. Each one has to do with the underlying piece of software that is being sold. For each major type of software there are actually specialized ESD tools and processes used to implement it. The forms of ESD are computer software, documents, graphics, audio, and video.

Computer Software

Any piece of computer software can be sold online and this is certainly the biggest part of the ESD revolution. In some ways computer software has been sold electronically for quite some time. The concept of shareware and "try-before-you-buy" marketing of programs has been used by many developers for over a decade. Shareware software reselling has the developer producing a piece of software that is given away for free. The developer then offers an enhanced version (and perhaps services, like free updates) to those users who send in payment to become registered users of the product.

It is important to understand that selling software through ESD may include shareware as a marketing concept. But the two items are entirely different. ESD may not involve the distribution of any free software. Formal ESD technology also tends to include features such as encrypted delivery and "digital wrappers" that enforce copyright compliance and protect against unauthorized use or piracy.

Software ESD also tends to include third-party reselling capability, whereas shareware registrations are done directly with the developer. Thus, shareware can be thought of best as a direct marketing method, while ESD is more akin to catalog or retail marketing as it may involve a store like yours or the developer's own internal store.

Recipe for Software-Based ESD:

1. Software publisher/developer prepares software master.
2. Developer partners with Resellers, third party clearinghouse, and ESD technology company.
3. Digital wrapper placed on product, vendors given software master.
4. Web retailer prepares site, accepts payments, and sends through software.
5. Clearinghouse provides digital key to unlock wrapper.
6. Web retailer provides follow-on support.

Documents

It is sometimes easy to forget how often products that are sold either in business-to-business markets or to consumers consist of nothing more than documentation. Whether it is a computer book, a market research report, a legal document, yesterday's news, or the latest issue of the *New Yorker*, words and pictures of a printed page are products that can be sold via ESD.

Most document-based ESD revolves around specialized document formats that render a document to a special file that, when viewed or printed, can actually reproduce the original layout, resolution, and complexity of the document. Two major technologies, Hummingbird's Common Ground and Adobe's Acrobat, are used by most developers. Acrobat is the market leader.

A product called Softlock can protect your documents from being routed around the world once someone buys a single copy. Softlock can be used in conjunction with Adobe Acrobat files to prevent piracy of the underlying Acrobat document.

Recipe for Document-Based ESD:

1 Prepare all content for publication.

2 Render document in either Common Ground or Adobe Acrobat format.

3 Apply copy protection (e.g. use Softlock with Acrobat).

4 Produce an abstract, table of contents, or index for Web site informational listing.

5 Produce a commerce system that accepts payment and returns document (via e-mail or password-protected site).

Graphics

Clip art, photographs, and other graphical software are already big sellers online and this will increase as better graphical-oriented ESD technology takes hold. The big issues with graphics are securing the graphic against copying and producing a way for it to support many different resolution styles. The first part, security, is handled by a graphical watermarking technology. This provides a constant copyright identifier with the image. No matter how often it is copied or changed, an artist or reseller will be able to identify improperly used product to help fight piracy. Leading the charge in digital watermarking is a company called Digimarc, which has a plug-in that is used in Adobe Photoshop 4.0.

In terms of resolution, the issue is that graphical content is often sold for different purposes. For example, a piece of clip art might be used for a Web site one day and a major magazine cover the next. Each use has extremely different resolution needs. For example, the Web image needn't be more than 72 dpi and low-resolution while the version for printing a magazine cover needs to be of a much higher resolution. Here too, there is an emerging solution. FlashPix (www.flashpix.com), a format developed by Live Picture, Inc. and backed by Microsoft, Hewlett-Packard, and Kodak, allows several resolutions of the same picture to be stored together. Once transferred, the format only presents the image data relevant to the underlying needs of the display technology.

By combining the high-end technology of the Flashpix format with digital watermarking available from Digimarc, there is a clear way to distribute high-resolution imagery via Internet stores.

Recipe for Graphics-Based ESD:

1. Prepare all graphical content by storing it properly in the Flashpix format.

2. Add a digital watermark for each product using Digimarc's plug-in for Photoshop.

3. Produce a lower-end version for the Web site for browsing purposes.

4. Produce a commerce system which accepts payment and returns image (via e-mail or password-protected site).

Audio

ESD-based audio distribution has taken several forms on the Internet. There are some specialized formats such as Liquid Audio's. There are also some companies looking at the RealAudio format. The big difference between the two is that Liquid Audio is seeking to provide perfect replications of CD-quality audio and specialized formats that better protect copyright. At some point though, RealAudio may offer such features. But for now, Real Audio is optimizing itself for streaming audio, which requires cutting some corners.

In terms of audio ESD, the major system being developed is by Liquid Audio. Examining its components allows you to better understand some of the overall issues involved in ESD. The system is comprised of three major components:

- Mastering software, called Liquifier.

- Server software, called MusicServer.

- Playback software, called the Liquid MusicPlayer.

In addition, the company supports a digital watermarking solution from Solana Technology. Solana has developed a system known as Electronic DNA (E-DNA) which embeds (unbeknownst to the listener) copyright protection and secure tracking into the music. One key item of this and other ESD schemes is to embed a special customer number right into the music file before it's delivered. That way if someone copies it, they may actually be spreading it to the point that the copying could be trace to the source.

This sort of responsibility and trace-ability makes it easy to go after people who illegally duplicate audio. While it is not meant to catch individuals who make a copy for a friend, it will be very good at preventing people from posting music publicly to the Internet. According to experts, there are more than 2,000 sites that are actively and illegally distributing music on the Internet.

The MusicServer software helps the merchant process the order, assemble it for delivery, and then send it down to the users' system, where it can be played back or written out to a CD. The server also works to record the song(s) that was sent and all the royalty information. The server manages the delivery of the content that, in the case of audio, can be significant.

On the other end the MusicPlayer software allows users to preview titles and interact with the MusicServer to order the product, get it downloaded, and then played back or recorded.

Real Audio based ESD products are primarily focused on content that is used for informational purposes rather than for recording or high-end replication. Audible, Inc. leads in the Real Audio ESD space, providing a handy portable playback device for Real Audio content. Content is bought from Audible then downloaded directly for playback on their device, which holds almost two-hours of content.

After software, music content could become the next major market for ESD. While computer software is growing fast, file sizes may be even bigger than most albums. A full audio album may be as small as 40–50 megabytes vs. 100 megabytes or more for a major software product like Microsoft Office. Indeed, music sold directly on the Internet is making some noise. Some companies are already saying that Internet music sales could exceed 1 billion dollars by 2002.

Recipe for Audio-Based ESD:

1. Record or obtain content for distribution.
2. Render content (Real Audio, NetShow, MPEG3, or Liquid Audio).
3. Apply copy protection (i.e. digital watermark).
4. Produce low-resolution version or sample for Web site preview.
5. Produce a commerce system which accepts payment and returns sound (via e-mail or password-protected site).

Video

Broad-based video ESD is still quite a ways off. While some simple video clips may be sold via clip-services, it can be expected that video will remain an ESD reach for at least ten years. However, it is clear that after all the above forms are conquered, video will be the remaining dominant software form to which developers will turn. When that happens, the ESD process and solution will be somewhat similar to its audio cousin.

A Closer Look at ESD

ESD is not a terribly difficult process once you've put together the content, the formatting tools, copyright protection, and an underlying commerce system. However, this chapter would be incomplete if it didn't delve a little more deeply into the process.

Making ESD Work Securely

For ESD to be successful, there needs to be secure delivery measures in place so that the product is delivered only to the intended recipient and only after the recipient has paid for the product.

One of the potential pitfalls of ESD involves unapproved reproduction of the product. Gone is the physical barrier provided by physical distribution systems so ESD needs to have a process that helps to block against widespread unauthorized piracy.

One of the biggest worries about ESD is in the accountability of the merchants who choose to use it. How does a developer actually know if a merchant sold 500 copies of a certain ESD delivered album if all the merchant tracks are downloads? This is where ESD proponents have introduced a third party to the equation to ensure against counterfeit by merchants. Without this, it would be much more difficult to get vendors to move their distribution to ESD and thus the overall ESD revolution would be hindered.

A clearinghouse company restores the barrier to counterfeit reproduction. The clearinghouse acts as an independent means of auditing product distribution and sales. The software vendor will also have a hand in controlling the validity of the software that is distributed.

If you are to provide ESD, you will be given a copy of the software master. Before you can send a copy of that software to a customer via ESD, you must also have a secure version of the product that is packaged in a digital wrapper. That package cannot be unlocked and installed until customer payment is approved. The customer then receives a key to unlock the product.

The best way to ensure security is to have the master registered with the vendor. An independent clearinghouse then handles the distribution of the "keys" used to unlock the software. A key that is specific to the transaction ensures that the end user license agreement is registered, the vendor receives payment, and the publisher receives proper compensation.

The clearinghouse maintains a database of licensed users that contains customer transaction information. The software publisher assures customers that they receive software rights granted by the publisher not by an intermediary. The vendor can also access the database when selling new software rights and returning or upgrading software to existing customers.

Clearinghouses are similar to digital certificate vendors mentioned in this book. They provide a means for everyone involved in the transaction to trust each other.

Stepping Through an ESD Transaction

Since you now have an understanding of the types of ESD and the role of clearinghouses, it is time to critically examine an ESD transaction.

A typical ESD transaction involves six steps:

1 The software publisher creates the software master.

A software master is nothing more than the final original version of the software, be it a computer program, audio file, graphical image, or document.

2 The publisher or its manufacturing partner prepares the master for electronic distribution. The protected master is registered with selected partners and posted to appropriate Web sites.

Preparation for electronic distribution can be done by the originator of the material. In some cases (primarily computer software) there are special vendors which help prepare the ESD version of the software. In the cases of art, audio, and documents, ESD usually involves the addition of a watermark that is a hidden attribute and can't be easily (if at all) removed from the file. Once the final files are ready, the product is digitally wrapped or encrypted into a single file that requires a password or key to be applied to it before it will release itself for absolute use. In terms of key-based orders, the keys can be stored at a clearinghouse that would then separately deliver that component to the user once a valid purchase is determined.

3 A customer orders the product.

A customer will typically first access a degraded, timed, or preview version of the underlying software before ordering the product. If the customer wants the product, she can then purchase it.

4 The retailer fulfills the order.

Once a customer has placed an order, the merchant must provide him with several items. Many vendors first opt to present the End User License Agreement (EULA) to the user. (The EULA is the legal document that describes the terms under which the customer may properly use and transfer the software). The customer must accept it before the transaction can close. The merchant will also have to verify the credit card and undergo any other process needed to ensure that the software is being transferred to a reputable customer.

5 The retailer notifies the publisher and the clearinghouse. After authorization, the customer is given the key that allows the downloading and installation of the product.

Fulfillment usually involves delivering a password-protected area where the user can download the software from the Web site. Many sites deliver the password and an authorization key via e-mail first. Some may opt to simply deliver the full piece of software via e-mail as well.

6 Returns, re-installs, and post-purchase marketing.

Returns are difficult in ESD in that, once downloaded and properly installed it is difficult for a merchant to insist on the uninstallation of the software. In terms of corporate buyers, this is somewhat easier as adherence to proof-of-destruction notices by reputable customers can be effective.

However the honor system won't regularly work with individual consumers. Instead, ESD vendors must substitute strict return policies for such products. In this case, users could be allowed one return for every X number of orders. Multiple returns would be frowned upon. Overall, the hope is that a merchant would be able to keep people from taking advantage of returns while leaving room to deal with loyal customers who make a small number of purchasing mistakes.

ESD Fraud and Other Concerns

When delivering software via ESD, make sure the software you sell is valid for sale outside of the country. The United States, for example, has strict rules against exporting software that provides certain levels of encryption and other security features. Serious fines and even jail time could result.

You might also have to deal with currency exchange, language issues, or local laws. For example, software depicting Nazi imagery is illegal in Germany. And while that might seem obvious, several years ago a WWII arcade game featured enemies with Nazi garb. It is difficult but very important to stay on top of these issues. You should make a concerted effort to keep from tripping in the global marketplace.

As with traditional online sales (if there is such a thing), credit card fraud is the most common form of crime associated with ESD. And, as with traditional online sales, the merchant is usually liable.

Because unscrupulous online merchants (not you of course) may not report the download transaction that was stolen through the use of an illegitimate credit card, the clearinghouse becomes more important as it looks over the shoulder of the merchant. The clearinghouse must work in cooperation with merchants not only to police them against high return rates, but also to assist them when legitimate returns or mistakes are made.

The other potential problem with ESD-based commerce is that goods are susceptible to hacker attack. Hackers can break through a site's protection and steal software. In fact, ESD vendors are prime targets for hackers. Hackers can also hurt merchants by cracking the digital wrapper that is used to protect the software.

While this is more the responsibility of the ESD technology company that protects the software, it is something you need to be vigilant about.

Coordination Is Key

It is impossible to open up an ESD store immediately on the Internet unless you offer products that you make yourself. Due to the technology involved and the potential for piracy, many vendors and publishers of software are working slowly toward ESD. Not only must you construct a good ESD commerce site, but you also need to work directly with the software publishers to make sure they approve you for ESD transactions. This might involve an audit of your site and company and a check to see that your site is properly configured for ESD transactions.

What this means is that if you want to implement ESD, you have to coordinate your efforts with the vendors and manufacturers. If not, you will never have the necessary stock. The Software industry has rallied around several major vendors, all of which make digital wrapper products, and some, like Portland Software, that make server systems that also help. In terms of the music industry, Liquid Audio is absolutely in the lead, but others may soon join it. Most of the major record companies are taking it slow. RealAudio-based commerce is currently slow with most of it revolving around Audible, Inc. However that will only takeoff if its player does.

The document-based ESD market has been primarily left to individual companies; most book manufacturers are uninterested. However, Adobe and its Acrobat product could begin to include some ESD features directly into Acrobat, making it even easier to begin selling documents over the Internet. Open Market has also begun to create specialized server software and back-end systems to facilitate large document-oriented Internet sales. This is important for companies with extensive of archives such as newspapers, or which generate large sets of information such as research companies and textbook manufacturers.

For graphical content (like market leaders Corbis and Photodisc), most vendors are themselves the licensors or developers of the content.

ESD Is the Future

A large part of the future of e-commerce will be totally electronic in nature. So much of what people consume is deliverable over the Internet given that connection speeds are good enough. Once some of the remaining distribution and copy-protection problems are solved, it will only require the major producers to begin supporting ESD en-masse. Once that leap of faith is made, expect this market to heat up considerably. Then stores will sell documents, music, digital stock art, and computer software as easily as they currently serve up graphics and text.

Being aware of the ESD universe and the basic framework of implementation places you ahead of the curve. As you explore ways to expand your store's offerings, you may want to consider the addition of digital goods and ESD.

ESD Terms

These are a few concepts that you might come across in setting up for electronic software distribution:

- **Digital Wrappers:** Digital wrappers provide a software shell around the code of a program that prevents it from being fully usable without the proper key to unlock the software.
- **EULA:** This acronym for End User License Agreement is simply the text that defines the terms of usage for the user. With ESD, you can create a screen that is displayed during ordering and includes the EULA and storing a record of the user's acceptance of it. This record can be used later to prove that the customer accepted the terms put forth during the sale. Some ESD solutions offer features to help with EULA implementation.
- **Clearinghouses:** A clearinghouse ensures that all transactions are valid makes them known to the software publisher and developer. They protect software developers from losing earned revenue.
- **Proof of Destruction:** This is the virtual equivalent of a customer returning a product. If someone receives a product via ESD but decides not to keep it, the customer provides a Proof of Destruction form guaranteeing the program's removal from the customer's hard drive.

CHAPTER SEVENTEEN

Everything About Shipping

Online means mail order, and mail order means shipping. And, being an online store, you will have customers all over the world—some in very remote places. And a significant number of them will be used to the immediate gratification of the Web and that means being able to get them your goods as soon as possible. The speed with which you can deliver their orders can be critical to your business' success.

Shipping is one of the few things that links you physically with your customers. While pricing, promotion, communication and order processing can be done virtually, the shipped package is what your customers will hold in their hands. The same level of speed, quality and attention to detail you put into the Web-based portion of your store needs to be applied to the shipping side.

You should understand that no single shipping option can cover you completely and provide maximum efficiency. The challenge is to stitch together the various services, software, Web sites, and your own store into a unified model that allows customers the best coverage, speed and pricing options. Then you have to display this "shipping stew" on your site in a manner that is easy to understand for your customers.

A Web site with too many options or ones that are poorly explained is confusing to customers. When someone looks lost in a real store, the owner will notice and be able to physically respond. On the Web you won't. Customers will turn away without you even noticing as they find that you don't offer a particular option for delivery. All you will notice is lower sales.

All of these are reasons why something as mundane and physical as how you organize your shipping plan is incredibly important to your store. So get to know your solutions inside and out, use the Web as much as you can, and make sure your plan is clearly displayed to users. If you maintain that and utilize the software the shipping companies offer, your customers will get nicely packaged, on-time products and you'll get repeat business. Many of the posts on newsgroups and much of the positive e-mail Tronix has gotten from its customers concerns its attention to the details of shipping.

Setting Up a Shipping Account

Surprisingly, a lot of account setup and management can be done via the Web. Setting up an account is especially simple online. The larger shipping companies have downloadable software on their Web sites, and you can also apply for an account by filling out a simple form online. To use the shipping software, you must have an account number.

FedEx and Airborne Express have a representative contact you by phone, and once your account is set up with these couriers, you'll be billed on a weekly basis. All three major private couriers will schedule a daily pick-up driver for your business. UPS requires a small weekly fee, whereas Federal Express and Airborne do not add any extra charges for this request (though you do pay for it with a higher per unit shipping charge). If your office is located near any of these major couriers, you can even drop off your own packages without the pressure of having the items ready for the driver and perhaps save a small amount of money.

TIP ▸ ***When opening new accounts, every courier will need to know a time of pick-up. It's essential that you try to schedule your packages to be picked up as late as possible—preferably about 30 minutes before you close. This will give you the much-needed time to pack your boxes.***

All major couriers (except the post office) want to know what kind of volume you intend on shipping per month or week. They may or may not offer a volume discount initially, but if you can eventually prove that you will move a decent amount of boxes per period, they'll work with you. At the beginning, you may be in a "Catch 22" situation. You'll need the discount to attract customers to your low-priced shipping, but the couriers want to see that you are moving volume before they offer that discount.

Here are some of the major shipping companies, how to contact them, some of their basic services and how to set up an account. Joe has also offered up his special take on each one.

FedEx

www.fedex.com

2005 Corporate Avenue
Memphis, TN 38132
Toll Free: 1-800-463-3339
Phone: 901-369-3600
Fax: 901-795-1027

Basic Services

FedEx is the leader in overnight shipping. FedEx Priority Overnight gets your package to most U.S. destinations by 10:30 A.M. the next business day. FedEx Standard Overnight gets a shipment to most U.S. cities by 3 P.M. the next business day and to most U.S. destinations. By 4:30 P.M. FedEx 2Day, their discount service, guarantees delivery by 4:30 P.M. the second business day to most U.S. destinations (up to 7 P.M. for many homes and residences). FedEx also has a freight service that handles packages from 151 to 1,500 pounds to most U.S. destinations. This service is available in overnight, 2Day and Express Saver versions. Advanced registration is usually required.

Internationally, FedEx offers International Priority, which gets customs-cleared packages to more than 200 counties within one to three business days. Most major European destinations require two business days. FedEx International Economy offers a lower-cost solution for packages to Canada (two to three days for delivery).

Web and Software Features

FedEx offers several software packages for its customers.

- **FedEx Ship 2.0** is the entry-level package available for download from its Web site. It lets you process shipments, track packages, create shipping labels and store frequently used addresses.
- **FedEx interNetShip** lets you process shipments directly on the Web site using any SSL-secure browser.
- **PowerShip** is offered in four versions, two of which are more useful for Web store proprietors. PowerShip 3 is available for shippers who send at least three packages per day. PowerShip 2 adds additional features such as customized shipping reports, and a customer database. This package is available for anyone who sends between five and 100 packages per day.

Setting Up an Account

Call FedEx's toll-free number (1-800-463-3339) and ask the operator to help you set up an initial account.

Special Services

- **FedEx First Overnight** service guarantees delivery by 8 A.M. the next business day to 90 major U.S. cities for packages and boxes up to 150 pounds.

- **FedEx SameDay** service gets shipments up to 70 pounds to almost any U.S. destination the same day depending on availability.

JOE'S TAKE FedEx services are nothing short of excellent, although their shipping rates can be on the high side. When you begin to move a substantial amount of packages, you can work on getting a very good volume discount from your FedEx representative. FedEx offices are prevalent in major cities, with some operating as late as 9 P.M. If you plan on having late business hours, you can still get orders out in the early evening.

TIP ▸ ***When you first set up shop, make sure you've checked the latest time for drop-offs and pick-ups for the local shipping companies. Times will vary from office to office and city to city. You never want to sprint to an office only to find you missed the final drop-off deadline by five minutes.***

FedEx International shipments are always reliable, but keep in mind that its international rates are a bit expensive. Generally, if you start shipping across the globe to entities that rely on getting their products on time and without fail, they'll lean toward FedEx.

Airborne Express

www.airborne-express.com

3101 Western Avenue
Seattle, WA 98121
Toll Free: 1-800-247-2676
Phone: 206-285-4600
Fax: 206-281-3890

Basic Services

Airborne offers traditional services including overnight, afternoon, and two-day service. Airborne also has international service to over 200 countries. It offers Sky Courier Next-Flight-Out International Service. It also has International Air Express Service, which provides door-to-door service within 24–96 hours, including customs clearance. The International Air Freight Service offers oversized and heavyweight freight shipping around the world, including customs clearance.

Web and Software Features

Airborne offers a number of software packages to help you better manage shipping products through its service.

- **Lightship Tracker** software provides basic tracking information, is downloadable from the Web site and runs on Windows 3.1/95.
- **The Lightship World Directory** helps you find any information pertaining to shipping to any of the more than 200 countries that Airborne serves.
- **Libra** system is a combination of tracking hardware and software that lets you weigh, rate and label every shipment. Libra also stores addresses, prints invoices and handles international forms and mailings as well.

Setting Up an Account

Airborne accounts can be opened by calling the toll-free number (1-800-247-2676).

Special Services

Airborne has a custom warehousing and distribution solution it calls Airborne Logistics Services. There are several variants of this service, but the one that might be of interest to store owners is Stock Exchange.

JOE'S TAKE: Airborne has very competitive rates—usually cheaper than UPS or FedEx—but one disadvantage is the slightly complicated rate chart. For instance, Airborne offers an inexpensive next day afternoon service, but many less-accessible areas in the United States are not eligible. Therefore the shipper must constantly refer to a large Airborne manual to look up the state, city and ZIP code to see which areas are highlighted for this service. If an area you want to ship to is not eligible, the customer must pay a priority price (usually a few dollars more) just to get it there in the afternoon. During very busy periods, this extra bit of work slowed me down, and I didn't like keeping a customer on hold while I referenced their city to determine their rate. You can, of course, decide on one flat rate per pound and simply charge everyone the priority price to save time and headaches.

DHL

www.dhl.com

333 Twin Dolphin Drive
Redwood City, CA 94065
Toll Free: 1-800-225-5345
Phone: 415-593-7474
Fax: 415-593-1689

Basic Services

DHL doesn't offer any second- or third-day delivery options; instead it only offers Worldwide Express and same day delivery.

Web and Software Features

Based on the volume you ship, you can set up shipping software that DHL calls Easy Ship. This lets you set up labels, tracking information, and fill out forms for fast and easy shipping within the DHL system.

Setting Up an Account

To set up an account with DHL, call 1-800-225-5345, and either a sales kit will be sent or an agent will visit you.

Joe's Take: *I've never used DHL because I'm relatively happy with what the other shippers provide for overseas service. DHL built a name for itself by being the company to use when shipping overnight overseas. However, now that FedEx, UPS and even the post office have beefed up their overseas operations, I—like many others—aren't as overwhelmed by their international prowess.*

U.S. Postal Service

www.usps.gov

(Address: Check Your Local Listing)
Toll Free: 1-800-222-1811

Basic Services

Not surprisingly, the United States Postal Service offers a wide range of services:

- **Priority Mail** is a good choice if you are mailing small packages such as documents, contracts or small items such as, in the case of Tronix, CDs. Packages weighing two pounds or less cost just $3 to ship. Rates for packages weighing up to five pounds do not vary by distance and there is a flat rate envelope available, for which you pay $3 no matter the weight.

- **Global Priority Mail** is available in two flat rate envelopes and ships to 31 countries.

- **Express Mail** offers guaranteed overnight delivery 365 days a year, morning delivery to 134 U.S. cities, automatic insurance and delivery to post office boxes. Rates for packages weighing between two and 70 pounds are based on whole-pound increments no matter how far the packages are traveling. A flat rate envelope costs $15 for however much you can fit in it.

- **Express Mail International** offers many of the same features, although delivery usually takes two or three days. You can make overseas deliveries to military installations at domestic rates and international delivery to nearly 200 countries and territories. Prices start at $15.

TIP ▸ ***To request a free Business Information Kit, call 1-800-THE-USPS (843-8777) ext. 2049 or visit www.usps.gov.***

Web and Software Features

Global Package Link establishes a direct link between your business and the U.S. Postal Service, enabling the post office to handle most of the documentation for international shipments. This is a worthwhile feature for high-volume shippers.

Part of the Global Package Link is the Customs Pre-Advisory System (CPAS), which relieves you of paperwork and helps speed your packages through customs. CPAS enables customs agents to review the contents of your shipment prior to its arrival and decide if the parcel requires inspection. Although CPAS provides a declaration of contents, all shipments are subject to search at the discretion of customs agents.

Setting Up an Account

Setting up an Express Mail Corporate Account helps you avoid weighing packages, affixing stamps and battling with postage meters. To set up an account, you can find the application on the Postal Service's Web site, fill it out and either mail it or take it to a post office. An account representative will contact you. To open an account, you must deposit $250 or your estimated Express Mail charges for four weeks, whichever is higher.

Once you have an account, enter your account number on the Express Mail label and drop off your package at any post office or Express Mail collection box. Each month you'll receive a statement detailing your mailing activity. You can pay for Express Mail with cash, a check or, in some cities, VISA, MasterCard or Discover.

Special Services

- **Express Mail Custom Designed Service** is tailored for your business's regularly scheduled, time-sensitive mailings and is available 24 hours a day, 365 days a year to meet your odd-hour mailing needs. You can have your shipments picked up or dropped off at any post office or airport mail facility offering Express Mail service. You can also have the package delivered directly to the addressee, have the addressee pick it up or combine any of these options. Custom Designed Service rates are determined by weight and option and start at $9.45 for shipments weighing eight ounces or less.

- **Express Mail Drop Shipment** allows you to pick cities around the country and send any class of mail to those cities in overnight Express Mail sacks. The next morning the sacks are opened and the individual pieces are delivered according to their class.
- **Express Mail Reshipment** accelerates the arrival of incoming mail and can be useful for businesses that receive payments and fill orders by mail for their products.
- **Express Mail COD** lets you rush merchandise to customers who order by mail or phone and request fast delivery.

Joe's Take *The U.S. Postal Service is generally a good choice and Priority Mail is a popular choice among Tronix customers. Keep in mind that, because of heightened security restrictions by the Federal Aviation Administration, any domestic mail other than Express Mail weighing 16 ounces or more and bearing stamps, or any international or military APO/FPO mail weighing 16 ounces or more, must be given in person to a retail clerk at a post office or given directly to a letter carrier. That means many of you will be scheduling pickups or making regular trips to the local post office.*

United Parcel Service
www.ups.com

55 Glenlake Parkway, NE
Atlanta, GA 30328
Toll Free: 1-800-PICK-UPS
Phone: 770-828-6000
Fax: 770-828-6593

Basic Services

As the largest shipping service, UPS offers a large number of services and is a very popular company, as evidenced by the broad effects its 1997 strike had on the shipping industry and UPS clients. The three basic services are GroundTrac, a reasonably priced two-day service known as "Blue Label" and overnight and early morning next-day shipping known as "Red Label." UPS also has a 3 Day Select service that guarantees delivery within three business days throughout mainland America.

TIP ▸ ***Depending on your account needs, you can schedule a daily stop by a UPS driver.***

UPS has begun aggressively building its international service. It offers Worldwide Express, which guarantees next-day delivery of packages to major cities in Mexico and Canada by 10:30 A.M., and to nearly 300 cities in the European Union by 10:30 A.M. the second business day. Saturday delivery to major cities in Canada is also available. Worldwide Express Plus can get packages to over 150 cities in 14 major European countries by 8:30 A.M. on the second business day.

The Worldwide Expedited service is cheaper and gets most shipments to Mexico and Canada in three days and to Europe and Asia in four days. For shipments to Canada, UPS offers Standard Service to Canada, which provides inexpensive service to every address in all ten provinces.

Web and Software Features

UPS has a number of software packages to help you better ship products, including a line of UPS Online software:

- **UPS Online Office** is free to every UPS account holder regardless of shipping volume. The package helps you process shipments, print address labels and pickup records, and track packages.

- **UPS Online Professional** requires a certain level of volume but offers increased options. You can generate detailed management reports, track multiple packages based on criteria and receive major updates automatically.
- **UPS Online Tracking Software** is available for download right from the UPS homepage. This product lets you or your customers track packages directly from a PC.

Setting Up an Account

A UPS regional representative will usually come visit a first time account to set things up. Tronix has an agreement with UPS in which our shipping charges are deducted once a month from our business account. UPS has a number of alternative payment plans, but anything automatic means one less bill to worry about at the end of the month. When business gets going, you'll thank yourself in the long run if you chose this option.

Special Services

Among UPS special services are Saturday delivery, COD service, and shipping insurance.

Joe's Take: *UPS GroundTrac is a great value for heavy items or for customers who aren't in a hurry to receive their order. Ground services go by truck, therefore it can take as many as five days depending on how far the recipient is from the shipper. UPS provides you with a zone chart for your area that will estimate time of delivery. A good rule of thumb is to use UPS for any item over 12 pounds—or simply very large in size—that is a domestic order. Let your customer know that UPS GroundTrac may be the most cost-efficient. UPS GroundTrac automatically insures packages for up to $100. Each additional $100 will cost you about 50 cents more to insure. As far as international shipping is concerned, you can work out a deal where your UPS representative will apply special discounts to countries to which you frequently ship. This is a good reason to monitor where the bulk of your international business is coming from.*

Utilizing Each Courier's Strengths

Each shipping company has staked out certain strengths. If you know precisely which ones are best for which situations and geographic areas, you can not only lower your overall costs but offer better customer service by providing the most flexibility and quickest service.

Post Office Domestic Priority Mail and Global Priority Mail are the two forms of shipping most often requested by Tronix customers. Domestic Priority Mail costs the customer only $3 for packages weighing two pounds or less, and only takes two to three days in transit, depending on the location. For each additional pound, it's an additional $1 to $1.50.

NOTE ▸ Priority Mail is great for items of low value. The only major drawback Priority Mail is the fact that there's no tracking number associated with the package—therefore you and your customer have no way of tracing a shipment if it's late or lost. The post office offers options like insurance and registered mail on Priority packages to keep your mind at ease. However, these additions involve extra charges, which put your shipment in the same cost bracket as the express couriers. Also, expect delays during the holidays and tax season. Priority mail is not a guaranteed delivery. Unlike express methods of shipping such as FedEx, UPS and Airborne Overnight and Second Business Day services, the post office will never guarantee a date of arrival on Priority Mail. You may want to remind your customer that Priority Mail can sometimes exceed the estimated time in transit, and if the package arrives later than expected, there's nothing that can be done in terms of a shipping refund to the customer. ▮

For small, international shipments, you can't beat Global Priority Mail from the post office. This shipping option is similar to U.S. Priority Mail, and the time in transit is anywhere from four to seven days. The post office will supply you with two types of mailers, which are good for magazines, books, CDs, jewelry and any other small, flat items. Both sized mailers have a low flat rate from $3.75 to $8.95, depending on the country to which you are shipping. Tronix is able to ship up to six CD games in the larger Global mailer and, within a week, an international customer will receive his or her package without spending a fortune on shipping. Because these flat rate mailers are normally meant for documents, be sure to wrap your goods with a sheet of bubble wrap. Don't wrap it too thick—otherwise you won't be able to seal the envelope.

If your item is fragile or exceeds the size and shape of a Global mailer, then you can pack your order in a small box. The post office provides Global Priority stickers for boxed items; however, there is no longer a flat rate involved. Now you will need to refer to a Global rates chart which increases in price every half pound. The savings are still quite good compared to other major couriers. The maximum amount for any Global Package is four pounds and is good only for selected countries.

Like the other three couriers, the post office offers its own Express Mail shipping for U.S. and international customers. Express Mail shipments have their own tracking numbers, and the air bills couldn't be any easier to fill out. For U.S. customers, most Express Mail shipments arrive the next day, but you may want to check with your local post office about the city to which you are shipping. Some cities require your package to be at the post office at selected cut-off times, otherwise the package will arrive on the second day. Be sure to make your customer aware of this.

TIP ▸ ***Separate your orders by courier. Work on the orders that need to be in at the earliest times first. In my case, it's the post office orders that require the most work, and have to be checked in first. If you are planning on using the post office for many of your shipments, be sure to call and check what time your local post office closes. The average closing time is 5:30 P.M., but many post offices in major cities have later hours.***

One major advantage of Express Mail is weekend service. If a U.S. customer places an order on Friday and wants it delivered on the weekend, FedEx, UPS and Airborne require an additional $10 fee for Saturday delivery, whereas the post office does not have any additional charges. Besides saving the additional fee, many customers will be surprised to know that Express Mail shipments include Sunday delivery. If a package doesn't make it to a customer on Saturday, it will certainly get there on Sunday. This is also a great option if you plan to ship orders out on Saturdays.

International Express Mail is a good bargain. Most of Tronix's international customers prefer using this service to using the other couriers. It might take anywhere from two to four days for Express Mail packages to get to the international recipient, but the difference in price compared to other couriers is substantial. Many international customers visiting your Web site may need a little extra hand-holding when choosing their courier. If they want their order to arrive fast, without having to spend too much money, Express Mail is the first option recommended. Offering a little help like this also shows your individual concern for your customers' needs and will most likely guarantee you a return customer.

Admittedly, the only downfall with Express Mail is the reliability factor. Whereas FedEx, Airborne and UPS International shipments are fairly expensive, they are generally accurate and arrive at the expected date, whereas the post office Express Mail shipments can experience delays. A lot of this has to do with how efficient a particular country's mail system is.

UPS and Airborne International Express shipments generally arrive in most major countries in two days. The shipper is required to include three copies of the original bill of sale for customs purposes. These copies should be placed together with the air bill in the supplied pouch, which is adhered to the outside of your box/envelope. FedEx and the post office supply their own customs form, so there's no need to print multiple copies of your customer's invoice for these couriers.

TIP ▸ ***Light items such as CDs, magazines and other small, flat goods, are great for shipping in FedEx, UPS or Airborne mailers. These envelopes allow up to eight ounces, with an overnight flat rate that is fairly inexpensive. Although this mailer is only meant for documents, you'd be surprised what can be shipped in a flat rate envelope. Once any small item is put into a box, the overnight price is automatically jacked up. So remember: if it's a flat, sturdy item weighing eight ounces or less, go for those mailers.***

Pitney Bowes Personal Post Office
www.pitneybowes.com

One Elmcroft Road
Stamford, CT 06926-0700
Phone: 203-356-5000
Fax: 203-351-6835

Pitney Bowes, the world's largest manufacturer of postage meters, has focused on the small-office and home-office markets. The company's new Personal Post Office for the PC allows small businesses to generate, address and meter mail from a desktop computer and an inkjet or laser printer.

The Personal Post Office is intended to allow users to manage multiple address books, import and export existing PC lists, verify addresses, design envelops and determine the rate for the class of service. Billing functions can be tailored or standardized and mail costs can be tracked and controlled with an accounting function.

The software determines the correct shipping rate for the user with service and rate information. The address verification function will correct incorrectly addressed mail with input from a CD-ROM of all know addresses in the United States. Secure encryption allows users to print envelopes with an address and the proof of postage simultaneously. Postage will either be downloaded over the Internet or through a direct network connection to Pitney Bowes' Postage by Phone System. In 1996, more than $10 billion of postage was downloaded in this matter, says Pitney Bowes.

Minimizing Your Shipping Rates

Courier rates are a private affair. Once you have obtained your personal discount rates for bulk shipments, you can decide on your own scale of shipping prices that can add a small profit to your orders. However, watch for the competition, especially well-established businesses that move mass quantities and already have frighteningly low rates.

In Tronix's line of business—primarily video and computer games—competition is intense. Tronix initially chose not to make any additional money on my shipping prices and that quickly attracted customers. If a customer has to spend a lot of money on shipping, then mail order may not be worthwhile, especially if the item is easily obtainable in their neighborhood.

TIP ▸ ***Mail-order houses that carry items which can be found in stores should always keep their shipping rates as low as possible.***

Originally, Tronix worked with a UPS and FedEx account and, when the number of orders began to increase, looked into working with Airborne Express, especially after hearing about their attractive rates. It quickly became obvious, however, that the savings would be minimal.

A representative will usually ask you which couriers you are currently using. You should tell the person the truth, while also mentioning that you would be willing to use their service over the others depending on their rate.

With this information, Airborne offered a substantial discount, and Tronix immediately added an Airborne basic rate chart to its Web site. Before long, there was a significant increase in overnight shipments and, more importantly, new customers. Using the same process above, FedEx eventually lowered its rates as well. Since it is hard to spread the business between the three couriers, each with a quota, Tronix uses FedEx and Airborne for express and second day services, and UPS for their inexpensive GroundTrac shipments.

TIP ▸ ***If there are a few mail order sites offering the same product, for the same price, a smart consumer will most likely drift toward the company offering the least expensive shipping and handling charges.***

Shipping Supplies: Easier to Get than You Think

All couriers are more than happy to send your business all types of free shipping supplies when needed.

A good thing about the post office is this: you don't need to have a special account to order your supplies. You can call and get supplies shipped to your business any time you need them. The post office offers a variety of shipping materials such as Express, Priority and Global Envelopes, rolls of Priority Mail tape, sturdy boxes for shipping garments, books and video tapes (to name a few items), and even pre-printed Express forms and self adhesive Priority Mail labels with your business address. In addition to packing materials, you will need a number of other things to make your shipping efficient.

Ordering Supplies

When ordering supplies, look at the range of items you'll be carrying and order boxes to accommodate each size (and even shape) of the item. Try to get an idea of the largest item you will sell and keep some boxes around that are at least two to three times larger. You never know when you may have to ship two or three of the same large item to one customer. Larger boxes can also be cut down so they never go to waste.

If you're working alone most of the time, it literally leaves all the shipping chores in your hands. You'll learn that boxing up orders soon becomes an art form. Try to stay away from very thick cardboard boxes; they'll only add unnecessary weight to your order, thus increasing the customer's shipping rate. Remember that you want these people to order from you again.

TIP ▸ ***In addition to its standard box, UPS has two types of boxes which your UPS supplier never speaks of and are not even mentioned in any of the UPS guide books. Tronix's UPS daily pick-up driver mentioned this when he noticed we were shipping fairly small items (generally no bigger than a paperback book) and the standard UPS boxes were a bit too large. These generally unmentioned containers are called security boxes and are usually best used for small items in need of good protection. The collapsible boxes come in two sizes with easy, interlocking folds, creating a solid container for protecting any small, fragile item. UPS does not publicize these boxes because they do not bear the UPS logo and therefore can be used for shipping with other couriers. If you need them, don't be afraid to ask your UPS supply house. Tell them that you are shipping a lot of small, valuable items and the smallest box they offer is too big for your shipments.***

Packing Boxes

Pack most of your boxes with Styrofoam when needed; it weighs next to nothing and protects fragile items quite well. Seal your packages with thin brown packing tape—the kind with a shiny surface. This type of tape is very flexible and is thin enough to mold around box corners to protect your shipment and make it look more presentable

Another excellent protective packing material is bubble wrap. It is great for wrapping any item, especially those needing extra padding. And who doesn't get a kick out of popping the stuff? It's almost an extra gift for your customer! One good place from which to order shipping supplies is U-LINE (1-800-295-5510).

TIP ▸ ***Try to buy tape, bubble-wrap, Styrofoam and boxes in bulk. Many office supply mail-order houses offer discount pricing on all types of box sizes, rolls of tape, and other related material. This will save you money in the long run, rather that buying small quantities at your local supply store.***

Your Shipping Area

Have at least two shipping tables in your work quarters and keep them as clear as possible. You'll use one for working on orders, the other for complete orders. Many large office superstores sell these types of inexpensive tables, which come in various lengths. Try to get them as long as possible without killing your office space. By keeping your shipping area clear you'll be able to pack boxes easily, and orders won't get confused. Eliminate unnecessary items—air bill forms, envelopes, paper clips, pens, music CDs—from your table. If you don't, when business begins to take off, your shipping table will become a nightmare collage of office supplies, making it more difficult to find things when you need them. The more room on the table, the more comfortable and faster it will be to pack your boxes If you work without a shipping table, you'll find the knees of your jeans wearing through in a hurry (okay, it's fashionable, but still...).

TIP ▸ ***Throw in goodies. Sometimes distributors will give out free catalogs or brochures on upcoming products. Make a habit of asking your distributors for any extra promo catalogs, advertisements, teasers, posters, or whatever they may have (which of course relates to your business). It's always a nice gesture to occasionally add a little something to your shipments, especially if it's something that may be of interest to the customer, which can be judged by what they're purchasing. On the other hand, remember that extra material can bog down your package. The next thing you know, you've charged the customer for a two- pound box, and now you are going to get charged for three pounds. Use your best judgement. If you can squeeze another ounce or two into your package before it jumps to the next weight, and then go for it.***

One of the most essential tools for shipping—and one of the first things you'll want to buy—is a good scale. Tronix started with a basic scale for under $30 that had a ceiling of 50 pounds.

With an average shipment in the one-pound range, we didn't need anything fancy. As the business grew, orders became bigger and the scale eventually wore down. There's nothing worse than an inaccurate weight reading that could result in overcharging the customer or shortchanging yourself. If you have the extra money, invest in a quality digital scale that will provide long-term, accurate read-outs.

Getting the Software You Need

As we mentioned, FedEx, UPS and Airborne offer their own software for entering, tracking and filing shipments. Once your account is set up, ask for the free software in case your representative neglects to offer it (reps are always on the move so when you pin one down, ask for the world if you can). FedEx, in particular, offers a package to their customers called Power Ship, which includes software, a laser printer, and a special terminal if you want to use it in place of your computer.

Power Ship allows you to automate all of your shipping, from keeping a customer database on file, to automatically printing out special bar coded labels and the customer's address. You simply pop one on each box, and there's no need to write a thing. FedEx encourages their customers to use Power Ship, as both the business owner and the FedEx clerk who checks your boxes benefit in speed. Power Ship is free, with the equipment basically being loaned by FedEx to all types of businesses. But you do have to be in business for at least a year and have a steady record of volume shipping. Even 15 to 20 boxes per day should do the trick.

Shipping Labels Made Simple

To make life simpler, make a return address template with your word processing software. Every few months, print out about 1,000 labels and simply peel and stick them on all of your UPS Ground or International Global Priority Mail shipments. Because you don't use pre-printed forms with these types of shipments, it saves time, rather than having to write your address on each box. Of course, you can also go to any stationery store and order a return address stamp and pad. But I you have a laser printer, designing your own return address logo is easy and it actually looks more appealing than a generic stamp. Plus, you have the advantage of changing your design any time you'd like. It all boils down to whatever is more convenient and less expensive for you.

Linking Shipping with Your Web Site

One thing you can do to make your Web site interesting is to add all the major shipping courier links to your Web site. Federal Express, Airborne Express, UPS and the U.S. Postal Service all have their own informative Web sites, which include package tracking features, and a wealth of information about their service. Customers who place orders through the express couriers can then click on these corresponding links and head over to their Web site. Now they're able to track their own packages, while learning more about the shipping service they chose. You'd be surprised how many customers find this exciting, as they're able to know exactly what's going on with their package.

If your company doesn't have a toll-free number, customers won't want to keep calling you to check on their order. Online tracking saves them the long distance call and you the extra time and effort trying to find their package. Automating customer service onto your Web site is key to keeping your operations lean and mean. When designing your web site, you can choose to add these links to any page you desire. You might want to copy and paste these links below your price lists, or have them on the bottom of every page along with your general links. Tronix felt it would make sense to keep all the shipping information together in one special shipping page (Figure 17.1).

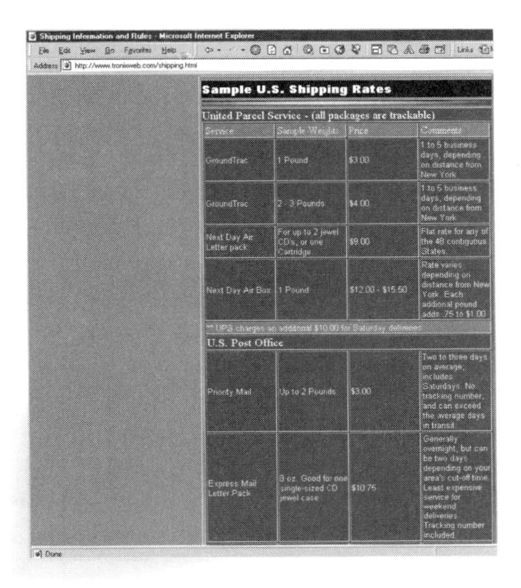

Sample U.S. Shipping Rates

United Parcel Service - (all packages are trackable)

Service	Sample Weight	Price	Comments
GroundTrac	1 Pound	$3.00	1 to 5 business days, depending on distance from New York
GroundTrac	2 - 3 Pounds	$4.00	1 to 5 business days, depending on distance from New York
Next Day Air Letter pack	For up to 2 jewel CD's, or one Cartridge	$9.00	Flat rate for any of the 48 contiguous States
Next Day Air Box	1 Pound	$12.00 - $15.50	Rate varies depending on distance from New York. Each addional pound adds .75 to $1.00

** UPS charges an additional $10.00 for Saturday deliveries

U.S. Post Office

Service	Sample Weight	Price	Comments
Priority Mail	Up to 2 Pounds	$3.00	Two to three days on average, includes Saturdays. No tracking number, and can exceed the average days in transit
Express Mail Letter Pack	8 oz. Good for one single-sized CD jewel case	$10.75	Generally overnight, but can be two days depending on your area's cut-off time. Least expensive service for weekend deliveries. Tracking number included

Figure 17.1
Tronix's shipping page is designed to give customers a multitude of shipping options.

Your Shipping Information Page

One of the most important parts of your Web site will be your shipping information page. You'll want to have a page which will list your company's shipping policies, along with some sample, cross-reference shipping charts showing the name of the courier service, a sample of your prices with corresponding weights, and the time in transit. You may even want to have all of your general company information—which will include your ordering and shipping policies on one page—and a separate page for your rate tables.

If you plan on having a large table of rates for each courier, you may want to have a page dedicated to each service so you don't bog down the user's browser. It would be nearly impossible to post every weight and price for each courier, so it might be a good idea to list the rates for perhaps the first five pounds from each service.

If the type of products you sell have similar weights, you may want to show rates that would only reflect that range of weights. For example, if your line of business is dedicated to specific types of antique desktop clocks, and you know all of your clocks range from four to six pounds, set up a rate chart to reflect the most-used weights. You might want to show rates from four pounds to 12 pounds in case someone orders two of your heaviest clocks. Of course, there may be orders that exceed the weight of any information you have provided on your sample rate chart, in which case the customer can call or e-mail you to inquire about that price.

Below your rate chart, it would be a good idea to add a linked message to your email in case customers need further price information on shipping or they need to know the weight of a specific item. If your line of business stocks only a small variety of items, you might even want to show the weight of each item right on your price list. Create your basic shipping chart using the table function in your HTML editor or a good word processor, which will allow you to easily create tables that can be converted into HTML format.

Pros and Cons of COD

You might choose to accept COD (Cash on Delivery) in your business. There are some advantages and disadvantages you should consider before deciding whether this payment option is right for your business.

One advantage is that you will certainly have access to a larger customer base. Many people either don't have credit cards or don't want to use them every time they place an order. By having customers not use credit cards, you also keep the percentage of your sale that would be taken by the credit card company. You also don't have to worry about fraudulent credit card orders.

However, there are also a number of disadvantages. First of all, the customer is charged an additional $5 by the courier for COD and a customer could change his or her mind while the order is in transit, thereby sticking you with the shipping charges as the order boomerangs back to you. Then you might need to ship that back to the distributor, incurring more charges and tying up capital.

The customer also has to be at home in order to pay the driver and, in some cases, it can take more than a week to get your payment and, of course, that has to get deposited in your bank account and the check has to clear. If a customer pays by cash, UPS will write a check to your company, but even UPS checks don't immediately clear in your account.

Joe's Take *When I began to take CODs, I used UPS because I was under the assumption that UPS was the only company that took CODs. The problem I had with this, especially being a small company (with an equally small business bank account) was waiting for payment to arrive. So don't expect that money to be available in your account for at least two weeks. After doing COD exclusively with UPS, I found out that FedEx also accepts CODs and your payment is delivered by a FedEx driver on the next business day after delivery. Unfortunately, FedEx does not accept cash, so you'll have to remind your customer to have a money order ready for the FedEx driver. You can accept a personal check if that customer is a trustworthy regular customer.*

Mistakes Happen and That Means a Refund

In this imperfect world, there will no doubt be many times when you make a shipping mistake on a customer's order, especially when you are a one-person operation, having to take on every possible angle of a small business. Late, lost or incorrect orders are probably the biggest reasons people are reluctant to use a mail-order service.

If you do happen to make mistake on a customer's shipping address, forget to check off the appropriate method of shipping, or send them an incorrect item or quantity, show your deep concern, apologize profusely, and offer the customer free shipping on the next order. If they paid to have the package shipped overnight, and it didn't get there because of a mistake made by your company, refund their shipping fee, as it will alleviate some of your customer's anger.

Most customers will understand the situation and they'll probably want to take advantage of the offer by placing another order. You may have lost some—or all—of your profit on this sale by refunding the current shipping fee and giving free shipping on the next order, but in the long run, you've probably gained a permanent customer and provided yourself some good word-of-mouth. Most reasonable people understand mistakes can be made. As long as you work to correct them, you can turn a negative into a positive.

TIP ▸ ***Be incredibly careful when filling out your address labels. Always double-check all your information before you plaster that label onto your box. Check for spelling, zip codes, spaces, and capitalization—and by all means, make sure your handwriting is legible. You don't want packages sitting in a warehouse for an extra day—or worse, having your courier return boxes to your establishment because your "D" in Delancy Street looked like an "O."***

As a Web-order business owner, you may become frustrated when packages shipped by your express couriers don't arrive at their destinations on time. This scenario is a common one for mail-order companies to experience, so you're not alone. A customer calls and complains he or she paid for overnight shipping but the package never showed. You put them on hold while you retrieve the copy of their air bill. You dash for your database or point of sale program to double-check their address, and everything checks out fine. Now what?

Well, you can start by patting yourself on the back, knowing it wasn't anything you did wrong—it was obviously the fault of the courier. When this happens, ask the customer for a phone number where she can be reached immediately. Let the customer know that you'll call the courier to find out where the package is because the copy of the air bill's information is completely correct. After learning why the package is late and when it will arrive, remind the courier service operator that your company should receive full credit for the shipping (remember, you're getting billed for it, even though you've already charged the customer).

Now you can call your customer, explain the situation, and offer a shipping refund. Sending e-mail with a full explanation is also a good idea in case the customer is not there when you call back. You can either give the customer a credit to apply toward the next order or simply refund the shipping amount. Unless the package was late because of an act of God, your courier should refund your money, and you should refund your customer's.

TIP ▸ ***Keep your most recent, already processed FedEx, Airborne, UPS or US Post Office Express Mail air bills handy. If a customer calls and requests his or her tracking number, or if a package is late, you can easily pull out the information without keeping the customer on hold. After a few days, you can file them away. Some of the more powerful shipping software will also help automate this process.***

Just In Case, Insure Shipments

Make certain that large ticket items are insured. Couriers generally have automatic insurance on your shipments, but they usually only cover the first $100. You should make it a habit to insure any orders over $300. When insuring a package, FedEx, UPS and Airborne will have a specific area on the air bill to fill out the amount of insurance you want to declare for your shipment. You will then be charged a small percentage for every additional $100 beyond the first $100. Be sure to tell your customer that this will be added to their charges. They shouldn't mind, knowing that if their package is lost or damaged in transit, there will be a full, hassle-free refund or replacement. After your business grows and you can afford it, you can always include this insurance without charging the customer, because it's a small fee to pay and yet another option that can make a customer happy.

TIP ▸ ***Watch for addresses that contain a Post Office Box. FedEx, UPS and Airborne will not deliver to these addresses—only the post office will. It's no fun to realize this after your local post office has closed for the day.***

Reinforcing the Shipping Link

As you prepare to launch your online store, it's to your advantage to set up all of your shipping accounts ahead of time—even if there is a service you don't plan on using immediately, it may be useful in the long run. You also want to know everything you can ahead of time because you never know when a particular shipper may offer the only way to get a product into the hands of a die-hard customer. For example, you should check with each courier about pick-up and drop-off times. In some large cities like New York, not all of the drop-off offices close at the same time. Knowing this ahead of time could be crucial to getting out an order at the last second—and it's this kind of attention to detail that will win you rave reviews by your customers on the Internet.

As this chapter stated at the outset, shipping is the physical link between you and your customers when everything else is so virtual. As the 1997 UPS strike showed, shipping is one of the most important aspects of many businesses, online stores included. Don't make the mistake of treating it as anything short of critical.

PART V

Maintaining and Growing Your Store

You have embarked on an evolutionary process. The stale store is the unsuccessful store. Part V shows you how to keep your store fresh, how to build loyal customers, and how to beat the competition. It also takes a look at some important issues in the emerging online legal landscape.

Part V Table of Contents

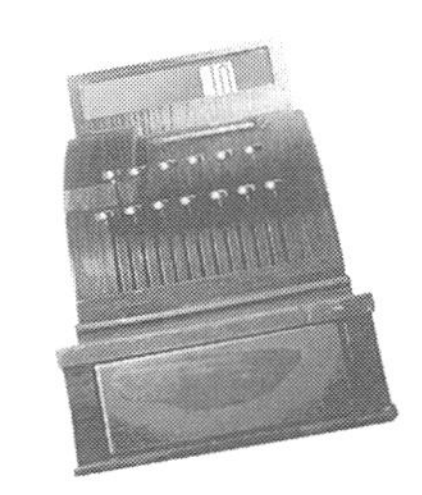

CHAPTER EIGHTEEN

Maintaining Your Store

You're up and running. Flying we hope. However, you can't just let your site sit there. Operating an online store involves a number of daily tasks that are easily scheduled. There are also a number larger, less frequent tasks. And of course there are those time-swallowing emergencies that you might as well count on. You never know when an order will get lost, you'll get scammed by someone using a fraudulent credit card, or even when a power failure will knock you out of work for a couple of hours. The more prepared you are for these instances of Murphy's Law, the better off you'll be.

This chapter will give you some tips on how to organize your day so you're not trying to pack 40 boxes an hour before they have to be out the door. You'll also get some tips on how to best deal with waves of e-mail, when to redesign your site, invoicing, and organizing your site's back end. Hopefully you'll reach peak efficiency. But remember, Michael Jordan still works on his jump shot. No matter how efficient you think you are, you can always get better.

Organizing Your Day

When you're running a small operation, the way to keep things running smoothly is by being organized. You can't show up in the morning without a plan and expect to be as efficient as is necessary. Everyone's schedule will vary. The important thing is that you have one and stick reasonably close to it. Of course there will be emergencies that will force you to be flexible, but if you have a solid schedule, it will be far easier to deal with these unannounced problems. This is how Tronix schedules its day.

Checking Your Voice Messages and Faxes

Tronix's day usually begins with a check for any new voice mail messages that have arrived after business hours from the previous day (or over the weekend). If you have a fax, check your machine for orders or announcements from distributors.

Joe's Take: *I use a PIM (Personal Information Manager) program to deal with day-to-day tasks and contacts. The program I use is Lotus Organizer, which eliminates desk clutter and helps you avoid losing a message when you get sidetracked by ringing phones. Organizer is a great tool to have readily accessible. I leave Organizer running throughout the day for note taking. You can add all of your primary contacts (distributors, credit card merchants, bank representatives, etc.) into Organizer's handy address book, with auto-dial features at the click of a mouse. If you're not a fan of Lotus Organizer there are other PIM programs including Microsoft's Outlook, and Sidekick that are also useful.*

Pull in Your E-mail, Extract Your Orders

After returning all of its business-related phone inquiries, Tronix begins pulling in morning e-mail, which takes 30–60 minutes. You should first concentrate on orders. Check out the products requested from each customer and carefully look over all of the information they've submitted. Make sure they provided a phone number, the issuing bank of the credit card, the type of shipping desired, and all of the product information. As submitted orders are read, Tronix adds each of the requested items to a blank page in Organizer, creating a master list of items needed.

Place Your Orders

Assuming there are orders for out-of-stock products, it's time to call your suppliers. You may have items in stock or may be selling products you have manufactured—if so, you won't have to worry about this.

When you call your suppliers, you need to find out exactly what they have in stock or when they will be getting restocked. If you work in a release-sensitive industry, you also need to ask what new products have arrived or will be arriving that day.

TIP ▸ ***Before finalizing your daily orders with distributors, check in with your customers. Is waiting an extra day for an out-of-stock order a problem? Why wasn't the credit card verifiable? Will the customer send a second e-mail for additional items to be shipped with the first order? The later your distributor allows you to complete the ordering process, the more changes or additions you can make. Generally, distributors don't mind last-minute additions to your orders. Cancellations are another matter.***

Update Your Site

After dealing with your distributors, you should have some time to update your Web site with news about the day's new arrivals. If you are not physically close to your supplier, you can announce the products as "Arriving Tomorrow" or whenever you expect them to reach you.

Unless you offer a very wide range of products, these updates are usually minor and only require about 30 minutes to be added to your What's New page and your price lists. A simple text editor like Windows Notepad or SimpleText for the Mac can make this job easy and quick. After you have made the changes, log on to your site to make sure the changes appear as you planned. If you make a change but forget to upload one of your updated pages, it could mean losing a sale.

Back to E-Mail

With your site updated, you need to go back to your e-mail and look specifically for orders placed by first-time customers. It's important to confirm that the credit card is valid by calling the issuing bank for address verification. Once those orders are verified, you can begin responding by e-mail to your customers to inform them of the status of their orders.

Process Your Invoices

Now you can begin processing sales for items that are readily available. If part of a current order is not expected in stock for a day or two, you can still process the order. You might wind up with a declined credit card and have time enough to cancel the order with your supplier. Orders expected to ship out that day should be separated from incomplete orders. You should also separate your daily outgoing orders by shipping type, since each method of shipping requires a different set of procedures.

Print Address Labels

If you are using UPS, Airborne, or FedEx online shipping software, you might want to process your address labels now since you will have to add any new customers to these individual databases. After your labels are printed, you can sort through any post office orders and begin filling out your domestic and international address labels.

If your point of sale program has such a feature, you can simply print those labels out. Tronix's day begins at 10 A.M. By 3 P.M., address labels have been printed and sorted by shipping type.

Pack and Ship

With your labels finished, you can begin putting together your boxes and packing any orders that involve readily available stock.

Set those completed orders aside and prepare boxes and labels for any orders involving stock that is expected to arrive that day. Once that stock arrives, you can simply place the newly arrived items into the pre-made boxes or envelopes. Whether couriers pick up your shipments or you drop them off, allow yourself enough time to get every order out before deadlines. You don't want to have to e-mail a customer and inform him that you didn't get his package out because you didn't have time. With experience, you will learn how to pace yourself. Orders will come in throughout the day. It's up to you to figure out how late you can accept an order and still get it shipped the same day.

TIP ▸ ***As discussed in Chapter 17, it is important to have a list of all your shipping outlets and their deadlines for shipments. You can either post this on a wall or have it easily accessible on your computer. This way if someone absolutely has to have something overnight, you can easily find the shipping company with the most convenient deadline.***

The Home Stretch

You've made your deadlines; all of your orders are out the door and on their way to your customers. You can breathe now. This is a good time to do a final e-mail check and some general organizing around your office. If you have a scanner at work, you can start scanning in photos of new products. You can do minor Web work now or save it for later tonight at home.

Expect the Unexpected

You can have an entire day planned out beginning to end and even arrive to your office earlier than usual. But there's always the possibility of an unwelcome time destroyer:

- **You may** have to spend time tracking down packages that did not arrive when or where they were supposed to.
- **You may** have to call a supplier after realizing an item is missing from your order or you were overcharged on a specific item.

- **You may** have bills or taxes to pay.

- **You may** need to call various shipping companies to find out why you were overcharged on a bill.

- **You may** have to deal with the dreaded charge-back from a credit card company, which means you'll have to fetch the original invoices from the sale in question.

Joe's Take: *The best way to deal with shipping pick-ups is to arrange a time at which the various drivers will stop by on a daily basis. If you call whenever you need a pickup, be sure you know how late you can call each courier and still have your packages picked up that day. The later you can have your orders picked up, the better. This gives you time to fill all your orders without having to neglect all other operational aspects. However, if you are in the early stages of operation and only need to ship a few orders a day you might want to arrange earlier pick-up times. Otherwise you might end up sitting around twiddling your thumbs until 8 P.M. waiting for your couriers to show up.*

Dealing With E-Mail

E-mail is perhaps the most important tool for your business; it is the essential avenue of communication between you and your customers. You will use e-mail on a daily basis to follow up on orders, handle problems, sort out pre-orders, and answer general customer inquiries. As your store grows in popularity, the amount of e-mail you receive can be nearly overwhelming.

If you can afford it, you should have a computer at home. Operating a small online business means you can't simply punch a clock at 5 P.M., go home, and put your feet up. Communicating with your customers from home, whether or not your home is your office space, is something you'll need to do nearly every day. As the e-mail begins to pour in, you will find less time to answer all your e-mail during business hours.

Joe's Take: *Once my business began to take off, I noticed I had very little time to ship out all of my orders after responding to all my e-mail. Eventually I found myself completely stressed out late in the day as I tried to fulfill all the orders and answer the phone. By the end of the day, I was both wired and totally exhausted.*

At Home, Leave Mail on the Server

Many e-mail programs give you the option of having your messages deleted from the server once you have downloaded them from the client. This option can allow you to easily access your messages from home. On your home computer, set your e-mail client to *not* delete messages once downloaded. This way you can safely download and answer mail at home. When you arrive at work the following day, your work machine will download all the messages again and delete them off your mail server. Once at work, quickly delete the messages you dealt with the previous night. This allows you to ignore messages at home that need to be dealt with at the office without having to forward all of them back to work. It's the best way to have two locations accessing the same e-mail account.

Prioritizing E-mail

Eventually you must prioritize your e-mail. Orders come first. Customers expect to receive a quick response, which is the whole point of shopping on the Web. Whether or not the customer's order is in stock, you should let them know as soon as possible.

You will also receive a number of general inquiries, such as "When will you have the latest version of EZMoneyManager?" or "Do you ship to North Africa?" General questions can be answered during business hours if you have some spare time, but once the tide rolls in, you should forward this e-mail to your home. That gives you more time to fill orders during business hours and answer non-urgent e-mail at your own pace in the comfort of your own home.

TIP ▸ ***If you work out of an office, keep a copy all of your shipping information at home so you can answer general shipping rate questions after hours.***

You should check your e-mail regularly throughout the day. If you have a phone line (or dedicated line) for Internet access, you can leave it running all day and have your e-mail program auto-check at regular intervals for incoming mail. Almost all e-mail programs have this option.

Filters

E-mail filters keep mail organized by applying a set of rules to all incoming mail. Filters look for keywords in the subject line, the body of text, and the sender's address. They trigger special events such as deleting, moving, or automatically responding to the message. You can design your online order form so that orders are sent to your e-mail address with the word "order" in the subject line.

By having the filter check for the word "order" in the subject line, the incoming message can then be sent to a folder for orders. Separating orders from all other e-mail eliminates the need to open every piece of e-mail in search of orders.

However, not everyone will use your order form to place an order. Some customers may use e-mail to submit an order. Regular customers might send a message saying something like "This is John Doe. Send me another one of those doggie beds using the same shipping, address, and credit card information as the last time." If John Doe's message has a subject line that reads "This is John Doe," the filter will not know to send it to the order folder. The message will simply be sorted with your regular messages in your incoming mailbox or main folder.

If the same message had a subject line reading "This is John Doe with a reorder," the filter would find the trigger word "order" in "reorder" and send it to the assigned folder. To limit the frequency of this problem, instruct your customers to use the word "order" in their e-mail orders. Because some people will fail to do so and therefore orders will slip past a filter, it's a good idea to occasionally check incoming e-mail for orders.

Filters for Automatic Responses

Another useful filter is one that triggers an immediate automatic response to the sender. This type of filter can be used to acknowledge that an order has been received correctly, especially if the order is placed during non-business hours when you are not checking your e-mail. For example, if a customer places an order on a Friday night and you aren't open on the weekend, the customer will at least be informed that the order reached its destination. A simple message stating that the order has been received and will be processed during business hours will do the job. This filter serves the same purpose during holidays or vacations.

Anti-Spam Filters

Using a filter to check incoming e-mail from a specific address can effectively eliminate messages from annoying individuals and spammers. You can use this filter to delete unwanted messages before they reach your mailbox.

TIP ▸ ***Be careful with filters. Choosing a word that is too general can do more damage than good. For example, how can you eliminate endless solicitations urging you to "Earn More Money Now." You could filter out any incoming messages containing the word "money." That will work, but it will delete all messages with the word "money." You could lose a potential customer who happened to us the word money in a message.***

Organizing Mail with Folders

Any good e-mail program allows you to set up a number of folders to sort your mail. You can create folders for any type of e-mail inquiry. For example, when a customer asks about an upcoming product, you can place the mail in a folder for inquiries about the particular item. When details become available, you can quickly go to that folder and forward the information to those people with messages in that folder. Your customers will be pleasantly surprised when the information becomes available and they are immediately updated.

Here are some other folders that Tronix has found useful:

- **Completed Orders:** After an order is processed, it is placed in this folder for future reference.
- **Unfinished/Undecided:** This is a folder for orders in limbo, such as those that need more information before processing or partially filled orders. If a customer fails to respond to a message that part of his order needs to be backordered, the order goes here. For whatever reason, the customer may be unable to get back to you for a few days. Because of this, it's better to store the message in a dedicated folder rather than delete it.
- **Money Orders:** This is a good folder for people who are mailing payment. When their payment arrives, you can quickly notify them by going to this folder. You can also use this folder to notify customers when their wired money has arrived in your account.
- **Fraud Attempts:** The folder says it all. Keep your fraudulent orders here. You can use this as a reference for all future orders and, if you have a relationship with other mail-order stores, you can forward and receive fraud alerts.
- **Web Additions:** This is where you can keep Web-related messages such as customer comments or questions about trading links.

TIP ▸ ***Construct a page of commonly used sentences and cut and paste them into your e-mail messages as needed. You can copy messages such as "Thank you for your order. It will be shipped today." from this page and paste them into numerous e-mails rather than repeatedly typing the information.***

Redesigning Your Web Site

The speed with which Web continues to evolve can make it difficult to keep pace. At one time, Web sites all looked relatively similar to one another with the exception of font sizes and specific images. Today, a plethora of tools help Web designers envision almost anything and place it on a page.

Your site will *always* be under construction. All businesses have to change with the times and your Web store is certainly no different. You can spend endless hours creating what you feel is a spectacular Web store, but one morning you will log on and think, "This looks stale." What was amazing six months ago has suddenly lost its kick. As you surf the Web, you come across features you've never seen before.

Start Surfing

When you feel your site is in need of an overhaul, start surfing. Search for sites or companies that are involved in Web development. Are there more advanced, sophisticated tools available than the ones you are using? Are there new Web add-ons available?

The more you see, the better idea you'll have of what's available for you. Embrace change.

Take Your Time

If you plan to reconstruct your entire site, take your time and spread the work out so it doesn't effect your current site. Change the look of your site as often as you feel it is necessary. Tronix redesigns its Web site about every six to eight months.

You can begin rebuilding your site by making a copy of your current site and using it for remodeling by working on one page at a time. Retain the general information and simply work on the cosmetics. All links can remain intact and your entire site will run exactly as it did before, but with a fresh, new look. You don't necessarily have to do a major overhaul each time you redesign your site. Experimenting with different colors, font styles and sizes and perhaps changing the structure of your price lists can breathe new life into your site.

Upgrading Technology

One thing to consider when retooling your site is upgrading the technology. As we've mentioned numerous times throughout this book, adding loads of automated commerce technology and other fancy site tricks can be a mistake because of the cost and the fact that this technology isn't always reliable. However, it is inevitable that better commerce tools will arrive and Web technology will fall in price, making these additions worthwhile.

If you decide to add display and multimedia features, you should do so sparingly to test the reaction of customers. Rather than redoing your entire Web site using the super-slick Flash product from Macromedia, add a single Flash object on a few pages and see how your customers respond. If your customers don't like it, or it causes their browsers to crash, you'll hear about it. Small tests will save you the pain of destroying your store with poor technology.

Regular Features

Daily, weekly, or monthly features keep your site fresh and give customers a reason to regularly visit your site. How often you add features depends on the size and type of business. Tronix receives new releases at least once or twice a week. Whenever you receive a new product, you can highlight it by posting photos and featuring the product throughout your site. The most important thing is to let your customers know about new products as soon as they arrive.

There are numerous types of regular features you should consider. For more about creating content, see Chapter 9.

Scheduling

Enhancing your site with feature articles, photos, and general graphical touches is best done at home or during non-business hours when you have the time to really focus on the task at hand. The weekend can be a great time to fine tune your site by scanning images, making small visual changes, uploading screen shots, changing fonts, and adding fresh content.

Invoicing

A good invoicing system is an important tool for processing and tracking all of your sales. Several invoicing programs are available for Windows or DOS-based PCs, as well as Macs. To get a feel for the type of invoicing program best suited for your business, you should search the Internet for any shareware or free trial versions that you can tinker with before making a final decisions. If you have experience with a good database program, you can even create a personalized invoicing program to handle your needs.

TIP ▸ ***If you choose to create your own invoicing system, one of the best programs is Filemaker Pro from Apple. This is an easy-to-use product that is available for both Mac and Windows systems.***

Key Features

Any good order-processing program should be able to cover all types of sales. Whether you purchase a program or design one of your own, here are the key features that should be included:

Customer Information

- Billing address.
- Shipping address.
- Phone numbers (home, business, fax).
- Credit card field.

Sale Information

- Quantity field.
- Item field.
- Price field.

- Discount field.
- Tax field.
- Shipping field.

Additional Information

- Purchase order field.
- Net field.
- Payment type (check, money order, cash, credit card).
- Credit card number and expiration field.
- No charge field (for free items).
- Store policy.

Optional Information

- Special announcements/upcoming events.
- General notes (an area where you can type a personal note to a customer).
- Customer's e-mail name.
- Issuing bank of the credit card.

Your invoices should display your company name, address, phone number, fax number, the date of purchase, and your Web address. Having your Web address on your receipt is important in case a customer loses a browser bookmark to your site. Whichever program you use, make sure you set it so it will print at least two copies of every invoice—one for your customer and one for your files. You can staple a copy of the customer's credit card slip to the invoice, unless you run a system that is automatically tied into a credit card terminal. In that case, the credit card approval code will appear on the invoice.

Your invoicing program should include customizable shipping and tax rates, a mailing list, and an easy-to-use inventory database.

JOE'S TAKE: *I've seen programs that handled almost everything perfectly, but when it came to something simple like allowing the user to define her own shipping methods, it didn't work. Imagine a mail-order company using an invoicing program that only handles UPS. The more flexible your invoicing program is, the fewer dead ends you'll run into, and the more flexible your business will be.*

Inventory

Your invoicing program's inventory capabilities should efficiently store all of your items in an easy-to-find fashion. The program should allow for a large number of additions and making new entries should be simple. Most stores use a bar code reader or a labeling system that separates each item by a part number. For these types of systems, all items must be labeled for identification.

You might want to abbreviate your item names. For example, a Sony Analog Control Pad would be SACP. A business specializing in PC multimedia accessories might have an item called SBA64 for Sound Blaster Awe-64 or CLSBA64 for Creative Labs Sound Blaster Awe-64. By using abbreviated item names as part numbers, you can simply look at the name on the packaging and easily access the item during a sale.

You should also be able to enter miscellaneous items on the fly. For example, a customer may phone in an order before you have the time to enter your new releases. If you are in the middle of a sale and you have already taken most of your customer's information, it would be inconvenient to keep your customer waiting while you suspend the sale in order to enter a new item. Having a program that allows you to enter a part during the sale will save time for you and your customers.

Organizing Your Site's Back End

Using a good File Transfer Protocol (FTP) program allows you can keep your site organized by getting a visual representation of your file layout. Tronix uses a shareware program called CuteFTP. You can have your entire site laid out in one main directory, but as your site grows you may want to separate specific files, such as graphics, into their own folders. Having separate folders eliminates the need to scan through dozens of files in search of the one file you need to update. You can keep all your HTML files in the main directory and all other file extensions out of sight.

When updating your files or adding new content, take note of any Web pages, screen shots, or other material to which you no longer link. Removing these unneeded files from the server will free up space and minimize clutter.

TIP ▸ ***Name your files logically for easy identity. For example, if you have a price list for gold earrings, a file name like goldear.html makes more sense than ge.html or golde.html. When it's time to locate that file for updating, you'll eliminate the need to load a number of files before finding the right one.***

Site Folders

Every site needs to be well organized on the back end. Your initial site design should have an organized directory system. In fact, your Web hosting company may already have some special requirements (such as where CGI scripts are stored).

Using folders is a good way to store various types of content. Graphics, audio files, video files, Photo-VR images, etc. should have their own folders. This system of organization allows you to quickly find whatever you are looking for. For example, if you need to address a graphical problem, you can simply go to the "Graphics" folder. Because you might want to use particular elements on different pages, organizing by content type rather than by site area is the way to go.

You can also create folders that split HTML files into different folders for your site's key categories. This isn't necessary for sites with only a few pages. But if you've got a site with four or five sections and 30 or more pages, you'll want to build in some organization. If you have a variety of content types, you can create separate folders for reviews, features, news items, and so on.

Analyzing Store Traffic

Analyzing your store's traffic is a crucial maintenance activity. Unlike other Web sites, a Web store has two types of information to analyze: sales data and site traffic data. Even if you don't specifically analyze your sales, you will certainly know what sells well.

If you run a Web server, you can use any of a number of major site log or traffic analyzers. Since most of you won't run your own server, you'll need to rely on the hosting company's efforts. Although all Web hosts are different, most provide traffic analysis assistance. Some companies will send you a daily report via e-mail. Other options include log files or links to pages that summarize your site's activity.

The optimum traffic report is a solid log file which you can analyze yourself using a tool such as WebTrends (Figures 18.1a and 18.1b). With a product like this, you can run more reports and examine the site logs as you wish. Table 18.1 shows the reports you can generate with the basic version of WebTrends. Learning which pages are most popular and when and where users are coming from is important.

The most interesting information results when you combine sales results and Web site analysis results. For example, having sold 20 copies of a certain CD, you can find out how many times that page was requested for you to reach those 20 sales. Dividing the results will give you the ratio of looks to buys. Finding out which countries are accessing your site can help you decide where you might want to advertise, which languages you should offer, or in which countries you should set up *mirror* Web sites.

FIGURE 18.1
Two sample reports by WebTrends.

Activity Level by Day of Week

This section shows the activity for each day of the week for the report period (i.e. if there are two Mondays in the report period, the value presented is the sum of all hits for both Mondays.) The Total Weekdays line indicates the number of hits occurring Monday through Friday of the report period. The Total Weekends line indicates the number of hits occurring Saturday and Sunday of the report period. Values in the table do not include erred hits.

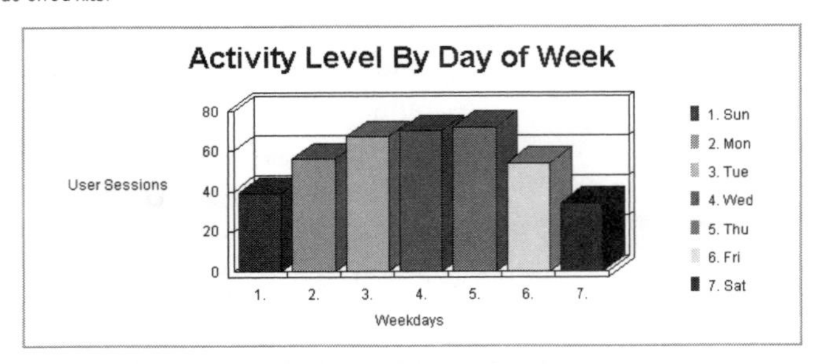

Activity Level by Day of the Week				
	Day	Hits	% of Total	User Sessions
1	**Sun**	327	10.13%	39
2	**Mon**	411	12.73%	56
3	**Tue**	492	15.24%	67
4	**Wed**	528	16.35%	70
5	**Thu**	712	22.05%	72
6	**Fri**	462	14.31%	54
7	**Sat**	296	9.16%	34
	Total Weekdays	2605	80.7%	319
	Total Weekend	623	19.29%	73

Single Access Pages

This section identifies the pages on your Web site that visitors access and exit without viewing any other page.

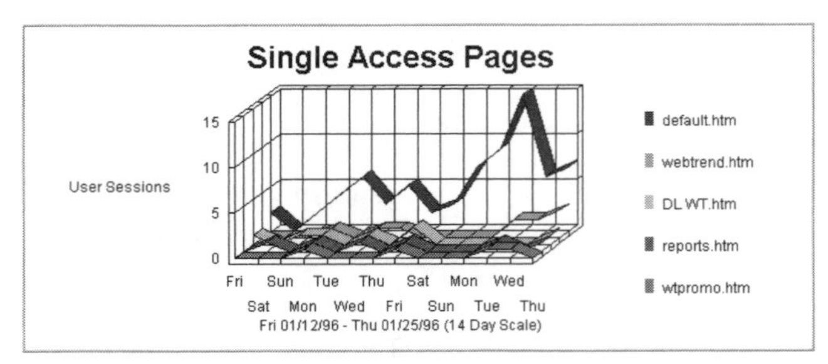

Single Access Pages			
	Pages	% of Total	User Sessions
1	**WebTrends Corporation** http://www.webtrends.com/default.htm	65.74%	71
2	**WebTrends** http://www.webtrends.com/webtrend.htm	9.25%	10
3	**302 Moved** http://www.webtrends.com/DL_WT.htm	6.48%	7
4	**302 Moved** http://www.webtrends.com/reports.htm	5.55%	6
5	**302 Moved** http://www.webtrends.com/wtpromo.htm	3.7%	4
6	**How can I order WebTrends?** http://www.webtrends.com/wtorder.htm	1.85%	2

TABLE 18.1 WEBTRENDS REPORTS

General Statistics	Client Errors
Most Requested Pages	Server Errors
Least Requested Pages	Most Downloaded File Types
Top Entry Pages	Organization Breakdown
Top Exit Pages	North American States
Single Access Pages	Most Active Cities
Top Paths Through Site	Bandwidth
Advertising Views and Clicks	Most Accessed Directories
Advertising Views	Top Referring Sites
Advertising Clicks	Top Referring URLs
Most Downloaded Files	Top Search Engines
Most Active Organizations	Top Search Keywords
Most Active Countries	Most Used Browsers
Summary of Activity by Day	Netscape Browsers
Activity Level by Day of Week	Microsoft Explorer Browsers
Activity Level by Hour	Visiting Spiders
Technical Statistics	Most Used Platforms

You should analyze your logs at least once a month—more often if you can manage it. You can also combine several monthly views to get a longer-term analysis.

JOE'S TAKE: *One particularly interesting statistic is the Top Paths Through Site statistic, which will show you what paths customers are taking before placing an order.*

TIP ▸ ***Don't spend too much time micro-analyzing every statistic; just make basic, solid decisions about your store. Eliminate poorly performing pages and give your customers more of what is popular. Statistics are meaningless unless you know how to use them.***

Backing Up

Backing up your site is *critical*. You may never need to use it, but having a backup is like having insurance. If you don't have it, that is exactly when something will go wrong. You should have at least two copies on your hard drive—one to alter as you try out new designs, and a permanent backup. You should also save a couple of backups on removable media such as a Zip disk.

Periodic Maintenance

Although there is a long list of tasks that you will perform on a daily basis, there are also a number of things you will have to do less frequently. These chores are just as important and can be scheduled at intervals throughout the month or year.

- **Check your competitors' sites each month.** See what they're selling, how their prices are, what new features have been added to their Web sites, etc. Keep up with the Joneses. Actually, keep ahead of the Joneses.

- **Check for dead links.** There are a number of programs that do this. You should also have a special e-mail link for people who want to report dead links or other problems with your site.

- **Do minor Web upkeep weekly.** This includes changing price lists and fixing minor errors as necessary.

- **Do a major site redesign a few times a year.** This doesn't mean completely changing the look of your site, but changing fonts, adding features, etc. You can experiment behind the scenes before actually presenting these changes publicly. The more you work on your design and HTML skills, the better you'll get. When redesigning your site, be careful about removing pages. If people were entering your site through a particular page and it suddenly disappears, they'll be told the page no longer exists. If you find it necessary to remove a page, use a redirect page to send people to your home page. The search engine Hotbot has a "check links to this domain" feature that allows you to see who is linking to your site. You can also check your log file to see where people are coming in. Don't close your store's door by removing commonly linked pages.

- **Update your content.** A What's New page that never has anything new is sure to make customers uneasy.

- **Check the speed.** If you use a high-speed connection such as a cable modem, periodically access your site with a dial-up connection to see how well it loads. Look for pages that are slow to load and do what you can to speed them up.

- **Check the search engines once a month to see where you're being listed.** Do what you can to improve your rating.

- **Ask for feedback.** When you have time, poll your regular customers about your store.

If You Fail To Plan, You Plan To Fail

Yeah, yeah, you've heard it before. And no, we're not trying to sell you a retirement plan. But if you arrive at the office every day without a plan, you'll leave the office every night with a little less hair—you'll have yanked it out. There will be plenty of emergencies that force you to stray from your plan, but if you are disorganized, an unplanned disaster will be even more disruptive. By the time you have put out whatever fire you were dealing with, you might return to work only to find the rest of the day has burned down around you.

The more organized you are and the better you use the available technology to speed up your daily work, the better you'll feel at the end of the day and the more you'll look forward to going to work the next morning. Take advantage of the available technology that allows you to organize your operations.

Next up is Chapter 19, which will show you how to use online technology to best serve your customers and how to keep them coming back to your store for years to come.

CHAPTER NINETEEN

Building Loyal Customers Through Online Customer Service

Customer service is the backbone of all businesses: no customers, no business. Although there are a number of traditional customer service tenets (which you can find throughout this book) that translate to Web business, there are also several aspects of customer service that are unique to the Internet. You can provide information to your customers without repeatedly answering the same questions. You can quickly respond to customer requests via e-mail and you can offer catalogs and updates on your products without the usual process of using the mail or buying advertising.

A loyal customer base can be the direct result of strong customer service. If you treat your customers well, don't insult their intelligence by being dishonest, and take advantage of the customer service advantages provided by the immediacy of the Internet, you'll eventually see the same people shopping repeatedly at your online store.

This chapter will show you how to get the most out of your e-mail program and the best way to handle all kinds of customer messages. We'll run through some of the most popular e-mail programs and also discuss how to deal with those pesky phones. Finally, Joe will provide the customer service keys that have helped Tronix survive and flourish.

E-mail Accounts and Customer Profiles

The key to providing good customer service is learning all the ins and outs of e-mail. As discussed later in this chapter, utilizing advanced aspects of e-mail products such as Outlook Express, Pegasus, and Eudora is a good way to deal with e-mail issues.

Another crucial element of customer service is learning more about your customers. Well-established stores do this by using personalization and profiling tools like Firefly, Likeminds, or Broadvision. However, these are expensive and intensive tools to use. If you are able to use them, you should. There are less expensive and less complicated ways to build loyal customer profiles and get that personalized relationship people seek on the Web.

Laying Out an E-Mail System

Most Web hosting accounts include e-mail in the package. A standard hosting package should allow you to set up as many as five different e-mail accounts for your domain. In addition, you'll have your dial-up access e-mail as well. Some more expensive packages will give you access to 10 or 20 e-mail accounts, giving you the ability to set up different e-mail departments to better handle user requests.

Here are five basic e-mail accounts you should have:

- **WEBMASTER@MYSTORE.COM:** Use this at the bottom of every page to collect information from customers about Web site difficulties, broken links, and so on.
- **CUSTOMERSERVICE@MYSTORE.COM:** Always have an address directly related to customer service issues and responses.
- **ORDERS@MYSTORE.COM:** A separate e-mail address for order inquiries will help you quickly sort incoming requests and mail that pertain to orders.
- **EDITOR@MYSTORE.COM:** Sites with a large amount of content and reviews might want to add a specific e-mail address for editorial content.
- **LIST@MYSTORE.COM:** If you want to run an e-mail mailing list, set up a specific e-mail account for the service.

These e-mail accounts give users a chance to send mail directly to an area in which it can be easily dealt with. It also gives the appearance that you have a large staff of people dealing with e-mail.

Answering E-Mail

Answering e-mail will be your most common daily task. No matter how slick your Web site is, the manner in which you answer e-mail can make or break your business. There are two key to answering e-mail—prioritizing e-mail and writing quality responses to your customers. In many cases it can boil down to two words: "Thank you."

Responses to e-mail orders should begin or end with a thank you. Although your order form will trigger a "Thank you for shopping at..." page, adding direct contact with the customer is essential frosting on the cake.

General inquiries are no different. If a customer is curious about a particular item and you don't have access to it, you should still thank him for his interest. You might even tell him where he can find the particular item. Although he'll be disappointed that you didn't have the item, your courtesy might encourage a return visit.

Cancellations

There will be many occasions on which you will be unable to deliver a requested item without a delay of a few days. In this case you should ask your customer if she wants to wait for the item to arrive or to cancel her order. If she decides to cancel, be sure to reply and confirm the cancellation. There is a right way and a wrong way to respond to cancellations.

The right way:

> *Dear Customer,*
>
> *Your cancellation has been acknowledged. We are sorry we couldn't fulfill you request, but we thank you for your interest.*

The wrong way:

> *OK. Order canceled.*

The incorrect way of replying to a canceled order sounds juvenile, shows no personality, and gives the customer the impression that the storeowner didn't care about the order anyway. Be careful not to develop these kinds of bad habits. The Web can be a fast and furious way to do business when you're the storeowner and your customers aren't sending and receiving hundreds of e-mails a day. Therefore they're not going to be happy with a terse response. It's easy to fire off a two-word reply, but it's not smart.

Even worse is not acknowledging a canceled order. This will not only upset the customer but it will give the impression that the credit card is now held captive to a sale.

Time Waits for No One

During the infancy of your business, answering e-mail is something you will look forward to. Detailed replies to e-mail make customers feel they are being treated with a personal touch. When business really heats up, you'll find yourself with much less time to respond to e-mail. What once was a detailed reply concerning an out-of-stock item can easily become "Sorry, we're out of stock." It's important not to neglect the art of e-mail correspondence, no matter how busy you are.

E-mail should be answered in a timely manner. Unless you are closed when an order is placed and that fact is posted on your Web site, replying to orders two days after they are made will not sit well with a customer. If for some reason your reply is late, be honest and let your customer know why. Be aware that e-mail speed varies between servers. If a server is having technical problems, whether it is on your end or your customer's, e-mail can arrive at its destination much later than scheduled.

Joe's Take: *I've had instances in which I received an e-mail order or inquiry from a customer, and 30 minutes after that e-mail arrived, a second message from the same customer came in, asking why he hadn't received a response. This usually means the person e-mailed you hours ago but a slow server kept the message from arriving promptly. You should make the customer aware of this, although people who are familiar with the Internet know e-mail responses don't always occur instantly.*

One way to make responding to e-mail easier is to create some templates with a simple ASCII editor. If you receive a number of e-mail messages with the same question, you can simply copy the answers from the template and paste them into your responses. These small templates can minimize typing, and the fact that it is a pre-written statement should give you more time to better word the response.

TIP ▸ ***An auto-responder is a good way to quickly reply to customers. This can keep your customers informed and relaxed knowing that their e-mail has been received. Even if you don't provide an immediate answer to the customer's inquiry, it will let the customer know you re working on it.***

Here is an example of an auto-response:

> *Thank you for your message.*
>
> *This is an auto-response to your message which was sent out immediately after we received your e-mail. Please understand that e-mail is not always instantaneous and it may have taken some time for us to receive your message. We are working to answer it as soon as possible.*
>
> *If you require immediate service, please call us at [phone number]*
>
> *Mystore.com is reachable by phone from 9:00AM to 6:00PM E.S.T.*
>
> *You may also want check the following sections of our Web site for the information you need:*
>
> 1. *Our store FAQ (Frequently asked questions) is located at www.mystore.com/faq.html.*
>
> 2. *All new store information is located at www.mystore.com/whatsnews.html.*
>
> 3. *You can find reviews and product information at www.mystore.com/reviews.html.*
>
> *You can also join our mailing list for news and product announcements by sending a message with the word "subscribe" in it to list@mystore.com.*
>
> *Thank you for your interest in MyStore. We will respond to your e-mail as soon as possible.*

General Inquiries

Not all e-mail messages will be orders. In fact, the majority of your e-mail will be inquiries. General inquiries are just as important as orders, so do not neglect them. Of course, there are exceptions to the rule, such as a question about how your logo was designed. These are the types of questions that you can answer at your leisure. They are also the types of questions you might want to add to your store's FAQ.

Back-Ups

Your e-mail program should be set up to retain a copy of all outgoing mail. You never know when you'll need to retrieve an old message. For example, if a customer presents you with a problem with her order, you can prove that you warned the customer about potential problems by referring to your original message. You should also archive and back up old e-mail (six months or older) on a Zip disk or tape backup.

Filtering for FAQs

An informative page of Frequently Asked Questions can deliver answers to the most popular questions about your business and minimize repetitious inquiries. You can also set up an autoresponding filter to send out a list of common questions (and answers) or general rules about your business. Have your filter search for a subject such as FAQ.

Creating E-Mail Mailing Lists

A mailing list is a great way to send information to your customers. It allows you to have contact with your customer, whether it is announcing an upcoming product, a special or sale promotion, a new arrival list with pricing, or even important information such as special hours or holiday closings. If your e-mail program features good filter capabilities (such as those in Pegasus Mail and

Eudora), you can easily set up a mailing list. By having your filter look for a trigger word such as "Mailing List," you can have your customers' e-mail addresses automatically sent to a specific folder for future mailings.

Once a mailing list begins to gain members, you can provide regular updates—daily, weekly, or as new products arrive. For a mailing list to be effective, your customers must be aware of its existence. You can do this in your signature or on your Web site.

Chose an E-Mail Program With Mailing List Capability

When deciding on an e-mail program for your business, it is important that it contains fairly extensive mailing list features. Using the carbon copy (CC) or blind carbon copy (BCC) function of an e-mail program is not the same as creating a mailing list. A carbon copy shows the original recipient's e-mail names and all other recipients who have received the same e-mail. A blind carbon copy solves that problem by hiding all the additional recipients' names. Both types work well if you want to send the same message to a small group of people. However, these are not effective ways to manage a mailing list that could eventually grow to hundreds of people, unless you want to be clicking on hundreds of names.

Managing Mailing Lists

The more mailing lists you offer, the more work you will have to contend with. If you run a business containing multiple formats, you can split your mailing lists. For example, a business that specializes in computer software should have one mailing list for Macintosh customers and another for PC users. A Mac user won't be interested in reading about "What's new on PC" and vice versa.

A mailing list has to be maintained, so consider the long-term effects on your business and the amount of time you'll need to spend working on it. Can you handle more than one mailing list? Between conducting sales, shipping boxes, and working on your Web site, you may not have the time.

NOTE ▸ Devote some time each week to cleaning up your mailing list. E-mail addresses can change like the weather. Customers might move to a new ISP or even cancel their accounts. When this happens, a message to that customer will simply bounce back with a "User Unknown" reply. The longer you let this go, the more unwanted "boomerang" messages you will receive. It's best to remove invalid e-mail addressed from your mailing list after several bounce backs. ▮

Outsourcing Your Mailing Lists

One option is to outsource the project to a mailing list vendor. A mailing list vendor will maintain the list for you and provide robust archiving and monitoring of list activity.

Mailing list vendors generally charge a monthly of about $25 for a list of approximately 50 people. The fee increases with the size of the mailing list. A mailing list with several thousand users might cost as much as $500 a month to operate, but the maintenance work alone on a list that size makes outsourcing the project worth the money.

A good outsourcer of mailing lists is Skylist, located on the Web at www.skyweyr.com/skylist/.

Top E-Mail Packages

As we've made clear throughout this book, e-mail is a critical asset to your store and selecting the right e-mail package for your needs is extremely important. The things to look for in an e-mail package are strong features for filtering, auto-responding, and accessing multiple mail accounts.

Here are some e-mail packages you should consider.

Pegasus Mail

Pegasus Mail is a continuously updated shareware package that has been around for several years. Pegasus offers a number of features that aren't available in many commercial packages, such as powerful filtering commands, mailing lists, and flexible forwarding and redirection of mail.

Forwarding and redirecting mail are two essential functions if you plan to answer e-mail both at work and at home. Forwarding simply moves e-mail to an assigned address. Every e-mail client has this function. However, the latest version of Pegasus Mail lets you forward your e-mail in a number of ways:

- **You can forward** each message individually to your personal account by typing in your own e-mail address. This is the conventional way of forwarding mail and is present in all e-mail clients.

- **You can forward** a group of messages to your e-mail address without working on each message separately. The e-mail arrives as individual messages.

- **You can send** off a group of mail in MIME format. This method allows you to select an entire group of mail and forward it as one attachment. When you retrieve this attachment, each message is shown independently from the others, retaining the original return e-mail addresses. If you are in a hurry, this is a quick way to send a chunk of e-mail to a different destination.

The redirect mail feature is another helpful tool. It allows you to redirect a message to another computer, while it retains the original sender's e-mail address in the "From:" field. If you simply forward a message from your office to your home, your business address will be in the "From:" box. If you want to reply to the original senders, you'll need to have a list of addresses at home. The redirect command eliminates this problem.

Pegasus mail also has a convenient notepad function. You can use this notepad to record information (phone numbers, Web sites, etc.) that you can eventually paste into a message to customers. You can also use the notepad to set up the template replies that were discussed earlier.

Netscape

Netscape's e-mail client is integrated with the Netscape browser, so alternating between Web browsing and e-mail is convenient. Folders are easy to create, and the drag-and-drop capability makes it easy to place messages into any folders. However, there are no mailing list functions powerful enough to be useful for a small business.

Eudora Pro/Eudora Light

Eudora Pro and the freeware Eudora Light are Internet-based e-mail packages. Eudora claims to be the most popular Internet e-mail software with an estimated 10 million users. Eudora Pro includes built-in spell checking, user-definable message filtering, color-coded message labeling and "hot link" Web page capabilities.

Eudora Pro's enhanced message filtering allows the user to use several filtering terms individually or together to sort messages into mailboxes, forward e-mail to other locations, send automated replies, or alert users when important messages arrive. Standard message filtering (also available on Eudora Light) sorts messages into mailboxes and modifies subjects and priorities based on certain criteria.

Eudora Pro allows users to send mail to multiple accounts at once and lets the user incorporate various fonts, colors, layout options, etc. Pro also has a customizable address book.

Some other features that Light shares with Pro include drag-and-drop support, nickname/address book support, and text searches within messages or headers.

Microsoft Outlook Express

Outlook Express is a free product that is also available bundled with Internet Explorer. Outlook Express automatically detects and offers users the opportunity to import Eudora, Netscape, Exchange and Windows Inbox mail messages and address books upon their first start-up. Users can create multiple hierarchical folders to e-mail. Users can also read e-mail and access newsgroups without having to switch windows or open new applications. You can create filters for each of their newsgroups to filter out postings that meet certain criteria. You can also sort their messages in a number of ways, including grouping messages by subject to keep related messages together for easy reference.

Microsoft Outlook

Microsoft Outlook manages e-mail, calendars, contacts, tasks and to-do lists, and documents or files on the hard drive. Outlook helps users communicate through e-mail, phone support and group scheduling capabilities. Outlook also helps users share information by means of public folders, forms and Internet connectivity. Among Outlook's key features are:

- **AutoName Check,** a feature that checks e-mail addresses against the address book to ensure that messages are being sent to the intended address.
- **Drag-and-drop capability** that allows users to drag information from a Word document into an e-mail message.
- **A message flag** that marks e-mail messages with due dates or specific follow-up actions and helps the user prioritize e-mail.
- **An AutoPreview feature** that displays the first three lines of each e-mail message so users can easily prioritize messages.
- **A voting feature** that allows the user to conduct polls and helps manage results.

How to Handle Phone Calls

Although e-mail seems to be becoming a preferred means of business communication, the telephone hasn't exactly gone the way of the hula-hoop. The way your business handles phone calls and the personality you project over the phone can be just as important as the manner in which you answer e-mail. When you're on the phone you can't always hide the fact that you're sick, tired, or both.

Be Happy! (Even if You're Not)

Responding to a customer by e-mail not only affords you the opportunity to respond at your leisure, but it allows you to think about what you want to say and change the message if you don't like the way it looks. Talking on the phone is a spontaneous situation. Assuming you can spell (or have a dictionary), handling e-mail in a professional manner is relatively easy. Your phone conversations should be no less professional.

Most people have had both good and bad phone conversations with stores, mail order houses, technical support lines, even friends. When you call a store and the person on the other end gives you the impression he could care less about your needs, do you quickly head to that store and spend a lot of money? Unlikely. Keep that in mind when you pick up the phone at your office.

However, we are sympathetic. You're only human and when the phones are constantly ringing as you are trying to maintain the rest of your business, it's easy to lose your patience. If you feel you are about to answer the phone in a snappy, impolite manner, let it ring a couple of times and consider the fact that the person on the other end is probably a customer. Answer politely, with a greeting ("Good afternoon, Tronix" rather than "Hello?"). Speak clearly and don't give the impression that you are in a rush (even if you are). Of course, if it's a solicitor, feel free to slam the phone down.

Crunch Time

As the clock winds nearer to pick-up time and the phones are still ringing, your life might appear to be spinning out of control. As you gain experience, you will be able to determine how late you can accept orders and still get the shipments in the mail that day. (This will depend on how many orders you are processing each day and whether or not you have any help packing the boxes.) For example, if your post office closes at 5:30 P.M. and your couriers arrive at 6 P.M., you might want to post a 4:30 P.M. deadline for orders. Any orders that are placed after 4:30 P.M. are not guaranteed to be shipped that day. This allows you to take a message and return any calls made after 4:30 P.M. after you have made your shipments. However, if you are not busy you might be able to fill orders placed after your deadline. Doing so will make your customer feel as if she is getting special treatment.

Joe's Take: *If you decide to take a message during crunch time, explain that your couriers are about to arrive and you want to be sure you get all of your shipments out on time. Don't ask the customer to call you back, especially if you don't have a toll-free number. Call her back as soon as possible. If you post your daily order deadline prominently on your Web site, you can cut down on phone orders made after that time. People who do call will at least be aware of the deadline and won't be disappointed if you can't fill their orders that day.*

May I Put You on Hold?

One of the most common (and annoying) situations customers have to deal with when ordering products by phone is sitting on hold for an inordinate amount of time. Putting someone on hold for a minute or two to see if you have what they want in stock or to check a tracking number from a shipment is fine. Otherwise, you're probably better off taking a phone number and calling the customer back as soon as you have the information he needs. In the age of automated phone systems, something as simple as taking a message and calling someone back can make your store seem more personable and caring.

If a customer inquires about a product you don't have and you have to check with your supplier, tell the customer she can either wait on hold for a few minutes or you'll call them back. Some people don't mind waiting on hold as long as they know it's going to be a few minutes.

Two Calls at Once

Depending on your phone system, you might find yourself taking one order only to have your other line start ringing. If you don't have voice mail or a second person to answer the second line, you're stuck. Ask the first customer if she minds waiting for a moment while you answer another call. Then you can answer the second call and tell the person you're in the middle of taking an order. Offer to put the second customer on hold or call him back. Then return to the first order.

How often you're forced to bounce back and forth between calls will not only be determined by your resources (voice mail, other employees, number of phone lines) but also by your store's popularity. If you're only filling four or five phone orders a day, chances are you'll rarely get two calls at once. However, if you find yourself constantly flipping back and forth between calls, putting people on hold, or returning calls, you have a problem that should be addressed.

Any customer who is repeatedly interrupted in mid-order so you can take a second call is going to quickly become annoyed with your service. This problem can be alleviated by installing a voice mail system or by hiring an employee to help answer the phones. Of course this depends on your financial situation. Keep in mind, every time you have to return a call, it costs you money.

Joe's Take: *International callers should not be left on hold for more than a brief time. The quicker an international order is handled, the lower the customer's phone bill will be, and the happier the customer will be. The more you can avoid returning international calls, the happier you will be.*

Encourage Other Means of Ordering

As you see, phone calls can be a bit of a hassle. At best, the order will be processed easily and without interruption and you will only lose a couple of minutes out of your day. At worst, you'll be frustrated by a crunch time interruption, the customer will be annoyed when you put him on hold to answer another incoming call, and everyone will walk away from the transaction with a bitter taste in their mouths.

Do whatever you can to encourage people to order via your online order form or fax. Make it apparent that ordering in either of these manners is advantageous for the customer in that it eliminates phone charges and the possibility of being placed on hold. You don't need to relate what a pain in the butt that phone orders are for you.

Joe's Customer Service Tips

- Pay for return shipping when a customer has to send back a defective item.
- Stay on top of lost, late, or incorrect orders. Don't leave customers hanging.
- Offer customers the best shipping option for their order. Not having to pay an arm and a leg for shipping will keep customers ordering online rather than shopping at a local store.
- Follow up on back-ordered items. Keep the customer apprised of the status of her order so that she knows you didn't forget about her.
- Don't try to push items on customers that they don't want or need. Leave that to the car salesmen.
- Quickly clean up any mistakes. If you send a customer an incorrect item, replace it immediately. If it was your mistake, don't make the customer wait until you get the initial shipment back.
- If a customer has a question about a product he purchased, offer any assistance you can. If you are in the middle of crunch time and can't spare a moment, call back as soon as possible. If you can't provide the assistance the customer needs, don't try to fabricate an answer just to give the impression that you know more than you really do. Offer them a phone number for technical support or of the product's manufacturer.
- Reply to all e-mail in a timely fashion.
- Inform customers, either by e-mail or phone, when pre-ordered items arrive.
- If you don't have a product in stock, say so. Let the customer know when the product will be in and how quickly you can get it to her.
- Don't leave customers on hold for long periods of time. Offer to call back if you think it will take some time to provide an answer for their question.
- Make sure your Web site is well maintained. Fix broken links, incorrect spelling and other miscues, especially when the problem is brought up by a user.

Tracking Customers and Building One-On-One Relationships

A store's ultimate success relies on its gathering a list of regular customers who are committed to your store as if it were a club. Your customer service efforts need to be aimed at these people. That requires you to identify these customers, track them, and cultivate them.

Larger stores can do this by building sophisticated tracking systems into their sites as well as by using personalization tools that provide automated forms of personalization to store customers. However, smaller stores must substitute sweat equity in return for less money invested in technology for their site.

Customer Database

You should build a database of everyone who orders from your store. Your ordering system should do this. Tronix does this by operating a separate order entry system for Web, e-mail, fax, and phone orders.

A good entry system will allow you to track each sale and retain information about the customer. This includes shipping information, phone number, address, and credit card information. More importantly, it will allow you to print out a list of customers and how many times they've ordered from you so you can easily identify key customers. For example, you can put a special filter on your e-mail package to notify you of priority mail from top customers. This lets you quickly prioritize e-mail in favor of your best customers.

TIP ▸ ***Let regular customers identify themselves by providing things like mailing lists and holding credit card information on file. People who plan to be regular customers will almost always sign up for these offers. You can also take it a step further by turning your store into a buyers club like retailing giant CUC does. In this case you offer customers a chance to get special offers, pricing, and service by paying a yearly club fee of $25–$75.***

Personal Attention

Once you've got a handle on who your main customers are, and as you identify new ones, the key is to keep them coming back. There are a number ways you can accomplish this:

- **Offer them priority on new products.** E-mail your top customers ahead of arrivals and allow them to reserve purchases.
- **Keep their order information on file** and let them easily order products by requesting them through email without re-entering all of their information.
- **Give them a special toll-free number to use.**
- **Offer them better shipping terms and/or pricing.**
- **Create a referral service for them.** For every customer they send you, give them a store credit. Your best customers are often your best spokespeople. Cultivate your ability to turn customers into supporters.
- **Create a private password-protected area** of your Web site with special content or invite them to join a mailing list reserved for your best customers.
- **Poll them occasionally** so they can have an impact on your store's content, service, and overall development.

Privacy

Another key to customer service is to sign on as a TRUSTe licensee. This new and popular service is a way to assure your users that you operate a site that adheres to welcomed principles regarding disclosure and use of personal information.

To join on as a TRUSTe licensee you must adhere to its principles:

Baseline Standards

- **THE SITE MUST EXPLAIN** and summarize its general information gathering practices.
- **THE SITE MUST EXPLAIN** up front what personally identifiable data is being gathered, what the information is used for, and with whom the information is being shared.
- **THE SITE MUST DISCLOSE** whether users may opt out of having their information used by the site or third parties, whether they may delete or deactivate themselves from the site's database, and whether they may update or change their information once it is disclosed.
- **THE SITE MUST DISPLAY THE TRUSTMARK** on its home page that discloses the site's overall privacy policy. (See the Sample Privacy Statement following this list.)
- **COMMUNICATION MONITORING**. The Site may not monitor personal communications to third parties such as e-mail or instant messages, except to the extent required by law, or as necessary in the process of maintaining the site.
- **THE SITE MUST ADHERE** to its stated privacy policies.
- **THE SITE MUST ADHERE** to its stated privacy policies, even after the site discontinues from the TRUSTe program unless consent is obtained directly from the user.
- **THE SITE AGREES TO COOPERATE** with all TRUSTe reviews and audits.

CASE STUDY

A Sample Privacy Statement Provided by TRUSTe

Company XYZ's Overall Privacy Statement

This Overall Privacy Statement verifies that Company XYZ is a member of the TRUSTe program and is in compliance with TRUSTe privacy principles. This statement discloses the privacy practices for the entire Web site.

TRUSTe is an independent, non-profit initiative whose mission is to build users' trust and confidence in the Internet by promoting the principles of disclosure and informed consent. Because this site wants to demonstrate its commitment to your privacy, it has agreed to disclose its information practices and have its privacy practices reviewed and audited for compliance by TRUSTe. When you visit a Web site displaying the TRUSTe mark, you can expect to be notified of:

- What information this site gathers/tracks about you.
- What this site does with the information it gathers/tracks.
- With whom this site shares the information it gathers/tracks.
- This site's opt-out policy.
- This site's policy on correcting and updating personally identifiable information.
- This site's policy on deleting or deactivating your name from our database.
- Questions regarding this statement should be directed to Company XYZ's site coordinator, or TRUSTe (www.truste.org) for clarification.

Information This Site Gathers/Tracks

Company XYZ is a Web site that allows users to buy Widgets. There is one Widget order form on the site that prompts users to give their name, credit card information, and postal address. This site also logs IP addresses.

Use of the Information This Site Gathers/Tracks

The information which is gathered on the Widget order form is used to process the order. Although Company XYZ logs IP addresses, we do not link it to any personally identifiable information. This means that users are anonymous. Our Web site logs IP addresses for system administration purposes.

Sharing of the Information This Site Gathers/Tracks

The postal address information gathered on the Widget order form is shared with Shippers Express. Shippers Express only uses the postal address to fulfill the transaction.

While navigating the Company XYZ Web site, you may find additional TRUSTe marks with links to privacy statements. These statements apply only to the page the mark is on and should not be construed as the Overall Privacy Statement.

Opt-Out Policy

If you would like to opt-out of being solicited by this site or third parties, please contact:

Webmaster
webmaster@companyxyz.com
1111 Company Way
Metropolis, CA 99999 USA

Correct/Update Policy

If you would like to correct and/or update your personally identifiable information, please contact:

Webmaster
Webmaster@companyxyz.com
555-1515

Delete/Deactivate Policy

This site does not offer a way to delete/deactivate your data.

How to Join TRUSTe

To receive the TRUSTe trustmark (Figure 19.1), you must send your signed legal agreement and payment.

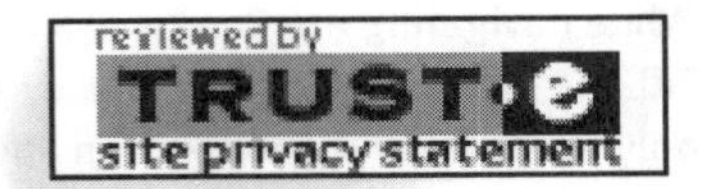

Figure 19.1
The TRUSTe trustmark.

You can print out an HTML version of the TRUSTe legal agreement or download a copy in Microsoft Word. In signing the agreement, you agreed to follow the TRUSTe standards and submit your site to the ongoing assurance process. An officer of your company must sign the agreement.

Once you've decided to become a TRUSTe licensee, go to the automated billing process to generate an invoice. TRUSTe will determine the cost of your license based on your company's revenue and type of business.

After you've completed those steps, you're ready to complete the TRUSTe application process by submitting the following information:

- Two signed copies of the legal agreement.
- A copy of your invoice.
- Payment, made out to TRUSTe.

Send the information to:

TRUSTe Application
4005 Miranda Ave., Suite 175
Palo Alto, CA 94304

Upon receipt of your application, an authorized TRUSTe representative will sign both legal agreements and return one to you for your records. A TRUSTe account representative will contact you and you'll be given a confirmation number. This number will provide you access to the For Licensees section of the TRUSTe Web site, where you'll build your privacy statements.

For a $10 million or less retail Web site, TRUSTe's yearly fee is $750.

Customer Service Is an Investment

Customer service is about being in contact with your customers as much as possible. This work is very time intensive. But if you lose one customer through poor customer service, you may lose many more as word spreads on the Internet.

Education is the best form of Internet customer service. The smarter you make your customers about how your business operates, the better. By convincing your customers to do things such as ordering online rather than over the phone, the less expensive your customer service efforts will be.

Customer service is an investment. If you correct one problem immediately, you can not only build a lifetime customer but, through that customer's recommendations, increase your customer base.

CHAPTER TWENTY

Fighting Off the Competition

You've done everything you can to attract customers to your store and provide them with an enjoyable shopping experience. Not only are your prices unbeatable, but you provide dedicated customer service, handle all complaints quickly and efficiently, and provide an unsurpassed selection of goods. Your Web site is attractive, easy to navigate, and a joy to visit. If they choose, customers can spend all afternoon bouncing around your site and checking out the new information before they even begin to shop. You tirelessly promote your store, you provide every shipping option known to man, and your site always appears fresh because of your willingness to update both its content and its look. You are organized and use the latest technology to maximize your efficiency. A minimal inventory minimizes your risk.

So what? Your competitors have the same things going for them.

Once you have built a sizeable customer base, you'll have to fight to keep it. Competing on the Internet involves a number of unique aspects that we'll discuss here. We'll also show you how to effectively track your competition, how to compete both offensively and defensively, how to find your competitive niche, and how to keep in touch with the Web community. We'll prepare you for battle.

Unique Aspects of Internet Competition

Although there are a number of competitive aspects of online business that are identical to traditional retailing, the Internet not only provides plenty of advantages for merchants but also a number of unique issues with which all storeowners must wrestle. The worldwide scope of a Web store's reach and the fact that the Internet allows smaller outfits to compete directly with corporate giants are advantages for your business. Starting a Web business is also generally less expensive than opening a traditional retail store. And once your store is off the ground, you can operate with a slim inventory. It's also much easier to track the competition and react accordingly. However, these are benefits that you share with your competitors. The businesses that best utilize the benefits of the Internet are the ones that survive and flourish.

There are also a number of issues that are uncommon for retail stores but important for Web stores to effectively deal with. The content of your Web site and your ability to promote your store is critical with so many competitors located all around you. The proximity of one Web store to all of its competitors also allows customers to more easily compare prices and take their business elsewhere if they don't like the prices, service, or selection you're providing.

Worldwide Customer Access

Unlike traditional retail businesses, Web stores have access to potential customers all over the world. Instead of competing with the store across town for a limited number of customers, you might be located in Vermont and find yourself battling with a California-based company for customers in Portugal. Any smart online merchant will use this to her advantage. You should obviously do the same.

Access to a wide geographical range of customers won't do you any good unless you work to utilize that aspect of online commerce. That involves promoting your store on the Internet through newsgroups and online forums, search engines, link exchanges and swaps, bounty programs, and banner advertising. It also includes advertising and promoting in traditional media as well as promoting your store and selling products on an international level. If you don't plan on taking advantage of these online-specific business aspects, you might as well open a traditional store in the local mall.

For more on taking advantage of worldwide customer access, see Part III of this book.

David vs. Goliath

Money (when used wisely) can help any business on the Internet. However, if you are a small company on a tight budget that presents the public with a professional-looking site, no one will know if there is one of you, 30 of you, or 300 of you. Unlike traditional retail, one person with the right knowledge, creativity, and drive can appear as big as any corporation. You needn't open stores in every state in the nation. Your one Web site resides in every state in the nation—and in every nation in the world.

Depending on your market, there might not be any huge corporations to compete with. Even if there are, don't throw up your hands and quit. It isn't like a superstore moving in next door and burying you. Find your niche and use it to your advantage. Remember: bigger doesn't necessarily mean better, especially in online retailing.

Lower Start-Up Costs, Minimal Inventory

One of the great things about operating an online store is the fact that start-up and inventory costs can be minimized. Rather than dumping thousands of dollars into inventory that might collect dust on a shelf, you can stock a few sure-fire big sellers and then add other items as they are ordered. As long as you know you can immediately procure the necessary items from your suppliers and quickly have them on their way to your customers, you needn't have the products sitting in your office. You can have them on your Web site (your virtual shelves) without assuming the risk of having bought them.

You also don't need to spend money on a snappy looking space. Assuming you don't have any walk-in customers, a cheap office (that can be as messy as you want) is fine. You can also run your store on your own without having to hire salespeople.

For more on stocking your virtual shelves and minimizing your inventory, see Chapter 8.

Web Content

Your Web site's appearance and layout is obviously an important factor in the competitive world of online commerce. An attractive Web site that is functional and easy to navigate will attract customers and keep them. All other things being equal—prices, customer service, shipping options, selection, etc.—customers will flock to the site that is the most enjoyable to visit and the easiest to use. Conversely, a visually unappealing site that is illogically constructed will send potential customers scurrying for a more enjoyable shopping experience. Why would anyone feel comfortable submitting credit card information to a store that looks like it was glued together by juveniles as an after school project? The outside retail world can be more forgiving in this sense, as a shabby store with good pricing can still attract customers. In fact, a ragged-looking store can be seen as having character and being free from corporate greed as long as it is clean and organized.

Here are some tips for setting your Web store's content apart from the rest:

- **Stay on top of emerging technologies.** Every day it gets easier to add snappy graphics and design flourishes to your Web site. Don't get caught listening to 8-track tapes when the rest of the world has CDs.

- **Don't get carried away with emerging technologies.** Although it's nice to have a bell here and a whistle there, too many of them will scare the pants off your customers. Either that or it will bore the pants off them as they watch paint dry and wait for site to load.

- **Keep everything fresh.** When you get bored with your site's content, assume your customers are equally as bored. That goes for colors, fonts, graphics, news items, features, etc. Change is good.

- **Make your site an informational destination,** not just a shopping destination. The more reasons there are to visit your site, the more people will visit. The more people that visit, the more you'll sell.

- **Make your site easy to navigate.** Your customers should be able to easily find whatever they want.

For more on creating content, check out Chapter 9.

The Enemy Next Door

Online shoppers have easy access to everything from cars to books without ever leaving their desks. In the real world, you can spend the day driving from store to store looking for the best price or just the right item and waste your savings on gas. Or you'll not feel like wasting a Saturday shopping, so you'll settle on an item that might be more expensive and of lower quality than one available across town.

If a Web shopper wants to comparison shop, she is just a new URL away from a whole new store full of options. Rather than using a car, cab, bus, or subway, customers can bounce between stores with the click of a Forward or Back button.

While the Web allows customers to easily hop from store to store, it also allows competitors to do so. Chances are your competition down the street in California is making the quick trip to your store in Vermont. You would be crazy not to pay her regular return visits. Within seconds, you can access any online retailer on the Web. You can find out what your competitors are selling, their prices, their shipping rates, their hit counter (if they have one), and the entire structure of their stores.

If you like certain aspects of a competitor's site, don't be afraid to incorporate the same ideas. Just look at Domino's, Little Caesar's, and Pizza Hut. When one comes out with a new idea (stuffed crust, double crust, recycled paper crust, whatever) the other two are sure to follow. However, copying proprietary Java Script code or VB Script code is technically illegal, not to mention unethical, lazy, and plain old sleazy. The last thing you want to do is get a reputation as a code thief. That would fall under the category of bad public relations.

Joe's Take: *Shortly after I began using alternate-colored bars on my price lists to highlight new releases, I noticed two other mail order companies using the same technique with the* same color combination! *I felt like somebody had stolen my car then driven up to my house and said, "Hey, how do you like my new car!" If you're going to be a thief, at least be a subtle thief.*

Tracking the Competition

Chances are when you set up your Web store, you'll think you have a truly unique concept. Then you'll start searching the Web and realize you're not alone. Well, at least you've found your competition. Not only should you visit these sites, you should bookmark the ones you find particularly interesting and visit them often. Assuming the owners of these stores have a clue, they'll be visiting you.

TIP ▸ ***Once you have found a search method that leads you to stores that are similar to yours, don't do it just once. Web commerce is growing at an alarming rate. You can be certain that the number of stores in your market will continue to grow. Check back every month or so for new competitors.***

Your potential customers are also your competitors' potential customers. They'll compare sites and shop where they feel their wants and needs are best met. You want that store to be yours.

Comparison Shopping

It's critical to identify precisely where your store is stronger (or weaker) than your competitors' stores. Another store might have better pricing, but you might have lower shipping rates and more shipping options. Another store might be open later but not accept credit cards, whereas you do. You probably won't beat a competitor in every category—if you do, then they aren't really competitive.

For a side-by-side comparison of your store vs. a competing store, use the following chart in Table 20.1. Give yourself a checkmark if you feel you are better than your competitor in a certain area, and vice versa. If you feel the two stores are even, give both stores a check. The only way this exercise can work is if you are honest. Giving your store the edge in every category is not only probably delusional but can cause you to be complacent. If you can find a friend who will be honest and whose opinion you value, have her fill out the chart.

TABLE 20.1 CORBIN, WE NEED A CAPTION HERE

		My Store	Store X
Availability	Representatives available via phone	☐	☐
	Longer store hours	☐	☐
Ordering	Better return policy	☐	☐
Fax orders accepted	Phone orders accepted	☐	☐
	International orders	☐	☐
	Secure order form	☐	☐
	More payment options	☐	☐
Inventory	More items available	☐	☐
	More items actually in stock	☐	☐
Shipping	Lower shipping costs	☐	☐
	More shipping options	☐	☐
	Latest shipping deadlines	☐	☐
	Better packaging	☐	☐
Web site	Faster to download	☐	☐
	Better presentation	☐	☐
Content	More product reviews	☐	☐
	More feature articles	☐	☐
	Informational content	☐	☐
	User created content	☐	☐
	Discussion boards	☐	☐
	Chat rooms	☐	☐
Customer Service	Direct customer service phone number	☐	☐
	Answers customer e-mail more quickly	☐	☐
	Customer FAQ available	☐	☐
	Privacy policy or TRUSTe participant	☐	☐
	Customer service chat rooms	☐	☐
	Promotion	☐	☐
	More advertising	☐	☐
	More associates/bounty sites	☐	☐
	E-mail newsletter	☐	☐
	Better newsgroup participation	☐	☐
Pricing	Average price discount	☐	☐
	More prices available	☐	☐

Following Your Customers

Usenet newsgroups are a great way to watch for customer comments. Take note of any headers that refer to purchases. A newsgroup topic that reads, "Where to buy...," or "I just purchased...," can lead you to information about your competitors. You might learn about a new store or find out which of your competitors are getting high marks (or low ones) from customers.

You can also track your competitors through your customers. If you feel comfortable doing so, ask some of your customers where else they have shopped or would consider shopping. If a new customer e-mails you asking if you can match or beat a price on a particular item, ask where he saw the price. Check the site and take a particularly close look at the shipping rates. Some online stores offer amazingly low prices but jack up the shipping charges. It's an easy switch; subtract most of the profit from an item and add it to your shipping rates.

TIP ▸ ***Picking up profits from low prices and high shipping rates might sound like a neat trick, but we don't recommend it. Most people will quickly figure out what's going on and just as quickly find someplace else to shop.***

Watch Your Competitors Watching You

Watch for any patterns that indicate how closely your competitors are following you. Is there are a store that seems to price its items exactly $1 less than yours? Do you see a store announcing the same new releases shortly after you do? Does a store respond to a new feature on your site by adding a similar one? If you see stores constantly making similar changes to keep up with you, that's a good sign. It means you are beating them to the punch and they are scrambling to keep up.

Joe's Take: *I have repeatedly seen competitors announce the arrival of new releases when they really didn't have the items available. We would get new product, announce it on our Web site, and within moments another store would announce the same information. When a customer calls to order the product, they tell the customer that the item "just sold out but more will be arriving soon." Eventually customers catch on.*

10 Keys to Tracking The Competition

Tracking the competition can sometimes be an overwhelming task. It is also one of the most important things you'll do. Keep the following in mind and you'll be in good shape:

- **Be a customer.** Either by yourself or via a friend, order something from a competitor and experience the service first hand.
- **Subscribe to every e-mail newsletter** or other service your competitors offer. Use a free e-mail service if you want to conceal your identity.
- **Use search engines or search agents** like Hotwired's Newsbot (www.newsbot.com) or Deja News (www.dejanews.com) to monitor Web articles or Usenet posts featuring your competitors.
- **Use the "search for links to this URL" feature** on Hotbot or other search engines to gauge the popularity of a site.
- **Ask customers** what other stores they frequent and what they like about those stores.
- **Collect horror stories.** Ask customers why they no longer shop at a particular store to learn what makes your site attractive.
- **Check as many** update, sale, and home pages as possible every day.
- **If your competitors** offer discussion boards, monitor them for dissenting posts or customer service complaints.
- **Strike up conversations** with your suppliers. They might let something slip about one of your competitors.
- **At least once each quarter,** evaluate your competitors' sites from top to bottom. Identify what has been improved, changed, eliminated, etc.

TIP ▸ ***If you have more than one e-mail account name, you can use your non-business alias to join the mailing lists of your competitors. This way you can keep up on what new products they are selling, where they are dropping prices, what new lines of products they are introducing, and so on, without their suspecting who you are.***

The Best Defense Is a Good Offense

As you prepare to launch your store, you should know what other similar stores are offering and be prepared to offer more. Open your cyber-doors with competitive, low prices even if it means sacrificing some early profit. You should also consider a Grand Opening special such as free Priority Mail shipping or a "buy one, get the second item at half price" promotion. You might also include a small gift for your first 50 or 100 customers. No matter what you do to add a spark to your opening, make sure your first customers leave feeling they've discovered a great place to shop online. This is how good word of mouth spreads. If your customers feel particularly excited about your store, they will quickly pass along a recommendation.

Look for your competition's weaknesses, and emphasize your strengths in that area.

If one of your competitors only accepts CODs, emphasize on your site that you accept major credit cards. If others only use UPS, let it be known that you provide a wide variety of shipping options.

Defense Wins Championships

You won't always be able to beat your competitor to the punch. In these cases you need to be ready to launch a counter-attack.

For example, an established competitor might receive product before you. Instead of losing potential sales, counter with a lower price. If people become aware that you have better prices, they might be willing to wait an extra day to get their shipment.

Another store might try to secure as many pre-orders as it can by offering a discount to anyone who pre-pays for a hot, upcoming item. You can counter that by offering the same price with no obligation to pre-order.

Defending your territory means never giving your competitors an easy opening to pummel you. Here are some points that will help keep the wolves at bay:

- **Only a catastrophe** should bring down your Web site. You store should be on a quality hosting service with complete backup. If your site goes down, your customers go elsewhere.

- **Answer e-mail as quickly as possible.** Do your best never to let an e-mail sit unanswered for more than 48 hours. If you don't take an interest in your customers, they won't take an interest in your store.

- **Never sell e-mail addresses** or other information about your customers to any other service without your customer's explicit permission. This is an easy way to annoy (and lose) customers.

- **Take orders securely over the Internet** using Secure Sockets Layer (SSL) and, when it is perfected and becomes the industry standard, Secure Electronic Transactions (SET). If you don't offer secure online transactions, you shouldn't offer any online transactions. If a customer has his credit card information stolen when dealing with your site, his next online purchase will be from one of your competitors.

- **Don't use hidden pricing techniques** such as inexpensive products and jacked-up shipping rates. If customers feel you are being dishonest, they will go to one of your competitors who is honest.

- **Never spam newsgroups** or customer e-mail lists. The result will be a bad reputation.

- **Check content and other postings** for validity, spelling, grammar, and other potential mistakes. If your content is unprofessional, customers will think your entire operation is unprofessional.

- **Make sure new items** and other inventory changes are posted as soon as possible. Don't let new items lag, especially in competitive consumer markets. If you have something, let people know. Otherwise, they'll find it somewhere else.

Finding a Competitive Niche

You can't be everything to everyone. Figure out what you do best and refine that area of expertise. Don't be afraid to break away from the standard online business formula and make your site different. Be honest rather than trying to fool the customer. You might not be known for rock-bottom prices, but you can do well by offering the best customer service. Although everyone likes to save a few dollars, many people don't mind spending a bit more in return for excellent customer service.

As your store becomes established, you'll find your own corner of the Web. Some qualities your store could become known for include:

- The lowest prices.
- Unbeatable customer service.
- The largest selection.
- Fastest E-mail responses.
- A well-designed site.
- A wide variety of shipping options.
- The most exciting sales.

- The best information and reviews.
- Flexible exchange polices.
- The first store with new releases.

Although you should do your best to provide all of the above, you probably won't be the best in every category. Whichever approach you take, stick with your plan and be the best at your specialty.

However, you may go after a certain niche only to find there is no way you can top a certain store. For example, you might design a beautiful Web site only to have a huge corporation with a 10-person Web development team come along and blow yours away. Be flexible. Don't trash your fine Web site, but don't sit around either. Shift your focus to another area and win there instead.

Keeping in Touch With the Web Community

Getting involved with the Internet community immediately elevates you above the pack of money-hungry retailers out to separate people from their money. Given a choice, people would rather give their business to merchants who share their interest in and passion for a subject. If you were shopping for rock climbing gear, would you rather deal with an out-of-shape salesman who says, "I heard these boots are pretty good," or one who responds with a story about how a certain piece of equipment worked particularly well for her while climbing in cold, wet weather?

There's no better way to make your presence known than by joining Usenet newsgroups and participating in various IRC chat sessions. Participating on a non-commercial level shows you truly care about your work. Offering your expertise to others—whether by answering questions, giving advice, or providing useful information—can give you an edge on the competition. With your signature attached, you have made people aware of your business without intrusive advertising.

If you become an informative, active presence, you will be a welcomed guest rather than an ignored or contemptible intruder. On the IRC, it's best to participate using your business name, rather than a nickname. If another member recognizes the name of your business, it might spark a conversation that leads to a plug. However, it's best not to initiate commercial offerings.

For more on newsgroups, see Chapter 10.

Fight, Fight, Fight!

Competition: it's the American Way. Running any business should be fun, but it should also provide you with a way to make a living. If you aren't ready to compete, fight, scratch, and claw for customers, you probably shouldn't be in sales. And if you are ready to go to battle, you should go to battle with a plan. We hope this chapter has instilled a bit of fighting spirit and has also given you some ideas for forming your own battle plan.

In athletics, some coaches say they only prepare their team and don't concern themselves with the opposition. In business, this is a mistake. Yes, your first concern should be with providing the best service possible. But there's no harm in taking a peak at the competition. Any professional basketball coach who says he doesn't pay particularly close attention to Shaquille O'Neal when preparing his team to play the Los Angeles Lakers is either lying or stupid. Don't let the online equivalent of Shaq sneak up and drop 60 points on you before you figure out what's going on.

The next chapter will present you with some legal issues to consider. With Internet law still developing, expect it to change rapidly and frequently. It is important to keep your eyes open and be aware of shifting legal winds. We'll provide you with some cases that provide a partial framework for Internet law.

CHAPTER TWENTY-ONE

Legal Issues

(This chapter was written by Peter S. Carlisle. Peter is an attorney in Portland, Maine specializing in the representation of small businesses. His e-mail address is **carlisle@maine.rr.com**.)

In January of 1997, the number of Internet users in the U.S. and Canada was estimated to be approximately 50 million—double the number reported in June of 1995. While this volatile industry expands unfettered, the traditional means of governance for social and commercial interaction—the law—struggles to keep pace; government legislation, the enactment of which is notoriously insensitive to the immediacy of social development and commercial innovation, and jurisprudence, a product of an even slower evolutionary process, must be applied to an industry that despite its ubiquity has only begun to define itself.

Introduction

Opportunity accompanies uncertainty in the wake of rapid and unmitigated growth. Both the European Renaissance and the Industrial Revolution bore cultural and financial riches that far surpassed the harvest of their times; arguably, the emergence of the Internet carries with it the same promise. Companies courageous enough to enter the fray of Internet commerce will assume the risks inherent in an industry where growth remains a step (at least a step) ahead of governance; at the same time, those companies will enjoy the potential for unparalleled growth.

The Internet dissolves traditional geographic barriers, increasing access and exposing a new crop of customers. Products and services can be advertised and sold in a geographic vacuum. But where do these transactions take place? Where are taxes due? What laws govern if there is a dispute relating to an Internet transaction? Naturally novel legal issues, such as those relating to jurisdiction and taxation, arise as business practices change. Unfortunately, given the rapid development of the Internet, it is difficult to predict how such issues will be resolved. Businesses participating in Internet commerce cannot refer to the law to conduct the typical actuarial analysis to weigh potential liabilities against potential gains. Until the law catches up with the expansion of the Internet, Internet commerce will require a roll of the dice.

Rest assured, the law will catch up. The development of the law will eventually correspond to the development of the Internet. Laws regulating static elements of commerce and society remain relatively static; laws governing developing industries must evolve accordingly. During the period of legal evolution, uncertainty is present. While that uncertainty cannot be eliminated, businesses can minimize the potential liabilities arising out of such uncertainty by gaining and maintaining awareness about how the laws governing Internet commerce are developing.

Jurisdiction

The most obvious legal issue that arises with the growth of the Internet is jurisdiction. In order for a court to entertain a lawsuit, it must have jurisdiction over the litigants and the claims; in other words, it must be appropriate for a particular court to decide a particular matter involving particular people. This issue arises in the context of Internet commerce where there is a dispute between people or businesses of different states. Is a customer in New York obligated to travel to Texas to defend himself against a company suing him for breach of a sales agreement? Reciprocally, is a company in Texas forced to endure the costs of litigating in New York? The answers to these questions should affect the approach a business takes in conducting its business over the Internet.

Both state law and the U.S. Constitution limit a court's jurisdiction over a defendant from another state. In order for a court to exercise jurisdiction over a defendant, jurisdiction must be authorized by the state's long-arm statute (state long-arm statutes authorize courts to entertain lawsuits involving non-resident defendants) and satisfy the Due Process Clause of the U.S. Constitution.

The Due Process Clause requires that a defendant have "minimum contacts" with the state within which the suit is brought (the "forum state"). The presence of minimum contacts is determined through a three part test: First, the defendant must be entitled to the protections of the forum state's laws by having purposefully conducted business in that state; second, the cause of action must arise out of activities related to the forum state; and third, the imposition of jurisdiction must "comport with traditional notions of fair play and substantial justice." (International Shoe Co. v. Washington, 326 U.S. 310 (1945)). These vague legal standards do not adequately resolve the uncertainties that have arisen in the context of Internet commerce. Nonetheless, it is important to review the handful of decisions that have confronted the challenging legal issues of Internet commerce.

In CompuServe, Inc. v. Patterson, 1996 U.S. App. LEXUS 17937 (6th Cir. July 26, 1996), the Sixth Circuit Court of Appeals found jurisdiction where the only contact between the parties was of an electronic nature. The court exercised jurisdiction over a Texan subscriber to CompuServe because he had entered into a "Shareware Registration Agreement" with CompuServe, an Ohio company through which he intended to sell his computer software. The court found significance in the fact that the defendant purposefully did business in Ohio—despite the fact that he never physically entered the state. The Court stated that CompuServe, in effect "acted as Patterson's distributor, albeit electronically and not physically." A significant element to the CompuServe court's rationale was the existence of a contract.

Interestingly, two years before the CompuServe decision, in Press Kap, Inc. v. System One, Direct, 636 So.2d 1231 (Fla. D.C. App. 1994), a Florida state court found jurisdiction lacking over a New York company that had entered into a contract with a Florida-based company (and had actually accessed the Florida company's database). Press Kap, Inc.'s apparent irreconcilability with CompuServe illustrates the uncertainty in the judicial treatment of Internet commerce.

In McDonough v. Fallon McElligott, No. 95 CIV 4037 (S.D. Ca. August 15, 1996), a case decided the same year as CompuServe, a federal court in California seemed to subscribe to the CompuServe court's requirement of a contract between the parties, holding that the creation of a Web site does not constitute the requisite "minimum contacts" to justify jurisdiction.

Despite the apparent importance of a contractual relationship, non-contractual activities such as advertising, which account f or a large percentage of Internet activity, may also lead to the imposition of jurisdiction. In Inset Sys. Inc. v. Instruction Set, Inc., 937 F.Supp. 161 (D. Conn. 1996), a Massachusetts company was subjected to personal jurisdiction for using a domain name inset.com when the plaintiff had a federal registration for "Inset." Despite the fact that it was never shown that the defendant made any sales in the forum state (Connecticut), jurisdiction was justified because the defendant company had "purposefully directed its advertising activities toward Connecticut, on a continuing basis." The Inset decision stands for the proposition that continual advertising can create sufficient contacts to justify the imposition of jurisdiction—despite the absence of a formal contractual relationship and a lack of sales.

In another recent case, Bensusan Restaurant Corp. v. King, 937 F. Supp. 295, 297 n. 1 (S.D.N.Y. 1996), a New York court adopted a more relaxed view on Internet advertising, holding that "[c]reating a site, like placing a product into the stream of commerce, may be felt nationwide—or even worldwide—but, without more, it is not an act purposefully directed toward the forum state." In Bensusan, the defendant advertised his business, but did not actually conduct sales.

In State of Minnesota v. Granite Gate Resorts Inc., No. C6-95-7227, 1996 WL 767431 (D. Minn. Dec. 10, 1996), Minnesota brought charges against the operators of a Web page that advertised a future online betting service. The Web site did not actually facilitate commerce, but rather provided information about the gambling service and created an opportunity to be put on a mailing list. The court characterized the defendant's actions in the following manner:

The defendants attempted to hide behind the Internet and claim that they had mailed nothing to Minnesota, sent nothing to Minnesota, and never advertised in Minnesota. This argument is not sound in the age of cyberspace. Once the defendants placed an advertisement on the Internet, that advertisement is available 24 hours a day, 7 days a week, 365 days a year to any Internet user (some of whom are Minnesotans) until the defendants take it off the Internet.

Despite the indirect nature of the solicitation (and the lack of formal agreements and sales) since the site provided consumers with phone numbers to call, the court held that the defendants had made "a direct marketing campaign to the State of Minnesota," and that "one who sets up his or her system...knows that anyone accessing his or her site will get that information, then the server ought to be held responsible for that information."

Similarly, the 1996 case of Maritz Inc. v. Cybergold Inc. Case No. 96CV01340 (E.D.Mo. August 19, 1996) held that the defendant's creation of a passive Web site triggered jurisdiction since the company's intent was clearly devoid of geographic restraint—despite the fact that the defendant had not made any sales.

In the 1997 case of Zippo Mfg. Co. v. Zippo Dot Com, Inc, 952 F.Supp. 1119, 1120 (W.D.Pa. 1997), the California court stated: "We are being asked to determine whether Dot Com's conducting of electronic commerce with Pennsylvania residents constitutes the purposeful availment of doing business in Pennsylvania." The court held that agreements with Internet service providers in a state, permitting that state's subscriber to access a company's news service, and advertising on its Web page in the state, were sufficient to establish jurisdiction. It should be noted that in Zippo, in addition to agreements, actual sales were shown.

In 1997, the same New York court that had decided Bensusan found an absence of personal jurisdiction where the defendant did not contract to sell or actually sell any goods or services to customers in the forum state. The court acknowledged but refused to follow the rationale of the Inset and Maritz decis ions. In Hearst Corp. v. Goldberger, No. 96 CIV. 3620 PKL AJP, 1997 WL 97097 (S.D.N.Y. Feb. 26, 1997) SITE, a New Jersey defendant had posted a Web site on the Internet that advertised future legal information under the name esqwire.com. Hearst Corp., owner of the trademark "Esquire" for magazines, sued in New York. The court declined to assert jurisdiction because the defendant's activities consisted solely of posting information, but no products or services were available for purchase by New York residents.

While the law of Internet jurisdiction remains confusing, these decisions constitute the existing jurisprudential framework for Web site businesses to consider when evaluating jurisdictional issues. These cases illustrate the unpredictable nature of the state of the law. Based upon the standards articulated in these cases, it would be advisable for a Web site holder to be particularly careful when utilizing interactive capability on a site. The cases in which jurisdiction has been found have one thing in common: the Web sites allowed for the immediate retransmission of information back to the Web site; the mere posting of information on a homepage is less likely to trigger jurisdiction.

Another consideration for a company that transacts business over the Internet is to limit Web site access from locales where they do not wish to be subject to jurisdiction. Indeed, businesses should not only gain an awareness of the potential costs of litigating in distant forums but also realize that the current state of the law may subject the company to the law of the state that is most favorable to the claim that plaintiff will assert.

Tax Issues

Similar to jurisdictional issues, tax implications relating to Internet commerce are fraught with uncertainty. The dissolution of meaningful geographical boundaries raises questions as to where a taxable event occurs in a commercial transaction over the Internet. While it is difficult to determine with certainty how tax implications will be resolved, it is important for a company to be familiar with the pertinent issues.

Federal

In Congress, a bill entitled the Internet Tax Freedom Act has been introduced, which recommends the imposition of a moratorium on state and local taxes on the use of the Internet. The bill also requires the President to prepare policy recommendations on the taxation of sales made on the Internet. The reasoning behind the bill is essentially to protect interstate commerce from the effects of taxation while a more sophisticated analysis is conducted.

The Treasury Department published a Discussion Paper, which is a fact-gathering effort designed to resolve the uncertainty about taxation of online commerce. Interestingly, the Treasury Department has advocated a principle of neutrality that rejects the need for new or additional taxes on electronic transactions. It recommends that all income be treated equally, regardless of the means by which it entered commerce. As authority for its position, the Treasury Department notes that foreign businesses are not taxed for soliciting and filling orders from U.S. customers.

Internationally, foreign companies typically pay taxes on income generated from the U.S. if the income is attributable to a "permanent establishment" located in the United States. Taxation of foreign companies is made possible by treaties with those foreign countries. Under the approach proposed by the Department of Treasury, a foreign corporation that advertised on a home page would probably avoid taxation. Issues that may arise in connection with international business include how a permanent establishment will be determined, and whether a foreign corporation's use of a United States server will lead to jurisdiction.

State

State taxation issues are similarly clouded. As a rule, a state must satisfy the nexus requirement under the due process and commerce clauses of the U.S. Constitution in order to tax an out-of-state business. The Commerce Clause, which would likely govern any Internet tax analysis, requires a "substantial nexus," and connection, for the imposition of taxes. In construing the meaning of "substantial nexus," the Supreme Court has relied upon the determination of physical presence. The Court has applied this test to the mail-order industry (which bears a strong resemblance to Internet commerce), where the only contact with the taxing state is by mail or "common carrier."

In the 1992 case of Quill v. North Dakota, 504 U.S. 298 1992, the Court held that simple contact with a common carrier does not constitute a sufficient nexus with the taxing state. The Court noted that the sufficiency of a nexus "may turn on the presence in the taxing state of a small sales force, plant or property." In fact, Quill has been interpreted as permitting taxation of a mail-order company that sent employees to install software and make repairs subject to a service agreement (Orvis Co. Inc. v. Tax Appeals Tribunal of the State of New York, 654 N.E. 2d 954, 962 (1995)). Other courts have held that maintenance of offices, warehouses, equipment, and personnel in a state create a sufficient nexus.

The logical argument in favor of Internet commerce holds that Internet commerce and the mail-order business are analogous. The argument posits that the Internet operates like a common carrier such as a shipper or courier. Obviously, states will attempt to discount the analogous nature of these two industries in an effort to protect their tax bases.

Some states have taken a more Internet-supportive stance. For example, New York Governor George Pataki proclaimed in January 1996 that he had directed the State Dept. of Taxation and Finance to implement recommendations for exempting Internet access service from New York sales tax.

Intellectual Property

Many legal issues relating to the Internet deal with measures of protection for ideas and information a person or company may release into cyberspace. Traditionally, the appropriate protections for intellectual property were copyright, trademark, and patent. While these mechanisms are applicable to Internet commerce, some new protections have emerged with the growth of the Internet.

Copyright laws protect original works of authorship fixed in any tangible medium of expression. While notice is not required for copyright to exist (as copyright subsists automatically the moment a work is created and fixed in a tangible medium) notice is required for one to bring an action for copyright infringement. Notice typically includes the symbol of a circled © the name of the author, and the date.

Proof of copyright infringement requires the following elements: a copyright owned by the plaintiff; access by the defendant to the copyrighted material; and a substantial similarity between the copyrighted material and the defendant's material.

Copyright grants the following exclusive rights to the owner of the copyright: reproduction rights; derivation rights (or the right to prepare works derived from the copyrighted work); distribution rights relating to the copyrighted work; the right to perform the copyrighted work; and the right to publicly display the copyrighted work.

A trademark is a word or symbol that distinguishes a good from other goods; similarly, a service mark is a word or symbol which distinguishes the services of one from the services of another. Trade names are names used to identify a business or vocation. Trade names are not protected under federal law, but only under state law.

As Internet addresses become identifiable with the names of certain businesses, those addresses, or domain names, acquire value and demand protection. Just as traditional storefronts battle for the rights to use certain names and associate those names with their businesses, so too do Internet businesses. Domain names have become an important aspect of Internet commerce; consequently, administration and regulation of domain names assumes a heightened level of importance.

Internic, the entity that currently administers domain names, will register domain names on a first-come, first-served basis only if the applicant warrants that 1) the applicant has a right to use the name; 2) the applicant has a bona fide intention to use the domain name regularly; 3) the use does not infringe upon any third party's intellectual property right, including those mentioned above; 4) the applicant does not intend to use the domain name for any unlawful use; and 5) the applicant agrees to resolve disputes through arbitration.

The cost to register a domain name is $100 for two years and $50 a year for each additional year. To register for a domain name, the registrant selects its domain name, and submits an application representing that the registration of the domain name does not interfere with or infringe upon the rights of any third party (to the best of the applicant's knowledge).

For businesses participating in Internet commerce, issues may arise where the use of a domain name conflicts with another's trademark. In such a case, the owner of the domain name can continue to use the domain name if the date he first used the name predates the trademark owner's first use of its trademark and/or the effective date of registration. The owner of a domain name may also enjoy continued use of the name if the owner provides Internic with a certified copy of its own trademark registration identical to the domain name showing that he is the actual owner of both the domain name and the trademark.

International Law

Any business planning to buy or sell its wares internationally must comply with all international import/export laws. Not only do individual countries each possess a distinct set of laws governing its particular commerce, but the United States regulates certain types of goods and services that companies may wish to export to these other countries. Given the esoteric nature of international business law, it is essential for a business desiring to reach out to other countries to consult an expert in the field.

It may be said that it is easier to run afoul of international commercial law in a cyberspace setting than it is to violate the same laws through traditional means of trade, given the ease with which information is communicated. The established infrastructure of international trade governance at present is not equipped to regulate Internet commerce. Import/export issues have traditionally been identified by third parties that facilitate and broker international commerce. Shipping companies and customs agencies process such transactions through a well-established system that has evolved over the years to guard against potential violations.

With Internet commerce, transactions may be consummated between private individuals or entities without the need for any third party to facilitate the deal—international commerce may take place in an instant, in cyberspace. The convenience of Internet commerce may seem like an advantage at first blush, but when that third party is a company's only insurance that international commercial laws have been satisfied, potential liabilities quickly multiply.

While it is impractical to outline the many potentially applicable regulations that may affect businesses participating in international commerce, a brief sampling of some of the obscure concerns should suggest to businesses that a tolerable comfort level is possible only with the involvement of appropriate experts. For example, any company selling goods in France may only advertise those goods in French (Is your Web site accessible in France?). Garments sold in Mexico must bear very specific labeling information (Have you ever shipped a T-shirt south of the border?). Certain software, computers and computer parts may not be exported to certain countries, as such exportation may threaten national security.

Just as our legal infrastructure is continually evolving, so too are the legal systems of other countries. The reconciliation of the laws of different countries and the facilitation of commerce between different countries are industries unto themselves, which should not be ignored by today's cyberspace companies. While the Internet may make it possible to bypass many of the traditional commercial procedures relating to international commerce, that fact offers no protection when a company is identified as having evaded international laws.

In addition to the complicated nature of international commerce, businesses must be aware of all laws and regulations governing their particular commodity—even when such business is consummated within the United States or even that company's home state. Food, alcohol, livestock, clothing, and nearly every other saleable commodity is governed by a unique set of regulations when it leaves a state, travels along federal highways to another state, and enters the destination state. It is important for an Internet company to view its export business, both international and intranational, as if it were doing business through the traditional avenues of commerce. A business would be well advised to consult a lawyer with a specialty in its specific industry to ensure that compliance with all pertinent laws is achieved.

Miscellaneous Concerns

Miscellaneous concerns continually emerge with regard to Internet commerce. For instance, unauthorized sites may be found to infringe upon trademark rights. The James Dean Foundation in Indiana has sued a California fan for using James Dean's name. In CMG WorldWide Inc. v. America Legends, defendant Ronald Martinetti is being sued for the unauthorized commercial use of James Dean's name and likeness by selling memorabilia over the Internet. Given the number of unauthorized fan sites, and links to sites containing the names and likenesses of celebrities, this may be an important issue for many businesses.

Links to other sites may also be the cause of litigation. Linking a Web page to another page within another site may cause people to miss the logo and advertisements present on that other company's front page. Since links are an important element of any company's Web page, it is important to consider the ramifications of linking to certain sites.

Many companies doing business over the Internet utilize standardized written agreements to structure relationships with their customers; oftentimes, this relationship is established and defined through standard terms and conditions to which the customer agrees in the initial session by simply clicking a button. These agreements are sometimes referred to as "click wrap" agreements. Because click-wrap agreements frequently go unread, there is some uncertainty as to whether an enforceable contract is formed through such a procedure. The click-wrap agreement is analogous to the "shrink-wrap" agreement used by software companies prior to the emergence of Internet commerce. Recently, in the case of ProCD Inc. v. Seidenberg, SITE the Seventh Circuit held that shrink-wrap agreements are generally enforceable. The same rationale employed by the 7th Circuit likely will be used to argue the enforceability of click-wrap agreements.

Conclusion

While it is uncertain how the law will evolve with regard to Internet commerce, companies may maximize their protection by remaining adequately informed of recent developments and trends. Canvassing some of the more reliable sites that track legal issues affecting the Internet should go a long way in alleviating the uncertainty that accompanies Internet commerce.

Some of the more helpful sites on the Internet are listed below:

- **Law of the Internet:** ljx.com/internet/ircomm.html
- **UF Law Internet & Computer Law Association:** grove.ufl.edu/~cmplaw/
- **Internet Law & Policy Forum:** www.ilpf.org/
- **Net Law News:** www.mindspring.com/~moceyuna/
- **Net Law U.S.:** www.netlaw.com/netwalus.htm
- **E-Commerce-The Legal Framework:** www.weblaw.co.uk/semb.htm

PART VI

Resources

We aren't so arrogant as to suggest you shouldn't continue to search for more information. Part VI offers a number of resources that might help make your store more efficient and profitable. There is also informationon some of the software companies that are important players in the online retailing world.

Part VI Table of Contents

CHAPTER TWENTY-TWO

General Resources

As an online storeowner, you'll spend nearly as much time learning about new technologies and new ways to better sell products online as you do actually selling products online. Not only is the Internet evolving with great rapidity, but the concept of selling on the Internet is even fresher and prone to dramatic change.

Throughout this book we have tried to combine research, technical information, and real-life experience to prepare you for your foray into the world of online retailing. However, it would be very arrogant of us (and foolish of you) to think there is nothing left to learn. The more time you devote to learning, the more successful your store will be. In this chapter we list a number of resources we think you should check out. This isn't intended to be a complete list of useful resources but represents some of the most helpful information we've come across.

Online and Traditional Information for Web Merchants

The magazines here exist online, offline, or in many cases, both. They provide a wide range of information, some of it specific to online storeowners, some of it more general but still useful. Some of these magazines could also provide a forum in which you can promote your store. We've listed the contact information for the various publishers and summary of what their publications have to offer the online storeowner.

CMP Media Inc./CMP Net

www.cmp.com

600 Community Drive
Manhasset, N.Y. 11030
Phone: 516-562-5000

CMP Media Inc. produces several publications, both online and offline. Of particular interest to online storeowners are *Internet Week*, *Information Week*, and *Techweb*.

Internet Week

techweb.cmp.com/internetwk/

E-mail: pbrown@cmp.com

Internet Week (online and offline) provides news, trends, and reviews. Telepath online provides daily updates on business and policy, technology platforms, information services. Edge of the Net updates readers on new Web technologies and allows users to get hands-on experience with some of these technologies. Insights & Incites provides weekly online industry features.

Among the resources in *Internet Week* are a collection of shareware downloads, commercial demos, career connections, and free product information. You can subscribe to receive an e-mail newsletter.

InformationWeek

techweb.cmp.com/iw/

E-mail: tuphoff@cmp.com

InformationWeek (online and offline) focuses on the concerns of business and technology managers and bills itself as "The Interactive Source For Managing Technology In Business." Like *Internet Week*, *InformationWeek* offers plenty of targeted news items. The Resource Center focuses on IT-related topics. IW Labs provides informative product reviews and news while the Date Book lists upcoming technology and business conferences and shows.

The IW Marketplace offers brief products descriptions, contact information, and links to a number of computer-related companies. You can also apply for a daily e-mail newsletter

TechWeb

www.techweb.com

TechWeb, updated throughout the day, is an outstanding resource for technology news, but doesn't stop there. TechTools provides Web development news, features, downloads, a database of nearly 300 tips and tricks, and a number of resource pages. There are also product reviews.

You can also check out the TechCalendar for trade shows in categories such as Internet/Online, Software & Services, Computing Platforms, etc. The TechWeb Technology Encyclopedia provides more than 10,000 definitions to technology terms and concepts.

As with *Internet Week* and *Information Week*, an e-mail newsletter is available.

Mecklermedia Corporation

www.mecklermedia.com

20 Ketchum St.
Westport, CT. 06880
Phone: 203-226-6967
Fax: 203-454-5840
E-mail: info@mecklermedia.com

Mecklermedia publications that are of interest to Web merchants *include Internet World*, *Web Week*, *Internet Shopper*, and *internet.com*. Mecklermedia is also the force behind Internet World and Internet Shopper conferences and exhibitions.

Internet World

www.iw.com

E-mail: letters@iw.com

Internet World analyzes industry issues and products for companies that use the Internet as an integral part of their business, helping those companies determine which new products are appropriate for them. *Internet World* has the largest circulation (350,000) of any Internet magazine.

Web Week

www.webweek.com

E-mail: letters@webweek.com

Web Week covers the latest innovations for the Internet. The *Web Week* Web site includes a database archive that provides an online directory of previously published Web Week articles, organized by subject and ranked according to timeliness.

Internet.com

www.internet.com

Internet.com is Mecklermedia's online news site and includes headlines, breaking news, and in-depth analysis of business-related Internet issues. InternetNews.com, which can be found at the Internet.com home page, features daily news in several categories including business and e-commerce. It also includes WebDeveloper.com and the E-Business guide, which online storeowners will find useful.

Ziff-Davis

www.ziffdavis.com

One Park Avenue
New York, NY 10016-5801
Phone: 212-503-3500
Fax: 212-503-4599

Among many other publications, Ziff-Davis publishes *Interactive Week* and *ZD Internet* magazine as well as producing the ZDNet Web site, which is jammed packed with information and resources.

Interactive Week

www.interactive-week.com/intweek

100 Quentin Roosevelt Boulevard, Suite 400
Garden City, NY 11530
E-mail: info@zdnet.com

Interactive Week is available online and offline. The online version offers daily news updates, Web reviews, and financial news. There are also available downloads and a calendar of computer industry events. *Interactive Week* covers all aspects of interactive technology products, issues, events, services, strategies, alliances, and key players.

Free subscriptions to the magazine are available through an application process in which the applicant must prove they make key decisions regarding interactive products and services for his or her company. *Interactive Week* is a joint venture with Interactive Enterprises.

ZD Internet Magazine

www.zdnet.com/zdimag

P.O. Box 55485
Boulder, CO 80322-5485
E-mail: info@zdnet.com

ZD Internet Magazine is an integrated print publication and Web site dedicated to reviewing Internet and intranet products such as Web servers, browsers authoring tools, Internet e-mail and traffic management software. The focus is business with information on new technologies, and creating Web sites.

There is an archive of labs (reviews) and Web site makeovers as well as a section dedicated to Internet Service Providers (ISPZone). The WholeWeb Catalog includes tips and tricks, product information, and zones dedicated to browsers, chat, e-commerce, HTML, mail, plug-ins, Usenet, and VRML. More than 10,000 titles are available for download.

ZDNet

www.zdnet.com

ZDNet is one of the Web's leading sources for computing and Internet information. ZDNet offers news, product information, a software library, a Web catalog, and Computer Shopper NetBuyer.

CommerceNet

www.commerce.net

4005 Miranda Avenue, Suite 175
Palo Alto, CA 94304
Phone: 415-858-1936
Fax: 415-858-1936
E-mail: info@commerce.net

CommerceNet is the leading industry consortium, dedicated to accelerating the growth of Internet commerce and creating business opportunities for our members. CommerceNet draws its strength from its broad base of members and global partners, comprised of industry and technology leaders. It creates value by bringing together Information Technology vendors and users who possess key pieces of the IMarket puzzle and helping them see where their pieces fit.

E Business Magazine

www.hp.com/Ebusiness/

E Business resides on Hewlett Packard's Web site and includes features such as "Small Business on the Net" and "Spotlighting Your Site" with continuing features E-Commerce, E in Action, E on the Edge, E Tools, E Talks Tech, and E Reads. This is an excellent resource for anyone conducting electronic business.

NeTProfessional

www.netprolive.com

612 Howard Street, Sixth Floor
San Francisco, CA 94105
Phone: 415.882.9502
Fax: 415.957.1911
E-mail: editor@netprolive.com

NeTProfessional is geared toward interactive professionals who work on the Mac.

Wilson Internet Services/ Wilson Web

www.wilsonweb.com

P.O. Box 308
Rocklin, CA 95677
Phone: 916-652-4659
E-mail: rfwilson@wilsonweb.com

Dr. Ralph F. Wilson is the director of Wilson Internet Services, which provides services and consulting in Web site design and for online stores. Among other things, Wilson Web offers the Web Commerce Today e-mail newsletter and the Electronic Commerce Research Room. Whether or not you seek Wilson's help in setting up your store, this site is a great resource.

General Business References

This book has focused on the unique aspects of starting and running an online store, but you should not ignore the more general challenges that face any new or existing business, whether it is online or not. The following Web sites, whether they deal directly with Web businesses or not, can be helpful.

The American Express Small Business Exchange

www.americanexpress.com/smallbusiness/

The American Express Small Business Exchange includes Business Planning and Resources, Expert Advice, Promote Your Business, Small Business Products and Services, Financial Planning Assistance, and Small Business News. There is also a guest column, a tip of the month, business-related features, and new product news.

EntreWorld: Entrepreneurs In Business

www.entreworld.org

EntreWorld bills itself as "A World of Resources for Entrepreneurs" and is presented by The Ewing M. Kauffman Foundation for Entrpreneurial Leadership. There are sections for starting your business, running your business, rapid growth, and supporting entrepreneurship. Each section is further divided into subtopics, which link you to relevant resources.

Hewlett-Packard's Small Business Home Page

www.hp.com/sbso

Hewlett-Packard weighs in with a Web site of its own that includes a number of areas of interest such as networking, computing, and information storage. Again, HP shows you which of its products can be useful for you in your business. There is also a small business resources section that links you to helpful sites for travel, marketing, financial, and more.

Home-Based Business Resource Center

www.be-your-own-boss.com

This site offers a number of inexpensive ($4.95 plus shipping) reports about, among other things, starting a mail order business. The reports on starting a mail order business include: "Mail Order Advertising Directory," "The Beginner's Mail Order Business Guide," "Mail Order Laws and Regulations," "Mail Order—Most Common Mistakes," "Controlling Mail Order's Key Expenses," "State Sales Tax Guide," "Create Circulars, Small Brochures and Sales Letters," "Mail Order Bookkeeping

Basics," "The Postal Savings Guide," "The Ultimate Profit Maker," "How To Write Order Pulling Ads," and "Mailing Lists Can Be Profitable." You can order any five reports for $14.95.

The Home Office Association of America

www.hoaa.com

The Home Office Association of America is, as the name indicates, for those of you starting or running a business from your home. Included is an online newsletter with features on topics such as marketing and technology. Membership is $49 ($79 for Canadian members, $100 for international members).

The Idea Cafe

www.ideacafe.com

The Idea Cafe aims to be a friendly source of business information and succeeds in that mission. The Idea cafe was founded by Rhonda Abrams, author of the best-selling book *The Successful Business Plan: Secrets and Strategies*. She also is a small business columnist and runs Abrams Business Strategies, a business-planning firm. The advisory committee includes HotWired President Andrew Anker, Internet Shopping Network Co-Founder Bill Rollinson and Randy Haykin, founder of Electric Minds and former vice president of Yahoo!. Abrams writes a regular column and features include the Cyber Schmooz, a networking opportunity for business owners looking for help or advice. Definitely worth a visit.

The Microsoft Small Business Resource

www.microsoft.com/smallbiz/

The Microsoft Small Business Resource includes timely information on topics such as changing tax laws and how they effect your business. Not surprisingly, the Small Business Software resource points you toward Microsoft products. Jane Applegate, author of *Strategies for Small Business Success*, has a Q&A column that includes issues such as online sales and marketing and business stagnation. You can submit business and technology questions to her through e-mail.

NetBITS

www.netbits.net/

NetBITS is a free, weekly, electronic publication that provides Internet information to people who spend significant amounts of time online for professional (or personal) reasons.

Research Institute for Small and Emerging Business

www.nemonline.org/sbfa/

The Research Institute for Small and Emerging Business (RISEbusiness) is an independent, nonprofit research and educational organization that focuses on nonpartisan policy research on small and emerging enterprises. Formerly The Small Business Foundation of America, RISEbusiness acts a research clearinghouse, sponsors and commissions studies, and gets information to policy makers, the media, and business advocacy groups.

SCORE (Service Corps of Retired Executives)

www.score.org

The SCORE Association (Service Corps of Retired Executives) is a resource partner with the U.S. Small Business Administration and is dedicated to aiding in the formation and success of small business. SCORE has more than 12,000 volunteer business counselors who provide free and confidential business counseling. You can get help through e-mail or locate a local chapter near you to meet with a local business counselor. You can link to your local chapter's Web site through SCORE's Web site.

Small Business Administration

www.sba.gov

The U.S. Small Business Administration (SBA) was created by Congress in 1953 to help entrepreneurs form successful small businesses. The SBA has offices in every state which offer financing, training, and advocacy for small firms. You can find information on your local SBA office here.

Smart Business Supersite

www.smartbiz.com

The Smart Business Supersite provides free how-to resources to help you run your business. A plethora of links sends you to various other Web sites for business owners. There are also daily tips and news and free business and computer catalogs available. An outstanding place to begin your search for help as a small business owner.

Visa's Small Business Site

www.visa.com/cgi-bin/vee/fb/smbiz/main.html?2+0

Visa's Small Business Site features a monthly commentary by a small business expert about a different topic. There are links that cover everything from business help for women and minorities to trademarks and tax codes as well as financing and venture capital. There's also a Success of the Month feature, a survey, and a newsletter.

Women Biz

www.frsa.com/womenbiz/

The WomenBiz site is maintained by FRS Associations, and intranet design and implementation company specializing in Database to Web Interconnectivity. The site includes the WomenBiz Discussion Forum.

Working Solo Online

www.workingsolo.com

Working Solo is a center for entrepreneurial resources. Working Solo helps entrepreneurs in all types of business, at all levels of experience. The company produces books, audio tapes, a free monthly e-mail newsletter, an online forum, and seminars, all specifically designed for solo business owners.

Online Legal Advice

The best legal advice you'll find will hopefully come from your lawyer. However, each time you sit down with your lawyer it costs you money. While there is no replacement for a good lawyer, these Web sites can provide some decent advice free of charge.

The Cyberlaw Encyclopedia

gahtan.com/techlaw/home.htm

The Cyberlaw Encyclopedia includes information on subjects such as copyright law, Internet and online banking, taxation in cyberspace and much more. The site is maintained by Alan Gahtan, who holds an M.B.A. from York University's Schulich School of Business and a B.A. from the University of Toronto. He graduated from Osgoode Hall Law School in 1987.

FindLaw

www.findlaw.com

FindLaw offers links to cases and codes, law firms, state and federal government resources, and more. You can also go straight to the Law Crawler at www.lawcrawler.com, a legal search engine powered by Alta Vista.

Internet Law & Policy Forum

www.ilpf.org

The ILPF has a number of working groups, the reports of which you can check out at this site. ILPF says it, "supports the development of an international network of reporters to provide timely and accurate information on legal and policy developments that affect the Internet around the globe." There are also links to Internet law resources including the World Internetworking Alliance, the World Wide Web consortium, The Internet Legal Practice Newsletter, and The Netlaw Library.

Law of the Internet

ljx.com/internet/ircomm.html

The Law of the Internet site offers Articles on issues such as click-wrap licenses, data security, Web site development, business on the Web, state and local taxes, and more from sources such as the *New York Law Journal* and the *National Law Journal.* You can also link to specific case briefings.

Net Law News

www.mindspring.com/~moceyuna/

Net Law News is exactly that. It's also a great place to keep up on the ever-changing Internet law. There are timely articles on new developments and you can also sift through archived news on contract, copyright, privacy, trademark, trade secrets, and civil procedure issues.

Net Law U.S.

www.netlaw.com/netlawus.htm

NetLaw U.S. is published by Lance Rose, author *of NetLaw: Your Rights in the Online World*. It includes features on legal issues and of course also exists to promote Rose's book.

The Nolo Press Self-Help Law Center

www.nolo.com

The Nolo Press Self-Help Law Center is a general legal resource site. Though it isn't focused on Internet law, it is helpful for any business owner. Not all your legal concerns will be related to e-commerce or the Internet. Nolo's legal encyclopedia has information pertaining to small businesses that is worth checking out. You can also download or purchase Nolo software.

UF Law Internet & Computer Law Association

grove.ufl.edu/~cmplaw/

This is an organization of the University of Florida College of Law. It includes legal resource links and a Supreme Court Decision search.

Web Law: E-Commerce—The Legal Framework

www.weblaw.co.uk/semb.htm

This site has some useful articles on Internet law and also provides a list of services that the form of Halberstam Elias & Co. can provide.

Research Firms

A number of research companies provide analysis of technology and its impact on various markets. Many of the reports generated by these companies are too expensive for small operations, but some of the Web sites provide key findings that in some cases are worth looking at.

Forrester

www.forrester.com

1033 Massachusetts Avenue
Cambridge, MA 02138
Phone: 617-497-7090

Forrester analyzes and predicts the impact of technology on large companies, consumers, and society. Forrester offers Senior Management Research, Information Technology Research, and New Media Research. In 1997, Forrester ranked number 12 on the *Forbes* list of The 200 Best Small Companies in America.

International Data Group/International Data Corporation

www.idc.com

Five Speen Street
Framingham, MA 01701
Phone: 508-872-8200
Fax: 508-935-4015
E-mail: idcinfo@idcresearch.com

International Data Corporation (IDC) and its subsidiary IDC/LINK, provide information technology data, analysis, and consulting. IDC provides continuous information services, consulting services, and interactive delivery.

Jupiter Communications

www.jup.com

627 Broadway
New York, NY 10012
Phone: 212-780-6060
Fax: 212-780-6075
E-mail: jupiter@jup.com

Jupiter Communications is a highly respected and growing new media research firm focusing on consumer interactive products and services. Jupiter's products are divided into four areas: consumer content, digital commerce, online advertising, and consumer Internet technologies. Jupiter organizes conferences and seminars, offers Strategic Planning Services, and publishes newsletters, a Web advertising data report, and in-depth research reports.

Zona Research

www.zonaresearch.com

900 Veterans Boulevard, Suite 500
Redwood City, CA 94063
Phone: 415-568-5700
Fax: 415-306-2420
E-mail: info@zonaresearch.com

Zona Research, a subsidiary of IntelliQuest, provides information and advice to the Internet industry through syndicated subscription services and reports as well as custom and proprietary consulting and panel services. Among Zona's key clients and customers are Microsoft, Sun, AT&T, Apple, Netscape, MCI, IBM, Hewlett Packard, and Silicon Graphics.

CHAPTER TWENTY-THREE

Software

Considering how quickly software changes, it would be unwise to recommend one piece of software exclusively over another without doing extensive testing. However, we do feel it is necessary to provide a list of options for those of you who are ready to open a Web store. This chapter provides contact information and a quick summary for a number of software options in various categories. This is not meant to be a complete list. If a product isn't mentioned here, that does not mean it is unworthy of your interest. As with all purchases, consider your options, read product reviews and know exactly what you are getting.

Merchant Servers/Storefronts

Most major merchant server offerings are not inexpensive. While the basic server market has seen prices go all the way down to free (Microsoft's Internet Information Server and Apache), merchant servers have remained at a premium. Three levels have emerged: Sub $5,000 offerings consist primarily of add-on server extensions that add robust commerce capabilities to existing Web sites. Full-fledged packages that are sold for between $5,000–$25,000 include such products as IBM's Net.Commerce and Microsoft's Merchant Server. Then there are the very high-end solutions that include offerings from Netscape's Actra Division, Open Market, and Broadvision. These typically include a wealth of additional commerce-specific features.

Breakthrough Software

www.breakthroughsoftware.com

2087 Landings Drive
Mountain View, CA 94043
Phone: 650-967-3700
Fax: 650-967-3735
E-mail: info@breakthroughsoftware.com

Product: Internet Business Breakthrough

Internet Business Breakthrough allows you to create your store, take secure orders, update your site with 50 design templates, and offer surveys and discussion groups. The product is geared toward business owners who have little or no Web design experience and costs $249.

Broadvision

www.broadvision.com

585 Broadway
Redwood City, CA 94063
Phone: 650-261-5100 or 800-269-9375
Fax: 650-261-5900
E-mail: Select "Feedback" from tool bar

PRODUCT: One-To-One Commerce

One-To-One Commerce is a turnkey solution that delivers secure and personalized commerce production systems. One-To-One supplies a packaged application that includes security features, personalization, and the Intuitive Dynamic Command Center and Content Management Center for ease-of-operation by non-technical merchants.

Forman Interactive

www.forman.com

201 Water Street
Brooklyn, NY 11201-1174
Phone: 718-522-2260
Fax: 718-522-0267
E-mail: mailto:sales@forman.com

PRODUCT: Internet Creator

Internet Creator is geared toward small and mid-sized businesses. There's no need to know HTML and a site-building wizard completes 50 percent to 70 percent of your site. Creator costs $149 and includes a shopping cart.

GoldPaint Systems Inc.

www.goldpaint.com

Phone: 909-693-0458
E-mail: contact@goldpaint.com

PRODUCT: GoldPaint Shopping Cart

GoldPaint Shopping Cart ($990) has the right price for a small startup operation. If you know how to program in HTML, the TAME HTML extensions allow you to easily add storefront capability.

IBM North America

www.ibm.com

1133 Westchester Avenue
White Plains, NY 10604
Phone: 800-IBM-3333
E-mail: ibm_direct@vnet.ibm.com

PRODUCT: IBM Net.Commerce Group

The IBM Net.Commerce Group includes a Web server and a server for store operations. Pricing begins at $4,995.

iCat Corp.

www.icat.com

1420 Fifth Avenue, Suite 1800
Seattle, WA 98101-2333
Phone: 888-533-8800 or 206-505-8800
Fax: 206-505-8810
E-mail: info@icat.com

PRODUCTS: Starter Store; Electronic Commerce Suite, Lemonade Stand

The iCat Starter Store program allows you to choose from 20 store designs and your store is guaranteed to be up and running within 30 days. Each store includes a product index, secure order placement, and basic search capabilities. Starter Store costs $4,695 and includes six months of hosting.

The Electronic Commerce Suite comes in two versions—Standard ($3,495) and Professional ($9,995). The Standard version is for business that want to create catalogs using predefined layouts. The Professional Edition is for Web developers who want high-end features and the ability to customize catalogs.

A promising new product code-named Lemonade Stand is also on the way. Lemonade Stand is an entry-level product geared toward the businessperson with limited technical ability.

Icentral, Inc.

www.icentral.com

World Headquarters
225 North University Avenue
Provo, UT 84601
Phone: 801-373-4347
Fax: 801-373-7211
E-mail: info@icentral.com

PRODUCTS: ShopSite Manager, Shop Site Pro

ShopSite Manager costs $495 and is recommended for smaller stores. No HTML is necessary and Manager can handle any HTML, Javascript, Java applet, or ActiveX control. Shop Site Pro costs $1,295 and is designed for the experienced Web designer or merchant. It handles larger databases than Manager and includes a fully integrated in-store search engine.

Inex Corp.

www.inex-corp.com

20 Toronto Street, Suite 400
Toronto, Ontario
CANADA
M5C 2B8
Phone: 416-214-2250
Fax: 416-214-4675
E-mail: info@inex-corp.com

PRODUCT: Commerce Court; Commerce Court for Site Server

INEX Internet Commerce Applications are geared toward small to medium-sized businesses. The host components of the two products provide multiple store environments. The clients components allow you to set up, modify, track performance, and download orders. INEX Applications utilize Microsoft's Active Server Pages.

The Internet Factory

www.ifact.com

6654 Koll Center Parkway #150
Pleasanton, CA 94566
Phone: 510-426-7763
Fax: 510-426-9538
E-mail: customer_service@ifact.com

PRODUCT: Merchant Builder

Merchant Builder comes with automatic catalog layout, customer service, advanced Web server, CyberCash, ICVerify and First Virtual payment solutions, financial reporting, and development tools for merchant applications. The single store copy costs $1,495.

INTERSHOP Communications Inc.

www.intershop.com

600 Townsend Street, Suite 500
San Francisco, CA 94103
Phone: 415-373-1530 or 800-736-5197
Fax: 415-373-1536
E-mail: info@intershop.com

PRODUCT: INTERSHOP Online

Online includes a database, online payment systems, and various Web servers. INTERSHOP Online uses Sybase's System XI database manager, one of the top SQL server products. The Windows NT version costs $4,995 while the Unix model is $7,995. INTERSHOP Online is recommended for larger stores.

Lotus

www3.lotus.com

55 Cambridge Parkway
Cambridge, MA 02142
Phone: 617-577-8500
E-mail: domino_server@lotus.com

PRODUCT: Domino.Merchant Server Pack

Domino.Merchant includes the Domino Web server. Sie Creator helps you register visitors, maintain a catalog, accept orders, process payments securely, calculate taxes and shipping charges, and generate invoices. Price for a single server is $3,495.

Mercantec, Inc.

www.mercantec.com

3080 Ogden Avenue, Suite 302
Lisle, IL 60532
Phone: 630-305-3200
Fax: 630-305-6065
E-mail: info@mercantec.com

Product: SoftCart

Softcart has a simple HTML-based approach. This is a piece of software for those who can deal with HTML code and databases. It can accommodate a wide range of payment systems, databases, Web servers and browsers, order delivery options, and tax and shipping options. SoftCart is recommended for medium to large stores. For $1,500, you get a single store license, free upgrades, and one year of technical support. You can also pay as little as $100 per month through selected Mercantec Premier ISP partners.

Microsoft

www.microsoft.com

One Microsoft Way
Redmond, WA 98052-6399
Phone: 425-882-8080
Fax: 425-936-7329
E-mail: info@microsoft.com

Product: Site Server, Enterprise Edition

Site Server's Enterprise Edition includes Commerce Server (formerly Merchant Server 1.0), a personalization system, site analysis, usage analysis, and improved order processing that includes tax calculation, inventory look-up, and sample software from VerFone for processing credit card transactions. Site Server's Enterprise Edition costs $4,999.

Netscape

www.netscape.com

501 E. Middlefield Road
Mountain View, CA 94043
Phone: 650-254-1900
Fax: 415/528-4124
E-mail: info@netscape.com

Product: Netscape Merchant System, Commerce Xpert

Netscape Merchant System provides companies with the ability to set up and manage their own storefronts on the Internet and other IP networks. It also allows enterprises to set up online electronic malls for hosting hundreds of stores and managing the sales of thousands of products. Merchant System is a suite that allows storeowners to display hundreds of products, update information easily, and handle transactions securely. It includes a shopping basket service, search capability, and shopping and sales monitoring.

Open Market, Inc.

www.openmarket.com

245 First Street
Cambridge, MA 02142
Phone: 617-949-7196
E-mail: investor@openmarket.com

PRODUCT: Transact

This award-winning Transact provides a complete set of end-to-end commerce services including online customer authentication and authorization; online order and payment processing; automated tax and shipping calculations; online order tracking and status; and online customer service.

O'Reilly

www.ora.com

101 Morris Street
Sebastopol, CA 95472
Phone: 800-998-9938 or 800-889-8969
Fax: 707-829-0104
E-mail: nuts@ora.com

PRODUCT: WebSite Professional, WebBoard

WebSite Professional is an award-winning Web server. This is a good alternative for someone who wants to buy a server while receiving a number of bundled tools. O'Reilly also offers WebBoard, which allows customers to interact through discussion forums and real-time chat.

Viaweb

www.viaweb.com

56 JFK Street
Cambridge, MA 02138
Phone: 617-876-2692
Fax: 617-354-2624
E-mail: info@viaweb.com

Products: Viaweb Store, Viamall

Viaweb Store has twice been rated the No. 1 online store software by *PC Magazine*. Viaweb Store allows you to create your site on Viaweb's server using a point and click interface on a normal browser. Viaweb hosts the finished site (on Viamall) and orders are accepted using SSL encryption. Viamall receives more than 8.1 million page views per month and grosses more than $1.6 million per month. Pricing is $100 per month for stores selling 50 items and 300 a month for stores selling up to 1,000 items.

Virtual Spin

www.virtualspin.com

1307 120th Avenue NE
Bellevue, WA 98005-2124
Phone: 425-974-1100 or 888-853-5600
Fax: 425-974-1200
E-mail: info@virtualspin.com

Product: Cartalog

Cartalog is a subscription-based service that offers a variety of online credit card processing options through Cardservice International and CyberCash. Cartalog can be used by people with little computer or Web experience. Pricing begins at $49 a month.

The Vision Factory

www.thevisionfactory.com

269 Mt. Hermon Road, Suite 105
Scotts Valley, CA 95066
Phone: 408-461-2100
Fax: 408-461-9255
E-mail: info@thevisionfactory.com

Product: Cat@log

Cat@log, with a cost of $4,995, is for those of you with big budgets. You can build a storefront using any database, HTML editor, and transaction processing software. This is a professional level tool that leaves a lot of the work up to you.

Wilson Internet Services

www.wilsonweb.com

P.O. Box 308
Rocklin, CA 95677
Phone: 916-652-4659
E-mail: rfwilson@wilsonweb.com

Wilson Internet Services will set up your online store with pricing dependant upon the size of your store and, therefore, the software needed. If you're interested in having Wilson Internet Services set up your online store, you can check out its list of clients and link to those sites to see samples of Wilson's work.

Site Analysis

For most small operations, WebTrends' low-end log tool will be plenty. However, as your store grows you may decide to move up to more robust solutions. Here are several leading products.

Accrue

www.accrue.com

1275 Orleans Drive
Sunnyvale, CA 94089-1138
Phone: 408-542-8900
Fax: 408-541-1874
E-mail: info@accrue.com

PRODUCT: Insight

Insight provides a picture of a visitor's travels, including where he came from, wait time, and how successful a visitor was in downloading a particular page. It also offers remote access and is password protected.

net.Genesis

www.netgen.com

215 First Street
Cambridge, MA 02142
Phone: 617-577-9800
Fax: 617-577-9850
E-mail: sales@netgen.com

PRODUCT: net.Analysis

net.Analysis helps provide information on your most successful marketing programs, how long visitors stay at your site, which parts of your site are most popular with visitors from other countries, and how many visitors who click through banner ads actually iew in-depth product information.

WebTrends Corporation

www.egsoftware.com

621 SW Morrison, Suite 1300
Portland, OR 97205
Phone: 503-294-7025
Fax: 503-294-7130
E-mail: sales@egSoftware.com

PRODUCTS: WebTrends Log Analyzer, Professional Suite, Enterprise Suite

WebTrends (formerly e.g. Software) provides site analysis tools ranging from $299 to $1,499.

HTML Editors

Most people have their own favorite HTML editor. Here are a few significant products worth looking into.

Allaire Corp.

www.allaire.com

One Alewife Center
Cambridge, MA 02140
Phone: 617-761-2000 or 888-939-2545
Fax: 617-761-2001
E-mail: info@allaire.com

PRODUCT: HomeSite

HomeSite is a powerful, easy-to-use, award-winning HTML editor. HomeSite's internal browser allows you to preview your pages as you work. It has support for various tags.

Bare Bones Software

www.barebones.com

P.O. Box 1048
Bedford, MA 01730
Phone: 617-778-3100
Fax: 617-778-3111
E-mail: sales@barebones.com

PRODUCT: BBEdit

BBEdit is the leader of the Macintosh HTML editors.

Microsoft

www.microsoft.com

One Microsoft Way
Redmond, WA 98052-6399
Phone: 425-882-8080
Fax: 425-936-7329
E-mail: info@microsoft.com

PRODUCT: FrontPage 98

FrontPage 98 is Microsoft's visual page editor. It has a lot of easy-to-follow wizards to help you get pages up easily. Additionally, many Web hosting companies feature FrontPage Web hosting extensions. These extensions let you insert special services such as CGI scripts and search engines.

Macromedia

www.macromedia.com

600 Townsend Street
San Francisco, CA 94103
Phone: 415-252-2000
Fax: 415-626-0554
E-mail: international@macromedia.com

PRODUCT: Dreamweaver

Dreamweaver is a new product aimed at people who don't like what visual editors do to your code. The product allows the user to visually edit pages without disturbing the underlying code. When editing HTML in text mode, Dreamweaver works directly with the two best HTML text editors on the market—HomeSite (Windows) and BBEdit (Mac).

Chat/Message Boards

Chat and message boards can help you build a community of loyal customers. These are some of the top packages that will help you take your store to the next level.

EarthWeb

www.earthweb.com

3 Park Avenue
New York, NY 10016
Phone: 212-725-6550
Fax: 212-725-6559
E-mail: info@earthweb.com

Product: Moderator

Moderator allows you to organize online events including discussion groups, marketing focus groups, interviews, etc. It is available in Java and HTML formats. There is a $5,000 licensing fee for an unlimited number of users and chat channels on a single server including one year of technical support.

Emaze

www.emaze.com

2007 Cutwater Ct., Suite 1000
Reston, VA 20191
Phone: 703-476-6665
Fax: 703-716-0691
E-mail: sales@emaze.com

Products: ScriptWizard, WebThread

ScriptWizard creates scripts to process forms and surveys. WebThread helps you create and manage Web-based discussion forums. Both cost $50.

eShare Technologies

www.eshare.com

51 Mall Drive
Commack, NY 11725
Phone: 516-864-4700 or 1-888-ESHARE4
Fax: 516-864-0833
E-mail: info@eshare.com

Products: Expressions Starter Suite, Expressions Interaction Suite, Expressions Advanced Community Building Suite.

eShare offers three levels of products. The Starter Suite base pricing begins at $995. It is an entry level, server-based software solution that adds real-time interaction to your site. The Interaction Suite and Advanced Community Building Suite both start at $3,995.

ichat, Inc.

www.ichat.com

11100 Metric Boulevard, Building 7
Austin, TX 78758
Phone: 512-425-2200 or 888-242-8669
Fax: 512-719-8225
E-mail: Go to www.ichat.com/sales/contact.html and fill out form.

PRODUCTS: Rooms, Message Boards

Expensive, but with high-end features and scalability, Ichat Rooms adds interactive, real-time communications to your Web site. Ichat Message Boards delivers a searchable, hierarchically organized discussion forum.

Paralogic

www.paralogic.com

2140 Peralta Boulevard, Suite 109
Fremont, CA 94536
Phone: 510-795-0559
Fax: 510-795-6181
E-mail: info@paralogic.com

PRODUCT: ParaChat Professional

ParaChat sells severs but also offers an inexpensive outsourcing service. ParaChat Professional has a room limit of 25users and costs $50 per month if paid annually and $75 per month if paid monthly. It allows you to customize and control your chat room, and offers chat transcripts. There is a $100 setup fee.

E-Mail

As we have emphasized throughout the book, e-mail is critical to the success of your Web store. These are a couple of packages to check out.

Pegasus Mail

www.pmail.com

Pegasus Mail is a freeware product, but one with a lot of powers. You can easily download off the Internet. Go to the Web site and download it.

Qualcomm

www.eudora.com

6455 Lusk Boulevard
San Diego, CA 92121-2779
Phone: 800-2-EUDORA or 619-658-1291
Fax: 619-587-1121
E-mail: eudora-rep@qualcomm.com

PRODUCTS: Eudora Pro, Eudora Light

Eudora Pro has more than 18 million users worldwide. It allows you to sort and manage your e-mail, access multiple accounts, and reply with automated responses to frequent requests. The price is $39 for one user. Eudora Light offers many of the same features for free.

Electronic Software Distribution

Providing Electronic Software Distribution can give you an advantage of your competitors. Here are a few companies that provide ESD tools. For more on ESD, see Chapter 16.

CyberSource Corporation

www.cybersource.com

550 S. Winchester Boulevard, Suite 301
San Jose, CA 95128-2545
Phone: 800-530-9095 or 408-556-9100
Fax: 408-241-9270
E-mail: Go to Contact CyberSource at Web site

PRODUCTS: CommerceEZ, CommerceFLEX

CyberSource specializes in secure electronic distribution of software and digital products over the Internet. CyberSource offers CommerceEZ, a service that is best used for straightforward product and pricing offerings and CommerceFLEX, which is for more complex commerce offerings such as shopping carts.

Maagnum Commerce Services, Inc

www.safesell.com

420 Highland Avenue

P.O. Box 339

Cheshire, CT 06410
Phone: 203-699-8225
Fax: 203-699-8235
E-mail: info@safesell.com

PRODUCT: SafeSell Service

SafeSell Service is the company's flagship product. Options include SafeSell Starter for smaller stores; SoftSell Service for delivering software, music, and information over the Internet; SafeHost Plan, a comprehensive commerce hosting solution; and AllCommerce, the company's highest-end product. Maagnum also offers custom solutions.

Portland Software

www.portlandsoftware.com

1000 SW Broadway, Suite 1850
Portland, OR 97205
Phone: 888-ESD-MADE or 503-220-2300
Fax: 503-525-6802
E-mail: service@portsoft.com

PRODUCT: ZipLock

ZipLock is one of the leading methods of selling encrypted software products over the Internet. ZipLock transforms commerce processes including inventory creation, inventory management, the purchase process, licensing and product fulfillment, and database management and sales reporting.

Preview Software

www.previewsoft.com

1601 South DeAnza Boulevard, Suite 100
Cupertino, CA 95014
Phone: 408-873-3450
Fax: 408-873-3465
E-mail: info@previewsoft.com

PRODUCT: TimeLock

TimeLock is a complete ESD solution that provides secure encryption, try-and-buy, and other purchasing options.

SoftLock

www.softlock.com

399 Alexander Street
Rochester, N.Y. 14607
Phone: 716-546-1970

PRODUCT: SoftLock

SoftLock offers publishers, developers, and online merchants the locking tools necessary to conduct ESD.

TestDrive Corporation

www.testdrive.com

1397 Charleston Road
Mountain View, CA 94043
Phone: 415-237-6700
Fax: 415-237-6705
E-mail: support@testdrive.com

PRODUCT: TestDrive/Internet

TestDrive/Internet allows software merchants to offer electronic software distribution trial securely over the Internet. The user can then purchase the product using TestDrive's secure transaction technology or execute an uninstall of the product.

Personalization

Personalization tools help you create profiles of your customers and direct them toward other products that they might be interested in purchasing. Personalization is the future of retailing on the Web. While most personalization tools have not yet matured, many are already being used effectively by major retailers such as Amazon.com, Barnesandnoble.com and CDNow.

BroadVision

www.broadvision.com

585 Broadway
Redwood City, CA 94063
Phone: 650-261-5100 or 800-269-9375

PRODUCT: One-To-One Commerce

One-To-One Commerce enables companies with large, rapidly changing product lines to handle high-volume transactions. One-To-One Commerce delivers secure, personalized commerce production systems.

Firefly

www.firefly.com

Firefly Network, Inc.
One Broadway, 6th Floor
Cambridge, MA 02142
Phone: 617-528-1000
Fax: 617-577-7220
E-mail: info@firefly.net

PRODUCTS: Passport Office, Catalog Navigator

Passport Office enables businesses to create, manage, and extend personal profiles for each customer throughout online or networked applications. Catalog Navigator advanced personalization software extends Passport Office's relationship management capabilities by capturing and adding preference and general interest-level information about your business and products to each customer's personal profile.

LikeMinds

www.likeminds.com

457 Bryant Street
San Francisco, CA 94107-1316
Phone: 415-284-0300
Fax: 415-284-6969
E-mail: info@likeminds.com

Product: WebSell

WebSell predicts in real time the products a customer is likely to purchase based on profiles and purchase history obtained from the customer's online interactions, implicitly and explicitly stated preferences, and transaction history.

Net Perceptions

www.netperceptions.com

11200 West 78th Street, Suite 300
Minneapolis, MN 55344-3814
Phone: 800-466-0711 or 612-903-9424
Fax: 612-903-9423
E-mail: info@netperceptions.com

Product: GroupLens Recommendation Engine

The market leading product, GroupLens allow Web sites to tailor information and recommendations to each customer's individual taste. It is designed specifically for the needs of commercial Web sites and Net Perceptions says it integrates into almost any online business.

Immersive Imaging

Immersive Imaging Tools such as QuickTime VR, Surround Video and PhotoVista can add flash to any Web store. These tools can provide more detailed views of products. Microsoft's CarPoint effectively uses Surround Video to offer a glimpse of a vehicle's interior.

Apple

www.apple.com

1 Infinite Loop
Cupertino, CA 95014-2084
Phone: 408-996-1010

PRODUCT: QuickTime VR

QuickTime VR is the original immersive imaging technology. Development kits available only on Mac but playback on both Windows and Mac. The technology is mature, but as Live Picture creates a totally cross-platform solution, QuickTime VR might suffer.

Black Diamond

www.bdiamond.com

Black Diamond
195 Hanover Street, Suite 22
Portsmouth, NH 03801
Phone: 603-430-7777
Fax: 603-430-7778
E-mail: surroundvideo@bdiamond.com

PRODUCT: Surround Video

Surround Video is a collection of tools that allows you to create fully navigable, 360-degree panoramic images for your Web store. Images can be generated via 3D rendering software or photographed using any camera.

Kaidan

www.kaidan.com

703 East Pennsylvania Boulevard
Feasterville Business Campus
Feasterville, PA 19053
Phone: 215-364-1778
Fax: 215-322-4186
E-mail: info@kaidan.com

PRODUCT: Power Rigs

Kaidan creates specially designed rigs that allow the user to create panoramic scenes by rotating the camera either around an object or within a scene.

Live Picture

www.livepicture.com

5617 Scotts Valley Drive, Suite 180
Scotts Valley, CA 95066
Phone: 800-724-7900 or 408-438-9610
Fax: 408-438-9604
E-mail: info@livepicture.com

PRODUCT: PhotoVista

PhotoVista allows you to add 360-degree panoramic images for visitors to experience on your Web site. Images are generally less than 100K. PhotoVista costs $79 to download or $99 on CD.

FTP

While some programs build FTP into their Web editors, having your own FTP product will be an important part of your toolbox.

GlobalSCAPE

www.cuteftp.com

12500 Network Blvd., Suite 402
San Antonio, Texas 78249
Phone: 210-691-8445
Fax: 210-691-8438

PRODUCT: CuteFTP

CuteFTP is the leading FTP package for Windows PCs.

Fetch

www.dartmouth.edu/pages/softdev/fetch.html

Developed in 1989 at Dartmouth by Jim Matthews, Fetch is now the leading FTP package for Macintosh.

Payment

Ah, payment...our favorite thing. As Web retailing grows, so too will the options for secure transactions and payment. Here are some of the current leaders.

First Virtual Holdings, Inc.

www.fv.com

11975 El Camino Real, Suite 300
San Diego, CA 92130
Phone: 619-793-2700
Fax: 619-793-2950
E-mail: info@fv.com

First Virtual's transaction system involves the distribution of a VirtualPIN. The customer's credit card information is stored offline and when she makes a purchase with a VirtualPIN, she receives an e-mail message seeking confirmation of the order. The customer's credit card is not charged until First Virtual receives an affirmative response to the e-mail inquiry.

GlobeSet, Inc.

www.globeset.com

1250 Capital of Texas Highway South

Building One, Suite 300

Austin, Texas 78746
Phone: 512-427-5100
Fax: 512-427-5101
E-mail: info@globeset.com

PRODUCTS: Wallet, POS, Gateway, CA

Wallet is a cardholder application that stores a buyer's account information and communicates with merchants via the SET protocol. POS is a point-of-sale device that connects the merchant to the customer's electronic wallets. Gateway aids payment authorization. CA is a digital certificate application that generates and manages the digital identification certificates.

ICVERIFY

www.icverify.com

473 Roland Way
Oakland, CA 94621
Phone: 510-553-7500
Fax: 510-553-7553
E-mail: info@icverify.com

PRODUCT: ICVERIFY

ICVERIFY can process all credit cards with automatic draft capture into an existing bank account. The software supports more than 80 major card-processing networks. Direct access is available to Visa, MasterCard, American Express, and Discover for authorization and settlement.

InfoDial

www.infodial.com

22761 Pacific Coast Highway, Suite 101
Malibu, CA 90265
Phone: 800-932-9311
E-mail: Go to Contact Us at Web site

PRODUCT: Cashier

InfoDial's Cashier allows real-time credit card authorization and supports most processing networks. You can combine shopping carts with transaction. Customers can fill up their shopping carts and buy them directly online. The system allows you and the customer to know whether or not the transaction was approved. The entire process is automated and the money from the transaction is transferred from the purchaser's account directly into your bank account.

Terisa Systems

www.terisa.com

4984 El Camino Real
Los Altos, CA 94022
Phone: 650-919-1770
Fax: 650-919-1760
E-mail: info@terisa.com

PRODUCT: SecureWeb Payments

The SecureWeb Payments toolkit provides the tools needed to add SET payment card security.

Transport Logic

www.transport.com

50 SW Second Avenue, Suite 510
Portland, OR 97204
Phone: 503-243-1940
E-mail: Support@transport.com

Transport Logic has a number of secure Web-based solutions. Transport Logic's secure transaction services start at $50 for setup and $25 per month. Transport Logic also offers online catalog solutions, and dedicated servers.

VeriFone

www.verifone.com

One Mountain Boulevard, Suite 201
Warren, NJ 07059-5613
Phone: 908-756-9300
E-mail: webmaster@verifone.com

PRODUCT: vPOS

VeriFone is a subsidiary of Hewlett-Packard. A leader in physical payment systems, VeriFone offers secure solutions for credit card payments. VeriFone's software is based on SET protocol. vPOS captures customer order and payment information, communicates with the appropriate financial system for authorization, and processes the transaction.

VeriSign, Inc.

www.verisign.com

1390 Shorebird Way
Mountain View, CA 94043
Phone: 415-961-7500
Fax: 415-961-7300
E-mail: info@versign.com

PRODUCT: Secure Server ID

VeriSign's Digital ID assures visitors that your organization is authentic and allows encrypted communications through SSL. Secure Server Ids are backed by VeriSign's NetSure Protection plan, which provides up to $100,000 of protection against loss due to theft, impersonation, corruption, or loss of use of an ID.

E-Cash

Credit card processing isn't the only concern when it comes to receiving payment. Here are some of the top e-cash players.

CheckFree Corporation

www.checkfree.com

4411 East Jones Bridge Road
Norcross, GA 30092
Phone: 770-441-3387
E-mail: info@checkfree.com

CheckFree has 15 years of experience in electronic commerce processing services and software products. CheckFree's Electronic Funds Transfer program deducts monthly payments from customers' checking accounts or credit cards.

CyberCash, Inc.

www.cybercash.com

2100 Reston Parkway
Reston, VA 20191
Phone: 703-620-4200
Fax: 703-620-4215

Or

303 Twin Dolphin Drive, Suite 200
Redwood City, CA 94065
Phone: 650-594-0800
Fax: 650-594-0899
E-mail: info@cybercash.com

CyberCash's CashRegister software enables secure, encrypted Internet transactions and the Wallet that allows shoppers to store their transaction information in one secure place. CyberCash also allows customers to make payments with the CyberCoin service and the PayNow service.

DigiCash, Inc.

www.digicash.com

2656 East Bayshore Road
Palo Alto, CA 94303
Phone: 415-321-0300
Fax: 415-321-0322
E-mail: info@digicash.com

DigiCash's ecash is a software-based payment system. Users and merchants open a bank account with a bank that issues ecash. The bank provides the merchant with the ecash Merchant Purse software with an Account Id and Password.

Digital Equipment Corp.

www.digital.com or www.millicent.com

130 Lytton Avenue
Palo Alto, CA 94301
Phone: 1-800-344-4825
E-mail: millicent@digital.com

PRODUCT: MilliCent

Digital's MilliCent allows customers to purchase less expensive items online without having to produce a credit card number for each merchant. MilliCent uses electronic tokens called scrip. Scrip is secure, is kept on the customer's disk and protected by a password. MilliCent supports single-click purchases as small as 1/10th of a cent.

Index

B

C

D

E

G

H

I

M

N

P

Q

R

S

T

U

V

W

X

Y

Z